25.00

The Dakota

The Dakota

A History of the Douglas Dakota in RAF and RCAF service

Arthur Pearcy Jnr, ARAeS

LONDON

IAN ALLAN

First published 1972

SBN 7110 0314 9

All rights reserved. No part of this book may be reproduced or transmitted in any form or by any means, electronic or mechanical, including photocopying, recording or by any information storage and retrieval system, without permission from the Publisher in writing.

© Arthur Pearcy Jnr, ARAeS

Published by Ian Allan Ltd, Shepperton, Surrey and printed in the United Kingdom by Morrison and Gibb Ltd, London and Edinburgh

Contents

To my wife Audrey
in appreciation of her devotion,
patience and long understanding

Foreword

by
Air Marshal Sir William Coles
KBE CB DSO DFC AFC
Controller RAF Benevolent Fund

The invitation from the author to write a Foreword to this book came as some surprise and I am delighted to do so. Having flown more than fifty types of aircraft, some 5,000 hours, over five continents, one develops a feel for certain aircraft, and the Dakota is one. Few who have flown the military versions of the Douglas DC-3 commercial airliner, known affectionately as the "DAK" to the Royal Air Force and to the United States Air Force as the Gooney Bird, would deny its great versatility.

It has been often used as an airborne Royal Carriage for members of our Royal Family, as a VIP transport for Prime Ministers and Presidents, Admirals and Marshals (Field as well as Air) and in many less glamorous roles, eg airborne horsebox carrying mules into Burma, flying Paratroops and towing Gliders to Normandy on "D" Day and to Arnhem, or as an airborne supply train in the Berlin blockade. On all these occasions and many others it invariably endeared itself to the crews who flew it, in any part of the world and in every type of weather.

My introduction to the Dakota came in January 1943 when Major Washburn of the 315th Troop Carrier Group US Army Air Force gave me an interesting 1 hour 20 mins. "Dual" when I was based at Marble Arch between Agedabia and Sirte, with a detachment of No 216 Squadron, during the final advance to Tunis. In April we were re-equipped and in the next eighteen months I flew 1,100 hours in 216, 117 and 233 Squadrons (in the last two as Squadron Commander), in the Mediterranean, Burma and European theatres of operations.

On several occasions there were odd moments for contemplation, although never the slightest doubt that the Dakota would meet all reasonable demands, or even unreasonable, that one might make on it.

It is now more than twenty-five years since many of the actions described in the book took place and over this period of time memories tend to grow dim, indeed this may account for minor inaccuracies in the text. Whilst no one would claim that the Dakota was the most exciting aircraft to fly, it was I believe one of the most reliable and, in its class, incomparable. The many varied and successful operations in which I took part, and the fact that it is still flying in many parts of the world, testify to its unique capability.

I congratulate the author, Arthur Pearcy, on the immense amount of detailed research which he has undertaken to produce a book which will, I am confident, commend itself to the thousands of crews who have flown the military and civil versions of the Dakota, as well as to many of the hundreds of thousands of passengers who have flown in them.

ACKNOWLEDGEMENTS

The author gratefully acknowledges the valuable assistance given by former Dakota aircrew and groundcrews, the Air Historical Branch, MoD, and its helpful staff, Specialist members of Air-Britain, plus many others in the preparation of this volume.

Chaz Bowyer kindly contributed the chapter on David Lord which was taken from his book *For Valour*; Ian James was responsible for the chapter on BOAC; the Canadian Armed Forces gave permission for the history of No 435 Squadron to be published, and friend Willis Nye from California in the United States supplied the information on the Douglas factory at Long Beach, and Dakota production.

The assistance given by the many members of the No 31 and No 194 Squadron Associations is greatly appreciated. Many Dakota crews supplied log-books and photo albums resulting in some of the photographs being published for the first time. The Photographic Department at the Imperial War Museum under Mr Brennan and Mr Hine, spent many hours of searching for my requirements, as did Mr JHG Bennett of 'Publicity 3' at the Ministry of Defence. For their patience and help my grateful thanks.

The item on Air Despatch was taken from a Short History of Air Supply by HO'N Drew, and the story of No 55 Company Royal Army Service Corps (Air Despatch) by Capt PH Houchin, Royal Corps of Transport. My grateful thanks to Capt GH Sims, RCT, for the information and photographs he kindly supplied. The Controller of H.M. Stationary Office kindly gave permission for extracts from their publication 'Wings of the Phoenix' to be used in the Air Command South-East Asia section.

The year 1970 was the 50th Anniversary of the Douglas Aircraft Company and the author appreciates their interest and co-operation during the preparation of this project.

Introduction

Few people have yet attempted to estimate what air transport contributed to the offensive and defensive operations of World War 2. The Royal Air Force took four years in building up a world-wide transport service, a service which could not have reached its peak strength without the help of the United States in providing nearly 2,000 Douglas Dakota transports under Lend lease agreement.

In the war the mission of RAF Fighter and Bomber Command was always to carry the fight to the enemy. The task of Transport Command in World War 2 was often vital – but it rarely made headline news. Against the flashing Spitfires and sleek Mosquitos, their aircraft were slow and lumbering. They were easy prey to the prowling Luftwaffe and Japanese fighters and a comparative "sitter" to enemy flak guns. The only "armour" of transport crews were their tin hats, which could either be worn or sat on according to the direction of the attack. Some crews wore flak waistcoats. Usually their only weapons were the revolvers they carried in their holsters.

The Desert Rats, the Chindits, the men who fought at Imphal, Sicily, Salerno, Anzio, on the Normandy beaches, at Arnhem and the Rhine all counted on them – and seldom in vain.

During World War 2 every theatre commander desired and needed the US built military variant of the famed Douglas DC-3, a two-engined aircraft without arms or armour but with an outstanding facility for carrying reasonable loads of supplies or men at reasonable speeds and often in unreasonable conditions. She served in every theatre of operations as a glider-tug, paratroop carrier, personnel transport, freighter and ambulance – and was the mainstay of all Allied transport squadrons.

My first flight in a Dakota is recorded in my log-book as having taken place during 1945 at RAF Melbourn in Yorkshire, in a Mk III KG655 on an air experience flight. The war in Europe was just over and all the Handley-Page Halifax units from No 4 Group Bomber Command were in the process of converting to transports – mainly Dakotas – to assist in the Far East under Air Command South-East Asia – ACSEA. Little did I realise that nine years later I would serve a four-year tour as a member of a United States Air Force squadron equipped with twelve Douglas C-47 "Gooney Birds". This was with the 7531st Air Base Squadron, 7500th Air Base Group, Third Air Force, based at RAF Bovingdon in Hertfordshire. A unique experience.

It was the squadron Engineering Officer, Major "Bill" Prather, who loaned me the Tech Orders relating to the C-47 series, after voicing my curiosity as to just how many of these transports were built. The documents revealed that approximately 10,000 military versions of the ubiquitous DC-3 were constructed by Douglas at factories located at Long Beach and Oklahoma City. This did not include the 800 odd commercial DC-3s manufactured at Santa Monica before the attack on Pearl Harbor in December 1941.

During 1954, eight years after World War 2, all and sundry were still using the many variants of the DC-3 as a transport. Of the fourteen countries comprising the North Atlantic Treaty Organisation, only one – Iceland with no air power – did not have the C-47 on its inventory. Even today many of the NATO countries still operate this famous Douglas transport. The US Navy at RAF Hendon were operating their version of the C-47, the R4D series, plus the Super DC-3 or R4D-8 as it was designated. Every base flight at every USAF airfield in Europe operated at least one C-47. At this time the Dakota was being phased out of squadron service with the Royal Air Force, whilst our squadron at Bovingdon was still taking delivery of re-furbished aircraft from Field Aircraft Services at Tollerton near Nottingham. It was a pleasant surprise to note on one such C-47 the Royal Air Force markings were still discernible under the highly polished natural finish – a sort of reverse Lend lease.

My service with the USAF has pioneered three momentous visits to the United States, during which I have toured the Douglas plants at both Santa Monica and Long Beach in California. At Santa Monica I was shown where the first DC-3 took off from on December 17, 1935. The airfield was then known as Clover Field. As friend Crosby Maynard and I stood talking about that historic event, the pilot of a Federal Aviation Agency DC-3 chose that time to open up the throttles of the two Pratt and Whitney Twin Wasps and take-off. Most appropriate.

During my second visit to Douglas at Long Beach, it was Ray Towne, Director of Public Relations, who persuaded me that it was time the long record of the Royal Air Force Dakota was put into print. Ray flew as a pilot during the Berlin Airlift and was General "Bill" Tunner's Public Information Officer. His wife, Dorothy, did a statistical survey of *Operation Plainfare* for the United States Government.

During World War 2 over fifty Royal Air Force squadrons and as many training and development units used the Dakota. I dedicate this book to all those connected with this workhorse of the sky. Among the four weapons listed by General Eisenhower which did most to win the war, one was the jeep and another was the Douglas Dakota, and to quote an unnamed pilot "You might wreck a Dak but you'll never wear it out."

ARTHUR PEARCY

CHAPTER ONE

The Douglas Commercial Transport

THE BIRTH OF THE DOUGLAS COMMERCIAL

In March 1920 an aircraft engineer and designer by the name of Donald Douglas decided that he wished his children to live in the warmth of Southern California, and his aeroplanes to fly in the same salubrious climate. That his total assets were in the order of less than 1,000 dollars proved no deterrent. He invested some of his savings in desk space at the rear of a downtown barber shop in Los Angeles and commenced to search for additional capital. It was a local newspaper reporter, Bill Henry, who introduced Donald Douglas to a well-to-do young man named David R Davis who would finance an aeroplane which could fly coast-to-coast nonstop. The first order to come to the barber shop was for 40,000 dollars, one aircraft.

The Davis-Douglas company was formed, and Douglas summoned from the east, six associates who had worked with him at the Martin company – he had designed a bomber for Martin which flew in August 1917. When the Cloudstar first took to the air on February 24, 1921, it achieved there and then, with no ceremony, one success that was of much greater consequence than any transcontinental records ever written. It was the first aircraft in history to airlift a useful load equal to its own weight. The Cloudstar was not the first to span the continent nonstop, but it started what is today, over fifty years later, the Douglas Aircraft Company.

In 1933, Douglas, then a comparatively small manufacturer specialising in torpedo and observation aircraft for the American armed forces, had bid successfully for a new passenger aircraft ordered by Transcontinental & Western Airlines. Known as the DC-1 in the earliest model, and as the DC-2 after it went into quantity production, this first Douglas entry into the transport field revolutionised the industry.

The birth of the Douglas Commercial is credited to Jack Frye who was vice-president of Transcontinental & Western Airlines in 1932, who realised that what was needed was a standardised "Model T" of the air that could operate at a profit. In 1932, TWA was subsidiary of North American Aviation, which owned 89,000 shares of Douglas. Frye was operating with antiquated tri-motored Fokkers and Fords, and knew his plight was desperate when he heard that United Air Lines had come up with the new Boeing 247. In fact they had invested $4,000,000 on a fleet of no less than sixty of these machines.

Frye took his problem to Donald Douglas, who consulted his chief engineer, a genius named Arthur E Raymond, whose idiosyncrasy was that he hated to fly. The result was the one and only DC-1, first of many DC series, a two-engined aircraft with a speed of 150 mph. When the DC-1 set up nineteen world records for speed and payload-range performance, even Raymond was astounded. On acceptance flight the DC-1 took off from Winslow, Arizona, and flew direct to Albuquerque, New Mexico, on one engine.

TWA immediately ordered twenty-six of the new transports and a total of 138 civil DC-2s were built plus 62 military models for the US Army Air Corps and the US Navy. Meanwhile the DC-1 had been sold to Howard Hughes in January 1936, and in May 1938 appeared in the United Kingdom and was registered as G-AFIF to Lord Forbes. Its last appearance was in the Spanish Civil War doing transport duties during 1939. During December 1940 it crashed on take-off from Malaga Airport whilst registered with Iberian Air Lines.

Douglas lost money on the DC-2, $65,000 on each in fact, and American Airlines wanted something better. They wanted to retain their luxury sleeper traffic, and the DC-2 was just too narrow to accommodate a comfortable berth. One summer afternoon in 1935, President CR Smith telephoned Donald Douglas from Chicago. What America wanted, specifically, was a larger, more comfortable aircraft which could lure the luxury trade. Result was the DC-3. Curiously, Douglas held out little hope for its success.

The first DC-3 went into service on American Airlines non-stop Chicago–New York run; other airlines quickly saw what they were looking for. An aircraft with a low operating cost and a cruising speed of 165–180 mph. The DC-3 was a dream ship from the start.

Douglas turned out 803 commercial DC-3 transports at its Santa Monica factory, besides over 10,000 military models at its Long Beach and Oklahoma City plants. On May 6, 1946, the last DC-3 rolled off the production line, destined for a Brazilian airline.

By mid-summer of 1939, Douglas had delivered a total of 1,503 assorted military aircraft to the Army, more than 300 to the Navy and Coast Guard, and a few hundred commercial transports to the airlines of the world. When the warclouds rolled over Europe in September of that fateful year, France had placed orders for 100 of the Douglas DB-7, to be known in the RAF as the Boston. The indefatigable DC-3, predecessor of the RAF Dakota, was in production for foreign and domestic operators, deliveries averaging six aircraft per month. Engineering design had commenced on the large four-engined DC-4 Skymaster.

With the fall of France and the almost desperate situation of the United Kingdom, the British Purchasing Commission in the United States took immediate steps to place large orders and to take over aircraft contracts placed by the French and Belgian Governments. On March 11, 1941, the Lend-Lease Act was passed which increased the flow of aircraft of many types to the RAF. These included many Douglas built Flying Fortress bombers constructed under contact from Boeing at the Long Beach plant, plus Liberators built under similar contract from Consolidated. During World War 2 Douglas turned out a grand total of 29,385 aircraft at plants located at Santa Monica, Long Beach, Oklahoma City, Tulsa, Chicago and El Segundo. These included 962 Liberators and 3,000 Flying Fortress bombers. The company had 160,000 employees spread over the six plants and much of the world.

During 1941 the British Purchasing Commission bought a number of surplus DC-3s from American Airlines and TWA for use by the RAF in India and the Middle East. They were dismantled and shipped as deck cargo to the Maintenance Units in the Middle East before allocated to RAF transport squadrons. Other DC-3s were taken over from Pan American Airways who operated them in the Middle East at that time; these supplementing the DC-2s already in service with the RAF. Nearly 2,000 Dakotas were delivered under Lend-Lease to the RAF, a type which until retirement in 1970 had spent a quarter of a century on the inventory.

MILITARY APPLICATION OF THE DOUGLAS COMMERCIAL

The transition of the world famous Douglas Aircraft Company DC-3 air transport into one of the vital strategic weapons of World War 2 is an interesting chapter in the revolution of the military air transport aircraft. In order to thoroughly understand this transition, it is essential that the reader review the actual genealogy of the Douglas Commercial series aircraft and how the Douglas C-47 – Dakota – was developed for the US Army Air Force.

The concept role of the military air transport in the US Army Air Corps started in the early days when the first Douglas DC-2s started to fly the airways with the scheduled airlines of the United States and abroad. The US Army Air Corps envied the airlines in the selection of the aircraft, and although the US Congress was miserly in those days for appropriations for aircraft, finally funds were earmarked for the purchase of Douglas air transports.

Fortunately the US Army Air Corps had long realised that logistical support of combat troops in the field by means of airlift was an essential part of the defence strategy of the United States. It seemed nearly axiomatic that troops and munitions could be airlifted from one coast to another in a matter of twelve hours or so if need be. In order to attain this objective and to implementate the strategy of airlift, the first aircraft purchased by the Army with its Fiscal 1936 funds was an example of the Douglas DC-2 commercial transport, which had first flown in 1934 and was bringing about a revolution in air transport. This procurement of the first modern air transport for the US Army was evaluated as the XC-32, the designation later changing to the C-32 when it went into service with a transport squadron. It was powered by two Curtiss-Wright 750 hp radial air-cooled engines, and weighed 18,200 lb gross. The US Army Air Corps at Wright Field had done static tests with a Douglas DC-2 during 1935, the aircraft finally breaking up under loads three times its design limitations.

The Douglas XC-32 proved so successful in the US Army Air Corps manoeuvres, that an additional twenty-four C-32A air transports were ordered. The Douglas C-32A was somewhat modified over that of the prototype in the interior arrangement. The aircraft were powered by two Curtiss-Wright 740 hp radial air-cooled engines, weighed 18,200 lb and high speed at optimum altitude was 210 mph. The entrance door was also enlarged to accommodate small cargo.

Then followed an order for eighteen Douglas C-33 air transports. These aircraft were basically an airline DC-2 configuration, except that the vertical tail surface was enlarged. A larger and heavier cargo door was also fitted. The C-33 was also powered with two Curtiss-Wright radial air-cooled engines of 750 hp each. The top speed was slightly better than 200 mph, or some 50 mph faster than transport built in quantity for the Army before 1936.

The concept of the cargo aircraft for the US Army Air Corps was by now well founded. Future procurement of air transport aircraft became a part of each succeeding budget for the military. Also purchased with 1936 funds were two Douglas C-34 air transports which were basically the C-32, which had the standard DC-2 tail and passenger door, except the interior was revised to meet increased requirements for the type.

By this time, the demand for military air cargo aircraft was great. As a result of past performance of Douglas aircraft, an order for a single C-38 was made. This aircraft was a C-33 converted in 1937 to have a DC-3 tail and sometimes called the DC-2½. Weighing 18,500 lb the engine horsepower for each radial air-cooled Curtiss-Wright was 950. The flight performance was somewhat improved. Then in 1939 followed the order for thirty-five Douglas C-39s, each being powered by two 925 hp radial air-cooled engines of Curtiss-Wright manufacture. The fuselage of the C-39 was a conventional DC-2 but the cargo door was enlarged and strengthened and the DC-3 type vertical tail was installed. It was mainly used for the transportation of vital US Army Air Corps high priority cargo.

The thirty-five Douglas C-39s, along with the C-33s, became the nucleus for the US Army Air Corps first systemised air transport operation. They called it the Tenth Air Transport Group, organised at Patterson Field, near Dayton, Ohio, in 1939. This was the home base of the Fairfield Air Depot, one of a whole nationwide system of Supply Depots under the Air Corps Material Division based a few miles down the highway at Wright Field, test and procurement centre for all Air Corps Operations. The Tenth Transport Group started their own airline, linking the Fairfield Air Depot with others located in Middletown, Pa., Sacramento, California, Oregon and Utah. The Douglas aerial freighters of the newly organised transport squadrons flew daily schedules between the depots. By the end of 1941, the 16-seat C-39s got a chance to prove themselves, when they were called upon to perform many rigorous transport operations in the early days of the war; they ferried supplies to Goose Bay, Newfoundland, and flew survivors out of the Philippines to Australia in December 1941.

It was found from experience, that additional cargo carrying capacity was necessary. However, this in turn would raise the gross weight and require additional engine power to maintain good performance. To this objective, the C-41 was the next aircraft procured which was the fourth C-39 converted at the factory before completion, with two Pratt & Whitney radial air-cooled engines developing 1200 hp each. This additional engine power raised the high speed to 225 mph and improved the take-off characteristics.

Then followed the C-41A, which for all practical purposes, was a DC-3 airline transport configuration with modified military interior for twenty-three passengers. The aircraft was also powered with two Pratt & Whitney 1200 hp engines. The high speed was 222 mph, and the gross weight rose to 26,314 lb. The Douglas C-42 was the fifth C-39 converted at the factory before completion, with two 1200 hp Cyclones and a gross weight of 23,624 lb. The interior was modified from that of the C-39. Only one model of the C-41, C-41A and C-42 was ordered.

Until the procurement of the C-41, C-41A and C-42, the general configuration of the air cargo aircraft was comparable to the airline DC-3 air transport, except that in some models cargo doors were installed. With the advent of war on the horizon, it was inevitable that modifications and performance compatible with military requirements would have to be made. On the C-41, C-41A and the C-42, the cargo floor of the fuselage was strengthened, tie down rings were made heavier and the aft fuselage structure strengthened. The cargo doors were also enlarged. All of these modifications to the basic structure increased the gross weight. Actually, these were only modifications to the basic structure only.

During 1942, twenty-four commercial DC-2s were amongst the transport aircraft impressed for military service from the fleets of the US domestic operators. These were generally similar to the single C-32 and were designated C-32A. They had 740 hp Cyclone engines which were designated R-1830-33 by the Army Air Corps, and differed from the C-33s in having no special door for large cargo. The RAF also operated the DC-2 in the Middle East and India, and the first to enter RAF service were undoubtedly the twelve received by No 31 Squadron in April 1941. They were designated DC-2K in the RAF inventory.

Late in 1939, the planners of the US Army Air Corps drew up the basic specifications of the improved cargo aircraft, the Douglas C-47. No aeroplane used by the US Army Air Forces has been more widely known, and probably none has been more widely used for so long an operational life, than the C-47. Produced in greater numbers than any other Army transport, the C-47 was used in every combat area of World War 2, and more than 1,000 remained in the USAF inventory in 1961. In this respect, Douglas engineers collaborated on the basic design of the airframe. The whole concept was based on an aircraft that could be massed produced for the impending war. Suffice to say, that coupled with the previous experience of Douglas technicians in the production of military air transports, and the fact that the basic DC-3 lent itself to a good production breakdown for mass output. However, manufacturing operations would have to be revolutionised to achieve mass production.

The aeroplane which was basically the prototype for the C-47 was first flown on December 17, 1935, by Carl Cover, from Clover Field, Santa Monica. Identified by the Douglas type number DC-3 – Douglas Commercial Three – and also known as the DST – Douglas Sleeper Transport – it had been produced for the US domestic airlines as a successor for the DC-2. From then until 1940, over 500 DC-3s were built for the airlines, including more than 100 for export. The US Army Air Corps, which had already bought a number of DC-2 variants as described earlier, was eager to buy the DC-3 also, and outlined to Douglas the changes that would be needed – stronger cabin floor, strengthened rear fuselage with large loading doors, more powerful engines and provision for carrying large cargo and supply packs externally. Most of the design work on the military version had already been completed when the first orders were placed, in 1940, for large numbers of C-47s.

Mention must be made of the whole series of Douglas DC-3 transports using the various and familiar DC-3 configuration. These aircraft commenced with the C-48 which was a military transport with the usual DC-3 interior. The designation applied to thirty-six DC-3s of various types taken over from US airlines in 1941 for use by the US Army Air Force. All had Pratt & Whitney R-1830 engines, like the C-47, but were limited to the commercial gross weight which varied from 22,650 lb to 26,850 lb according to type. Only one C-48 with twenty-one seats was acquired having R-1830-82 engines. The next in the series was the C-48A the interior of which was modified for air staff transportation. The three models impressed had R-1830-51 engines and eighteen seats. The C-48B was simply a commercial version of the DC-3 sleeper, and the sixteen of this model – DST – had fourteen berths. Then followed the C-48C, of which sixteen were procured, which were simply twenty-one passenger seat configuration, based on airline experience. With R-1830-51 engines these were used for troop transport only.

The C-49 was a commercial version of the DC-3, except it was powered by Curtiss-Wright radial air-cooled engines in lieu of the Pratt & Whitney engines, hitherto used exclusively on Douglas airline transports. The C-49 was a hybrid. This configuration required that all control cables for the tail surface were re-routed. Then the C-49B had the cargo door located on the right side of the fuselage. The C-49C was a so-called DC-3 Trooper version with formed plywood bucket seats on a bench along each side of the passenger compartment. This kind of seating permitted rapid bail-out of paratroops in an airborne operation. The C-49D was a commercial DC-3 with a modified interior arrangement for the transportation of combat troops. The interior, however, was lined with a dark green olive kapok insulation to ward off cold and noise. Equipment for the troops for field use and airborne operations plus a static line was included. Some of these aircraft had cargo doors, whereas others had the conventional door for boarding of passengers.

As mentioned earlier many of the aircraft of these various designations were commandeered from the scheduled airlines of the United States and modified for military use with Air Transport Command and for utility purposes. Towards the latter days of World War 2, many of these aircraft were returned to their original owners, in good flying order.

Pan American Airways was contracted to deliver twenty Lockhead Lodestar airliners, bought by the British Purchasing Commission in May 1941, and deliver them to Africa. The aircraft were delivered in the autumn of 1941, and the operation had started the powers in Washington to thinking about setting up a regular service to and across Africa in case the US should get involved in the war. Pan American Air Ferries was organised for ferrying aircraft across the South Atlantic and Africa, and Pan American Airways Africa was similarly created to shuttle the spares and return the flight crews. PAA-Africa actually started operations from Takoradi to Khartoum on October 21, 1941, with seven DC-3s, also running a flight to Fishermens Lake in Liberia to connect with Pan Americans Boeing 314 flying-boats on the South Atlantic route. RAF ferry crews often used the PAA-Africa DC-3s and on October 29, 1941 a flight from Takoradi to Cairo involved a C-49F 42-256623, whilst a visitor to No 2 Aircraft Delivery Unit at Cairo on May 26, 1942, was a C-48C 42-38333. As recorded later, a quantity of these hybrid types were later impressed into service with the RAF.

Besides the foregoing transport aircraft commandeered for US Army Air Force use, there were others. All of these aircraft had been constructed at the Douglas Santa Monica factory. Various aircraft had varying gross weights and engine installations but all of them had the same structural and aerodynamic configuration. In fact, beginning with the model C-49E, the C-49F, C-49G, C-49H, C-49J, C-49K, C-50, C-50A, C-50B, C-50C, C-50D and the C-51, all were powered with the Curtiss-Wright radial air-cooled engines.

Beginning with the one C-52, the one C-52A and the two C-52Bs, this was another series of commercial DC-3s with Pratt & Whitney R-1830-51 engines and improvements to suit them for a military role.

But the Douglas C-53 started a whole new series of air transports. A total of 193 C-53s were procured and were called the Skytrooper in contrast to the C-47 which was called the Skytrain. But ever on the alert to develop the maximum potential use, Douglas produced the XC-53A. This aircraft was basically a C-53 except that the wing was built with full span trailing edge flaps. However, it was not developed as a production model and only one aircraft of this type was built. The C-53B had extra internal long-range fuel tanks and a navigator's position. Eight of this model were ordered. The seventeen C-53C aircraft were paratroop transports equipped with side bench seats, as were the 159 C-53D aircraft, basically a commercial DC-3 modified to carry paratroops in aerial assault operations. Aircraft from the C-52 onwards reverted to the use of the Pratt & Whitney radial air-cooled engines.

The C-68 designation reverted to airline transports impressed for wartime service and had twenty-one seat configuration. Two were impressed in 1942. The C-84 transports were older Douglas DC-3B configuration impressed from the airlines for war time service. The four aircraft of this type were 1937 model DC-3Bs, had Wright R-1820-71 engines and twenty-eight seats.

Produced at the Tulsa Douglas plant, the C-117 was a variant of the C-47B. It had an airline interior for use as a staff transport. Only seventeen of the C-117A were built from an order for 131 which was cancelled after VJ Day. In later years, some of these served as C-117B transports, having the high altitude superchargers removed from the R-1830-90C engines. Another model followed in 1953 when eleven non-standard VC-47 staff transports were redesignated C-117C. They were the last examples of the DC-3 designated by the US services; they were still in service in 1962, some as the VC-117A and VC-117B aircraft.

The XCG-17 was a C-47 converted into a glider configuration in the course of a series of trials by the Air Technical Service Command at Wright Field in 1944. The aircraft was a conventional C-47 except that two water tanks were faired into the two engine nacelles to provide the balancing components. The idea was to use the glider for airborne assault operations being towed behind two C-47s or a C-54 transport. It had the flattest glide of any cargo glider tested up to that time, and could have been even better had not the specification required that it be possible to reconvert the XCG-17 to a C-47. In consequence, the engine nacelles were retained on the wing, less engines. The prototype was reconverted back to a C-47.

Aircraft intended for the US Navy Air Transport Service were diverted from the production runs at the Santa Monica and Long Beach plant, being designated as the Douglas R4D with the appropriate dash number to indicate their production block. First ordered in 1941 for Navy use, versions of the famous Douglas twins are still operating thirty-one years later, and it was indicative of the widespread use of this type that no fewer than sixteen Navy variants qualified for redesignation in the unified system introduced in 1962.

The six hundred odd model R4D aircraft were procured by the US Army Air Force Material Command for the US Navy. Funds were allocated from the Navy appropriations to the USAAF to pay for the aircraft. Various models of this coterie of aircraft were used for personnel transport, air medical evacuation, cargo transportation, etc. The US Navy maintained a representatives office at the Douglas Long Beach plant. The personnel of the office functioned in a liaison capacity between the company management and the resident USAAF office.

Prior to the advent of World War 2, purchase of naval aircraft from the Douglas Aircraft Company was handled entirely by naval procurement agencies. At the advent of World War 2, it was considered more expedient to allocate one large contract, or a recurring series of contracts for orders of aircraft, and then to allocate blocks of aircraft for US Navy use in accordance with their logistic requirements.

The basic naval R4D designation for the DC-3 aircraft configuration was simply commercial DC-3 transports fitted with an oversize loading door and were comparable to the Army Air Force C-53 transport. The R4D-1, powered by two Pratt & Whitney R-1830-82 engines, was a cargo counterpart of the C-47 Skytrain. Two R4D-2 transports were ex-airline DC-3s – Army Air Force C-49 – and were later designated R4D-2Z and R4D-2F to indicate their VIP flagship interiors; they were the only R4Ds with Wright R-1820 engines. Also ex-airline and used as personnel transports were the R4D-3 and R4D-4 which were equivalent to the C-53 and C-53C Skytrooper. Major US Navy cargo transport variants were the

R4D-5 with R-1830-92 engines and 24-volt electrical system, matching the C-47A Skytrain; the R4D-6 with R-1830-90B engines – C-47B – and the R4D-7, which matched the TC-47B navigation trainer. The wartime exterior paint pattern was olive drab camouflage type. Spare parts were interchangeable with the C-47 as were the various accessory components.

Prior to World War 2, the US Navy had purchased Douglas model R2D-1 air transports powered by two Curtiss-Wright 710 hp radial air-cooled engines. These aircraft were of the same configuration as the DC-2 airframe, and five were purchased in 1934 by the US Navy. It was from the superior performance of these air transports that the US Navy made the choice of the type for World War 2.

PREPARATIONS FOR PRODUCTION

The parent Douglas factory at Santa Monica, California, had grown up over the years. The factory had continually expanded since the time it was built during the Golden Years of aviation, prior to the great depression in the United States. It had been continually expanded with the growth of commercial and government production programmes. In 1939, it was clogged with production contracts for commercial, military, naval and Lend-Lease aircraft contracts. The airfield at the factory for conducting test flights was beginning to be too small for fast attack bombers such as the A-20 Boston. It was these obvious deficiencies that required that the Douglas C-47 programme be conducted with plant facilities entirely new in concept. For an increased tempo in production, the need for interchangeability of assemblies and parts, made it mandatory that steel production tooling and assembly jigs be designed and built. Space was at a premium in the parent plant. The whole concept of production tooling had to be radically improved to accomplish mass output of assemblies to the aircraft production line, and subsequently the flight line. It would have been foolhardy to expect that the parent factory could produce the C-47 in quantities desired with the existing facilities. The Douglas El Segundo Division was busy with the production of the SBD Dauntless and could not therefore function as a feeder facility for the C-47 programme.

Study of mass production methods on a large scale would require a new concept in aircraft plant layout. To this objective, architectural plans were completed in 1939 for the construction of the Douglas Long Beach plant on the north boundary of the Long Beach Municipal Airport. At the time of the conception of the layout, it was intended to be the most modern factory of its kind in the Free World. And it was. The newspapers referred to it as a "black out" plant because it was built as a windowless structure. The United States Government supplied the funds through the Defence

Plant Agency. The land was leased from a subsidiary of the Douglas Aircraft Company, the Montana Land Company. The plant consisted of several long buildings for production, plus a coterie of smaller structures for technical, administrative, purchasing and executive personnel. The factory as it is today was eventually purchased from the United States Government in recent years and is the main West Coast plant for the Aircraft Division, McDonnell Douglas Corporation. Two larger assembly buildings were also built in which the Douglas jet transports are built and assembled.

The accession and awarding of large contracts in quantity for the Douglas C-47 caused the creation of the Tooling Division as a separate autonomous corporate division of the parent company. The sole function of the Division was to design and build the necessary tooling to produce the assembly facilities for government contracts for aircraft. New tools for manual use, new tools for the machine shops, new assembly and mating fixtures, handling dollies, racks, drill jigs and templates as well as new methods of optical and collimator application, all of these and more were developed to reduce man-hours required, increased production poundage coupled with interchangeability of assemblies and parts by means of precision tooling design.

The function of this division was multitudinous. Aside from the development, design and procurement of aircraft much of the strategic programmes for waging global war were originated at the Headquarters of the division at Wright Field, Dayton, Ohio. But with the war clouds gathering on the horizon and approaching ever closer to the United States, serious consideration on part of the strategic thinkers in the Material Division was given to the role of air transport and the part it was to play in any eventuality. Proposals were made to the Douglas Aircraft Company at the Santa Monica plant to submit technical data for the complete production redesign of the basic DC-3 configuration into a troop and cargo transport. Actually, this was not beyond the capability of the Douglas Aircraft Company. They had built the first basic cargo transport for the US Army Air Service, the C-1 and the C-1A. These two aircraft models were simply improved versions of the Douglas World Cruiser adapted to light cargo or limited troop transportation in 1924. Then followed the Douglas XC-32 and its sister aircraft that followed, all based on the parent DC-2 and DC-3 aircraft configurations. The company responded with production data and technical drawings of an aircraft that was eventually to become the Douglas C-47 or Dakota as it was known in the Royal Air Force.

Although the Douglas C-47 had limited capability, nevertheless, there was no time to design and develop a new larger cargo aircraft. In this respect, the Douglas C-47 and the Douglas C-54 were primarily commercial aeroplanes with revamped designs for mass production for military airlift operations.

Prior to the advent of the Douglas C-47, all air transports were constructed at Santa Monica. The new proposals for mass production of the C-47 was based on the construction of the new high volume plant intended to be built at Long Beach Municipal Airport, California. This meant that much of the original wooden tooling on which the ancestral DC-2s and DC-3s were fabricated and assembled, would be redesigned by the newly formed Tooling Division to simplify high volume output. In short, the whole concept as presented by Douglas engineers was based on new and advanced concepts. These proposals for the Douglas C-47 were readily accepted by the Material Division, US Army Air Corps.

The whole design of the airframe of the C-47 while based on the DC-3 configuration, was radically changed to achieve fast production and minimum amount of hours invested to build the aircraft to the scheduled requirements. For example, the original DC-3 had tubular steel engine mounting rings. This was a costly assembly to make. Therefore the engine mounting rings were made in two halves of a steel forging and bolted together at the centreline. The supporting tubes were of high strength steel tubing. The substitution of a forging for the tubular structure accomplished two objectives, ie it speeded production of the finished article and it also eliminated the steel tubing required for the engine mounting ring. Steel tubing at that time was a critical material and in short supply. Another dividend of this type of design was that instead of a skilled and specialised welder being necessary to produce the part, a semi-skilled production worker could be utilised. The same technique was used for the components of each landing gear assembly. Other minor assemblies such as fairings, wing fillets, inspection access panels, engine cowls, all parts hitherto being manually produced, were formed to the required dimensions by hydraulically or pneumatically actuated presses or stretch formed over a die. Powered bending and spinning tools were also employed. In short, wherever possible machine tools were used to produce parts which before were produced by manual means. The precise interchangeability of parts also made for faster assembly and installation. Then an expanded programme for the use of die and sand castings was also inaugurated where hitherto formed heavy gauge sheet metal parts had been used. Other parts were redesigned so that they could be produced by the use of sand casting, investment castings, die castings or forgings all in ferrous or non-ferrous metals. One object to be achieved by redesign of these parts would be that these parts or fittings could be subcontracted to small suppliers and then funnel them into the main production plant in the vast quantities so required. Some of these parts were supplied in rough form and some were finished in entirety ready for use, while others had to be machined to the fine tolerances required by the engineering drawings for usability.

All of this redesign for gearing to a high production tempo required countless hours of production engineering and production planning to an intense degree in order to obtain the necessary diversification and simplification of the various production processes. But it was all done on great haste prior to the advent of the United States entrance into the war in December 1941. But by January 1942 the C-47s began delivery to the armed forces and foreign allies in volume.

But this was not all. There were the various processes to be considered such as the plating, pre-painted ferrous and non-ferrous metals, anti-corrosion coatings, degreasing, painting, insulation, head lining, fabric treatment, fungus treatment, organic protective paints, threaded parts, pickling, anodic treatment of non-ferrous metals, coding of lines, placards, finishing and forming of lines, cable protective coatings, priming materials, slushing materials, doping of fabric, cotton materials, leather materials, synthetic rubber materials, lacquers, primers and aqueous cleaners to name a few. For all of these technical specifications, procurement procedures, and testing had to be formulated for vast-scale procurement, hitherto unheard of. But it was all part of the overall production operation.

Then there was the order of familiar A-N (Army and Navy) standard parts in sufficient quantity to assure volume production. These parts had to be obtained from outside vendors. Each part had to comply with the quality and inspection standard set forth in US Government drawings and material specifications.

In order to attain quality standards, rigid inspection methods had to be compiled and disseminated to the parts vendors. Production gauges made to great accuracy were distributed to the various vendors to assure accuracy and interchangeability. All of these functions had to be undertaken in order to maintain the necessary quality standards and uniformity.

The secondary part of the search for quality was to enlist vendors who could comply with the rigid A-N inspection standards, yet at the same time, could guarantee delivery as per schedule without a high percentage of rejection of the parts when they arrived at the Receiving Department of the Material Department of the Douglas factory.

The design of production tooling and procurement were not the only factors to be concerned with in volume production of the C-47. The personnel factor was also one of great importance, because without skilled and experienced personnel in engineering, administrative, procurement and production aspects of the total productive effort, no volume production of aeroplanes could be achieved. The whole solution to the problem of manpower centred around a skilled core of specialists from the parent plant at Santa Monica who were assigned to work at the Douglas Long Beach facility.

Great effort and means at hand were expended to obtain competent workers in aircraft tooling, production operations, process knowledge and blueprint reading. Newcomers who had never worked in production operations prior to their employment were given training and indoctrine in various production operations and then given on-the-job training as well. New workers were trained to use the various hand tools proficiently. Those who had prior machine tool experience were assigned to machine fabrication operations. The workers came from all walks of life, from near and far, all anxious to work and to speed the production effort of vital aircraft for the armed forces.

The technical manpower aspects also played an important role in attainment of the desired objective and production schedules. The engineering department at the Douglas Long Beach plant was expanded around a seasoned core of old time and experienced aircraft project engineers, to name a few, Fred Herman as Chief Engineer, Fred Steinman as Assistant Chief Engineer, Jack Bromberg, Gordon Farquhar, etc, plus many others too numerous to mention, all of them being key personnel in the parent factory at Santa Monica. All of these individuals were steeped in technical experience relating to the DC-2 and DC-3 air transports. Coupled with engineering design aspects was the Douglas Inspection Department at the factory, the function of which was to maintain the quality and accuracy of parts that comprised the Douglas C-47. This department performed inspection of all parts, either those procured from vendors and subcontractors as well as parts fabricated in the plant. The various inspection operations involved parts, production, assembly and finally flight inspection.

One phase of the entire operation seldom mentioned in the factory history was the staff of company test pilots who performed the first and second test flights after the aircraft were serviced and flight inspected and prepared for the company acceptance flights. Usually not more than two test flights were required to certify that the aircraft was ready to be turned over to the USAAF test pilots. They in turn performed two test flights before returning the aircraft to the company for final delivery to Air Transport Command. Of the thousands of aircraft produced at Long Beach during World War 2, only one test flight fatality occurred and that was not on the initial test flight. When it is considered that two- and four-engined aircraft were also produced in great quantity besides the C-47, this proved that Douglas management as a whole, and their concept of volume production was exemplary.

C-47 PRODUCTION AND ITS TECHNIQUES

It is not generally realised that the military version of the Douglas DC-3 had every reason to be rejected when the United States entered World War 2. Early Army Air Corps attempts to develop transport aircraft had produced no satisfactory model, and, in spite of redoubled efforts, no successful design was produced during the war years. So, inevitably, the Army Air Force turned to civilian models already in production and the various modification of heavy bombers. The early standby, and indeed the most dependable aircraft within its capacities throughout the war, was the Douglas DC-3, known alternatively according to its special modifications, as the C-47 and the C-53, and with the Royal Air Force and Allied Air Forces as the Dakota.

Long successful in civilian passenger service but already obsolete at Pearl Harbor time, the two-engined DC-3 had many features ill suited to the convenient handling of bulky freight, and its payload was too light for the new tasks. But it was flyable under almost any conditions, was easily maintained, and above all, was in production.

The DC-3 was a low-wing monoplane whose fuselage stood so high off the ground that loading from an ordinary truck platform was impractical. Also the door was narrow and the floor lacked the strength to support heavy cargo. A larger door, reinforced floor, special loading equipment, and other improvisations were devised for the C-47, but it was natural that Air Transport Command should have sought an aircraft better suited to its needs. Desired characteristics included a low-swung fuselage to facilitate loading, especially of such bulky equipment as jeeps or small tanks, a higher payload, the ability to operate from small unsurfaced airfields, and a ferrying range of at least 2,500 miles to permit delivery of the aircraft from factory to the front under its own power. It was desirable, furthermore, that the aircraft be constructed of non-critical materials, such as plywood, plastics, fabric, and tubular steel, in order not to compete with combat types at the factory.

Much time and money went into the search, before and after Pearl Harbor, for a two-engined aircraft that would meet all these requirements. The Budd C-93 of stainless steel construction was developed but engineering problems and shortage of stainless steel led to the cancellation early in 1944. The Waco C-62 project was an experiment in the construction of a wooden transport aircraft. Engineering problems proved difficult, and the C-62 rated a lower priority than wooden gliders and in late 1943 the project was dropped. The Curtiss-Wright C-76 Caravan, identical to the C-62, met with little more success. In July 1943 after the first aircraft had crashed, orders for all but twenty-five aircraft were cancelled and the Chief of the Material Command estimated an unrecoverable loss of 40 million dollars.

Better success was had with the Fairchild C-82 Packet, but even though this design was presented to the Material Command shortly after Pearl Harbor, the first C-82 was not delivered until June 1945.

It seemed that the answer to Air Transport Commands need would be found in the Curtiss-Wright C-46 Commando. After the first encouraging reports, however, came discouraging ones. In heavy rain the fuselage leaked like a sieve because the joints had not been properly sealed, the camouflage paint began to peel, and much more serious trouble developed with the hydraulic and fuel systems. In August 1942 it became necessary to ask for fifty-three immediate modifications, exclusive of winterisation, and to recommend forty-six additional changes as desirable. The first thirty aircraft delivered to Air Transport Command had to be returned to the factory. They began to return in early 1943 as the C-46A, a modified version which was flyable but still far from satisfactory. As late as April 1943 when many of these defects became known, Brig Gen Cyrus R Smith, Chief of Staff of the Air Transport Command and one of the ablest airline executives in the United States, declared that for hauling cargo over distances of 1,500 miles or less, the C-46 was more efficient than the four-engined C-54 Skymaster. For short hauls of around 1,000 miles, he insisted that the C-46 offered twice the value of the C-47. The War Production Board, too, had gone out for the C-46, declaring it to be the most efficient and economical cargo aircraft then in production, and the C-47 the least efficient of the short-haul carriers.

Amongst Air Transport Command pilots the C-46 Commando was known with good reason, as the "flying coffin". From May 1943 to March 1945 ATC received reports of thirty-one instances in which C-46 aircraft caught fire or exploded in the air. Still others were listed merely as "missing" in flight, and it is a safe assumption that many of these exploded, went down in flames, or crashed as the result of vapour lock, carburettor icing, or other defects.

After the disappointment with the C-46, Air Transport Command had no choice but to place its heaviest dependence for medium-range transport on the under-valued C-47. At the peak of operations in August 1945 well over a third of the Command's major transports – 1,341 out of 3,090 – were Douglas C-47s. In addition the type was in use in large numbers by the Royal Air Force and the air forces of the Allies – South Africa, New Zealand, Australia, Canada and even Russia. The C-47 or Dakota remained in demand for many years.

However, let not all the glory be showered on the Douglas DC-3 airframe. Without the engine development of Pratt & Whitney and Curtiss-Wright, no DC-3 could have lifted from the runway with the greatest of ease.

The development of the 1,000 hp radial air-cooled engines, endowed with a high degree of reliability and a moderate fuel consumption, gave the Douglas C-47 the boost it had to have to generate high lift with the wings. Coupled with that would be the development of 100 octane aviation fuel, the development of the Hamilton-Standard Hydromatic quick feathering propellers and instrumentation and communication equipment. As such this was a team effort of American technology at its best. All of these components when blended together in a clean aerodynamic air transport design made it possible to transport twenty-one passengers at 195 mph across the United States in comfort and at a profit to the airlines. Suffice to say that the DC-3 is still the epitome of luxury air travel in many parts of the world today, over thirty-five years later.

But in order to continue with the story of this miracle of Douglas technology, which produced thousands of the "Gooney Bird" as the C-47 was affectionately known in the US Army Air Force and the Royal Air Force, it is fitting to review how the transport was produced.

In order to perform a fast and vast production, the airframe was broken down into fifty major assemblies and sub-assemblies. These in turn were further broken down into sub-sub-assemblies and so on to the fourth quantity, it being the smallest and simplest. Actual production of the C-47 started prior to the participation of the United States in World War 2. When the Japanese launched the attack on Pearl Harbor, many Douglas C-47s had already been delivered to the armed forces of the United States. These transports were ready to perform their appointed rounds on December 7, 1941, a day of infamy in American history. The C-47 and its forebear was the only cargo aircraft available in quantity in the US Army Air Force inventory. The brunt of air cargo transport operations was imposed on the shoulders of the "Gooney Bird" and it did not falter.

But how was an aircraft as large as the Douglas C-47 to be assembled so easily and in such large quantities? Prior to the war, the assembly jigs were mainly constructed of easily available wood structural members. Wood was a low cost material and it could be easily replaced when the jig was worn by constant and repetitive use. But to produce aircraft on a vast scale required the utmost in technical design and accuracy. The entire Douglas C-47 production jigs and fixtures were constructed of steel. In fact, the Douglas Aircraft Company established a corporate autonomous division to manufacture the tooling jigs, assembly jigs, handling tools, assembly fixtures, hoisting tools and rigs, etc. The tooling division of the company was responsible for the production of all tooling for manufacturing in conformity with the engineering drawings.

The Douglas Aircraft Company is above all an aircraft and aerospace engineering firm that welded skilled engineering and tooling talent together to produce the Douglas C-47 in quantity. Suffice to say, the company accomplished this with several other aircraft programmes under way, it being the only aircraft company in the world that manufactured three different types of four-engined aircraft at the same time.

One can surmise that care and co-ordination of the production programme was the order of the day in order to establish that record. This in itself was no easy task. The acquisition and training of technical personnel was a programme of vast import as well as the training of a vast army of production workers and still build and deliver aircraft in compliance with the production schedules of the armed forces. But it was done. Time was a factor and military aircraft were needed post haste. But between the genius of the company technical personnel working side by side with the technicians of the Air Material and Air Service Commands, all production goals were eventually effectuated within the allotted time.

The Douglas C-47 structure is broken down into five major assemblies, ie the fuselage, the centre wing, the tail surfaces and the outer wing panels. The two engine nacelles are attached to the centre wing structure as are the two landing gear assemblies. All of these major components when joined together comprise the completed article, the Douglas C-47.

The fuselage is of all metal, semi-monocoque construction, almost circular in section and built up of channel-section transverse frames, or formers, and extruded bulb angle stringers. There is a limited number of rolled alloy channel members running longitudinally to provide additional stiffness. The framework is covered with an Alclad skin of varying gauges and is riveted with snap rivets. There are six compartments in the fuselage, which are, from forward to aft, cockpit; port and starboard baggage compartments; radio operator's compartment; main compartment and lavatory.

Conventional in layout, the pilot's cockpit accommodates the first pilot on the port side and the second pilot on the starboard side. Full flying controls are provided for each. The control columns are of the usual type, but are cranked so that the column itself is outboard of the seat in order to provide more room and greater freedom of movement of the pilot. All the electrical controls are positioned in panels above the windscreen and are separate from other services.

The baggage compartments are situated each side of a central gangway leading to the cockpit. Behind these, on the starboard side, is the radio operator's station. The port side is available for an additional fuel tank, if required. At the aft end of the main compartment, on the port side, are a pair of large doors for cargo loading and unloading. In the forward door is inset a smaller single door for use when passengers are carried instead of freight. The lavatory, in the aft end, contains a chemical disposal type toilet and a wash basin.

The nose section assembly of the fuselage is a complex production assembly, and is produced on a separate production line, away from the aircraft assembly hall. The floor of the C-47 is sub-divided into fourteen sub-assemblies for production. The floor sections are attached together, and these and the longerons are joined in the first major position of a nine position moving assembly line.

By far and large, the fuselage is the major structural assembly of the C-47. It has a top section that extends from the circumferential ring at the tail stub section to the pilot's escape hatch circumferential ring.

The wings are of full cantilever design, of all-metal stressed-skin construction and consist of a centre section which passes through the lower part of the fuselage beneath the flooring. The engine nacelles are mounted on the centre section. Attached to the centre section are the outboard sections which are tapered along the leading edge. Each outboard section is fitted with detachable trailing edges and wing tips.

The centre section is of constant chord and is built up on three main spars of aluminium alloy extruded booms and sheet Alclad webs. The ribs are sheet Alclad pressings with pierced lightning holes. Aft of the rear spar the wing is reinforced with extruded alloy sections running longitudinally as is the underside of the forward section. Between the spars the top skin is reinforced by corrugated sheeting, the corrugations running spanwise and thus forming a tremendously strong compression structure. Two main fuel tanks and two auxiliary fuel tanks are fitted in the centre section. The attachment of the centre section to the fuselage is affected by eight vertical fittings, there being two each on the three main spars and two on a forward auxiliary spar. In addition there are skin attachment angles and the fixings are covered by a fillet fairing, giving a smooth contour from the wing aerofoil to the fuselage.

The engine nacelles are constructed as separate units, but are assembled to the centre section before the final assembly and so they can be classed as part of the wing structure. They are of monocoque construction, with pressed channel-section formers and top hat stringers. In each nacelle are mounted two rubber fittings on the lower stringers, against which the undercarriage axle rests when retracted. These, as well as providing a support for the landing gear, also serve to protect the nacelle structure in the event of a wheels-up landing.

The outer wing sections are of similar construction to the centre section, except that transverse bulb angles and "Z" section stringers are incorporated instead of the corrugated sheeting. The trailing edge of the outer section is divided into inboard and outboard portions. The outboard portions are riveted to the main wing and form an integral part of the structure. The inboard portions are removable.

Metal frame, fabric-covered ailerons are fitted and are hinged at six points on self-lubricating bearings. The flaps are of the split trailing-edge type, extending between the inboard ends of the ailerons. They are operated hydraulically and are in four sections which function as a single continuous unit. The maximum downward movement is 45 degrees, which gives an increase in lift of approximately 35 per cent, and approximately 250 per cent increase in drag. A flap position indicator is provided for the pilot. The flaps are of all-metal construction with pressed aluminium alloy ribs.

The tailplane is of full cantilever, all-metal construction, consisting of extruded framework and sheet Alclad skin. It is made in two halves, bolted together at the fuselage centre line and attached by four flange plates in fixed alignment to the fuselage. The elevators are metal-framed and fabric-covered, attached to the tailplane by four forged aluminium alloy plate hinge brackets. An 8-lb counterweight is embodied in each elevator. The elevators are pivoted on self-lubricated ball bearings. Trim tabs, controlled by the pilot, are fitted to each.

The fin is of similar construction to the tailplane and is bolted to the fuselage. The lower part of the leading edge fits over a false fairing and is attached by machine screws. This fairing, which extends along the top of the fuselage, is made up of pressed formers, bolted to the fuselage frame and covered with an Alclad skin. It gives additional directional stability and increases the rigidity of the fin proper.

The rudder is constructed of aluminium alloy pressed frames and is fabric covered. It is balanced by an 11-lb balance weight secured in the leading edge and is carried on Fafnir self-lubricating bearings, similar to those on the elevators.

Of the conventional tail-wheel type, the main landing wheels of the undercarriage retract forward into the nacelles. When fully retracted, the wheels project slightly below the nacelles and no doors are fitted. Bendix aluminium alloy cast wheels, complete with Duo-Servo brakes, are fitted and carry Goodrich tyres, with an air pressure of 43 lb per sq in. Two Bendix Type EH-3C air-oil shock-absorber struts are fitted to each main unit, one each side of the wheel. A tube connects the struts at the top to balance the pressure in each. A safety latch is fitted in each nacelle to lock the gear when extended. The latch control system is connected by levers to a catch on the landing gear control valve in such a manner that the latch must be raised before the landing gear control can be moved in the "up" position to retract the wheels.

A flight wheel brake, consisting of heavy, flexible belting with sheet steel facings, is attached to the firewall in each nacelle. When the wheels are retracted, these brakes engage with the tyres and prevent rotation caused by outside air pressure on the exposed portions of the wheels.

The landing gear is actuated by means of an hydraulic system. This system consists of a control valve and two actuating struts, one strut for each gear. When the control valve handle is placed in the "up" position, fluid, under pressure from the hydraulic system, is directed to the bottom of each strut, forcing the piston and piston rod up and pulling each gear into its nacelle. The fluid in the top of the struts is directed through the control valve into the return manifold as the piston is forced up. The landing gear is not mechanically locked in the retracted position, but is held up by the fluid pressure in the lower end of the strut. In flight the undercarriage lever is kept in "neutral" which blanks off both lines from the strut this retains the pressure in the lower end of the strut. To extend the gear the control lever is placed in the "down" position and the reverse procedure takes place.

In order to prevent the landing gear from extending too rapidly, due to combined forces of gravity, hydraulic pressure and outside air pressure, an elastic bungee cord is attached to each gear through a mechanical linkage, the resistance of which has to be overcome by the hydraulic pressure. The wheel brakes are operated hydraulically by toe pedals on the rudder controls. Each brake can be operated independently for taxiing.

The Dakota Mk I – C-47 – is fitted with Pratt & Whitney Twin Wasp R-1830-92 fourteen-cylinder radial motors, with single speed blowers. The Dakota Mk II – C-53 – and Dakota Mk III – C-47A – are fitted with Pratt & Whitney Twin Wasp R-1830-90C engines, with two-speed blowers, while the Dakota Mk IV – C-47B – is fitted with Pratt & Whitney Twin Wasp R-1830-90B engines. They have a compression ratio of 6·7:1, an impellor gear ratio of 7·15:1 and an airscrew reduction ratio of 16:9. Each engine is rated at 1,050 hp at sea-level, 1,050 hp at 2,550 rpm at 7,500 ft and 1,200 hp at 2,700 rpm for take-off, using 100 octane fuel. All engine types are equipped with combination electric inertia, direct cranking starters. The induction system is controlled by PD-12H Stromberg-injection carburettors.

Prior to the advent of the entry of the United States into World War 2, the Douglas Aircraft Company had devised the demountable engine power plant assembly for airline use. This feature was made a design component of the DC-3 airline transport and was included in the C-47 design. It permitted quick removal of a defective engine and the quick installation of a new engine if required. It made engine removal a routine flight line operation and reduced greatly the time on the ground for aircraft with engine malfunctions.

The engines are mounted on tubular mounting rings, which are interchangeable left and right. An air scoop on the nacelle supplies air to the carburettors. On early Dakotas the induction is of the simple, direct ram type, but later aircraft have a modified system whereby air can be supplied, unfiltered, by direct ram, or by a non-ram filtered system.

Each engine has its own fuel supply, consisting of a main fuel tank, an auxiliary tank, a tank selector valve, fuel strainer, wobble pump, fuel pump and primer, and operates at a pressure of 15 lb per sq in. The two engine systems are interconnected by lines running from the selector valves to tee unions on the other system's supply line, thus making it possible for each engine to be operated from any of the four fuel tanks. There is also a separate cross-feed system connecting the pressure side of the engine-driven pumps.

The two main tanks each have a capacity of 168 Imperial gallons, and the auxiliary tanks each have a capacity of 167 Imperial gallons, giving a total tankage of 670 Imperial gallons. They are constructed of welded aluminium sheet and each is fitted with an electric contents gauge connected to the pilots' indicator, a water-collecting sump and drain cock. The main fuel tanks are mounted between the front and centre spars of the wing centre section, on each side of the centre line. The auxiliary tanks are mounted directly aft of the main tanks, between the rear and centre spars. They are secured with padded metal straps. Additional long-range fuel tanks can be carried in the fuselage.

A complete oil system is provided for each engine. The system consists of the oil tank – which is of the "quick warm-up" type – an oil temperature regulator, a drain valve, provisions for oil dilution and the necessary controls, lines and connections.

The oil flows from the tank through an oil dilution tee and then direct to the engine crankcase. From the crankcase it passes through the manually controlled oil cooler and back to the oil tank where it circulates through the "quick warm-up" hopper and again enters the system. An oil temperature regulator valve in the oil cooler by-passes the oil directly to the tank instead of to the oil cooler if the oil temperature is below 71 degrees C. The oil tank is of the saddle type, fitting round the undercarriage jack in the aft end of the nacelle. It is of welded aluminium sheet construction with riveted internal baffles and hopper. Each tank has a capacity of 24 Imperial gallons, exclusive of foaming space.

The "quick warm-up" hopper in the tank is merely a cylindrical inner container isolating a small quantity of oil which is circulated through the system. Due to the small quantity of oil in circulation, it attains a working temperature at a much quicker rate than if the full quantity were in use. Any oil loss in the system is replaced in the hopper through an opening above the outlet.

The oil cooler is manually controlled from the pilot's position by a series of cables and pulleys which actuate a bell crank on the aft face of the engine firewall. This bell crank opens and closes the oil cooler shutters by means of a flexible push-pull rod in a protective housing. An oil-pressure gauge for each engine is fitted in the pilot's cockpit and is operated by a ¼-in pressure line running from the oil sump to the instrument. The oil pressure varies between 75–90 lb per sq in. An oil-dilution system, for cold weather starting is provided.

Pressure for the hydraulic system, which operates the landing gear, brakes, cowl flaps, wing flaps, carburettor non-ram filter mechanism and windscreen wipers, is supplied by means of two motor-driven pumps, one mounted on each engine. Normally, the pump on the port engine supplies fluid to the main system and the starboard pump operates the automatic pilot. There is, however, a pump selector valve which provides a means whereby the flow from the pumps may be reversed.

When operating, the hydraulic fluid passes by gravity from the reservoir to both pumps and then to the motor pump selector valve. Special valves are installed at the engine firewall to enable the motor unit to be disconnected and removed without the necessity of draining or plugging the lines. From the pump selector valve the fluid from the pump supplying the main system flows through the pressure regulator to an hydraulic pressure accumulator and, from there, into the main system at an operating pressure of 600–875 lb per sq in. The pressure regulator controls the pressure in the accumulators and correspondingly in the system itself. In the event of the pressure regulator failing, a relief valve opens when the pressure builds up to 1,000 lb per sq in and by-passes the excess fluid to the reservoir. A hand pump is provided to operate any hydraulic mechanism if the pressure in the system is insufficient, or if the engine-driven pump ceases to function.

There are two types of oxygen installations: a high-pressure system, which is installed in the earlier models; and a low-pressure system installed in subsequent models.

The high-pressure system operates at a pressure of 1,800 lb per sq in and consists of an oxygen cylinder aft of the rear bulkhead of the cockpit, a regulating valve, three bayonet-type plug-in valves with regulator openings and the necessary oxygen lines and connections. With this system oxygen output is controlled manually.

The low-pressure system operates at a pressure of 400 lb per sq in. The system is known as a demand system and supplies oxygen, diluted with air, only when the user demands it, ie at altitudes over 10,000 ft and during inhalation only.

The oxygen is stored in cylinders beneath the floor of the main compartment. It flows through the lines of the regulator which is connected to the mask. The oxygen is automatically diluted with air to the correct ratio for that particular altitude and is delivered automatically with each inhalation of the user. A panel, containing flow indicator warning lamps and a pressure gauge is fitted at each station. The flow indicator is in the form of a blinker or mechanical eye which blinks every time the oxygen is inhaled. By this device the user can tell immediately whether oxygen is being delivered. The warning lamp is operated electrically when the pressure falls below 100 lb per sq in. A control is fitted whereby the user can obtain pure oxygen if necessary.

A steam-heating system is embodied in the earlier model of Dakota, the later series being provided with a hot-air system. The steam-heating system incorporates a boiler in the starboard engine exhaust tail pipe in which water is converted into steam by the heat of the exhaust gases. The steam is passed into a radiator where it transfers heat to air entering through a scoop from outside. This heated air is circulated through the aircraft by means of ducts. The temperature can be regulated by introducing cold air into the ducts in a suitable ratio to the heated air.

The hot-air system incorporates a muff-type heat exchanger which is an integral part of each engine exhaust tail pipe. Outside air enters these and is heated. It is then passed to a mixing chamber – one for each engine – where it is mixed with cold air to provide the desired temperature. Ventilation is accomplished by allowing unheated outside air to pass through a ventilating duct system.

On the aircraft assembly line, when the transport is theoretically complete and has been functionally checked for proper operation, the aircraft is run onto carriers that run on a rail and steel plate secured to the factory floor. A dolly is placed under the tail wheel. Although the carriers run straight, the aircraft is turned 30 degrees in relation to the final assembly line in order to conserve floor space.

Then the initial factory inspection takes place. All functional systems and flight controls are checked for correct operation. Auxiliary electrical power is supplied to the aircraft to perform checks and to energise the hydraulic system so that the landing gear may be checked, wing flaps operated and other hydraulically operated systems worked. The same check is made for all of the electrical and radio components and systems.

The electrical storage batteries are installed. The company inspectors note any discrepancies and these are corrected. After these inspectors have certified the aircraft as being correct and airworthy it is moved to another position so that the military inspectors may examine the transport. Any further discrepancies are noted and corrected.

At the last and final position on the assembly line, certain painting and markings are performed. However, the major assemblies were all previously painted in a spray paint booth provided with a water recovery system for excess protective or camouflage painting. Any markings are made by means of templates and colour charts to Army Air Force specification, and before the end of World War 2 were to include the insignia of many nations.

After the company's inspection team has certified that the C-47 is airworthy and all the Army Air Force inspection teams agree, the transport is accepted for delivery. It is towed to the flight line for preliminary servicing, fueling and engine run-up. Additional checks may be performed on the flight line by company personnel prior to the first flight. If the supervisor deems the aircraft as airworthy, the first company test flight is made. On this flight an inspector makes any notes necessary, and at the conclusion of the flight, the pilot submits a report to the supervising crew chief inspector. Any discrepancies noted are corrected. After a second test flight the aircraft is signed off ready for delivery to the military test pilots who make two test flights. On the final test flight all discrepancies are corrected and the C-47 is made ready for formal delivery to the Army Air Force acceptance team.

After refuelling, all loose equipment items are stowed on board along with a complete "G" file of inspection forms, Tech Orders and weight and balance forms. In the instance of C-47s manufactured at the Long Beach plant, the aircraft was taxied around the edge of the airfield to the Air Transport Command Base at Long Beach Army Air Field, ready for its ultimate destination.

Mention must be made of the major sub-contractors who supported the massive production programme involving the Douglas C-47. These were Beech, Cessna, AO Smith, Murray Body, Fleetwings, Pullman-Standard and many more. Note that these vendors were all located in the mid-west part of the United States.

The initial C-47 transports were designed and intended for the transportation of troops, either combat or medical evacuees, medium and light cargo support for airborne assaults. However, the air transport configuration of the C-47 proved to be so successful that it soon became a jack of all trades in the Army Air Force and the armed forces of the Allies including the Royal Air Force. It must be remembered that the C-47 has served the US armed forces in three wars. The C-47 that was basically the DC-3 airframe progressed from an initial weight of approximately 18,300 lb to a gross weight of 29,200 lb. As the tactics for airborne warfare evolved, so did the multitudinous functions of the C-47. The demand far exceeded the supply and so to eliminate the shortage, the Army Air Force built the Douglas Oklahoma City facility as a secondary source of production. This former plant is now Tinker Air Force Base.

In order to improve the basic C-47, there followed the C-47A which had an improved 24-volt electrical system. Then followed the C-47B which was intended to be used to fly the Hump to China. The gross weight on this model was raised to 30,000 lb and the two radial air-cooled engines were centrifugally supercharged to obtain the extra power to fly the Hump air freight route over the Himalayas to Chungking in China to support the 14th US Army Air Force. These two latter models were produced at both Long Beach and Oklahoma City plants.

For the first two years of combat the US Army Air Force had a shortage of experienced transport pilots. To alleviate this shortage of pilots with multi-engine ratings, more than 133 model TC-47B air transports were fitted for dual piloting and navigational training purposes.

With the war raging around the world and in various climates, came the possibility of using the C-47 as an amphibious float plane. One model of the C-47 – XC-47 – was fitted with Edo floats for landing on water. Two floats were substituted for the landing gear. However, the military situation changed before the need for the XC-47 was required. The gross weight of this model was approximately 34,000 lb. However, although considerably heavier than the land version, the transport had a remarkable performance for a cargo amphibian. Only one model of this transport was converted and it did not see combat.

The model C-47D followed next in the development of the type. This was an improved version of the C-47B except that the engines were not supercharged. It was intended for normal air support operations.

All wartime C-47s had windows equipped with rifle apertures in the perspex. It was thought that if a troop carrying transport was attacked in flight by hostile aircraft, the troops aboard with rifles could drive off an attacker with combined fire. While this was good in theory it was not very useful in actual service. It is doubtful whether the rifle ports justified their cost and installation. In India and Burma the early Dakotas used by No 31 Squadron carried Vickers "K" gas operated machine-guns mounted on pivot supports and protruding through the window frame aft of the wing port and starboard, the perspex having been removed.

When it is considered in retrospect, the capacity of the Douglas Long Beach plant complex as originally constructed was far beyond the comprehension of the layman. During the month of May 1945 more than 415 C-47s were delivered by the factory to Air Transport Command. This is no small programme when it is considered that at that time the factory was also building approximately 120 Boeing B-17 Flying Fortress aircraft per month. All aircraft built were ready for delivery by air.

LICENCE TO BUILD

The merits of the Douglas DC-3 were recognised by the foreign companies who were licensed by the Douglas Aircraft Company to build the DC-3 transports. These companies in Japan, our enemy, and in Russia, our ally, were granted the manufacturing and patent rights. Licence to manufacture was granted to the Dutch Fokker company, but they never went into production. Instead Fokker became the Douglas agent in Europe, and so handled all the DC-3s which were shipped over from the USA to the ports of Rotterdam and Cherbourg. After final assembly the aircraft were delivered to the airlines; these included KLM in Holland, ABA in Sweden and many other of the European operators of the DC-3. Sales were so good that Fokkers held a pool of DC-3s. The purchase price of a DC-3 was then approximately £30,000 or $115,000.

Nakajima in Japan held the licence to manufacture the DC-3 and on September 30, 1938, the assembly of the first aircraft was completed at Hanedda Airport for Dai-Nippon Airways. A quantity of DC-3 type transports were built for the Imperial Japanese Navy, who preferred the Douglas type. Many of these Nipponese transports served on the Japanese war front in the South Pacific and performed meritorious service in their assigned functions.

A third licensee was the State Aircraft Plant in the USSR who not only bought large quantities of jigs and tools from the USA, but purchased a total of eighteen DC-3s from Santa Monica between November 1936 and March 1939. These were delivered by Douglas in the name *North Eastern* and *Excello* both of which were represented by Amtorg the prewar purchasing agency. There is considerable reason to believe that these were paper organisations of the Russian Government. The first aircraft had constructors number 1589 registered NC14995 in the USA with *Excello*, followed by a block of eleven delivered between May and August of 1938 and concluded with a block of six, the last of which was delivered in March 1939. Of the eighteen DC-3s, two were delivered disassembled ostensibly for use as spare parts.

The State Aircraft Plant's leading aviation expert, Boris Lisunov, spent two years studying with the Douglas Company at Santa Monica, before returning to Russia to supervise production. Small-scale production did not commence until 1940, but it is believed that by the summer of 1941 about thirty to forty aircraft per month were being produced in the USSR. Designated the PS-84 and later the Lisunov Li-2 the aircraft was for use by Aeroflot the Russian State airline.

It is not known how many DC-3 type transport aircraft were built by the Russians and how they served the forces of the USSR on the Eastern front. The transport is still in use by the USSR and its satellite forces, and carries the code-name *Cab* in the NATO aircraft vocabulary.

In waging global war, it was necessary to modify the Douglas C-47s for geographical as well as combat functions. In order to accomplish this objective, a modification centre was established by the US Army Air Force at Daggett in California. The C-47s were flown from the factory to the modification centre. Here in assembly line operations, the transports were fitted for various roles dictated by geographical operational requirements. For example, aircraft intended for Alaska, the USSR, or the North Atlantic air ferry route were winterised for low temperature operation with special hose lines, high capacity heaters, de-icer boots, special engine oil dilution systems, special tyres, added interior insulation, etc. Aircraft intended for operations in North Africa were fitted with special carburettor dust exclusion systems, etc.

Aircraft undergoing these modifications were usually selected in certain numerical blocks and modified accordingly. But while the whole concept of theatre modification and specialisation was to achieve a specific objective, sometimes in practice this did not always hold true. The Operations Officers in the various theatres would occasionally receive an aircraft modified for the tropics of North Africa at a unit serving in sub-zero temperatures in the Arctic theatre. This was no doubt caused by the Pentagon's habit of selecting aircraft by serial number blocks without determining before assignment to what theatre the aircraft had received modifications. But such are the exigencies of air warfare that frequently ideas that appear logical do not always function to complete satisfaction because of the human factor involved.

Dakotas intended for the Royal Air Force were delivered from the production lines at the Long Beach and Oklahoma factories under Lend-Lease agreement. Alongside the initial Dakota Mk Is on the production line at Long Beach in January 1943 were similar transports for the Royal New Zealand Air Force, the USSR and China. All carried the US Army Air Force designation C-47-DL. Oklahoma manufactured C-47s carried the designation C-47-DK. Some of the RAF Dakotas went through the modification centre at Daggett, others were flown direct to Mobile Air Force Base in Alabama, for US ferry crews to fly to the east coast embarkation points.

Responsibility for RAF Dakotas at the Douglas factories was vested in the US Army Air Force who also issued the contracts on behalf of the British Government, the first for 200 aircraft being issued on June 28, 1941, under contract No DA167, followed by DA1043 on February 7, 1942, for a further 150 aircraft. This was preceeded by a small contract for 40 aircraft on the last day of January 1942 – DA1040 – and a further 25 transports under contract DA1047 on February 7, 1942, both the latter contracts including three aircraft for the US Navy. Many more contracts were issued before the final Dakota was delivered to the Royal Air Force, this being a Mk IV KP279 a C-47B-40-DK 44-77249 manufactured at the Oklahoma factory.

So that a close liaison with both the US Army Air Force and Douglas could be maintained, a British representative was based at the factories involved in producing the Dakota for the RAF. In the same respect Douglas had their representatives based in all theatres of operations where the transport operated. The files of No 31 Squadron record the visit by Mr Achelle, a Douglas representative, to their base at Khargpur in connection with tool kits which were missing from new Dakota aircraft delivered to the unit. During the same month, November 1943, the squadron Engineering Officer recorded that he deplored the shortage of American tool kits, and maintained that American tools for American fittings and aircraft is half the serviceability battle. Two Dakota Mk Is, FD811 and FD844, were cannibilised because of this problem. The story is told in California of a similar situation with missing Dakota tool kits which occurred at the Long Beach plant involving Lend-Lease C-47s for the USSR. The Russian Colonel, who was acting as liaison officer, called in the OGPU secret police.

A function of the manufacturing facilities of the factory was to engineer and produce special maintenance handling tools for field maintenance and depot functions. Each of these tools were given a part number and would then be made part of the basic aircraft procurement contract. Certain special hand tools for maintenance were either manufactured in the tooling facility of the factory or were designed by the tooling engineers and obtained from outside vendors.

At the factory each Dakota as it was delivered to the Army Air Force, had to have a "G" file as an item of the loose equipment stowed on board. This file consisted of technical aircraft data, operational forms, flight manuals and erection and maintenance manuals, etc. No aircraft would be accepted from the factory unless this data was included.

The preparation of the technical manuals and data was undertaken by the Douglas Engineering Department in a special group trained for this kind of technical handbook preparation. The technical data was made part of all aircraft contracts.

A Weight and Balance Handbook was also included in the "G" file and the data prepared by the company for each individual transport aircraft for subsequent use of the unit involved. This usually travelled with the aircraft.

It is not generally known that the Douglas Aircraft Company was the first to produce an airframe parts catalogue which was originally prepared for airline use with the DC-3 series. Each component of the aircraft was numbered in accordance with the part number so that procurement could be facilitated. Each handbook was numbered and also coded as to what series aircraft it was applicable to. All parts of the airframe and accessories bore a Douglas part number regardless whether it was in fact a Douglas part or a product of some other manufacturer.

The engineering data contained in the technical manuals was voluminous, and all were grouped into the Army Air Force Technical Order system for distribution to personnel in all categories whose function was to keep the aircraft in commission. The costs to produce these handbooks were made part of the contract for aircraft purchase by the US Army Air Force. The Douglas company supplied the engineering data, drawings, photographs and art work to the US Air Service Command for reproduction into the Tech Orders. Compilation of these engineering manuals required the employment of competent engineering personnel to assist in the production of the handbooks. This work was of a very specialised nature.

As with all Lend-Lease aircraft the Royal Air Force produced its own technical documents in the Air Publication series, including the pilot's notes for the Dakota which were printed in the United Kingdom and India as AP2445.

The US Army Air Force Material Command was originally charged with the purchase of aircraft, spare parts, special tools, technical data, etc, for air war functions of the US Army. When the vast expansion of the Army Air Corps took place, it became necessary to divorce some of the functions of the Air Material Command relating to maintenance and field flyability operations. Thus the Air Service Command was organised as a separate command of the US Army Air Force. The functions relating to aircraft supply, maintenance and operational ability were delegated to the functioning groups of the new Air Service Command.

Air Service Command operated the main depots of the Army Air Force as well as the specialised depots. It co-ordinated with Material Command in the supply of all spare parts, engineering data and special tools and made these items a part of the aircraft contract. The two commands were in very close contact with each other.

At the Long Beach and Oklahoma factories the Air Service Command had a coterie of civilian employees assigned to supervise procurement of supplies, spare parts on production contracts, special tools and technical data. Once the aircraft was delivered to the Army Air Force they had to depend on the Air Service Command for their logistics at home and overseas.

It had long been recognised that aircraft in the combat zones required supporting activities such as performed by Air Service Command in order to attain a high percentage of availability for operational missions. Without replacement parts, damaged or grounded aircraft could not fly. It was the function of the civilian employees on the staff of Air Service Command in the Douglas plants to see that all items on demand relating to spare parts, special tools, engineering data and Tech Order compliance kits were delivered in accordance with the concurrent requirements of the contracts. Weekly statistical reports were transmitted to HQs Air Service Command by teletype from the factory. Thus the teamwork exhibited by the Army Air Force civilian staff and the Douglas personnel made it possible to effectuate the C-47 programme to the scheduled requirements.

It had long been a requirement of all Army Air Force procurement contracts for aircraft that 10 per cent of the total contractual expenditure funds be devoted to the purchase of spare parts for field support, depot and routine maintenance in the operational theatre. This provision applied to aircraft such as the C-47 Dakota built in quantity and did not necessarily apply to experimental aircraft where limited production was programmed.

As to be expected, the production of aircraft spares imposed an additional work load on the factory facilities in order to keep delivery of the parts to the Army Air Force depots. The production of spare parts could not fall behind aircraft deliveries. There were times when to keep all operations in balance, each facility borrowed parts from each in order to comply with the programmed delivery. Suffice to say, the delivery of spare parts from the Douglas plants was always in line with the programmed schedules.

Coupled to the insistent demand for aircraft and then more aircraft by the armed services, there were also two other production programmes that consumed much productive manpower, scheduling, engineering manhours, purchasing of materials for these items and finally shipping and packing. These two programmes, the production of spare parts for maintenance and support by field activities and the Tech Order compliance kits had to be considered in the overall manpower and order programmes for compliance with Government contracts. Each of these classes of material would be delivered either to the Army Air Force depots or to the using field activities for support operations.

Requests for immediate shipment of spares usually came through the Army Air Force network of teletypes to the Air Service Command representative in the factory. These TWX requests were handled and expedited in the shortest possible time to their destination. No request was made from the factory unless the parts were not available through the normal channel of supply. AOOC (aircraft out of commission) requests could only be made where the transport was grounded or not safe to fly, unavailable for operations, or involved the safety of the aircrew. These requests were given top priority handling, regardless of the factory schedule of production or delivery.

The provision of the Tech Order compliance or modification kits was initiated by HQs Air Service Command. Each kit contained a specific number of parts, tools if these were required to install it, and the engineering or technical data for the installation or modification. Attached parts were also included. The kits were shipped to the depots or direct to units when directed to do so. Sometimes the kits were placed on board transport aircraft as they were delivered from the factory to Air Transport Command. In this instance field personnel would perform the modification or installation. In some instances the kit contained only technical data.

As deliveries of the Dakota to the Royal Air Force increased, Maintenance Units in the various theatres of operation prepared to receive the new transport, and to stockpile spare parts. Dakotas initially delivered to the United Kingdom were ferried to Doncaster in Yorkshire for modifications which included installation of British VHF radio sets. During the latter stages of World War 2 an MU in the Middle East built a complete Dakota transport from spare parts.

RAF airfields used by Douglas Dakota units in the UK during World War 2

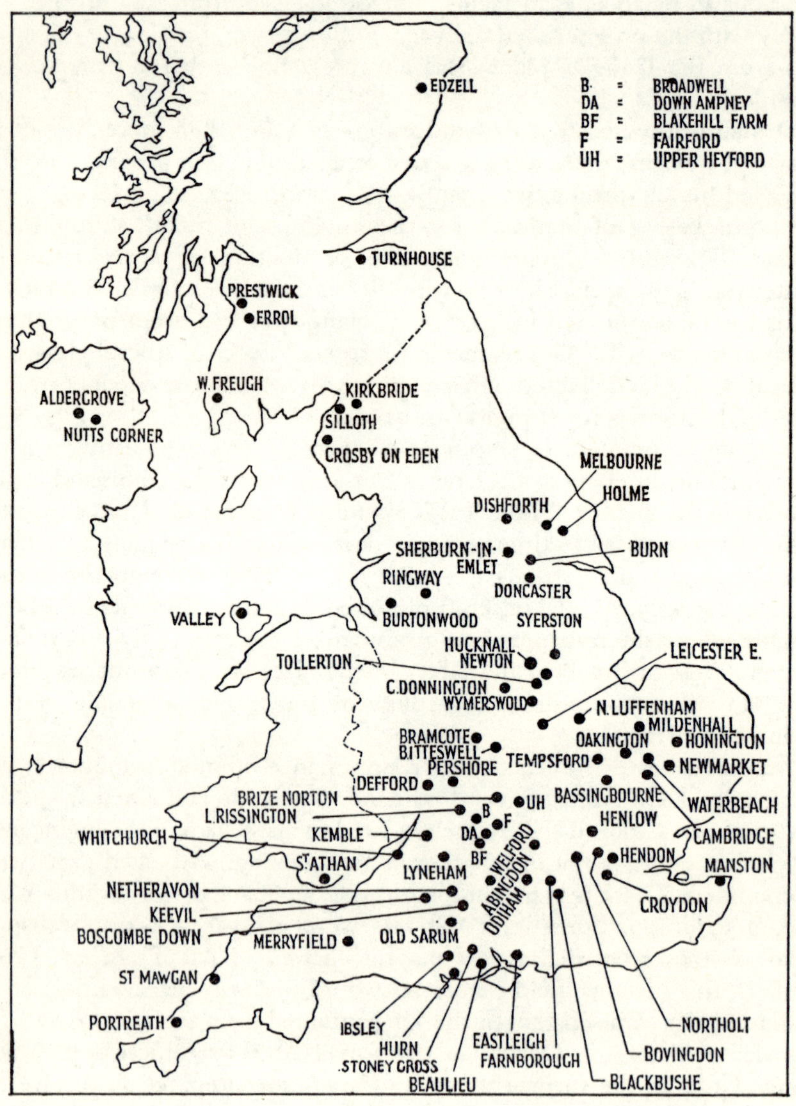

CHAPTER TWO

The Douglas Commercial Joins the RAF

The first Douglas transports to enter Royal Air Force service were undoubtedly the twelve received by No 31 Squadron in April 1941 – all Douglas DC-2s. A total of twenty-five DC-2s were bought by the British Purchasing Commission in Washington, DC, during 1941, the first fifteen being earmarked for the Government of India who originally intended their use by Tata Airlines and Indian National Airways. In the event, only the first twelve reached India and they were diverted to the Royal Air Force before seeing service with either airline, so that their original allotted civil registrations VT-AOQ to VT-APB were dropped in favour of the military serials DG468 and DG479. However log-book entries from at least one of the pilots from No 31 Squadron shows that some of the DC-2s were flown by the unit whilst they still had their Indian civil registrations. This was in May 1941 and included VT-AOT, U, V and Z plus VT-AUU.

For the record, the last three DC-2s from the batch of fifteen were allotted the civil registrations VT-APC to VT-APE and the military serials DG480 to DG482. Although they never materialised, it is known from the Trans World Airlines archives that NC13720, NC13726 and NC13784 were sold to the Indian Government for Tata Airlines. After a change in the United States policy they were retained by TWA until 1942, when they were sold to Northeast Airlines and the Defence Supply Corporation, finally going to the Army Air Force as C-32A transports.

The period commencing April 12, 1941, was spent by No 31 Squadron to converting "B" Flight crews to the first six Douglas DC-2Ks as the new transports were known in the Royal Air Force inventory. Sq Ldr WH Burbury was the Flight Commander and they became operational on April 16. Rashid Ali had started his rebellion in Iraq at this time and "A" Flight with seven Vickers Valentias and "B" Flight with four of its DC-2Ks – DG468, 469, 470 and 471 – were detached to fly further reinforcements to Shaibah the following day, where they remained as a detachment. During the next three days four more American civil Douglas DC-2s were taken over at Shaibah from their American crews. The detachment moved to Basra on April 19 and continued flying men, stores and equipment to Habbaniya daily with the loss of one DC-2K – NC14290 –

and two Vickers Valentias during a low flying attack made by six Luftwaffe Messerschmitt Mf 110s from Mosul. No one knew of the presence of German aircraft in Iraq, and at the time of the attack No 31 Squadron had six of its transports lined up on the aerodrome at Habbaniya.

May 1941 saw the detachments return to Karachi and in September the squadron moved to Lahore, but in late October another detachment of DC-2Ks consisting of DG468, 469, 471, 473, 476, 477 and 478 were flown to the Canal Zone and based at Bilbeis, where they were joined by a detachment of DC-2Ks from No 117 Squadron. Here they were used for supply carrying and evacuating casualities. The Douglas transports of No 31 Squadron returned to Lahore early in February 1942. During the period of their detachment one DC-2K was shot down and another crashed on take-off. DC-2K AX755, piloted by Wg Cdr Lord Forbes took General Sikorski the Polish Premier to see Marshal Stalin at Kuibishev, which was the temporary capital of the USSR whilst Moscow was threatened by the Germans. A flight was also made to Stalingrad. One of the two pilots of DC-2K DG475 "X-Xray", which was shot down by three Messerschmitt Bf 109s ten miles north-east of LG 138 on December 8, 1941, was Warrant Officer DSA Lord, who along with Flt Lt Howell, crash-landed the aircraft and escaped serious injury.

Meanwhile, Japan had entered the war in December 1941. Only two of the DC-2Ks of No 31 Squadron were serviceable at Lahore and these kept open a service between Rangoon and Calcutta, although one aircraft – DG474 – was destroyed during an air raid on Mingaladon airfield in January. The following month the whole squadron moved to Akyab, on the Burma coast, where they operated mainly in evacuating the air forces from Burma during February and March. When Akyab became untenable through Japanese air raids, the squadron moved back to Dum Dum, near Calcutta, and operated from here. Their principal task was carrying reinforcements and stores to Shwebo and Mandalay with casualty evacuation on the return flight. A DC-2K flew each evening to Akyab until the port finally fell to the Japanese and veteran DC-2K AX755 was lost on one of the last sorties. Another DC-2K was badly damaged at Chittagong, but was patched up and eventually flown out.

No 117 received their first three DC-2Ks – AX767, 768 and 769 – in October 1941 and were later joined by HK821 in November; HK837 and HK847 in December, and HK820 in July 1942, the latter after extensive airframe repairs. But in April 1942 the aircraft were allotted to No 31 Squadron in India, although HK820 and HK837 were retained on loan until July and May 1943 respectively.

It must be remembered that these Douglas DC-2Ks and DC-3 transports used by the Royal Air Force were already veterans. Some of the engines, a mixture of Wright Cyclones and Pratt & Whitney Twin Wasps, already had a history of 10,000 hours when the RAF took them over from the United States. They arrived in the theatre of operations at a time when they were required almost incessantly in deteriorating weather, and therefore inspections, which were routine elsewhere, had to be skimped. In any case there were no spare parts for replacements and the Douglas Commercials had to keep on flying. Everything was a matter of improvisation; different types of engines and propeller would be on the same aircraft. It was not out of the ordinary for an aircraft to have a 550 hp engine on its port side and a 700 hp on its starboard.

The Royal Air Force pilots had great faith and affection for their new transport aircraft. On March 14, 1942, DC-2K AX755 was being flown to Akyab from Dum Dum when an oil pipe to the starboard engine burst midway across the Bay of Bengal. The DC-2K only had fine and course pitch, with no feathering facility and the aircraft lost height rapidly. The co-pilot was ordered to throw all the freight out of the rear door while the pilot jettisoned fuel and AX755 managed to limp into Akyab at about 100 feet. The starboard engine had been windmilling without oil for nearly an hour, and the pilot fully expected the engine to be a write-off, but, after refilling with oil and repairing the damaged pipe, it was discovered the engine ran perfectly and AX755 continued flying.

More Douglas DC-3s were impressed from Pan American Airways who were operating the type in the Middle East, and both the DC-2K and DC-3 flew throughout the war in the Middle East, India and Burma, serving with Nos 31, 117, 194 and 267 Squadrons.

Three DC-3s were received by No 267 Squadron in August 1942, one of which had its single door on the starboard side. Unfortunately their military serials are not quoted. HK867 was a Dakota Mk II used by No 267 Squadron in 1942 and in June 1944 was based along with another Mk II – FJ711 – at No 1 (ME) Captain's Course Unit at Bilbeis. HK983 was a Dakota Mk I made up from the scrap heap, while HK993 was a C-47-DL – ex-Army Air Force serial 41-38625 – which was finally purchased by Ambica Airlines and registered in India as VT-CLE in May 1947. The origins of DC-3s LR230 and LR234 are not clear. Both MA928 and MA929 were C-53s flown from California to Lahore via Cairo, and were allotted to No 31 Squadron on June 12, 1942. MA928 crashed on take-off from Agartala on March 25, 1943, and MA929 was missing on a flight from Tezpur to Dinjin on January 27, 1943.

The chief task to which the DC-3s and their crews were called, with the help of Westland Lysanders plus any other aircraft which could make the trip, was the extrication of the wounded, the ailing and the weak. Thousands of these refugees had been carried on stretchers to the high village of Myitkyina during the closing stages of the retreat in Burma. On three sides of the refugees were jungle and mountains; on the fourth were the approaching Japanese. Women, children, fever cases and wounded were lined along the airstrip, waiting.

Weather worsened with the approach of the rains, but the DC-3s, unarmed, continued to make the crossing of the Naga Hills, which jutted up to 17,000 feet between the Brahmaputra and the Irrawaddy. Pilots flew mostly blind in cloud, seeking security from marauding enemy fighters. The sortie rate demanded of each crew was high, but the crew themselves asked to increase it after witnessing the plight of children and the dying near the runway.

As mentioned earlier No 31 Squadron had taken delivery of its first DC-3 in April 1942. By the time three DC-3s arrived on May 7, making six in all, the squadron detachment was operating from Dinjin in North Assam, busy ferrying evacuees and wounded from Myitkyina. The weather and the Japanese moved in, and bombardments of the airfield increased in intensity, but the rescue work continued through the gathering storms until May 6, when the first two Royal Air Force DC-3s to land were attacked by Japanese dive-bombers. In one aircraft two women passengers and a child were killed.

As the remainder of the refugee passengers tumbled out of this aircraft the Japanese returned and machine-gunned them. In another raid on May 8 two DC-3s from No 31 Squadron – LR231 "E-Edward" and LR230 "D-Dog" – were destroyed by two Japanese dive-bombers while embarking refugees and wounded. Casualties in the aircraft were heavy. A third DC-3 from Dinjan landed at dusk and evacuated the crews of the destroyed aircraft plus sixty-five refugees and walking wounded. The pilot was Flt Lt Howell who had only just rejoined the squadron after recovery from his experience in the Middle East as recorded earlier. The following day aerial reconnaissance showed the air strip to be occupied by the Japanese.

With the arrival of the DC-3s more pilots were required and some of the crews from No 31 Squadron were trained by United States military crews at Karachi on Santa Monica built Douglas C-53-DO transports, an example being 41-20081 which served with No 31 Squadron at Dinjan and was used on supply dropping sorties on refugees walking out of Burma. The early Douglas types continued to give valiant service both in the Middle East and India. It was to be another year before the first Royal Air Force C-47 Dakota would be available.

FERRY AND TRANSPORT COMMAND

The possibility of a regular airmail crossing of the Atlantic had in 1939 been discussed by the postal authorities of the United States, Canada and Great Britain. It was not considered feasable to carry mail during the winter months and the project was abandoned. Discussions were revived early in 1940, but the emphasis had shifted from mail to aircraft. At this time the US built Lockheed Hudson was a vital weapon for Coastal Command. Britain was purchasing them and shipping them by sea from the United States under the system of cash and carry. Something like three months was elapsing between test flights in the US and the operational destination in the United Kingdom – usually Aldergrove in Northern Ireland. By flying them across the Atlantic, shipping space was saved and the three months was reduced to less than ten days.

The Canadian Pacific Railway Company were suggested as the best agency to operate a ferry-bomber service with headquarters in Montreal. The British Purchasing Commission in New York issued the contract for the first delivery by air, BOAC assisted with their technical experience, the Air Ministry paid all expenses and supplied such flying personnel who could be spared and the new Canadian Pacific Air Services Department was formed.

By mid-September 1940 the first of the Lockheed Hudsons was ready and deliveries of fifty within two months was promised. The aircraft were flown to Pembina in North Dakota, on the international border about sixty miles south of Winnipeg, and there, since the United States were not yet at war and custom properties had to be observed, they were drawn across the frontier by horses. The crews employed to ferry these aircraft came from many countries and many walks of life.

The first Atlantic ferry crews were returned from the United Kingdom by boat, a journey which took anything from ten days to a fortnight. This caused hold-ups and on several occasions so many ferry crews were tied up at sea that there were none to fly aircraft which were ready. In May 1941 a return ferry service was initiated with Consolidated Liberator transports operated by BOAC.

Quick expansion of the ferry, together with political and military considerations in North America and Britain, made it essential that control should be directly rested in a Ministry of the British Government, and in May 1941 the Canadian Pacific Railway were notified of the termination of the agreement. The Atlantic Ferry Organisation or ATFERO, came under the control of the British Ministry of Aircraft Production but the arrangement was short-lived for in June President Roosevelt informed Mr Churchill that he was prepared to help with the ferrying of all aircraft destined for the United Kingdom. It was, however, a condition that the hand-over must be to a military command instead of a civil authority.

It was for this reason that on July 20, 1941, ATFERO became the Royal Air Force Ferry Command. Air Chief Marshal Sir Frederick Bowhill, who had been directing RAF Coastal Command in the Battle of the Atlantic, became C-in-C at Montreal. These changes in direction did not affect operations or staff. A mixture of civilian and service personnel continued to work together both in the air and on the ground.

The autumn of 1941 saw the completion of the great Royal Canadian Air Force base at Dorval, and Ferry Command moved out from Montreal on October 4 and this airfield became the hub of the whole organisation under Sir Frederick Bowhill. The flying ranks of the command were still mainly civilian as the Royal Air Force could not spare service crews in any numbers. There were something like a hundred trained crews at that time, and it was evident that this number would have to be doubled. The shortage of men led to an amazingly daring improvisation.

In Canada, airmen from all over the world were being trained under the Commonwealth Joint Air Training plan. These men were learning everything which they would need to know on operations in Europe and the Middle East. Within the space of one year, after undergoing elementary, secondary and operational training, they became operational units. Sir Frederick suggested that these newly trained crews should be entrusted with the task of delivering operational aircraft, including Dakota transports. The "one-trippers" as they were called, took on the Atlantic crossing even in winter, when many experts still considered it impracticable.

The Atlantic ferry had operated under a number of titles, and under several immediate controls. This was the result of a natural and logic growth. It was the Secretary of State for Air, Sir Archibald Sinclair, who first announced the change of title from Ferry to Royal Air Force Transport Command on March 11, 1943, in the House of Commons.

> "All transport aircraft which we now possess, or which we shall produce here, or obtain from America, will be used to meet urgent requirements. With these increased number of transport squadrons an organisation will be required to control their operations throughout the world. I have, therefore, decided to establish a Royal Air Force Transport Command. To create such a Command sooner would have been to put the cart before the horse. It has not been Commanders and staff that we have been short of, but aircraft. Now the Command will come naturally into being through the process of bringing supply and organisation into focus. In addition to controlling the operations of RAF transport squadrons at home, the Command will be responsible for the organisation and control of strategic air routes, for all overseas ferrying and for the reinforcement moves of squadrons to and between overseas theatres."

Sir Frederick Bowhill took command of this world-wide organisation and Montreal remained the headquarters for the North and South Atlantic. Apart from the steady expansion the changes in Command had not affected the flying.

By this time the first batches of Dakota Mk I transports for the Royal Air Force were leaving the Douglas factory at Long Beach in California. The first aircraft – FD768 – was delivered at the factory on January 9, 1943, and the second – FD769 – arrived in the UK on February 11 by the North Atlantic route into Prestwick, now well established as the transatlantic aircraft control point. Deliveries to the Middle East by the South Atlantic route were also in progress, FD774, the seventh Dakota Mk I arriving on the last day of March 1943. On the first day of April, FD781, FD786 and FD787 were delivered to India. Ferried in twos and threes, the flow of a suitable transport aircraft for the Royal Air Force had begun.

With the formation of Ferry Command in July 1941, in order to administer the whole business of ferrying aircraft across the Atlantic, No 44 Group was formed in August at Gloucester to take over from the Overseas Air Movement Control Unit responsibility for all non-operational flights in and out of the UK, which included Transatlantic delivery flights, the preparation and despatch of aircraft to overseas commands, and the ferry training of aircrews.

The Group grew rapidly and from time to time was called upon to perform duties other than ferrying and in 1942 when Malta was short of supplies, flew a regular shuttle service between the UK, Gibraltar and on to Malta carrying spares and stores to the garrison.

During the build up for *Operation Torch* – the Allied landing in North Africa – the Group was charged with the despatch of aircraft to Gibraltar and a joint operations room with the US Army Air Force was established. Extra briefing parties were set up at the despatch points and in November alone 254 RAF and 491 USAAF aircraft, many of the latter Douglas C-47 Skytrains and C-53 Skytroopers, were sent to the North African theatre.

A highlight of 1942 was the conveyance by air of Mr Churchill to and from Moscow. In January 1943 Mr Churchill was again transported, this time with the Chiefs of Staff to the Casablanca Conference.

On March 23, 1944, No 44 Group was transferred to the newly formed Transport Command. From April the function of the Group changed slightly to include a greatly increased training and ferrying programme. Aircraft of all types were ferried to the UK by various transatlantic routes and despatched to all theatres of war in increasing numbers. The shorter range aircraft, such as Dakotas, were despatched from Portreath, and the heavier longer range aircraft from St Mawgan, both in Cornwall. Because of the increase in air transport activities, Dakota Operational Training Units were formed in No 44 Group to provide the specially trained crews required for the increasing number of transport squadrons.

In June regular scheduled services to Gibraltar, North Africa, Cairo, the Azores, Malta, Colombo, India and Iceland were operated. The air transport operations of the Group continued to expand and in 1944 it was decided to transfer these operations to a separate formation operating under the direct control of Transport Command, and in September operational control of all transport services was handed over to No 116 Wing.

Although the Group relinquished scheduled services, the control of aircraft entering or leaving the United Kingdom was undertaken by the Group through Overseas Aircraft Control located at Prestwick. These two controls were responsible for the safety of virtually all non-operational aircraft flights which took place directly between the UK and overseas bases. The list of passengers on these flights was endless and included Heads of States, plus political and military leaders of many nations. Aircraft continued to be ferried to various places after the end of the war but reduced commitments made the existing ferry organisation uneconomical and the Group was disbanded on August 14, 1946. Dakota squadrons which came under the jurisdiction of the Group included Nos 24, 271, 510 and 511. Just prior to the disbandment, the last Dakota – KP231 – for delivery to the UK, having arrived with No 45 Group Atlantic Transport Group at Dorval on June 15, was ferried across the Atlantic.

With the formation of Transport Command, a world-wide organisation, Ferry Command became No 45 Group with headquarters at Dorval, and responsible for all Royal Air Force Dakotas delivered. Within the Group No 231 Squadron was reformed in September 1944 and operated from Dorval with various transport types including Dakotas, providing a vital airline type service schedule between the factory plus many points in the United States and No 45 Group headquarters.

No 46 Group, Transport Command, was formed on January 17, 1944, with headquarters in Uxbridge Road, Stanmore, Middlesex, and Air Commodore – later Air Vice-Marshal – AC Fiddament as Air Officer Commanding.

The 150 Dakotas allocated to the Group were hardly sufficient for the task it was to perform with its five squadrons. These were to operate from airfields located at Broadwell, Down Ampney and Blakehill Farm, selected because of their proximity to other Royal Air Force stations to be used in launching airborne operations.

On D-Day, June 6, 1944, 108 Dakotas from Nos 48, 233, 271, 512 and 575 Squadrons, under the operational control of No. 46 Group, dropped the main body of the 3rd Parachute Brigade in Normandy, and also towed Airspeed Horsa gliders into action during *Operation Overlord.*

Nearly a year later, the SEAC – South East Asia Command – Commander, Lord Louis Mountbatten, required more transport squadrons to assist with the Allied advance in the Far East. In this context, in the United Kingdom, No 4 Group Royal Air Force Bomber Command occupied the Vale of York with its bases and Handley Page Halifax squadrons – resting after the cessation of hostilities in Europe. On May 7, 1945, which was the eve of VE-Day, headquarters No 4 Bomber Group at Heslington Hall, York, was renamed headquarters No 4 Transport Group.

Units and bases involved included No 10 Squadron at Melbourne, No 51 at Leconfield, No 76 at Holme-on-Spalding Moor, No 77 at Full Sutton, No 78 at Breighton, No 102 at Pocklington, No 158 at Lissett, No 466 Royal Australian Air Force at Driffield, Nos 346 and 347 Free French Air Force at Elvington, No 640 at Leconfield and No 1689 Bomber Defence Training Flight, all of which were disbanded on May 7, 1945.

On transfer to Transport Command, the squadrons enumerated above, with the exception of the two Free French units, were ordered to be prepared for re-arming with transport types of aircraft and for further transfer to operational duties with the new command.

Priority as regards rearming was given to Nos 51 and 158 Squadrons, each to re-equip with thirty Short Stirling Mk V transports for operation on the trunk routes to the Far East. Nos 10 and 76 Squadrons were each to re-equip with thirty Douglas Dakota Mk IV transports for support work. Rearming squadrons were to be trained for transport duties with the exception of No 466 Royal Australian Air Force who was to re-equip with Consolidated Liberators at a date to be decided. It was hoped to re-equip all units eventually with Dakota Mk IV transport aircraft. Meantime they were to continue to operate with an establishment of twenty Handley Page Halifax Mk VI bombers for training.

All equipment no longer required was to be concentrated at the airfield at Snaith, whilst Burn was reduced to care and maintenance – C & M. Training on Halifaxes continued pending the arrival of the Dakotas and No 78 Squadron at Breighton collected its first two aircraft from Down Ampney on June 30, 1945. On July 5 a Mobile Transport Training party arrived for crew conversion, and the flying hours for the month showed 1,638 on the Dakota and 171 on the Halifax. By September with training completed, No 78 Squadron was despatched to the Middle East and based at Almaza with No 282 Wing as part of No 216 Group. On September 4 the first flight of five aircraft under Sq Ldr Beattie departed for their new home. Squadron headquarters at Breighton were closed on September 17 and reopened at Almaza three days later. An early mishap was Dakota Mk IV KP235 piloted by Fg Off GE Venables, which crashed on take-off from Istres in the early hours of the morning of September 5. All crew and eleven passengers were killed, nine passengers injured of which two died later.

Dakota Mk IV – KP233 – with Flt Lt Bell opened up the squadron operations with a special flight to Catania, and by the end of September No 78 Squadron had its six Dakotas of "A" Flight based at Maison Blanche, Algiers, taking over the transport duties previously carried out by

No 28 Squadron, South African Air Force. The Dakotas came under No 284 Wing. Transition from bombers to transports was partially complete.

At Holme-on-Spalding-Moor, No 76 Squadron was preparing to dispose of its four-engined Halifax bombers for Dakota transports and the units RAF Form 540 records the following message:

> "VE-Day. What a great day for the squadron to become a new member of Transport Command, having completed our duties as a bomber squadron. We now turn to our new life knowing that our aim in the past has been reached and that some results will be obtained in the future."

On May 21, 1945, five Dakotas arrived for ground instructional use, and on the first day of June a Link trainer arrived in preparation for the conversion programme. By the middle of the month cross-country flights were taking place with the new transports, more pilots were detached for Dakota flying and on June 19 four Dakotas were ferried in from Wymeswold. Records show that by the end of the month training flights were being undertaken over once familiar territory – Germany. Early in July the squadron still had a few Halifax bombers on strength, but also had nineteen Dakota aircraft and crews.

Wg Cdr PA Nicholas, DFC, was in command and before the squadron departed for warmer climes, issued a résumé at the completion of flying for July, flying which consisted of 800 hours on Dakotas and only 27 hours on the Halifax. "This month has seen the completion of the training programme for No 76 Squadron before it departs for Broadwell early next month. The early parts of July saw a large number of flying hours completed and then all personnel proceeded on embarkation leave. Thus No 76 Squadron says good-bye to Holme-on-Spalding-Moor where it has completed a very fine job of work and anticipate with some degree of pleasure the execution of equally sound work in a different sphere."

To ensure that the finest training facilities were available for these new Transport Command squadrons who were soon to embark for SEAC, experienced crews were withdrawn from operational units in the Far East theatre and based in the United Kingdom with No 42 Transport Supply Training Unit – TSTU – at Broadwell.

During August 1945 crews and aircraft from Nos 10, 76 and 77 Squadrons were given close support training at this unit which included glider towing, paratroop and supply dropping, all under the guidance of specialists. When training was completed the crews and aircraft were prepared for their long flight to their new theatre of operations.

By the end of August No 76 Squadron was ready for transit from Portreath, Cornwall, and by the first day of November was based at Poona.

No 77 Squadrons first five Dakotas departed Broadwell on September 23 enroute to SEAC and these were followed by daily waves of five aircraft when the weather permitted. The route from the United Kingdom was via Elmas, El Adam, Lydda and Karachi. The month of October found the squadron at Kargi Road under No 229 Group of Air Command South East Asia. No 10 Squadron had flown out from Portreath and was based at Delhi. The conversion was now complete.

FERRY ROUTES

As early as November 1940 the Royal Air Force had undertaken to fly bombers built in the United States across the Atlantic from Canada by way of Newfoundland to Scotland. When the responsible agencies in the spring of 1941 found it difficult to recruit a sufficient number of qualified pilots for the transatlantic flight, General Arnold proposed to lend the assistance of the US Army Air Force. The Royal Air Force had been accepting delivery at the factory, and thus might have to provide pilots for flights extending all the way, which in the case of Douglas Dakotas was from the new factory at Long Beach, California, to Prestwick in Scotland. By having US Army Air Force pilots fly aircraft built on British contracts from the factory to the eastern seaboard port of embarkation it would be possible to enlarge the number of pilots who would be available for employment in flights across the Atlantic. The proposal found its technical justification in the need for US Army Air Force pilots to secure all possible training. As mentioned earlier, President Roosevelt readily endorsed the suggestion. As a result the United States Army Air Force Ferry Command was established on May 29, 1941, under the command of Col Robert Olds, who four years later was to be connected with the joint Combat Cargo Task Force in Burma.

The idea of a northern ferry route, which could enable aircraft such as the Dakota, with its shorter range, to fly the Atlantic as it were by stepping stones, and would provide diversionary bases useful to all aircraft in bad weather, had been under consideration by the United Kingdom, Canada and United States authorities for some time. In March 1941 the ferrying of medium and light bombers via Greenland and Iceland came under review.

Across the top of the world the Great Circle routes, dreamed of by seekers of a North-West passage for four centuries were now being rapidly realised. Through the silent north, through Greenland and Labrador, lay the paths for express traffic from Europe and North America, the Orient, India and Australia by way of the Atlantic and the Yukon. Work was started by the Americans in Greenland, while in Labrador, in a sandy plateau of muskeg and virgin forest there was built one of the loneliest, largest and most important of long-distance air bases. It is close to the outlet of Goose River and therefore has the perfectly complimentary name of Gander.

Goose Bay was discovered in July 1941 and the Newfoundland Government agreed to grant a lease of the area to the Canadian Government who bore the cost of the construction of the airfield. Never had so vast an undertaking been carried out in the wilds with such precision and speed. Within a month three temporary runways, each about 7,000 feet long, were ready for the largest type of aircraft. The work had gone on by day and night and snow was falling and the runways being rolled, when on December 9, 1941, the first aircraft arrived. The Labrador base was becoming one of the busiest airports in the world.

The Royal Canadian Air Force, under whose command the airport came, had carried a great part of the burden and materials into Labrador with the proud record of never having lost an ounce of freight or scratched a wing-tip. The Royal Air Force ran a scheduled service or "milk-run" of freight and passengers from Montreal.

After the winter of 1940 the Canadian Government was approached with a request for an airport in the vicinity of Montreal. On flat country some ten miles from the city, adjoining the groups of French-Canadian villages which fringe Lake St Louis, a great airport was planned. This was Montreal Airport – Dorval – which later was to house the headquarters of No 45 Group of Royal Air Force Transport Command who were responsible for the delivery of Dakotas and many other types to the United Kingdom.

After passage of the Lend-Lease Act early in 1941, the United States assumed an active part in the joint effort to take full advantage of the "stepping stone" provided by Newfoundland, Labrador and Iceland and so make possible the ferrying of short-range fighters from North America to the United Kingdom.

During the preceding July the United States had sent engineers to Narsarssuak in Greenland for the building of the air base that came to be known as Bluie West One – BW-1 – and in the following September work began on BW-8, a much more northerly base on the west coast of Greenland. United States forces had taken over the defence of Iceland in July 1941, where they improved the airstrips previously occupied by the Royal Air Force and began in the spring of 1942 to build two new airfields – Meeks and Patterson – near Keflavik.

Prestwick, in Scotland, had been developed in 1941 from an ordinary airfield to the key terminus for democratic Europe and was to be the final delivery point for many Dakotas. The US Air Transport Command shared the facilities at Prestwick. The aircraft were serviced by civilian personnel and those intended for the Royal Air Force were distributed throughout

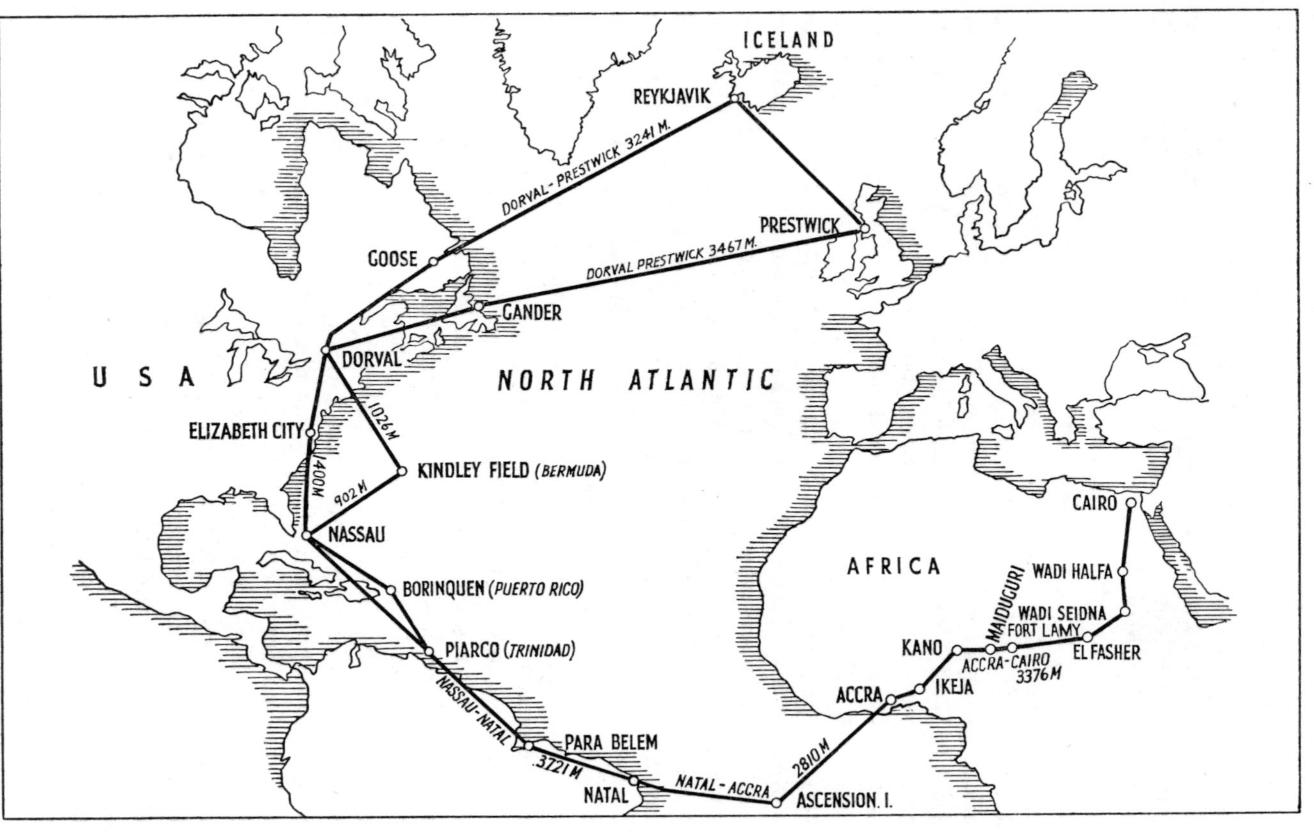

The Atlantic Bridges

the United Kingdom by the gallant men and women in the dark blue uniforms of the Air Transport Auxiliary. During 1940 only twenty-six aircraft were ferried across the North Atlantic route, 722 in 1941, 1,163 in 1942 and 1,450 in 1943. A Dakota Mk III FZ676 was lost after leaving Reykjavik en route for the United Kingdom. The route was open, losses were few, and the route was being put to good use by both the Royal Air Force and the US Army Air Force.

By agreement with the British and American governments in the early summer of 1941, three subsidiaries of Pan American Airways had been established. Pan American Air Ferries for the delivery of United States built aircraft from Miami, Florida, to Khartoum in the Sudan; Pan American Airways Company for the operation of a transport service from the USA to West Africa, and Pan American Airways – Africa Limited, for a transport service across Africa. Soon after Pearl Harbor the services of PAA-Ferries and PAA-Africa were extended by contract from Khartoum to Cairo and Tehran.

Ferrying operations over the South Atlantic route had begun in June 1941 when Atlantic Airways Limited, a Pan American Airways subsidiary corporation organised especially for the job, undertook to deliver twenty transport-type airliners, mainly Lockheed Lodestars, to the British in West Africa. The British Purchasing Commission had bought the aircraft in May, and they were delivered between June and September of that year.

Shortly after the passage of the Lend-Lease Act on March 11, 1941, the British Government had requested, under the terms of the act, a minimum of fifty transport aircraft for its trans-Africa operation. These aircraft were to be placed on the run between Takoradi in the Gold Coast colony and Cairo – an airway of the highest strategic value in the line of communications between the British Isles and the Middle East. With the loss of the French fleet in 1940 and the growing activity in the spring of 1941 of the German air forces based in Sicily, the line of air and water communications with Egypt by way of the Mediterranean was virtually closed. Fortunately, the existence of the trans-Africa route enabled the Royal Air Force to avoid shipping aircraft by water all the way around Africa and up through the Red Sea to Egypt.

The South Atlantic route to Africa had been initiated by the United States over territory which was partly British, partly American and partly Brazilian. In December 1942, agreement was reached between the Royal Air Force and the US Army Air Force that the responsibility for delivery of RAF aircraft from United States production plants across the South Atlantic should fall upon Ferry – later Transport – Command. Along the route much of the equipment, maintenance and supervision was that of the United States, often shared but sometimes running parallel with the British organisation. An RAF receiving point was established in Nashville, Tennessee, with twenty-five fully trained aircrews from Dorval, Canada. US Air Transport Command loaned the ground administration staff some offices. The main base for the South Atlantic was at West Palm Beach, on the southern tip of Florida.

The first main staging post across the treacherous air of the Caribbean was in Trinidad, though RAF aircraft had the use of an American post in Puerto Rico, a little more than halfway across. From Trinidad usually they flew in one hop to a point in Brazil near the mouth of the Amazon. The next leg brought them to Natal, near the most easterly tip of Brazil. Here aircraft were prepared for the 1,400-mile flight across the Atlantic to Ascension Island, which lies several hundred miles north of St Helena. The route from Ascension Island is direct to the Gold Coast. It was a longer route than the North Atlantic. Its advantages were shorter hops, fairer weather, and more direct access to Africa without hazards of the Bay of Biscay. In February 1943, the receiving point was moved from Nashville to Nassau in the Bahamas, conveniently sited upon British territory, one hour's flying time from Miami. Losses were few, although KG508 – a Dakota Mk III – crashed off the Brazilian coast on delivery. In 1942 the Royal Air Force ferried 127 aircraft across the South Atlantic, compared with 1,336 in 1943, many of these being Dakota transports.

The origin of the ferry routes across Africa dates back to the mid-1920s when members of Nos 45 and 47 Squadrons with Vickers Vimy and Vernon aircraft, undertook a number of pioneering long-distance flights, the major one being to West Africa. It was from these flights that the foundation of the routes used during World War 2 had their beginning.

In the early days of the war in the Middle East during 1940/41, a number of aircraft flew up from South Africa, landing at airfields that had been surveyed in the 1920s, checked by the Royal Air Force through the years, and now were to prove very valuable. In addition a number of aircraft were assembled at Port Sudan and ferried to the North African front, or the Western Desert as it was called in those early days, via Abara, Wadi Halfa, Luxor and so into lower Egypt.

Control of flying in the early days was vested in the Officer Commanding Khartoum, and later, in the Commanding Officer of the Communications Squadron looking after the route. This state of affairs existed until late 1941 when No 2 Middle East Ferry Control was established to take command of all the posts in the Sudan Sector – the majority of staging posts and all flying within that area; a similar control was formed from Takoradi the main assembly base, to cover West Africa.

Two aircraft delivery units were formed of pilots and other aircrew to ferry the large variety of aircraft from assembly point to the maintenance units near the front line. The main unit was No 2 Aircraft Delivery Unit – ADU – which was based on a house-boat in Cairo. The aircraft were

North Africa with ferry routes and major airfields used by the Douglas Dakota

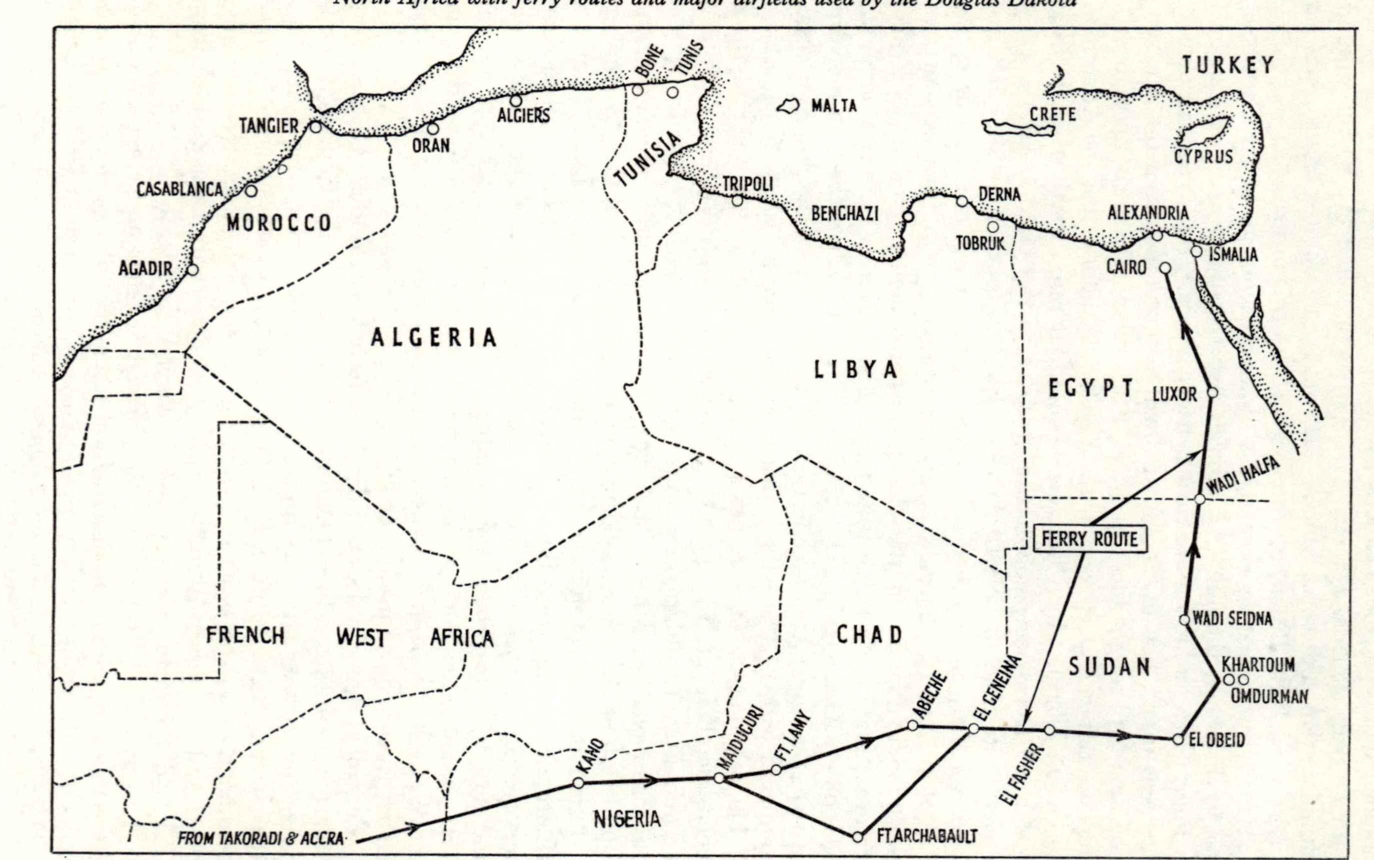

ferried in convoy with "mother" aircraft and "chicks". The "mother" aircraft was either a Bristol Blenheim, Douglas Boston, Martin Baltimore, Marauder or Maryland, or sometimes even a Lockheed Lodestar. The timing depended very much on the weather but basically it was a day's hop between staging posts. The navigation equipment on the route was very limited and the most one could really hope for were medium frequency beacons on continuous wave – CW – and, therefore, the main method of navigation was dead reckoning – DR – and local knowledge. The number of aircraft lost through errors of navigation were comparatively few.

A large base and an assembly plant was established at Takoradi by the Royal Air Force; built on top of red cliffs on the outskirts of the vivid Gold Coast bush. The existing facilities had to be rapidly extended; new workshops, hangers and runways were made. Living accommodation had to keep pace with a staff which by 1942 had been increased to more than 3,000 men. From Takoradi fighters, bombers and transport Dakotas were ferried in the many air convoys across Africa to Cairo.

Across the waist of Africa, airfields had been cut from the jungle or laid out on the desert like at Kano, one of the most romantic cities in all Africa, built of reddish clay and compassed by a wall eleven miles in perimeter, and ruled by an Emir from a palace covering 33 acres. Delivery crews encountered the harmattan, a persistent wind which raises a haze of Sahara dust sometimes to 10,000 feet, often blotting out visibility. Only constant cross-checking with the aircraft by radio kept the convoys together. The next leg after Kano was over dense jungle before reaching Maiduguri, over territory which was so dense as to make a forced landing inconceivable. It was possible to fly direct from Kano to Fort Lamy in French Equatorial Africa, where the maintenance men who refuel the aircraft spoke only French. Into Anglo-Egyptian Sudan with stops at El Geneina, El Fasher or El Obeid, to the confluence of the White and Blue Niles by Omdurman and Khartoum. El Fasher was the capital of Western Dafurand and the Governor, Phil Ingleson, was a great friend to the Royal Air Force. One of the added attractions on landing at El Fasher, apart from its excellent breakfasts, was a tame lion, which used to be handled like a small cat by a Polish cavalry lieutenant with most enormous hands by the name of Tadeuc Milenski. The lion eventually became too playful and big so was sent to a zoo. At the staging post located at Abéché which was in Chadd, the French commissioner had a number of lions chained underneath his stilted house. An additional and slightly more southerly route was founded after the bombing of Fort Lamy, which went south from Maiduguri to Fort Archabault, eastwards to My Ala, north to El Obeid and on as before. The last leg was the magnificent flight down the Nile until the Pyramids loomed ahead, followed by the sprawling city of Cairo, and a let down into Cairo West, or LG224 as it was known to many.

A second category of ferry aircraft naturally developed with the creation of the South Atlantic route. Besides the fighters and light bombers which could be spared from the United Kingdom, the Desert Air Force needed the Martin Marylands and Baltimores, North American Mitchells and the Douglas Bostons and Dakotas, all of which were manufactured in the United States. For these aircraft the southern route across the Atlantic was open. They arrived in one piece, their arrival base being Accra, a peacetime airfield built by the Gold Coast Public Works Department and extended at British Government expense to be an important airport, with the Americans supplying some of their own equipment.

Within three months of their arrival at Takoradi, the advance party sent off their first reinforcement aircraft, and within fourteen months more than 1,400 had passed "up the line" as they called it, to the Middle East. Royal Air Force crews who ferried the assortment of aircraft in convoys to Cairo made their own way back to base at Takoradi by varied means of air transport. Pan-American Air Ferries with Douglas DC-3s established a base at Accra on October 8, 1941, and thirteen days later a DC-3 took off on the first scheduled flight from Accra to Khartoum. By the end of that month, seven aircraft and thirty pilots were maintaining regular scheduled operations.

One of the first recorded use of this scheduled service by RAF ferry crews was on October 29, 1941. After delivering a "mother" Bristol Blenheim Mk IV Z7621, with five Hawker Hurricane Mk IIs as "chicks", the crews flew by BOAC Lockheed Lodestar G-AGCT to Khartoum, connecting with the PAAF Douglas DC-3 N25623 piloted by Captain Fowler. The route was El Geneina, Maiduguri, Kano and Accra. Captain Brenner took the flight on to Takoradi. Total flying time from Khartoum was 14 hours with a night stop at Kano. At least five of the seven Douglas DC-3s used by PAAF on this route were later handed over to the Royal Air Force.

This return journey for the ferry crews varied with both route and the aircraft used. During August 1942 one crew took the BOAC Empire flying-boat G-AEUE from Mombassa to Kampala, then Sabena Lockheed 14 OO-CAH from Stanleyville to Takoradi. The services of Sabena, who were still operating in the Belgian Congo, although their homeland was in possession of the enemy, were used under charter to British Overseas Airways Corporation.

By June 1942 when the US Air Transport Command commenced to take over the Pan American operations, the fleet of Douglas DC-3s had increased to forty-eight, some of them military Douglas C-47 Skytrains and C-53 Skytroopers, plus the odd Douglas C-48C and C-49F which were commercial airliners impressed into service and all variants of the now famous Douglas Commercial Three. When Air Transport Command took over from Pan American an attempt was made to standardise the fleet of transports for reasons of reducing the spares problem, and it is suspected that this is when the five aircraft mentioned earlier were handed over to the Royal Air Force.

A ferry flight of an unusual nature which must be mentioned is that involving a Waco CG-4A glider, known in the Royal Air Force as the Hadrian – FR579 – which, fully laden with vaccines for the USSR, plus urgent radio, aircraft and motor parts, was towed across the Atlantic by a Dakota Mk I – FD900 – of Royal Air Force Transport Command during June 1943. The flight from Dorval, Montreal, to Prestwick was done in stages totalling twenty-eight hours flying time to cover 3,500 miles. It was an experimental flight, the first of its kind and no special emphasis was laid on the accomplishment. It provided information regarding the possibilities of an Atlantic air train service.

Captain of the glider was Sq Ldr RG Seys of the Royal Air Force with Sq Ldr PM Gobeil of the Royal Canadian Air Force as co-pilot. The Dakota tug was captained by Flt Lt WS Longhurst, a Canadian, and Flt Lt CWH Thomson, a New Zealander, both serving in the Royal Air Force. Mr HG Wightman was the Radio Officer and Plt Off RH Wormington the flight engineer.

The CG-4A 84-foot span glider was designed by the Waco aircraft company and built by a piano manufacturer in New York. The freight load was one and a half tons. For the flight it was equipped with rubber dinghies, the ordinary ocean emergency equipment carried by bombers and transports crossing the Atlantic, and flotation gear. The steel attachments were designed to take a pull of 20,000 lb. Loading and unloading was carried out through a hinged nose which opens and closes with a jaw-like action. Modifications to the Dakota tug included special tanks for extra fuel, so made that they could be jettisoned intact, with their contents, should the need arise. Petrol could not be jettisoned loose, as it would spray back on to the glider and atmospheric electricity may ignite it. Drill in the Waco glider itself, in case of being forced down in the sea, was to be a routine matter between pilot and co-pilot. The first essential was to cut the fuselage open, and through the hole the freight and pilot would go, so that the flotation apparatus would function. The glider and its tug were in communication by radio, but this was switched off most of the time to save batteries. When the Dakota pilot wished to speak to the glider pilot he waggled his wings.

The flight set up a world record in total distance for a glider carrying freight. The non-stop record flight had already been made by Sq Ldr Seys, who began the actual experiments for the crossing six months beforehand. All trials were made with the glider fully loaded, and some of the worst weather known in North America for fifty years was met during the experiments. Once the glider force-landed in deep snow, during a blizzard, in mountainous country sixty miles from Montreal. The first major achievement was a triangular course flight from and back to Montreal by way of Newfoundland and Labrador. The last stage of this flight, 820 miles, set up a record for a glider fully laden with freight, beating the United States record of 670 miles. Longer flights followed. On one, southwards from Canada, 1,177 statute miles were covered non-stop at an average speed of 150 mph. This flight provided the data for the Atlantic venture.

On the journey from Montreal to the United Kingdom, conditions were mainly favourable, except on the first leg when progress was extremely slow due to head winds. After the first three hours the pair had reached 9,000 feet in an attempt to get over the cloud tops. At 13,000 feet it was decided to descend through cloud to 1,500 feet.

The glider had to be flown all the time as there was no automatic pilot. The pilot could not take his eyes off the Dakota tug, nor the tow-rope if the tug was in cloud. The physical strain was considerable. Concentration became almost hypnotic. There was no heating system in the glider. Out of the sun, in cloud or snow, the outside temperature could drop to 30 degrees below zero. At one time there was snow inside the Waco glider, yet in clear sunshine the glider cockpit was as hot as a glass-house.

Departure from Dorval was June 24, 1943, and there was no incidents. Landings were good and without mishap, except that once the towrope had to be spliced before take-off, and on another occasion the coupling was damaged by being dropped on a rack. It had to be straightened and rewelded. Precisely on ETA – Estimate Time of Arrival – the Waco glider and Dakota tug circled Prestwick for the final landing on July 1, 1943.

Unfortunately, Royal Air Force Transport Command never propounded the advantages of towing a load instead of carrying it inside a Dakota with extra tanks fitted.

THE MIDDLE EAST AND THE BALKANS

Twenty millions pounds of freight and war supplies were carried to the Russian, Mediterranean and Indian war fronts during 1943 by No 216 Group of Royal Air Force Transport Command based in the Middle East and commanded by Air Cdr Whitney W Straight. The Group's aircraft also carried 100,000 passengers and 3,400,000 lb of mail.

Casualties evacuated from the battlefields of the Western Desert, Sicily and Italy and the Dodecanese Islands totalled 16,400. To do all this, Douglas Dakotas, Lockheed Lodestars and Hudsons, Avro Ansons and other aircraft of the Group flew for 70,000 hours and covered 10 million miles – forty times the distance to the moon. In addition over 8,000 aircraft were ferried through the Mediterranean theatre to Russia, Malta, Italy and other battle fronts.

These figures illustrate the growth of this Air Transport Group from small beginnings – a Delivery Flight from West Africa to Cairo in the early days. At this time the only headquarters organisation was a small liaison section attached to the Movements Branch in Cairo. Even when the Delivery Flight was expanded into a Group, it remained a very small one, concerned with ferrying aircraft only. The invasion of North Africa opened the Mediterranean as a delivery route for aircraft and the Group expanded for the third time. In addition to ferrying new aircraft, it dealt with air transport with Bristol Bombays, Lodestars and Hudsons, Dakotas and other aircraft.

Based in the Middle East since 1922 in the transport role, No 216 Squadron flew Douglas DC-2K and DC-3 aircraft, re-equipping with Dakotas in 1943 while at Cairo West, then known as LG224 or Kilo 26 on the road from Giza to Alexandria. Under the newly formed RAF Transport Command it began operating new scheduled routes – the normal "territory" covering Egypt, Italy, West Africa, Iraq and Persia, but was particularly concerned with the Western Desert.

After the Salerno landings the squadron flew in reinforcements and supplies. In the autumn it flew in support of the Aegean campaign dropping Greek paratroops it had assisted to train earlier in the year at No 4 Middle East Parachute Training School located at Ramat David, near Haifa in Palestine.

On April 30, 1941, the formation of No 117 Squadron at Khartoum from a detachment of No 216 Squadron was effected, and became famed as its worthy forbear. Originally it had an odd assortment of aircraft including Bristol Bombays but, on moving to Bilbeis – between Cairo and Alexandria – it began training on newly acquired Douglas DC-2Ks for the squadron's future role of transport support. At this time civilians were evacuated from hard-pressed Malta and the squadron took on charge its first Dakota. Wherever the advancing troops went the Dakotas followed, ferrying stores, food and ammunition and evacuating the casualties – often under fire. Even before Sicily fell, a detachment of Dakotas was based at Catania.

During April 1942 No 267 *Pegasus* Squadron was based at Heliopolis and was made up of two flights, one of Lockheed Lodestars, the other a miscellany of light aircraft including one Messerschmit Bf 109. The Commanding Officer was Wg Cdr Wynne-Eaton and during August the first of three Douglas DC-3s allocated to the unit arrived. By September the squadron had moved to Bilbeis and was flying the Malta schedule, a typical sortie with DC3 HK867 being recorded on September 10. The transport was positioned at Shallufa, fully fueled and heavily loaded for the flight to Luqa, Malta, departing late afternoon so as to pass Crete, which was still occupied by the enemy, after dusk. Flight time was 8 hrs 45 mins. Cargo included one torpedo. After unloading the DC-3 was refuelled and left so as to be east of Crete by dawn arriving at Cairo West 7 hrs 50 mins later.

Using mostly Lockheed Hudson transports on airline type work, No 267 Squadron continued to support the 8th Army in the desert until Alamein. During May 1943 it began to re-equip with the Dakota Mk I, supplies of which were being ferried via Takoradi and Cairo. Two of the units first Dakotas were FD863 "A-Apple" and FD926 "B-Baker".

Meanwhile a detachment from No 267 followed the 8th Army to Tunis using the advanced base at Marble Arch, dropped paratroops in the invasion of Sicily, and landed on the beach-head in the invasion of Italy, with part of the squadron still maintaining the ever-lengthening supply line from Cairo West. By October the re-equipment with Dakota Mk Is was complete.

These were the initial three Dakota squadrons which made up No 216 Group, although No 117 Squadron was transferred to India and subsequently SEAC during October 1943 whilst based at Bari in Italy.

The desert and North African campaigns over, the Group prepared for the invasion of Sicily, Dakotas being the first transport aircraft to land when they moved fighter squadrons to the first airfield captured on the island. Air Cdr Whitney Straight led this task himself when the Dakotas moved an American fighter group from Gozo, Malta's other island, to Sicily – from an aerodrome which had been constructed in twenty days and had been in use for twenty days. The Dakotas moved seventy-five men and their baggage and equipment to Licala, Sicily, landing on a specially made strip beside the main blitzed aerodrome.

A regular service between Malta and Sicily was established by the Group and many Army casualties were brought back to Malta.

Mediterranean Air Command praised this work. The rapidity with which the air-carrier services have been established between the various Headquarters in Sicily and North Africa, Malta and Egypt had earned the Allied Air Forces full praise by the British and American Armies. The air courier services were organised with such speed and efficiency that communications were kept up throughout the continuous movement of the various army headquarters.

During the invasion of Sicily, the Dakotas moved men, light equipment of fighter squadrons, fighter wings and fighter control staffs, ammunition, a whole headquarters consisting of over one hundred men, and 40,000 lb of baggage and equipment, Jeeps, motor-cycles, trailers, and casually filled a random demand for 15 tons of boots and socks for the 7th Army.

Altogether the Dakotas carried 763,230 lb of war supplies and evacuated

2,476 casualties. They flew 1,390 hours. The "lifts" soared with the invasion of Italy to a total of 3,460,000 lb involving flights totalling 400,000 miles. Over 700 sorties were made by the transports and over 2,000 casualties evacuated.

The transport squadrons with their aircraft and crews were in from the start. They moved four squadrons from Malta to Sicily for the protection of convoys. This involved carrying 600 men and 150,000 lb of baggage and equipment. At Salerno as soon as a landing strip had been prepared, the Dakotas flew an American fighter group and two squadrons from Termini in north-west Sicily to Paestium, carrying 225 men and 50,000 lb of baggage and equipment, five jeeps, four trailers and three water trailers. This move took four hours from the time of loading in Sicily to the time of unloading at Paestium, 250 miles away.

Altogether two American fighter groups, two RAF fighter wings, two American dive-bomber groups, and three other squadrons were flown into Salerno area by Dakotas of No 216 Group between September 13 and 26, 1943. Another big "lift" was 100 tons of ammunition. These Salerno lifts were made under exceedingly hazardous conditions, particularly in the early stages. Landing strips were narrow and dusty and barely out of reach of enemy guns. Once again, this time in the Taranto area, the Daks helped to keep the enemy on the run. They moved a fighter wing headquarters and two squadrons of fighter-bombers and another of Supermarine Spitfires from Sicily to Taranto, together with one day's supply of ammunition and bombs. The transports were loaded at midday in Sicily, and the Spitfires were on patrol four hours later around Taranto – where the Germans least expected them. This lift involved the transport of 210 men and 40,000 lb of freight.

But this was only the beginning. The Italians capitulated and the 8th Army advanced so fast that the Desert Air Force decided to fly four more squadrons into the Taranto area immediately. The Dakotas carried 300 men and 100,000 lb of baggage, tents, signals equipment, rations, and also three RAF Regiment detachments complete with their guns to protect the airfields. For the next two and a half days they flew in all the ammunition, petrol and rations that the squadrons needed – 250 tons in all.

It was entirely owing to the work of the Dakotas at Salerno and Taranto that our fighter-bomber squadrons were able to keep within range of the enemy as he retreated, and only airborne supplies enabled fighters to maintain continuous operations. This achievement was in good measure responsible for the quick advance of the 8th Army to Foggia and the acquisition of the valuable airfields in that area. A single Air Despatch and Reception Unit put up records. In September 1943, on four days, they loaded more than 100 tons a day. On one day they dealt with 137 tons between dawn and two o'clock in the afternoon.

Cos, Leros and Samos provided the transports with further exciting action. They dropped paratroops, carried 1,226 Army and RAF personnel to the islands, and 807,000 lb of supplies of petrol and ammunition for the Spitfire detachment operating there. The Dakotas, often laden entirely with petrol and explosives, had to penetrate the heart of the German Aegean defences in broad daylight. They were ground strafed and lost several aircraft. When the landing ground at Cos became unfit for use from bombing, the Dakota crews threw supplies out through the aircrafts cargo doors.

During November 1943 No 267 Squadron moved its base from Cairo West to Bari in Italy along with its detachment at Catania. The winter was spent in semi-airline duties in the Mediterranean area until March 1944 when alternate halves of the unit began supply dropping and landing in Yugoslavia to assist Marshal Tito and evacuate his casualties. For the remainder of 1944 the squadron with its black horse with wings insignia painted on the nose of its Dakota transports, maintained supply dropping or landing in Greece, Yugoslavia, Austria, Northern Italy and Southern France. On March 19, 1944, several aircraft made a second attempt to reach target "Cyanide" behind the enemy lines, Air Cdr Whitney Straight and Grp-Cpt Muspratt-Williams, who was commanding No 249 Wing, joining in as co-pilots.

On the evening of April 18 Dakota Mk III KG475, fitted with eight overload tanks in the fuselage, giving an endurance of approximately 19 hours, flew to a field near Warsaw, and evacuated personnel and equipment. The following day the Dakota landed at Gibraltar before arriving at Hendon in the United Kingdom with its vital load of passengers and cargo on April 20. This was the first of three such flights to Poland carried out by aircraft and crews from No 267 Squadron.

"Pick-up" operations were an integral part of the activities of No 334 Wing, which operated mainly from Brindisi, using the Special Operations aircraft of Nos 148 and 624 Squadrons, No 1586 Polish Flight, all ably supported by fifty C-47 Skytrain transports of the 62nd American Troop Carrier Group plus some transports of the Italian Air Force. Agents could be dropped by parachute easily enough, but if they were to be brought out, then an aircraft had to land within enemy territory. On the evening of July 25, 1944, Dakota Mk III KG477 of No 267 Squadron, fitted with four long-range cabin tanks, and flown by Flt Lt SG Culliford, took off on *Operation Wildhorn III*, a pick-up in Poland. The second pilot was Fg Off Szajer from No 1536 Polish Flight, the navigator Fg Off Williams and wireless-operator Flt Sgt Appleby were from No 267 Squadron. The cargo consisted of four passengers and twenty suit-cases weighing 970 lb. An anti-night fighter escort of one Consolidated Liberator aircraft from No 1586 Polish Flight stayed with the Dakota until darkness, by which time it was approaching the Sava River. The Hungarian plains were crossed at 7,500 feet, the Carpathians reached, and then the transport Dakota headed for the target area rapidly losing height. At the estimated time of arrival – ETA – the recognition letter "O-Orange" was flashed and received the answering letter "N-Nuts". Much traffic was noticed moving westwards along a road as the Dakota landed on the improvised landing strip. Three green lights had indicated the best approach, three red lanterns its end, and the runway was marked by a lamp every 75 yards. These were ordinary stable lamps, each attended by a local peasant, but a strong electric lamp was available for signalling.

In five minutes the aircraft had been unloaded and reloaded and was ready to take-off again. However the wheels had sunk in the soft earth. The passengers disembarked and the parcels off-loaded whilst the wheels were dug out, and space cleared in front of them. After reloading the aircraft still refused to move, so preparations were made for the destruction of the Dakota. A request for one more attempt was agreed by the pilot. As the doors of the aircraft were closed a warning came of a German patrol approaching. The Dak moved slowly forward, taxied around the landing field twice, and then rushed forward over the rough turf and was airborne. Just as the sun was rising the aircraft landed safely at Brindisi. The ground on which it had landed had a few hours before been used for practice circuits by Luftwaffe pilots under training.

On one of the three "pick-up" operations successfully completed by Dakotas from No 267 Squadron, important equipment relating to the V2 rocket was brought back.

It was in June 1944 that the Chiefs of Staff informed Marshal Tito of the formation of a Balkan Air Force. Its commander, Air Vice-Marshal W Elliot, was placed in control of a miscellaneous force made up of pilots and ground crews belonging to different nationalities operating aircraft of ten different types. The nationalities were British, South African, Italian, Greek, Yugoslav, and for the supply dropping operations, American, Polish and Russian. The aircraft at the formation were Supermarine Spitfires, North American Mustangs, Hawker Hurricanes, Bristol Beaufighters, Westland Lysanders, Handley-Page Halifaxes, Martin Baltimores, Douglas Dakotas and C-47s, Consolidated Liberators, but by the end of that year the total of types had risen to fifteen with the additions of Boeing Flying Fortresses, Martin Marauders, Savoia-Marchetti SM 82s, Cant 1007s, and Bell Airacobras.

The Russians some eighty strong, with twelve Dakota aircraft and twelve Yak fighters, were based at Bari with orders to maintain communications with their military mission and to participate in the supply dropping operations. They were under the control of the Balkan Air Force from their arrival early in June 1944.

Care of the wounded is perhaps the biggest problem of guerilla warfare, for troops who would otherwise be fighting have to be used to guard and transport them. To take them out by air was the best and most obvious solution, but this was no easy matter. At the request of No 37 Military Mission, RAF personnel had arrived behind the enemy lines in Yugoslavia on August 11, but the first landing strip they constructed came under shell-fire and had to be evacuated. A four-day march to Brezna was made by the column of wounded, now numbering about 800, and on arrival all who had the physical strength to do so, set to and cleared the corn from two chosen fields. At 0900 hours on August 23 six Dakotas, escorted by eighteen Mustangs and Spitfires, landed on the new strip. Within twenty minutes they were airborne again carrying 200 wounded, and in the course of the day twenty-four C-47 Skytrains of the 60th Troop Carrier Group evacuated 721, a further six Dakotas from No 267 Squadron brought out 219, and during the night an additional 138 wounded were carried by the Russian Air Group. In all, 1,087 persons were flown out – 1,059 Partisans, 16 Allied aircrew and 3 members of the Allied Control Commission.

During the last six months of 1944 about 8,000 tons of materials were flown to Yugoslavia under the auspices of the Balkan Air Force. A large share of this load was carried by the Dakotas of No 267 Squadron, who had a detachment of its transports under the operational control of the Balkan Air Force for the supply of German occupied Balkan territory.

For these special operations two methods were used. The dropping of men and supplies by parachute, and landing on secret airstrips built under the direction of RAF and Army personnel who in the case of Yugoslavia worked with Marshal Tito's forces. Naturally the landing and unloading of aircraft was the more effective method, for a return load was then possible. However, in the mountains and in winter, and districts thickly infiltrated by the enemy, para dropping is often the only means of operating.

The *Pegasus* squadron flew on an average 1,000 hours a month. During October 1944 it flew several flights to target "Towan Bucket" on the promontory west of Patras in Greece. On the first day of October Bucharest in Rumania was relieved by the Russians and Sq Ldr McLannahan took the first RAF flight over, repeated with a second flight on October 4. Later in the month the Dakotas from No 267 made the first RAF flight to Sofia in Bulgaria.

By November 5 the first Dakota had flown into Belgrade. But by mid-December the uprising in Greece caused attention to be transferred to flights direct to Athens. Two incidents at the end of the month showed the ability of the Dakota to operate on one engine. Flt Lt AL Firth had an engine failure near Patras which involved jettisoning the cargo and a flight of 1 hr 50 mins on one engine back to Brindisi. The following day

Fg Off Baker had an engine failure at 200 ft on take-off, laden with 5,000 lb of ammunition and the pilot managed to make a circuit and crash landed on the airfield, nobody being hurt.

No 216 Squadron had supported the 8th Army in its advance to Tunisia and beyond, whole fighter wings being moved by air on the heels of the retreating enemy. A detachment from the squadron went to South East Asia Command during 1944 to operate from Agartala for supply dropping missions to the Chindits.

During January 1944 a Dakota from No 216 Squadron and flown by the Commanding Officer, Wg Cdr EM Morris, made the long flight to Moscow to bring back a sick man. Regimental Sergeant Major Stanley Bulmer, a peace-time journalist and serving in Moscow as confidential clerk to the Head of the British Military Mission to the USSR was taken ill and both the Soviet and British medical authorities agreed that his removal to a warmer climate was necessary as soon as possible.

Air Commodore Whitney Straight approved the flight which at that time, made the longest flight – 5,000 miles – by the Royal Air Force to evacuate a patient, and was the first wholly RAF-manned aircraft to fly to Stalingrad and Moscow.

At one time the Dakota was flying through heavy cloud above the pass in the Elburz mountain range which is the "road to Russia" for lorry convoys, and it had to climb to 17,000 feet to get over this belt of bad weather. Outside Stalingrad the transport was flying at less than 200 feet through snowstorms.

After a night stop at Stalingrad the Dakota continued its flight to Moscow, flying blind through snowstorms and experiencing strong headwinds, before arrival at the capital in clear cold weather. The temperature was 12 degrees below freezing.

Air Cdr DN Roberts, OBE AFC head of the RAF section of the British Military Mission entertained the crew until completion of the necessary planning for the return flight. This included a further night stop at Stalingrad and Tehran. Dust storms caused a diversion to Baghdad, but by the the time RSM Bulmer arrived safely in Cairo he had flown 2,750 miles through the capitals of Russia, Iran, Iraq and Egypt, whilst the Dakota transport and crew had flown twice that number.

By early 1945 there was a great need in Air Command South East Asia – ACSEA – for more Dakota squadrons, and during February No 267 Squadron was transferred to Imphal near the Burma border with India.

Many pilots and aircrew from No 216 Group were decorated for their work in the Middle East, Italy and the Balkans. For the most part the work of the transport pilot was hard and monotonous. Every day they flew war supplies along many thousands of miles in the Mediterranean theatre of operations on schedules which were continued even after victory.

At the end of World War 2 No 216 Squadron was still based at Cairo West, having maintained regular Middle East routes and many special flights. Detachments were operating at Habbaniyah in Iraq, Eastleigh near Nairobi, Khartoum, Aden and Karachi.

No 216 Squadron moved to Almaza in July 1945, to Fayid in September 1946 and in February 1947 to Kabrit. In 1948 it participated in evacuation flights and flew arms to Transjordon. Valettas replace the Dakota workhorse at the end of 1949.

CHAPTER THREE

Airborne Forces

The only aircraft that were available to the British Airborne Forces from their inception in 1940 were those that could be spared reluctantly from the hard pressed RAF Bomber Command. Some of these aircraft were already obsolete at this time and all of them unsuitable for dropping parachutists by present-day standards. These aircraft were cramped and uncomfortable for the parachute troops and exits could be extremely dangerous. However, it was a case of "needs must when the devil drives", and such aircraft as the Armstrong Whitworth Whitley, Vickers-Armstrong Wellington, Vickers Valentia and Lockheed Hudson, to name but four of the earlier types, were used, not only to drop parachute troops but also to act as glider tugs.

In May 1942, Churchill was investigating the possibility of providing more aircraft for airborne training. However, although the RAF was prepared to provide aircraft for specific operations, it was not in a position to make further provision for training. The real solution to the problem lay in increasing supplies of transport aircraft, such as the Dakota, from the USA. The Prime Minister cabled President Roosevelt explaining the position and the President's reply was a promise of indirect help only. It was impossible to supply transport aircraft to the RAF because of the tremendous demands of the US forces but he promised that four Transport Groups of the US Army Air Force would be arriving in the United Kingdom during June–July 1942. These four groups would be equipped with 208 aircraft and by November it was hoped that the arrival of further groups would increase the total to 416 aircraft. On reaching the UK all these groups would be available to assist the British Forces both in operations and in training.

Throughout 1942–43, requests were made by No 1 Parachute Training School at Ringway, near Manchester, for the allocation of a Dakota aircraft so that door jumping experience could be gained by the instructional staff. The experiences of the 1st Parachute Brigade in North Africa during November 1942 added weight to this appeal for during their operations this Brigade was making its first descents from this type of aircraft, and casualties were high because of this.

Even an old or even a crashed aircraft or fuselage would have satisfied the PTS instrctors who were anxious that door jumping experience could be gained. But the request of the Parachute Training School was not granted until September 1943. The few Dakotas available to the RAF were urgently required for transport work, and the transport pilots did their work so well that not even a crashed fuselage became available.

The RAF used the Dakota Mk I, III and IV for airborne duties, principally for resupply duties and for the carriage of troops plus towing gliders such as the Airspeed Horsa and the US built Waco CG-4A Hadrian. Twenty paratroops in full equipment could be carried seated in the fuselage and exit was made from the door on the port side of the aircraft.

It was on June 22, 1940, that the Prime Minister sent a brief instruction to his Chief of Staff. "We ought," he wrote, "to have a corps of at least five thousand parchute troops – I hear something is being done already to form such a corps but only, I believe, on a very small scale. Advantage must be taken of the summer to train these forces, who can none the less play their part meanwhile as shock troops in home defence. Pray let me have a note from the War Office on the subject."

On April 26, 1941, the Prime Minister witnessed a well-combined exercise for his benefit at Ringway. It was no more than a demonstration. A formation of Armstrong Whitworth Whitley aircraft dropped their full complement of parachute soldiers, each carried eight plus several equipment containers in the bomb racks. Five sail planes landed in formation, and one General Aircraft Hotspur glider was towed past the visitor. By then it had been realised that to train 5,000 airborne soldiers was a task requiring a great deal of time. Soon after this demonstration a Glider Exercise Unit was formed, and the technical and tactical problems connected with the use of gliders were worked out. It was then that the foundations of what was to become general practice were laid. Expansion continued, and the number of glider-training units considerably increased, until they occupied several stations of the RAF.

By November 1941 the initial period of experiment was drawing to a close. The foundations had been laid strongly and well. Now at last the house could be built. In that month Major-General FAM Browning, CBE DSO MC was appointed General Officer Commanding Airborne Forces and provided with a skeleton staff. From that time on, despite a multitude of difficulties and disappointments, there was no looking back. Airborne Forces were now an integral part of the British Army and presently wore on their heads the maroon-coloured beret soon to become famous and on their shoulders Bellerophon astride winged Pegasus.

A conference had been held at the Air Ministry early in June 1940 to consider the air requirements necessary to the development of parachute troops. By the end of the month the Manchester Corporation's civil airport at Ringway had been decided upon as the home of the new unit to be known initially as the Central Landing School. The selection of Ringway was influenced by the necessity for keeping away from operational areas. The RAF and Army were to work together on the staff. The RAF was to be responsible for the air side of the development and training, and the Army for the military subjects.

As from September 1940 Ringway became the Central Landing Establishment which soon included a Development Unit, a Glider Training Squadron and a Parachute School under Group Captain Newnham with Group Captain LG Harvey as Station Commander. Close liaison was kept with Henlow which was the home of RAF parachuting, and the Airborne Forces Experimental Establishment which was formed at Sherburn-in-Elmet, Yorkshire, during 1941.

At first, the CLE was conspicuous mainly for an almost total lack of the equipment necessary to train parachute soldiers, glider pilots and air-landing troops. Information was equally scanty. A damaged parachute and jumping helmet captured from the Germans were the only models available, and the Armstrong Whitworth Whitley Mk II and III aircraft were seldom simultaneously serviceable. Material in the form of parachutes was presently provided by the energetic labours of two commercial firms, trade rivals, but firmly united in their determination to endow their country with the finest airborne equipment which could be devised. The principal of the statichute – that is, a parachute which opens automatically – was already known, and was rapidly being developed till it became as near fool-proof as any man-made device can be.

Parachute training had been carried out at Henlow by the RAF for many years and aircraft used included the Vickers Vimy and Virginia which were the standard RAF bombers between the wars. The author can recall a parachute dropping demonstration held at Driffield during 1938 involving the Virginias of No 51 Squadron. The parachutists were strapped to the struts of the lower wing and at a given signal the pupil pulled the rip-cord, the parachute was ejected from its container bag into the slipstream, the pupil let go his strap to the strut, and he immediately became a parachutist. This was known as the "pull-off" method.

At Ringway it was soon realised that for operational purposes a number of men must be carried in each aircraft and they must be able to make their exits in very rapid succession so that they would land near together. The most suitable type of aircraft for the purpose would have a deep fuselage with a large door so that men could move about freely and follow each other quickly when making their exits.

In this respect, the Armstrong Whitworth Whitley was about as awkward and uncomfortable for the task as could be imagined. The door was much too small to allow men to pass through it quickly when wearing parachutes and equipment, and the only practicable alternative was to make a circular hole in the floor of the fuselage. The cramped interior into which the men had to crawl on their hands and knees was dark, draughty and smelly. The exit hole was for all the world like an outsize in those manholes which give access to drains or coal cellars. No wonder the Douglas Dakota was in such great demand. Although designed in the mid-1930s as a civilian transport aircraft, it was easily modified for paratroop dropping and glider towing. When No 46 Group RAF Transport Command was formed in January 1944, it was completely equipped with Dakotas and the five squadrons subsequently formed contributed enormously to the success of Airborne Operations from then on.

On July 9, 1940, the first pupils arrived at Ringway, and four days later the first parachute descent was made at nearby Tatton Park which was to be used by No 1 Parachute Training School until it moved to Upper Heyford in March 1946, a complicated move which took three months to complete. It was in 1950 that the Parachute Training School moved to its present home at Abingdon in Berkshire.

Late in 1941 the first parachute brigade under Brigadier (later Major-General) RN Gale, DSO OBE MC was formed, shortly to be followed by the first air landing brigade under Brig GF Hopkinson, OBE MC. Half and presently more than half of Browning's command consisted of airborne troops carried to battle in gliders. A Glider Pilot Regiment was therefore formed in January 1942. Glider pilots had to reach as high a standard on the ground as they attained in the air. How they conducted themselves in North Africa, Sicily, Normandy, Holland and the Rhine shows with what fortitude and unanimity it was reached. In the glider the tow pilots sit side by side, the first pilot being on the left. The controls are similar to those of a power-driven aircraft except that there are no throttles. The correct position to be assumed by the glider is either slightly above the tug, high-tow, or slightly below it, low-tow. The glider must never be directly behind the tug, for the slipstream would cause it to oscillate so violently that the tow rope would soon snap. The breaking of the two rope is naturally the chief fear of the pilot, and it may assume the proportions of a nightmare if he is flying in cloudy and bumpy weather. The strength of the rope depends on the strength of the tug's fuselage and the nose of the glider, to which it is attached by a simple bolt-and-shackle device. Too strong a rope would mean putting too great a strain on the tug; too weak would lead to a frequent snapping. For the Airspeed Horsa the circumference of the tow rope is nearly four inches, 350 feet long, and contains within it the telephone wires connecting the pilot of the glider with the pilot of the tug. The Airspeed Horsa is fitted with large flaps, which enable them to be dived at a comparatively steep angle and thus, if necessary brought quickly to the ground after being cast off. The landing speed in still air is not less than 70 mph. No glider pilot or glider-borne soldier carries a parachute, but all wear mae wests. Escape hatches are fitted so that, if the glider falls into the sea, the occupants can leave it quickly. One great advantage possessed by gliders is that their wooden construction gives them buoyancy. Some of them have been known to float for twenty-four hours.

Major (later Brigadier) George Chatterton, DSO was given the task of raising the Glider Pilot Regiment. Out of the many thousand volunteers interviewed for the purpose of choosing glider pilots, only a very few were accepted. Of these, a third failed to pass their qualifying tests or to reach the military standard required. It was thus only a chosen band who were judged worthy to follow the arduous and gallant call. As with the parachute soldier, they represented every regiment in the British Army. Later, in SEAC, there was a shortage at one time of Dakota pilots, so it was proposed to train glider pilots to fly this unique transport.

Another problem of great though more technical importance was how to arm the parachute soldier – to supply him with weapons and ammunition so that he would be in a position to fight unaided by the regular supply services until such time as the army on the ground had made contact with him. There is a limit to what can be carried by a man descending by parachute. How great it was had to be discovered. A method was devised at Ringway of dropping with as much as 100 lb weight of extra supplies attached to the parachutist. The ammunition or machine-gun was put in a bag attached to one end of 70 feet of rope, the other end being secured to the jumper's waist. After leaving the aircraft, the bag was allowed to fall the full length of the rope, thus increasing the speed of descent. The bag, being below the jumper, was the first to strike the ground; its weight was thus neutralised, the speed of descent of the parachutist was checked, and he could land safely. This method of carrying arms and supplies supplanted to some extent the use of containers, which were often hard to find, especially in close country.

However, on resupply missions the use of containers was a necessity. The precise method of waging air warfare is to make use of specialised aircraft for the various functions. In this respect, the Douglas Dakota was no exception. For airborne operations which involved the dropping of paratroops, the underside of the fuselage was provided with containers which were aluminium cannisters known as parapacks. Each cannister contained medical supplies, ammunition, food, communications equipment, etc, for paratroop use once they were deployed on the ground. Each parapack was attached to a special rack to the underside of the fuselage by means of an electric jettison release, operable and controllable by the transport pilot. It was possible to jettison the parapacks within the designated drop zone (DZ) occupied by the paratroops. Each parapack was painted and marked in colour to designate medical supplies, ammunition, food, water, etc, as the case may be. The release of the parapacks was governed by a timing device known as an intervalometer. This device controlled the jettison and spacing pattern in which the parapacks were to be dropped. The entire operation was under the control of the pilot. Only Dakotas intended for airborne assault operations carried parapacks or were equipped to receive them.

At the end of May 1941 information was received that a similar parachute training school was to be formed in India. The Commanding Officer and a nucleus staff were to be provided by Ringway. On September 22, 1941, an Air Landing School was established at Willingdon Airport, New Delhi. During October 1942 the school was transferred some 350 miles north to Chaklala near Rawalpindi where it remained until October 1945. Pupils were Indians and Ghurkas, and initially the aircraft used consisted of aged Vickers Valentias, the Vickers-Armstrong Wellington which was a particularly difficult type from which to jump, and the Lockheed Hudson which were not used for regular paratroop work, but they were the most suitable aircraft for flying agents to Burma and dropping them behind the Japanese lines. The school was later designated No 3 Parachute Training School and most of the SEAC Dakota squadrons found themselves detached to the school for training and exercises. In October 1943 No 194 Squadron was seconded for jumpmaster training to Chaklala and the official records show that forty-seven of the fifty Wireless Operators completed the course voluntary. As "A" Flight from No 194 Squadron moved into the school, the Dakotas and crews of "A" Flight from No 62 Squadron moved out after a period of airborne forces training. On September 20, 1943, Grp Capt George Donaldson, Officer Commanding No 177 Wing at Rawalpindi, had signalled that this unit, which was known throughout SEAC as "The Friendly Firm", be designated No 194 Airborne Forces Squadron.

There was little publicity given in the United Kingdom to *Operation Dracula*, the operation that led to the capture of the important city of Rangoon in May 1945. But the Ghurka paratroops were there and played an important part. A report of their participation describes it thus: "In one of the most successful paratroop operations of this war 800 paratroops, 18 door bundles and 221 packages were put down by the initial group of aircraft. The air discipline of the paratroops was very good and they seemed eager to go. The results were nearly 100 per cent successful – only eight minor injuries being reported among the men – while no mechanical or maintenance difficulties marred the operation."

The history and adventures of No 4 Middle East Training School, as the parachute unit came to be officially designated, were perhaps more varied and romantic than those of either the English or Indian establishments.

In August 1941, when the school at Ringway was hearing rumours about the formation of a parachute brigade and plans were being made for the RAF to assume full responsibility for training, Capt David Stirling thought it would be a good idea to do some parachuting in the desert. He was an extremely gallant and enterprising officer and commanded a unit of the Special Air Service whose function was to carry out raids on Commando lines in the desert and along the Mediterranean coast.

There was no official policy for parachute training in the Middle East at that time, and as several requests for assistance to form a school produced no results it was decided to try and create one without it. A small supply of parachutes was acquired by some unorthodox means and the use of several old Bristol Bombay aircraft was arranged with a local RAF squadron. The lack of knowledge and experience soon resulted in several fatal accidents, but as there was nothing so effective as a few deaths during training to arouse the attention of higher authority the casualties were not in vain.

Ringway, as the fount of parachute training and learning, was called upon to provide an officer who knew something about the requirements. It was an Army officer, Peter Warr, who was sent out to Kabrit on the Suez Canal to render what assistance he could in October 1941. With the help of Staff Sgt Kennedy and Flt Sgt Spencer he set about the task of improvising the parachute equipment to conform as closely as possible with the methods used in the United Kingdom.

A fortnight after Warr's arrival arrangements were made for a parachuting demonstration to be carried out before Gen Auchinleck. By dint of much enthusiasm and hard work five Bristol Bombays were borrowed from the obliging RAF and equipped for the occasion. Flying in close formation they made a mass drop of seventy-five men which in those days was an impressive sight.

The official recognition of parachuting as a necessary military adjunct at home, as evidenced by the decision to form an Airborne Division and the setting up of a school in India, gradually percolated through the departments of Air HQ in Cairo. In May 1942 Wg Cdr Warne was sent to command a new unit to be known as No 4 Middle East Training School at Kabrit and shortly afterwards the nucleus staff was augmented by more Army and RAF personnel.

The work of the new unit was carried on in the face of various and considerable difficulties. Parachutes had to be serviced and stored at a RAF Maintenance Unit some miles away. The three Vickers-Armstrong Wellington aircraft were more often unserviceable than serviceable, and their meagre flying hours had to be divided between operational and training demands. The dropping zone was four miles from the camp and could only be reached by traversing a stretch of particularly rugged desert.

In spite of the difficulties and frustrations the work of the school went on with that concentrated enthusiasm and determination which seemed to animate all who were actively engaged with military parachuting throughout World War 2. The first commitments of the newly formed No 4 METS included the training of two squadrons of Special Air Service troops and considerable numbers of Greeks, Italians, Yugoslavs, Germans and Frenchmen who had volunteered for special clandestine operations against the common enemy.

Then came the news of the defeat at Bir Hachim followed soon afterwards by the fall of Tobruk. The situation was so serious that all aircraft were withdrawn immediately for belligerent action against the enemy. The soldier pupils, too, were needed for more urgent duties than parachute training. Wg Cdr Warne was transferred to an RAF squadron for operational duties, and as the threat to El Alamein developed the school virtually disentegrated. The RAF instructors joined their good friends of the Special Air Service company.

Had it not been for the devoted interest and staunch support of a Ringway graduate in the person of Lt-Col Kenneth Smyth it is doubtful whether No 4 METS would ever have recovered from the grievous disruption of affairs. Smyth had been sent out by the War Office to fill a staff appointment at the Middle East headquarters which included the difficult task of spreading the gospel in regard to airborne forces in general and parachute troops in particular. He agitated for the resuscitation of the school and for it to be organised on proper lines. His efforts were so successful to the extent that Ringway was called upon to provide a chief instructor and in August 1942 Flt Lt Phil Murphy arrived at Kabrit.

There were signs that parachute training would be required on a large scale in the near future. The SAS was in the process of being expanded; Smyth had been appointed to raise and command the 10th Parachute Battalion, and a semi-trained parachute battalion was on its way from India. In addition, the various secret organisations and partisan movements intimated that they would require increasing facilities for the parachute training of their agents.

The dropping of men and supplies in Yugoslavia, Greece and other parts of Southern Europe went on apace, and the instructors found themselves employed in an operational role one day and a training role the next. Many well-known names appeared among the pupils, including those of Maj Randolph Churchill and Brig McLean.

At the end of December the school was set another unusual task. This was to teach a party of Arabs how to parachute and then drop them near Tripoli which involved a round trip of nearly a thousand miles. Despite the language and other difficulties the training was successfully accomplished.

In March 1943 No 4 METS left its home in the desert and moved to greener and more agreeable pastures at Ramat David near Haifa in Palestine. The Parachute Brigade units also moved to camps in the same area. Wg Cdr Warne, who had returned from his operational duties with a DSO and a DFC, resumed command of the unit.

The RAF was, as usual, extremely short of aircraft, and the school was most fortunate in arranging with a squadron of the US Army Air Force to have their Douglas C-47 transports co-operate in their work. The pilots and aircrews were able to gain experience in the dropping of parachutists and also in fairly long cross-country flights across the desert.

Early in 1943 No 216 Squadron, based at Cairo West, re-equipped with the Douglas Dakota, and during August "A" Flight was detached to No 4 METS with its Dakota Mk Is – FD805, 806, 807, 816, 829, 866, 923, 963, 778 – and during the three months detachment, in addition to many hours of training, made operational sorties to Salerno, Taranto, and the beach-head at Catania. In October it flew in support of the Aegean campaign dropping Greek paratroops which it had assisted to train earlier at Ramat David. Many resupply missions were flown to the islands including Leros and Samos.

There were no British aircraft suitable for parachuting operations, and the diversion of improvised bombers from their proper functions was considered to be inexpedient. Until the RAF received the Dakota in quantity it was arranged that the US Army Air Force should provide the majority of aircraft and crews, both for the transportation of the paratroops and the towing of gliders. The transport used was the Douglas C-47 Skytrain and the C-53 Skytrooper, and this meant that our men had to learn a completely different aircraft drill because the Douglas transport had a door in the side of the fuselage instead of a hole in the floor.

At the end of 1943 No 4 METS moved to Italy, and in April 1945 was based at Goia Del Colle near Bari. A small detachment carried on with the 2nd Independent Parachute Brigade until June 1945 at Lido Da Roma.

Back at No 1 PTS at Ringway the first Canadians arrived for training in August 1942, afterwards returning to Canada to form the nucleus of a Canadian Parachute Battalion and a parachute school at Camp Shilo. A year later they were using the versatile Dakota for paratroop training.

Long before the United States was engaged in active war with the Japanese after Pearl Harbor, we were extending hospitality and supplying information to her Service officers, war correspondents, and others who showed interest in the new Airborne Forces activities. The most important of the early visitors was Mr Averill Harriman who accompanied Mr Winston Churchill on that momentous day in April 1941 when Britain's airborne potential was demonstrated by five obsolete Armstrong Whitworth Whitleys and a few single-seat gliders.

In August 1942 Ringway welcomed a party of visitors from the US Parachute School at Fort Benning. They stayed for a week or so, made jumps from the balloons and the aircraft and generally studied our methods. The experts at No 1 PTS were naturally interested to know what other countries had done and were doing in regard to military parachuting so that they might have a yardstick by which to measure our own results. A reciprocal visit by a party from Ringway to airborne establishments in the USA was warmly welcomed. This included a visit to the Canadian establishment at Camp Shilo.

The Parachute Training School, which started as the progeny of No 22 Group and the Central Landing Establishment, became the problem child of a long succession of parent formations. In June 1943 it was, inaptly enough, under the temporary jurisdiction of Fighter Command. Later in the year the PTS was transferred from the jurisdiction of No 70 Group and Fighter Command to No 38 Group and the Tactical Air Force.

Throughout the summer, autumn and winter of 1943 and the spring of 1944 the great hangar-gymnasium at Ringway echoed and re-echoed with the incessant clatter of the training apparatus, the commands of the instructors and the thuds of the pupils' tumbling bodies. At Tatton Park men jumped from balloons and Dakota aircraft by day and night, weekdays and Sundays, whenever weather conditions were suitable. A thousand men at a time were housed and trained at the Parachute Training School in preparation for the tremendous events which were drawing near.

Men of many nations, nice men, brave men – all learning to parachute because they believed it would enable them to inflict greater harm on the enemy; fair Dutchmen and Norwegians; swarthy Czechs and Yugoslavs; Poles from Warsaw and Poles from Galicia; a battalion of Green Howards; Naval men and smart Marine Commandos; Canadians, trained in the US style, being converted to British methods; BBC and Press reporters; all found their way to Ringway to acquire the confidence and skill that would enable them to parachute down on enemy soil with the minimum risk of injury.

In May 1943 when plans were being made for the assault upon Europe a new organisation was formed to deal with the greatly increased numbers of airborne soldiers that would be required. This was the Airborne Forces Depot and Development Centre, responsible for recruiting, military training, and the co-ordination of arrangements with the RAF for parachuting and glider-flying instruction. In the same month Richard Gale left the War Office and commenced to form the 6th Airborne Division with the knowledge that its specific objective was participation in the attack on Europe. The nucleus of this new command was provided by the 3rd Parachute Brigade which had been left in the United Kingdom when the rest of the 1st Division went to Africa.

No 38 Wing was formed at Netheravon on January 19, 1942, its initial function being to Control Nos 296 Glider and 297 Parachute Squadrons and to provide for the air requirements of the Airborne Division, both in training and for operations. The Wing was located with the Airborne Division and its first Commander Gp Capt Sir Nigel St V Norman Bt.

Aircraft and gliders of No 38 Wing were involved in a series of operations against Sicily, which were given the overall codename of *Husky*. The first operation was against Syracuse on July 9–10, 1943, to which the Wing contributed twenty-eight Armstrong Whitworth Albemarle and seven Handley Page Halifax aircraft from Nos 296 and 297 Squadrons. The operation was mounted from Kairouan but was not a great success because of the 137 gliders, mostly towed by Douglas C-47 Skytrain aircraft of the US Troop Carrier Command, landed in the sea.

On July 13–14, 1943, there was a further operation in which No 38 Wing were involved. The objective was an important bridge over the River Simeto. A total of 107 aircraft were involved – Dakotas and Albemarles – in paratroop dropping and 17 gliders were towed by Halifax and Albemarle aircraft. Of the paratrooping aircraft 27 were lost and 19 returned to base without dropping because of intensive flak. One of the tug aircraft was lost.

An examination of the results achieved by the Wing in the Sicily operation revealed that these were very creditable. In the first operation, 35 aircraft of the Wing were involved and 26 released their gliders over the correct zone. Of the 17 gliders towed in the second operation, 13 landed in the correct area, two were lost and two were damaged on take-off.

As a result of the lessons learned in *Operation Husky*, it became apparent that, for later operations, the Wing would have to be considerably expanded and reorganised. Eventually, after many meetings, the Wing was given Group status on October 11, 1943, and Air Vice-Marshal LN Hollinghurst, CB OBE DFC became the first Group Commander in place of Air Cdre Primrose. The new Group absorbed all stations in No 38 Group and a strength of nine squadrons were authorised, comprising four Albemarle, one Halifax and four Short Stirling squadrons, all to be formed by February 1, 1944, to an establishment of sixteen front-line and four reserve aircraft. Reorganisation was completed by November 22, 1943, when the Group came under the control of Headquarters Allied Expeditionary Force.

Throughout March and April, 1944, the Group along with the Dakotas of No 46 Group were engaged in exercises and training practises in preparation for *Operation Overlord*, the landing of British and American forces on the mainland of Europe. Training was completed by the end of April and continued at a reduced tempo throughout May, the last large-scale exercise being held on the first day of May, when seventy-four

Airspeed Horsa gliders landed by night in a small landing zone at Netheravon.

After the end of World War 2, the Dakota continued in use as the main aircraft used by Airborne Forces. Training and exercises were carried out in the paratrooping role in Palestine, Egypt and Europe. Just before the cessation of hostilities in the Far East, Dakotas and their crews were being trained in glider-snatch operations at Ibsley, Hampshire, using Waco CG-4A Hadrian gliders loaded with concrete blocks in preparation for the invasion of Japan.

The last operational drop carried out by the RAF Dakota was in Malaya in February 1952 when personnel of the 22nd Special Air Service were dropped into primary jungle. As a fitting tribute to all those "Red Berets" who gave their lives for the cause of freedom, a Dakota C.4 – KP208 – stands outside the Airborne Forces Museum at Aldershot in Hampshire. Aldershot is the home and depot of the Parachute Regiment and Airborne Forces, and one or two of the senior instructors have vivid memories of No 1 Parachute Training School with its motto "Knowledge Dispels Fear".

AIR DESPATCH

It was within the framework of Airborne Forces that Royal Army Service Corps – RASC – Air Despatch was to be born. In June 1940 the first parachutists were trained at Ringway and by 1942 the first Airborne Division was taking shape, and it was then realised that once on the ground these airborne troops would need supplies so the Air Despatch Group was formed under control of the War Office.

During World War 2 two main air supply organisations were formed, one in the United Kingdom and one in Burma. Although the responsibilities of the army in each were identical, the organisations had many differences. By 1943 Army responsibilities were clearly defined in South East Asia Command and by 1944 the formation of the Air Despatch Group relieved the RAF of a commitment that it could not readily undertake in Europe. From the very beginning the RASC played an important part and throughout the war was the only arm to provide despatching crews for aircraft. By the end of hostilities the Army responsibilities for air supply were almost totally in the hands of the RASC and have remained so ever since.

The primary units in both these wartime organisations were the Air Despatch Companies which were responsible for delivering all stores required by the Army, Military Missions, and Resistance Groups, whether landed, dropped by parachute or free dropped. In order to do this they had four main tasks. First they were responsible for loading all aircraft engaged in resupply sorties. To do this simply, without wasting manpower or time is not an easy task. Not only has the aircraft a fixed payload for a given distance, above which it may not be loaded, but different parts of its fuselage floor take different strains. Thus, although a loaded aircraft may be within its weight limits for take-off, a badly positioned load may become a serious hazard. Also, it must be loaded so that it balances within its centre of gravity limits, and finally the freight must be so securely lashed that it will not come loose however violent the strain upon it. An aircraft might be forced to take evasive action almost as soon as it left a rear airfield; unarmed, an easy target, eluding the enemy might impose a strain upon it five times the weight of the load. In war, most demands for air supply are the result of emergency, so care must be tempered with speed.

Secondly, the Air Despatch Companies were responsible for packing and storing the containers used for dropping supplies. During World War 2 there were three of these. The airborne pannier, in shape and size almost identical to a wicker laundry basket, could take a load of 500 lb and being too heavy to be despatched by hand was usually loaded on to a roller conveyer fitted into the aircraft. The bombcell container was originally designed as a free fall container, that is designed to be dropped without a parachute. It is a cylinder of sheet metal hinged to form two parts, approximately four and a half feet in length. Although it was found necessary to fit a parachute to this container it was particularly useful to resupply resistance groups as it could be fitted to any aircraft with a universal bomb rack. Also it was the only container long enough to hold ·303 rifles or Bren guns. As fighter bombers could readily carry three or four bombcell containers, the device proved its value time and time again. The SEAC pack was designed for use in the Far East and many hundreds of thousands of these were dropped in Burma. Made of canvas, it could bear a load of a little under 200 lb. The packing of these containers had its own particular problems. If the container is too heavy, the canopy of the parachute may rip and the speed of descent will increase so that on impact the stores will be damaged. If too light, payload is wasted and it may drift away from the dropping zone, there is also a danger that on ejection the pack or partially developed parachute will hit the tailplane. At the beginning of the war no load tables were in existence and these had to be worked out for each container. This is only a fragment of the problem of packing containers that was overcome by the Air Despatch Companies during 1944.

Thirdly, they were responsible for providing the air despatch crews that flew with the aircraft and despatched the loads over the dropping zones. In 1944 this could be done in three ways; either by fitting the loads on roller conveyors or ejecting them manually or releasing them from the bomb racks on the underside of wings and fuselage. When the aircraft reached the dropping zone a red light followed by a green signalled by the captain were the indications used. Although it may appear a small matter to eject stores from an aircraft in flight, experience shows otherwise. Dropping zones in the European theatre were invariably large enough to allow slight errors in despatching, but dropping zones in Burma and those used by Military Missions and resistance groups were usually very small. Thus the slightest error by the navigator or delay by the despatchers might result in the packs being widely dispersed or caught in the trees or jungle outside the DZ limits. When an aircraft travels at 150 feet per second, about the slowest despatching speed during the war, a high standard of training is necessary to ensure that the loads land within the boundary markers. The operation was often complicated by attack by enemy fighters or anti-aircraft fire. In order to obtain accuracy, supplies were dropped at either 600, 400 or 50 feet above ground level, the height dependant on the type of parachute used, the lowest height being reserved for free fall containers. Even at night, flying at these heights, only a little above stalling speed, unable to alter course until free of its load, often presented an easy target to ground attack which a fighter escort, however watchful, could do little to prevent.

During the summer months despatchers wore a Denison Smock, a loose fitting camouflaged jacket worn by airborne troops, and in winter, depending on the theatre of operations they were issued with flying-suits, fur-lined boots, sweaters and gloves or mittens. Throughout any operation they wore parachutes, safety belts, paratroop helmets, mae wests and were armed with ·38 revolvers. No 1 despatcher wore a flying helmet and was connected to the aircraft's inter-comm system. After a while it was found that the "O"-type parachute fitted on the chest was too bulky and impeded movement. To discard it while over the DZ was unwise as the large buckle on which it rested readily entangled itself with the packs. Thus it became a simple matter to involuntary despatch oneself with the food, weapons and ammunition. The odd one in fact did. An American parasuit was substituted, fitted with a parachute in the seat and it was found to be more satisfactory.

Finally the Air Despatch Companies were responsible for packing the parachutes used for supply dropping. Originally an RAF responsibility, this was the last of the tasks given to air despatch ground personnel. During World War 2 there were four main types of parachute. Two were used in Europe, one British and one American, of 28 and 24 feet diameter, and two in the Far East, both of 18 feet diameter. The British parachutes were designed at the Royal Aircraft Establishment, Farnborough, and by a civilian manufacturer. They were made of cotton, nylon or silk. Shortage of cotton never forced the country to develop a paper parachute although some experiments were carried out with limited success. Packing parachutes in Europe was no great problem as they could be dried and stored without difficulty. In the Far East lack of suitable storage space and the humid climate combined to make drying the parachutes almost impossible. The cotton parachutes readily absorbed moisture which prevented the canopy fully developing on ejection. But this in time was overcome and of the millions of parachutes dropped in Burma during the campaign only a small proportion "candled". When the static line to the aircraft extracts the parachute from the pack and the canopy fails to develop the parachute is said to "candle". This is usually caused by dampness.

These then were the tasks that the RASC were given.

It was in the Far East that supply by air reached its greatest value. In Burma there were no metalled roads of any length but only wide mud tracks cut through the jungle and twisting and turning up the hillsides. During the monsoon they were either washed away or made impassable by rain. There was only one solution; to maintain as far as possible all the fighting troops by air. In 1942 there was no equipment designed for dropping supplies, there were no parachutes, no containers, and no roller conveyor. But fortunately there were transport aircraft; the Douglas DC-2 and DC-3 followed in large numbers by the Douglas Dakota. It was these aircraft that were to be used in the next three years to carry the supplies, thousands of tons, to the armies in the Burma jungle. There was at that time no other aircraft available in large quantities comparable in size, range or strength. Its reliability in the damp climate was proved over and over again.

The importance of air supply in Burma will be realised when one considers the primary danger of jungle warfare. With each step advanced, the line of communication becomes longer and more fragile, the supplies have farther to travel, and troops have to be held back to defend the communication zone. An army in the jungle is forever looking over its shoulder lest its lines of communication be cut. If this happens it is without sustenance of any kind. Shortages will be felt almost at once and without sufficient food and ammunition defeat in battle is a certain conclusion. All along this line of communication, whether it is rail, river or road, are supply dumps ever decreasing in size but all requiring an organisation to staff and administer them. The result is a costly and fragile line of communication.

For the Burma campaign the lines of communications started in India, and until the later stages of the war the front was divided into two, North Assam and Arakan. For the army in North Assam the supplies had to pass along a broad-gauge railway as far as the Brahmaputra River and thence on a narrow gauge. Such was the congestion of this single line of communication that sometimes supplies had to be despatched by river. On one particular route there were nine transhipment points and delays were often caused by the railway being washed away or the rivers being in flood. Railhead was Manipur where supplies were lifted by a transport column operating on the only route available, the famous Manipur road. To add to the congestion, reinforcements passed along the same route.

The use of supply by air could cut away this disastrously long and complicated supply line. By 1943 it had been proved that an army in the field need not be dependant upon its ground line of communications nor need it hold large stocks of supplies. In this way it had no fear of encirclement for provided it could defeat the enemy in battle it could be supplied indefinitely from the air. Also it became more mobile, staging posts and advanced bases being dispensed with, and its administrative tail extensively reduced.

The first air despatch operation took place in Burma during its evacuation in 1942. Large numbers of European and native refugees trekked through the jungle to India. At the same time irregular forces attempted to delay the Japanese in the Chinwin valley. Owing to the lack of equipment all but the most valuable items had to be free dropped. Some 3,000 tons of supplies, mostly food and medicines were dropped at irregular intervals during the long march to India. It was a result of this operation that the need for standardised containers and parachutes was realised, and it became accepted that the air could be used to maintain formations without any other lines of communication.

In order to carry out this first air supply operation in Burma a Royal Indian Army Service Corps general transport company was hurriedly trained, as far as there could be training in a branch of the service bristling with new problems, and gained very valuable experience in packing and despatching techniques. Known at first as an air supply company it was then the first unit in SEAC to be trained in air despatch.

As the war developed eight RIASC companies and two RASC companies, No 61 and No 799, were air-despatch trained and operated in Burma until the end of the war. The 14th Army was the largest formation to be supplied by air and it became apparent that a special unit would have to be formed. This was called Troop Carrier Command and consisted of RAF, RCAF and US Army Air Force squadrons. At first a branch of headquarters 14th Army called "Q" Air was responsible for the administration of all air supply. This system proved satisfactory until operations in Burma were intensified. Then a new headquarters was formed called the Army Air Transport Organisation. At about the same time the United States sent reinforcements to SEAC and Troop Carrier Command was increased and renamed the Combat Cargo Task Force.

The new AATO controlled the supply by air organisations which were called Rear Air Maintenance Organisations. They included Air Despatch Companies, General Transport Platoons, Supply and Petrol Platoons,

Pioneer or labour units, and detachments from other arms when required. On forward airfields, supplies were handled by Forward Air Maintenance Organisations which were commanded not by AATO but by the formation with which they were placed. When the supplies were dropped, small units were responsible for laying their own markers and for the operation of the dropping zone. Of the total tonnages lifted, approximately 60 per cent was dropped by parachute. At the time when supply by air was in the greatest demand over 2,500 tons was air transported daily.

Some idea of the enormous quantities of supplies dropped and landed in Burma can be gained by a comparison with the tonnage of bombs dropped on Germany. A report of No 223 Group, part of the Combat Cargo Task Force, stated that bombs on Germany in 1944, the year of the greatest obliteration raids, weighed 47,000 tons. In the same year cargo aircraft dropped or landed 600,000 tons of supplies in Burma alone. The standard operational payload of a Dakota aircraft is approximately three tons. It would have required 200,000 Dakotas to have removed that tonnage in one lift. Nose to tail they would stretch over 2,500 miles.

By 1944 most of the difficulties first encountered had been overcome; dropping zone markings had been standardised, the SEAC pack and 18 foot cotton parachute were in general use, light aircraft were employed to evacuate casualities, and the early difficulties of the new air supply organisation were things of the past.

Although the 14th Army had been supplied by air before 1944 it only became vital to its existence when it was encircled in the Arakan that year. Enormous tonnages were flown in, the majority dropped, but whenever possible landed on airstrips. Aircrew were often asked to fly in impossible conditions and land their Dakotas on jungle clearings that bore little resemblance to runways. They frequently landed and took off from uneven strips covered with pierced steel planking, known to many as PSP. During the Arakan operation, dropping zones were frequently extremely small and difficult to locate. The dropping zones operated by the 7th Indian Division were particularly awkwardly placed, most of them between high ranges of hills. During the monsoon, clouds as thick as 30,000 feet prevented aircraft from flying to the dropping zones. But at every opportunity the Dakota transports delivered their loads. Only nil visibility prevented flying.

At the height of the monsoon, British troops operating near Imphal were dropped over 14,000 tons of supplies in the month of June alone. During the sixteen-day siege of Kohima both the garrison and relieving troops were supplied by air until the Japanese withdrawal.

Owing to the lack of suitable roads for motor transport, mules were in universal use with units operating in the jungle. Although they could easily be transported in aircraft or gliders a need sometime arose for mules in areas without landing strips. It was decided that a method of dropping them alive should be devised. Dropping of animals had never been carried out on a large scale, though during the Italian campaign in Ethiopia live sheep had been despatched from aircraft to feed the troops taking part. Although animals had never before been dropped successfully and lived after the ordeal, the Royal Army Veterinary Corps in India devised a satisfactory method. A mule was strapped down to a platform and covered with inflated rubber bags. Six 28-foot silk parachutes were attached, and, narcosis having been effected, whole contraption was loaded on to a Dakota. On the first experiment, it was found that although the mule remained prone for about ten minutes after impact it could carry a load within half an hour. Later experiments with younger animals – the first one used was very old in case of mishap – proved that they suffered no ill effects from the descent and required only a short time to become acclimatised to their new surroundings. Goats were also air dropped to the Ghurka troops to be used for their meat supply.

No 61 Company RASC was trained in Air Despatch duties to support Special Force. Not only was it responsible for packing and despatching the loads but for helping to operate the landing zones within the strongholds. It was rare that sufficient tonnage could be landed by day and so large quantities were dropped by night, the sorties sometimes carrying on until dawn. Often DZ markings would be unnecessary as a battle would be in progress. The flashes from the artillery would clearly show the Dakotas where to fly, and not infrequently ammunition would be carried straight from the DZ to the gun lines. This Company was also responsible for casualty evacuation as RAF Casualty Air Evacuation Units were not available. During the advance to the Chindwin early in 1945 this company alone landed or dropped 100,000 tons of supplies. A little later it supplied the armour engaged in the push on Meiktila, when there was a shortage of petrol. Once again the figures are high, for during the operation the Company landed 25,000 gallons of petrol.

No 799 Company, originally a part of the Air Despatch Group in the United Kingdom, moved to Burma in January 1945, and was soon involved in the routine of large supply drops. It only remained in Burma a short time and in July moved once again, this time to Singapore. As the military position in Java had deteriorated, the unit was ordered to assist in the maintenance of the 23rd Indian Division and 5th British Parachute Brigade, and to do this the whole unit moved yet again, to Batavia. There it remained until the end of the war. During its nine months in Batavia, it dropped or landed 50,000 tons of equipment.

It is easy to overlook the real value of air supply in considering a mass of facts and figures. It is true that in Burma the figures are quite staggering. The number of parachutes expended during the Far East campaign must total several millions. It is no exaggeration to say that supply by air was the greatest single contributory factor to victory in the Far East and helped to shorten the war as much as the two atomic explosions over Japan.

The development of an Air Despatch Organisation in the United Kingdom was very much slower than in the Far East. No 48 Air Despatch was formed from a troop-carrying company, a lines of communication column and a driver training battalion. These were transformed into three Air Despatch Companies which when they were fully manned consisted of four air-dropping platoons in each company. Each platoon comprised of 15 air despatch crews of four men. Thus 48 Air Despatch could put in the air 180 crews at any one time. A total of 360 tons could be despatched with the use of these crews. The whole group was at one time 5,000 strong with approximately 1,500 vehicles. Six general transport companies were under command and these performed the details required by the group. The headquarters was located with the RAF Air Freight Control Centre near Swindon. No 48 Air Despatch had its headquarters at Ashton Keynes, close to the Transport Command airfields from which the crews would fly. The three Air Despatch Companies – Nos 233, 799 and 800 – were located at Burford, St Margaret and Down Ampney. The main airfields used by the companies were Broadwell, Blakehill Farm and Down Ampney, although occasionally during a large operation Lyneham and Fairford would be used. Training of the Air Despatch crews was carried out initially at the Air Training Centre at Leicester.

The Group's first operation was to resupply the 6th Airborne Division on and after D-Day. By comparison with the larger operations of the future it was well within the Group's capacity and gave the Air Despatch Companies valuable operational experience. Although the Airborne Companies had been able to give the new organisation valuable assistance in the way of technical information, very little actual experience had been gained in Europe before *Operation Overlord*.

It was during the attempt to close the Falaise Gap that all three companies were involved in an operation of any size. So fast was General Patton's advance with his US Third Army that his armour became seriously short of fuel. Thousands of gallons were loaded onto Dakotas in Wiltshire and a steady stream of transports flew to airfields within the Third Army's perimeter. So fast did this army outstrip its supply line that enormous tonnages had to be despatched to the divisions at the front. No 799 Company alone supplied 140 men to fly with the aircraft. On August 7 a battalion of the 120th Regiment was surrounded by the Germans. For six days the lost battalion refused all demands for surrender and held grimly to its position. On August 8 it radioed for medical supplies of plasma, morphine and shell dressings. A flight of Dakotas attempted to resupply the battalion, but enemy anti-aircraft defence was so effective that over half the load was dropped wide and only a small amount reached the American troops. General Bradley described their exploit as "one of the epochal struggles of the war" and the battalion was awarded the Presidental Unit Citation.

As the advance through France continued, the logistic problems increased as the supply lines lengthened. Originally No 21 Army Group had demanded 170 tons to be dropped each day and a further 700 tons a day to be landed. As the land tail became stretched more and more taut, this was increased to 350 tons and 3,000 tons per day respectively. After the fall of Paris, the problems of supply were further aggravated by the necessity to feed the four million population of the city. Once again the Air Despatch Group were involved, ferrying in 500 tons of flour and food daily for a fortnight. Although as much as possible of the 4,000 tons of food required every day was brought in by convoy it strained and overworked transport companies to the limit. The Air Despatch Group continued to load aircraft for despatch to France and Germany until the end of the war in Europe.

The gallant stand by the Airborne Forces at Arnhem is now a legend. On September 17, 1944, the 1st Airborne Division, 10,000 strong, landed near Arnhem. Nine days later, one-fifth of them recrossed the Rhine to a spearhead a few thousand yards wide held by the 2nd Army. Although the bridge at Arnhem had been captured and held for forty-eight hours, the 2nd Army had failed to break through as planned.

A total of 900 all ranks of Nos 48 and 49 Air Despatch flew 600 sorties during the attempts to resupply the Airborne Division. Most of them did two sorties and some of them three. Two hundred and sixty-four were shot down, of whom 116 were eventually missing or killed. Despite their sacrifices all attempts failed. Over sixty aircraft were destroyed by the enemy.

When the roller conveyers were shot away, the panniers were despatched manually. Sometimes one or two of the despatchers were wounded, sometimes all. Rarely during the last attempts did an aircraft get through unscathed. Many times young RASC soldiers did their first parachute jumps over enemy territory, and some of them delayed the canopy opening for as long as possible for fear of attack on the way down.

The losses had indeed been heavy and the gain small. Through the long summer days of 1944 the men of Nos 48 and 49 Air Despatch had packed and loaded the supplies on airfields in Essex and Wiltshire. And then they had waited. Sixteen times an Airborne operation had been planned and cancelled and they still waited to perform the job for which they had been trained. Finally the call had come and it was answered: no matter the sacrifice, no matter the wounds, no matter death itself, the call was answered. The exploits of these men shall pass into history. Those that came back, limping across the skies of Europe, brought with them a little of the immortality that will forever be linked with the name of Arnhem.

As a result of its part in the Arnhem operation the Air Despatch Group was at last awarded the right to wear a formation sign of its own. It was designed by the Commander of No 48 Air Despatch and it represents a yellow Dakota on a blue background. Depicted in two of the RASC colours, this flash has, since Arnhem, been worn by all personnel instead of district or War Office controlled signs. It is believed that this is the first formation sign granted the RASC which is their right alone to wear.

During the German counter offensive in the Ardennes in December, a large-scale operation was planned by the Air Despatch Group as it appeared inevitable that some of the American force would be surrounded. Of these the 101st United States Airborne Division in Bastoigne was in the most critical position. A large part of No 48 Air Despatch was moved to US airfields in the South of England to prepare 100 aircraft loads, mostly for C-47 Skytrain transports. The three companies worked day and night packing the containers. Dense fog made this task more arduous. But at the last moment Bastoigne was relieved and a large part of the operation was cancelled.

During *Operation Varsity*, the code name given to the airborne assault across the Rhine, the 6th Airborne Division was supplied by air by US Consolidated Liberator aircraft with British Air Despatch crews. A total of 250 aircraft were loaded, the despatchers briefed and standing by when once again the majority of the operation was cancelled. Some crews flew with loads and the operation was carried out without loss.

By the time the Air Despatch Group was formed in the United Kingdom, large and determined resistance groups had collected in France. After D-Day it became practicable for the first time in the war for the French patriots to openly rise against the Germans and increase their sabotage activities without incurring too much risk. For this they required large amounts of explosive; also rifles and machine-guns with an adequate supply of ammunition. Clothing was also required urgently, especially boots. Wireless sets and radio valves, dropped in special containers designed for the purpose, were needed, as was medical equipment and occasionally food. Nearly every night a Dakota, Anson, Halifax or Stirling, would depart from one of the Wiltshire airfields for a DZ somewhere in Europe. Not infrequently they were forced to turn back, either because of weather over the DZ, or lack of signals to indicate it was safe to drop. The despatching crews for these sorties came from No 48 Air Despatch and the Air Service Group.

In Italy No 352 General Transport Company was trained in Air Despatch duties early in 1944 and in March a detachment was attached to

Special Operations, Mediterranean Theatre of Operations – SOMTO – to resupply allied prisoners of war and patriots in Italy, and partisans in Yugoslavia. After Italy became a co-belligerant a number of resistance groups formed in the north to expedite the German withdrawal. Their demands were similar to those in France and large amounts of equipment were dropped to them. During the winter of 1944–45, No 352 Company dropped over 300 tons a month to patriots in Italy, aircraft making as many as forty sorties a day.

A military mission in Albania had a demand unique in the history of air supply. In order to pay locally raised forces and for their food and accommodation, thousands of pounds of golden sovereigns were required, paper money being worthless. This valuable cargo was safely delivered as the occasion demanded. Safely delivered, that is, to the DZ, but panniers of bullion occasionally disappeared to the satisfaction of some patriots and the discomfiture of the Military Mission.

In Yugoslavia it was not until the country gave all its support to Tito in 1944 that large supply drops started to take place. It is difficult to work out figures of tonnages dropped to the patriots of any country but in the case of Yugoslavia the figures are available and are very impressive. Among other things, there were dropped in 1944, 100,000 rifles, 50,000 Bren and Sten guns, and over 1,300 mortars with proportionate amounts of ammunition for them. Also 700 wireless sets, 26,000 pairs of boots and 175,000 suits of battle dress were safely dropped from the air. These figures indicate that the aid given to occupied countries resisting the enemy was much larger than is generally supposed. No 353 Company operating in Italy supplied the crews for the Dakota aircraft for many of the sorties carried out by the British-trained Balkan Air Force.

The emergency was declared in Malaya in June 1948. One platoon of No 55 Company RASC was sent to Kuala Lumpur and was located at Dour Grange near Batu Caves. Initially this platoon carried out motor transport details but the need for air supply gradually developed. At first the requirement was very small amounting to about two sorties a week to patrols operating in the jungle. The platoon also carried out a certain amount of loading for air freighting.

During 1949 the operations against the communist terrorists – *Operation Firedog* – increased and were of a more offensive nature. The patrols began going deeper into the jungle and so demands became greater as many more units became dependant on air supply. By the end of the year there were very few operational units which had not learned what a satisfactory feeling it is to be supplied by air when deep in the jungle.

The air supply requirement continued to develop and soon became a major feature of the campaign forming 90 per cent of the air transport support effort. The anti-terrorist campaign could not have been conducted without the widespread use of air supply. Without it patrols would have been unable to penetrate the thickest parts of the jungle where the terrorists were most active and had their camps and arms dumps. The troops knew from experience that, wherever they were patrolling in this wild country, they could rely on the Dakotas coming over an agreed point at a prearranged time and dropping to them food, arms, ammunition, medicines, mail, newspapers and many other things.

During 1950 the air supply commitment increased to an average of 300,000 lb per month. Sometimes the Dakotas from No 52 Squadron at Kuala Lumpur were used to drop oil bombs as markers for strikes by the Avro Lincoln bombers of the Royal Australian Air Force. In August 1950 a Dakota caught fire whilst dropping oil bombs and crashed in Kelantan killing both the RAF and the RASC crews.

During 1952 the Dakotas which had served so well were replaced by Vickers Valetta aircraft. This meant a small conversion course for all despatchers. However the Royal Australian Air Force continued to use the Dakota, and the last Dakota sortie was flown from Butterworth on December 10, 1968, when a drop was made to a Police field force fort along the border of Thailand and West Malaysia. By this time the RASC had been renamed Royal Corps of Transport – RCT – but it was No 389 Air Despatch Troop who had provided the despatchers for this final operational air supply mission.

It is no exaggeration to say that the Berlin airlift was one of the most outstanding world events during 1948/49. During the thirteen months of *Operation Plainfare*, British aircraft alone ferried 350,000 tons of supplies into Berlin.

The first air despatch troops flew from Netheravon to Wunstorf on the evening of June 29 and immediately reinforced the detachment already in Germany. It was soon apparent that trained Air Despatch personnel were wasted on this task which was in no way specialised. It was, therefore, decided to employ the trained despatchers with the RAF Air Movements Staff in supervising the loading and manifesting the aircraft. German labour was employed for the manual work.

At each airfield – Fassberg, Lubeck, Celle, Fuhlsbuttel, Schleswigland – a control room was set up which organised the servicing and loading of aircraft as they came in. The aircraft captain informed the control room when he was twenty miles away from the airfield. Servicing, refuelling and marshalling crews would then stand by to meet the aircraft. RASC despatchers would supervise the loading and prepare the manifest so that delay in turn round was cut to a minimum. This system was proved to be efficient for as many as 120 sorties were made a day from Wunstorf and 1,000 tons of freight transported into Berlin.

The story of the development of supply by air is mainly one of hard and often unrewarding labour, of patience and of industry. The use of air supply in World War 2 gave to the soldier a better chance of survival or victory, and in peace gives the civilian the knowledge that flood or snow will not isolate him.

Because of the long association the RASC has had with the Dakota a silver model of this ubiquitous transport was presented to the Corps by the Douglas Aircraft Corporation and is kept in the Headquarter's Officers' Mess, Royal Corps of Transport, Aldershot, Hampshire.

INTO BATTLE

On November 8, 1942, great operations of war, for which many preparations had been made both in the United Kingdom and America, were launched. That day saw the landing of the Allies at several points on the coast of French North Africa. Not all the troops were carried in ships. Some arrived on the field of battle by parachute, transported by troop-carrying aircraft. The troops were British and belonged to the 1st Airborne Division; the aircraft were American and came from three groups of the 51st Transport Wing of the US Army Air Force.

The object of the Supreme Commander, General Eisenhower, was to occupy all that part of North Africa which owed allegiance to Marshal Pétain and the Vichy regime. By the evening of November 10 the port of Oran was in our hands, American troops were in Casablanca and both British and Americans in Algiers. Rather more than halfway between Algiers and Tunis, the latter port being the object of the Allies, lies the port of Bone, which possessed a good airfield. To take it was an immediate and obvious object. Plans to do so had been maturing for some time. On November 12 they were put into execution.

On that day a task force consisting of two company groups and a headquarter's group, comprising some 360 officers and men belonging to the 3rd Battalion of the 1st Parachute Brigade, under the command of Lt-Col RJ Pine-Coffin, arrived over the airfield in the early morning. They were carried in Douglas C-47 aircraft from No 60 Group of the US Army Air Force. They had left England three days earlier, and had rested en route at Gibraltar to check their equipment and make final preparations. The airfield at Maison Blanche near Algiers, was their next stop. Leaving at first light they reached Bone but by then their numbers had been reduced from 450 to 360. Two C-47s had developed defects and been unable to leave their base in the UK, and two more had fallen by the way, one having crashed in flames between Gibraltar and Algiers. The occupants of the other were picked up by an American ship on her way to New York. The paratroops rejoined their regiment two months later, travelling to North Africa via the USA and the United Kingdom.

The detachment of the 3rd Battalion were well aware of what was expected of them. The drop was made in a scattered pattern covering some three miles of stony ground. Some containers fell a mile short. Moreover, the air in Africa is thinner than the English air and the paratroops were heavily laden. Each man was carrying a considerable quantity of small-arms ammunition, and this was over and above what was in the containers. The drop was made from a height of 400 feet. There was only one fatal casuality, one man accidentally shot himself with his Sten gun during the drop, but thirteen men were injured.

The operation was successful, for the airfield was captured. Together with No 6 Commando the task force held the airfield for a week, despite constant attacks by enemy aircraft, till they were withdrawn and joined the remainder of their battalion. They had accomplished their task, thanks to the co-operation of our American Allies, who provided all the aircraft necessary to transport them and their comrades in the other battalions. This they did despite the fact that many of the US crews had not been trained to carry and drop paratroops. British aircraft and trained crews were not yet available in sufficient numbers, for the requirements of Bomber Command were still paramount.

While two-thirds of the 3rd Parachute Battalion were engaged at Bone, the 1st and 2nd Battalions and the remainder of the 3rd had arrived successfully at Algiers by sea. Between November 13–15 they collected their equipment and stored it in readiness at Maison Blanche airfield. The parachute packers went to work in a requisitioned cinema and worked day and night until every parachute, over 3,000, had been repacked for instant use.

On November 16, after an unsuccessful attempt on the previous day, the 1st Battalion, under its Commanding Officer, Lt-Col (later Brigadier) Hill DSO MC and transported by No 64 Group of the US Army Air Force with its Douglas C-47s, were dropped on the plain near Souk El Arba. This was successful, but one man was killed and two others, victims of what is known as "Roman candling", severely injured. This mishap occurs when the parachute leaves the pack but fails to open, its wearer hurtling to earth with a long and useless streamer of silk fluttering from his shoulders.

Kept in reserve at Maison Blanche was the 2nd Battalion, and it was decided to use them to attack two enemy airfields, one at Pont du Fahs and the other at Depienne, both almost due south of Tunis. Having destroyed the German aircraft and stores on these airfields, the Battalion was to move to Oudna, still nearer to Tunis, repeat its performance then join the leading elements of the British 1st Army.

On November 29, shortly before they were due to take-off, information came to hand that the airfields at Pont du Fahs and Depienne had been abandoned by the Germans. It was decided, therefore, that the battalion should land near the third objective, Oudna. The force, carried by the Douglas C-47s of No 60 and No 64 Group, under the protection of long-range Hawker Hurricanes, Supermarine Spitfires and Lockheed Lightnings, was on the way to its objectives by noon. Bad weather had made previous reconnaissance impossible, and it was left to the battalion commander, Lt Col JD Frost DSO MC who travelled in the leading C-47, to share with the pilot the responsibility of choosing the dropping zone from the air. The force flew high to clear the mountains; it became very cold; the air was bumpy, and some of the men suffered from air-sickness. About 30 miles from Depienne they began to descend until they were at 600 feet. The dropping zone chosen was mostly ploughland with a watercourse dividing it: The first stick was dropped at three in the afternoon, followed quickly by the remainder. One man was killed in the drop. A number were injured in the operation, but were well treated by the local French inhabitants. That evening the battalion formed up to begin its advance to Oudna.

The historians have already recorded in detail what happened to these gallant men. The 1st Parachute Brigade earned in ninety days a reputation for gallantry, discipline and initiative unsurpassed by any other troops in Africa. In three months' fighting the awards consisted of eight DSOs, fifteen MCs, nine DCMs, twenty-two MMs, three Croix de Guerre, and one Legion of Honour.

During 1942 the Commander of the Airborne Forces and his staff had been struggling with three main difficulties, shortage of men, deficiency of equipment and lack of aircraft. Many of the men who had just completed their training had had to be sent to North Africa to replace the casualties suffered by the 1st Parachute Brigade. There was a shortage of glider pilots, mainly owing to training difficulties. Vital items of equipment were scarce. By the beginning of 1943, 132 jeeps had not yet come to hand. There were too few six-pounder anti-tank and 20-mm Hispano guns.

As with men and equipment, so with aircraft. No tug aircraft capable of towing a fully loaded Airspeed Horsa any length of distance had yet made their appearance. This lack of aircraft put a heavy brake on training, particularly on the training of the glider-borne troops who were now beginning to come forward in considerable numbers. Fortunately, the situation was relieved by our American Allies, who were able to place a considerable number of Douglas C-47 and C-53 transports at our disposal. They were suitable both for parachuting and for towing gliders, but their crews, though keen and determined, lacked training.

Plans were being made to include an Airborne Division in operations against Sicily during June and July 1943. It was realised that the attack would certainly prove a complicated and difficult business for the airborne troops. They would have to fly 350 miles, partly over sea, in a semi-tropical climate. They must travel in a type of transport and glider to which their training had not accustomed them. The paratroops would have to leap from a door, not drop through a hole, while other troops would be passengers in Waco CG-4A Hadrian gliders. They held at the most eighteen men, as compared with the thirty-two carried in the Airspeed Horsa. The C-47 transports were not powerful enough to tow the heavier glider the required distance.

The Glider Pilot Regiment, under the command of Maj George Chatterton, were ordered to North Africa, where it arrived at the end of April for intensive training. They exchanged the comparative comfort of Salisbury Plain for two airfields in the Mascara area of Algeria, both of which had been condemned by the French as too badly infected with malaria to be serviceable. Such was the physical fitness and mental stamina of the glider pilots, and the aircrew of the US Army Air Force C-47 tugs who accompanied them and worked with them, during the whole period of training, sickness from all causes was almost nil.

Difficulties were many, but they were all overcome. Most of the pilots had never flown a Waco Hadrian, and due to the great heat in the cockpit none of them were able to do so between the hours of ten in a morning and five in the evening. The gliders had not been unpacked, and although they lacked previous experience, the pilots assembled fifty-two in ten days.

Chatterton concentrated the attention of his first pilots on learning how to take off quickly and easily in formation and, above all, how to land both in moonlight and in darkness. The training of the second pilots was devoted to map reading, pin-pointing and general navigation, and also in manipulating the trimming tabs of the glider and the "Spoilers", a special apparatus fitted to enable the speed of the Hadrian to be checked.

It was evident that a certain number of Airspeed Horsa gliders would have to be used. The Hadrian was not large enough to take both a jeep and what it was required to tow, an anti-tank gun. Separated, the uses of both were limited; together they formed a mobile and effective combination. The Horsa was large enough to transport the combination. The question was, how could a sufficient number be brought to North Africa. They were both large and fragile, and this made their transport by ship difficult. Grp Cpt Cooper, with Sq Ldr Wilkinson, proved by a series of flights round the United Kingdom that a Handley Page Halifax could tow an unloaded Horsa 1,400 miles and still land with a small reserve of fuel. Final destination would be Kairouan in Tunisia and finally, when the operation began, to Sicily. Each tug had to fly seventy hours, of which fifty were spent in towing.

Despite all the difficulties of distance, weather and enemy action, more than 80 per cent of the gliders thus ferried to Africa arrived. The first

Horsa reached Kairouan on June 28, twelve days before the invasion of Sicily began.

The remainder of the Airborne Division had not been idle. By the end of May it was concentrated in the Mascara area, where it liaised closely with No 51 Troop Carrier Wing of the US Army Air Force, who were to provide nearly all the air transport for the invasion.

Training of the paratroops continued side by side with those of the Air Landing Brigade and was equally strenuous. Altogether, from May 8 to June 30, 8,913 jumps were made. By then the plans for the invasion of Sicily were almost complete.

The airborne attack on Sicily consisted of four operations, two carried out by the British – *Operation Ladbrooke and Operation Fustian* – and two by American troops. The first operation took place on the night of July 9–10, and was carried out entirely by glider-borne troops. Their object was to secure the Ponte Grande, a very important bridge near Syracuse, and to attack the western outskirts of that city to create a diversion so as to ease the task of the seaborne forces. The Air Landing Brigade, consisting of two battalions with anti-tank guns, sappers and a medical unit, were to be carried in 129 Waco Hadrian and 8 Airspeed Horsa gliders, towed by 109 Douglas C-47 transports, 7 Handley Page Halifaxes and 21 Armstrong Whitworth Albemarles. The tugs were to release the gliders off the coast, the Hadrians at 1,900 feet and the Horsas at 4,000 feet. The ground chosen for all landing zones was partly cultivated, partly pasture, and thickly strewn with orchards.

Six airfields were used for the take-off, the first combination becoming airborne at a few minutes before seven in the evening. At the last moment bad weather nearly wrecked the expedition. A strong south-easterly wind sprang up which caused a number of the combinations to be blown off course. The strength of the gale reached at times 45 mph, and flying conditions were rough. It was necessary to fly low to escape detection by enemy radar. Off Malta the wind moderated, and the whole force arrived off Sicily at the right time, and the gliders were released. Due to the off-shore wind, many gliders were parted prematurely from their tugs. Not many of the gliders which succeeded in reaching Sicily made the designated landing zones. Some came down as far as forty miles away.

It was a bitter struggle for the Ponte Grande. The airborne troops had captured the bridge without loss, only to be over-run by the enemy after suffering heavy casualties during a heroic defence. But their splendid defence had not been in vain. Patrols from an Infantry Brigade which had landed by sea soon arrived in the area, and in a few minutes the leading elements of the Royal Scots Fusiliers had won back everything which the gallantry of the airborne troops had originally taken. The success thus more than justified the hazards of the operation.

Operation Fustian, involved the next objective, Primosole Bridge, where the main road from Syracuse crossed the River Simeto. Involved were three Parachute Battalions, the 1st Parachute Squadron of the Royal Engineers, an Airborne Anti-tank Unit of the Royal Artillery and the 16th Paratroop Field Ambulance. This Brigade was to be carried in 105 C-47s of the US Troop Carrier Command, 11 Albemarles, 8 Waco Hadrians, 11 Horsa gliders with their Halifax and Albemarle tugs. The six airfields used four nights earlier were used. It was now the night of July 13–14, 1943.

Anti-aircraft fire, some of it heavy, was opened by Allied naval forces on the Allied airborne force. Considerable damage was caused and 27 aircraft carrying paratroops lost their way, 19 returned to base without dropping their troops, and 10 C-47s, 1 Halifax and 3 Albemarles were shot down. In all fairness this mishap must be attributed for the most part to the fortunes of war. The enemy's Junker Ju 88s had been operating sporadically over the beach-heads, and the naval gun crews were eager to defend their ships. Aircraft recognition, at all times difficult, was especially so that night, for there was haze over the coast. Moreover, no small proportion of the transport aircraft were off course and flying in the danger zone, a belt five miles wide running along the coast of Sicily. To experience anti-aircraft fire is always unpleasant, and when flying an unarmed and unarmoured C-47 transport with no self-sealing tanks, it is more than usually so.

Once more an airborne operation had been successful despite mistakes which had caused only one-fifth of the force despatched to arrive at the right place at the right moment. In this operation disorder in the air meant confusion on the ground; the assembling of the Brigade at the rendezvous near the dropping zones did not take place according to plan.

The operation against the Primosole Bridge was successful, but the margin between success and failure was very small. This was accomplished at the cost to the 1st Parachute Brigade of 12 officers and 283 other ranks, of whom more than one-third were killed or wounded.

Mention must be made once more of the gallantry of the Dakota crews of No 216 Squadron. Shortage of shipping placed a great responsibility on transport aircraft for keeping the invading forces supplied and in these operations the squadron played a notable part. Many of the flights involved had to be undertaken by aircrew inexperienced in supply dropping. Altogether from the night of October 5–6, to that of November 19–20, 1943, when the last sortie was flown to the third of the ill-fated islands in the Aegean, Samos, regained by the enemy on November 22 – these supply dropping missions were attempted on twenty-six occasions, involving a total of eighty-seven sorties.

The outstanding achievement of No 216 Squadron was the dropping on two nights of two hundred officers and men of the Greek Sacred Squadron onto the island of Samos, from which they were very soon withdrawn. It appeared that the Allies were trying to accomplish too much. The Aegean episode was a setback, with fortunately no effect on the final issue.

Nos 38 and 46 Groups of RAF Transport Command, who were to carry the 6th Airborne Division on D-Day, June 6, 1944, had undergone many weeks of intensive training which culminated in Exercise *Mush*, carried out on April 21 over an area stretching from the Severn estuary to the borders of Wiltshire and Oxfordshire. Such exercises, of which the frequency increased as the great day grew near, were difficult and dangerous; both Lt Gen Browning, commanding the Airborne forces, and Air Vice-Marshall Hollinghurst, commanding the air transport groups, took the view that it was better to run considerable risks rather than to send half-trained and inexperienced soldiers and aircrews into battle. This decision was abundantly justified, for the task facing the Groups was heavy. Not only must the 6th Airborne Division be taken to the right place, it had also to arrive at precisely the right moment, if surprise, essential to success, was to be achieved. Correct timing was essential. The use of different types of aircraft and different types of combinations complicated matters because of the different speeds.

On D-Day, 108 Dakotas from Nos 48, 233, 271, 512 and 575 Squadrons, under the operational control of No 46 Group, dropped the main body of the 3rd Parachute Brigade in Normandy and also towed Airspeed Horsa gliders into action during *Operation Overlord*. Seventy-one of these Dakotas conveyed the principal group to Zone "V" by the River Dives, but only 17 aircraft dropped their troops on the correct spot, 9 within one mile and 11 within one and a half miles. The landing of the Horsa gliders, one of them within 50 yds of the swing bridge across the Caen canal, had been successful.

The 5th Parachute Brigade, taken into action by 129 aircraft from Nos 38 and 46 Groups found their dropping zone correctly marked; 123 aircraft dropped their loads accurately, though a high wind scattered the paratroops far and wide. Out of the 2,125 paratroops belonging to this Brigade, 2,026 were dropped and 702 out of 755 containers.

A total of 264 aircraft and 98 glider combinations was despatched by the two Groups. Altogether 4,310 paratroops were dropped and gliders carried 493 troops, 17 guns, 44 jeeps and 55 motor-cycles successfully released. Seven aircraft and 22 gliders were lost.

Four and half hours before the first seaborne troops set foot upon the shores of France at 0630 hours, the air transport commands had commenced dropping the airborne assault forces on either flank of the invasion zone. In this operation, the biggest of its kind ever to date attempted, were included in addition to the RAF aircraft, 1,662 aircraft and 512 gliders of the US Ninth Troop Carrier Command, most of these tugs being Douglas C-47 Skytrains and C-53 Skytrooper transports.

While the airborne forces were being conveyed to France diversionary forces of the RAF were jamming enemy radars with "Window" the metallic strips from Avro Lancasters. These strips produced on the enemy radar screens a response similar to that created by a ship or aircraft. Off Boulogne other aircraft dropped dummy parachutes, rifle fire simulators and other devices, such as squibs and fireworks, which produced the sound of gunfire. The object, which was largely attained, was to create the impression that an airborne landing in north-west France was taking place.

Over 1,000 bombers of Bomber Command were playing their part in the prologue to the invasion with attacks on the principal batteries. Unfortunately the bombing in certain places was very far from accurate. A party of the 9th Parachute Battalion on their way to join the main body in the assault on the battery at Merville suffered heavy casualties in killed and wounded from our own bombing. Such tragic mishaps were inevitable.

D-Day closed with *Operation Mallard*, the flying of 256 gliders bearing reinforcements and stores to the British 6th Airborne Division. A total of 246 of them arrived at the chosen landing zone. Close fighter escort by fifteen squadrons of No. 11 Group was given to this slow-moving force towed to its destination by the aircraft from Nos 38 and 46 Group. They landed just north of Ranville and between Ouistreham and Benouville. The operation was successful, 95 per cent of the gliders reaching their destination, much to the joy of the hard-pressed men of the 6th Airborne Division.

Dakota aircraft from No 46 Group took part in the work of preparing for the day of liberation by assisting two British organisations, the Special Operations' Executive (SOE), which was concerned with acts of subversion and sabotage, and the Special Air Service (SAS), whose members wore uniform and were in touch with the Maquis and the French Forces of the Interior. Before the necessity was over, there were more than 5,500 dropping grounds in France and Yugoslavia, besides those in Norway and other occupied countries.

On the night of August 14–15, *Operation Dragoon* was launched in southern France. In the early hours of the morning, following a small Pathfinder force dropped earlier, the first elements of the Task Force of Paratroops carried by some 400 aircraft of the US Army Air Force dropped silently to earth through 500 feet of dense fog and dispersed about their allotted tasks of securing fields for the arrival of the glider force. With daylight, in improved weather, the first of the gliders slipped its tow and made a safe landing. It was one of 407 which landed at intervals throughout the day. Altogether, including resupply missions, 987 sorties were flown. Some 9,000 airborne troops, with 221 jeeps, 213 items of artillery and many thousand pounds of petrol, bombs, ammunition and rations – a total weight, exclusive of men, of over 1,000 tons. At dawn on August 15 the first beach landings took place between Cannes and St Tropez against no opposition in some sectors and only slight resistance in others.

It fell to the aircraft of Transport Command to render a determined but, as fate would have it, a far from fruitful service to the troops in the field. The operation to seize the bridges over the Rhine was made up of two parts. The airborne operation, known as *Market*, had as its purpose the capture of the vital bridges over the Mass, the Waal, and the lower Rhine at Grave, Nijmegen, and Arnhem. The forces employed in the airborne operation included the US 82nd Airborne Division, the 101st Airborne Division, the British 1st Airborne Division, and the Polish 1st Paratroop Brigade. On September 17, 1944, Nos 38 and 46 Groups towed the main glider-borne element of the 1st Airborne Division to the town of Arnhem. The former, commanded by Air Vice-Marshal Hollinghurst, was composed of two squadrons of Albemarles, six of Short Stirlings and two squadrons of Handley-Page Halifaxes; No 46, under Air Commodore L Darvall, supplied six squadrons of Dakotas. In addition, the 1st Parachute Brigade was carried in C-47s and C-53 of the US Ninth Troop Carrier Command. To mount airborne operations was a complicated business which needed time for planning. Postponements for one reason or another were frequent and all this time the aircraft and crews were inevitably kept idle. No 48 Squadron at its Down Ampney base had prepared its aircraft and gliders in readiness for *Operation Market* after numerous exercises which had commenced on September 7. On the great day twenty-three out of the forty-nine crews detailed took part, the first Dakota being airborne five minutes before 10 am and the last one eighteen minutes later. The official history covering the operation states that RAF Transport Command could not take the whole airborne division to its destination in one lift, due to not having sufficient transport aircraft.

The first lift to Arnhem which carried part of the Air Landing Brigade was composed of 320 tug-glider combinations. It was preceded by a Pathfinder Force of 12 Stirlings, and from these, elements of the 21st Independent Parachute Company were dropped to mark the landing zones. This they did successfuly, and the lift arrived, losing en route, mostly through bad weather in the United Kingdom, 23 gliders, of which the loads of 21 were recovered and sent on with the second lift, plus a further 12 between the shores of the UK and the woods of Arnhem. Altogether, that September morning, 3,887 aircraft, British and American, and some 500 gliders, became airborne. Of this total, 1,240 fighters and

1,113 bombers supported and protected the landing. It was the largest airborne operation undertaken by the Allied forces up to this time.

One of the pilots flying a Dakota in the airborne armada was Wing Commander WE Coles, who, on June 6, 1944, relinquished command of No 117 Squadron in SEAC. Earlier that year, during *Operation Thursday*, he had flown many missions in and out of all the airstrips located behind the Japanese lines. Bill Coles arrived in the United Kingdom during July and took over command of No 233 Squadron which was based at Down Ampney along with Nos. 48 and 271 Squadron. On *Operation Market* he flew Dakota Mk III KG559 towing an Airspeed Horsa glider. He was one of the many who gained decorations for their gallant part in this fateful operation, and was awarded the DSO. Four days later, on a resupply mission his Dakota was damaged by flak, his co-pilot Flg Off Sharpe was wounded and he was forced to land at airstrip B56 at Evère.

The second lift to Arnhem, on September 18, was delayed five hours by weather. By then the situation in the battlefield had deteriorated. On this occasion 296 tugs and gliders took off, 200 landed in one zone and 69 in the other. One tug aircraft was lost and another Dakota, belonging to No 575 Squadron based at Broadwell, was brought back to the UK by the second navigator, Warrant Officer AE Smith – the pilot being killed and the first navigator wounded – and successfully landed, though he had never flown an aircraft before.

Despite mounting casualties, and an almost impossible task, the supply aircraft continued day after day in their gallant if fruitless efforts. The operation cost No 38 and 46 Group a total of 55 aircraft lost with a further 320 damaged by flak and seven by fighters, many of these being Dakotas. On September 21, No 48 Squadron lost 6 Dakota Mk IIIs – FZ620, KG346, KG350, KG404, KG417 and KG579.

Between September 17–30, a total of 20,190 troops had been dropped by parachute, 13,781 had landed in gliders, and 905 were landed on a strip made ready by the preceding airborne troops. In addition to this total of 34,876 troops, 5,230 tons of equipment and supplies, 1,927 vehicles, and 568 artillery pieces were transported by air. In all, the supporting air forces flew over 7,800 sorties with supplies.

As operations in Europe had now moved further eastwards, the range for aircraft based in the United Kingdom was greatly increased and it was decided to move No 38 Group and its squadrons to East Anglia to facilitate future operations. The move took place early in October 1944.

To assist the advance of the Second Army, the First Allied Airborne Army was to drop No 18 Airborne Corps – comprising the US 17th and British 6th Airborne Divisions – north and northwest of Wesel to seize the key terrain in that area. This airborne operation known as *Varsity* was, unlike those previously conducted by the Allies, timed to follow the commencement of the ground assault, it being hoped to achieve an additional element of surprise.

Punctually at 0600 hours as planned, on March 24, 1945, the British 6th Airborne Division took off from their East Anglian airfields. The ground crews of No 38 and 46 Group had made an effort to put every available transport and glider into the air. So successful were they that only one glider combination failed to take off. A total of twelve Dakotas from No 271 Squadron towed gliders to a point just north of Wesel on the east bank of the Rhine. The aerial fleet set course for Brussels where it joined the Douglas C-47s and C-53s carrying the US 17th Airborne Division from their bases near Paris.

Unfortunately the gliders and tugs arrived over the battle area seven minutes early, this preventing the fighter-bombers from the 2nd Tactical Air Force from completing their task of attacking anti-aircraft defences, so the paratroops and gliders had to descend through air still obscured by dust and smoke from the bombing of Wesel. Nevertheless, the landing of the gliders was exceedingly accurate, many touching down within yards of their objective. About 300 gliders were damaged, more or less severely, and ten shot down.

Operation Varsity was the most successful airborne operation carried out to date, and its brilliant results reflected the great strides made in this aspect of warfare since the Normandy landings on D-Day, nine months earlier. The 6th Airborne Division had been carried in 669 transports and 429 gliders from Nos 38 and 46 Group with support from the US Ninth Troop Carrier Command, while the US 17th Airborne Division was carried in 903 C-47s and C-53s plus 897 gliders from the US Ninth Troop Carrier Command.

By this time the 2nd Tactical Air Force was being supplied with petrol, oil and ammunition largely from the air by Nos 38 and 46 Group, 280 transport aircraft being available every day for these operations. During April, No 46 Group with its Dakotas carried nearly 7,000 tons of supplies while No 38 Group carried 514. Nor did the transports return empty, for, during that period they brought back to the United Kingdom 27,277 British and American prisoners of war and 5,986 casualties.

The struggle for Europe was over, but the Dakotas of Transport Command were required elsewhere. The SEAC Commander, Lord Louis Mountbatten, required more Dakota squadrons to assist with the final Allied onslaught against the Japanese in the Far East. Bomber squadrons were re-equipped with Dakotas, and veteran units such as No 48 Squadron ceased their scheduled duties with No 46 Group, and commenced training for transport duties in the warmer climate of South East Asia Command.

They bade farewell to the *Red Devils*, a name bestowed on the British airborne troops by the enemy in March 1943. A term derived from the colour of their berets. These were the valiant men who wear the badge of Pegasus, the winged horse and its rider, brandishing a lance, singularly appropriate. It is the emblem of which they are justly proud.

DAVID LORD, VC

If an individual had to be selected to epitomise the dogged courage and splendid devotion to duty displayed by the many Dakota supply captains throughout the 1939–45 war in the air, then probably no finer pilot could be chosen than Flight Lieutenant David Samuel Anthony Lord. His career extended over five years of the conflict, a continuous record of operational flying stretching from lumbering Vickers Valentias to Douglas DC-2Ks, DC-3s and C-53s over India, Egypt, Iraq, Libya, Burma and Germany. Although Lord would have been the first to deny such praise, his was a career of patience, resolution and sheer determination in the face of myriad dangers. Genuinely modest, somewhat shy and self-effacing almost to the point of introspection, David Lord was highly respected and immensely popular with all whom he came into contact. With no conscious effort on his own part he inspired complete confidence in others by his cool acceptance of what he regarded as his clear duty. And, maintaining his private code of that duty, he died in a manner still regarded as one of the greatest acts of individual heroism of the war.

Born in Cork on October 18, 1913, David Lord's background had a military foundation for he was the son of a serving Warrant Officer in the Royal Welch Fusiliers. He received his first schooling at the Lucknow Convent School in India and, on returning to England, continued his academic education at St Mary's School, Wrexham. He next attended St Mary's College, Aberystwyth, from where he matriculated to the University of Wales. On leaving university, Lord made a decision which might well have altered his complete future. He entered the English Ecclesiastical College at Valladolid, Spain, with the intention of studying philosophy and eventually becoming a priest. It was no sudden decision but an extension of a childhood ambition. But after two years he decided he had not found his vocation and therefore returned to Wrexham where he took employment as assistant to a pharmaceutical chemist. In his spare time Lord tried his hand at writing, mainly short stories, and in 1936, encouraged by having several of his stories accepted for publication, he travelled to London to work as a freelance journalist. In September of that year he changed his mind and enlisted in the Royal Air Force.

For some two years Lord continued to serve in the ranks before being accepted for aircrew duties and on October 6, 1938, he commenced pilot training at No 3 Elementary and Reserve Flying Training School, Hamble, making his first solo flight on October 20 in a de Havilland 82a Tiger

Moth. On January 2, 1939, he reported to No 2 Flying Training School, Brize Norton, and trained on variants of the Hawker Hart and was awarded his "wings" as a Sergeant pilot on April 5, 1939. Continuing his advanced aspects of his training at Brize Norton, Lord completed an armament course at Warmwell in the July and was then posted to his first squadron, No 31, based at that time in Lahore, India. He arrived at Lahore on October 7 and was introduced to the Vickers Valentia transport – a trundling wood and fabric biplane which was already obsolete. Despite their age No 31s Valentias were needed for supply and transportation in support of units of the Army and RAF still attempting to control the fighting tribes along India's North West Frontier and it was not until June 1941 that the squadron finally received modern replacements for their vintage aircraft. The new equipment was the Douglas DC-2 transport and in the December Lord, by then a Warrant Officer, qualified as a DC-2K captain.

Meanwhile the war situation in North Africa necessitated reinforcement of the few supply units there and accordingly in October 1941, No 31 Squadron supplied eight DC-2s with crews for support of the land operations in northern Egypt and Libya. One of the DC-2 skippers was Warrant Officer David Lord. The detachment lasted some four months but was by no means without incident. On December 8, for example, Lord was captain of DC-2K – DG475 "X-Xray" – on a routine supply sortie to LG – Landing Ground – 138. Carrying nine passengers, some 1,500 lb of stores and a crew of three – Flt Lt Howell, Sgt White and AC Shaw – Lord's unarmed aircraft was jumped by three Messerschmitt Bf 109s and forced to land ten miles north-east of their objective. Although slightly wounded, Lord gathered crew and passengers together and walked the last ten miles. On the following day he was flying again – a supply sortie to an Eighth Army forward unit.

Returning to India in February 1942, Lord continued the daily routine of transport, supply and communication flights and on April 28 qualified as captain on Douglas DC-3 aircraft. On June 14, 1942, he also qualified as captain on the C-53 Skytrooper and in the following month was commissioned as Pilot Officer. With the gradual return of the Allied Armies in Burma to the offensive, Lord and his fellow Dakota crews soon found themselves in constant demand for air supply of the many individual units operating deep in Japanese-held territory, well behind the so-called "front lines". Implementing Orde Wingate's inspired decision to maintain those forward troops solely from the air, the Dakotas were called on to deliver and collect almost every imaginable item of military and domestic equipment to the courageous Chindits and similar guerrilla fighters. The overall task meant spot accuracy in supply dropping, needle-sharp navigation and no little courage to take a relatively slow unarmed Dakota between the lush green carpeted mountains and into the dank, steaming valleys of Burma day after day, but every supply skipper was only too conscious of his responsibility to the men on the ground and each discharged that responsibility faithfully. Lord's personal prowess was recognised officially by an Air Officer Commanding's Commendation and later he was Mentioned in Despatches for his long record of devotion to duty. Finally in July 1943 he was awarded the Distinguished Flying Cross. A few months later, after four years continuous operational service overseas, David Lord, by then a Flight Lieutenant, returned to England, arriving home on January 6, 1944. Following a brief disembarkation leave, he reported to No 271 Squadron at Doncaster on January 29.

Flying Dakotas, Lord spent the next few weeks training for the role of airborne equipment supply and, on February 29, the unit moved to Down Ampney where its role was extended to include paratroop dropping and glider tug duties. With the near certainty of an imminent invasion of German-occupied Europe, No 271s crews trained hard and well. As his personal crew at this time, Lord had Flying Officer Ager as second pilot, Flying Officer DI MacDonnell as navigator and, as wireless operator, Alec Ballantyne, an ex-Warrant Officer now commissioned as Flying Officer. On the eve of D-Day, June 5/6, 1944, Lord and his crew were detailed to convey a load of paratroops to a point six miles east-north-east of Caen. Despite flak damage to the Dakota's rudder, elevators and hydraulic system, Lord completed his small part of *Operation Neptune* successfully. For the next few weeks life for No 271s crews comprised a succession of supply and resupply to Allied troops on the Normandy beach-head.

After some two months of bitter fighting from June to August 1944, the Allied invasion armies finally broke out of the beach-head and thrust inland towards Germany. The headlong rush soon liberated several major cities such as Paris and Brussels and by early September General Eisenhower, Supreme Allied Commander, was considering the possibility of "one final blow" to demoralise the enemy and thus bring hostilities to a rapid conclusion. Unable to strike such a blow, Eisenhower chose instead to attempt a bypassing of the fortified Siegfried Line at its western end and thereby "roll up" the German west flank; at the same time establishing a foothold on Germany's borders from which to spring a final offensive into the German homeland. The plan to outflank the Siegfried Line – originally submitted by General Montgomery – would, if successful, not only provide such a spring board but would isolate German forces in Holland and, even more important, free the port of Antwerp thereby solving the increasingly difficult supply route to the advancing Allied armies. The plan for an airborne assault – *Operation Market* – entailed a triple attack at Arnhem, Nijmegen-Grave and Eindhoven with the primary objective of capturing bridges across the Lower Rhine, Waal and Maas rivers respectively. Meanwhile 30 Corps of General Dempsey's 2nd Army were to penetrate from the south and link up with the airborne troops – *Operation Garden*. On September 10 the decision to implement *Market Garden* was taken and immediately ran into its first snag. Ideally the whole airborne forces were to have been carried in one day's operations, but there were insufficient transport aircraft available for such an operation. Instead it was decided to have three consecutive air drops on September 17, 18 and 19 – a circumstance which in the event was to prove a primary reason for the failure of the operations.

On Sunday, September 17, the first mass air drop set course for Arnhem. From No 271 Squadron twenty-four Dakotas were contributed to the air armada, one of these piloted by David Lord. He was without two members of his usual crew. MacDonnell had gone on leave to be married, while Ager was replaced by Pilot Officer REH Medhurst, son of an Air Marshal and fresh to operational flying. The day's operations went smoothly, meeting little opposition and achieving 98 per cent success. The following day saw Lord acting as tug pilot to an Airspeed Horsa glider crammed with troops of the 1st Airborne Division, bound for LZ – Landing Zone – "S", six miles from Arnhem and just north-west of Wolfhezen. German opposition had stiffened considerably since the previous day and Lord's Dakota came under a hail of flak, resulting in its rear fuselage and tail unit being peppered with shrapnel. The reception did not deter Lord. In the words of one member of his Horsa crew – Staff Sergeant F Rye DFM – who wrote later to Lord's parents: "I flew in a glider behind your son at Arnhem on September 18 . . . I guess I owe my life to his determination to 'press on regardless'. Through most of the journey a fault in the starboard engine made the journey difficult. His words to me and my glider pilot through the intercom were a great encouragement and helped to accomplish a very difficult trip."

Tuesday, September 19, dawned bright and clear over the besieged 1st Airborne at Arnhem and the Red Berets looked forward cheerfully to their promised resupply air drops scheduled for 10 am. But in England a thick mist of fog and low cloud forced a postponement of the planned early take-off. At Down Ampney No 271s crews waited impatiently. Detailed to fly Dakota Mk III KG374, David Lord had asked Flying Officer HA King to fill the vacancy left by MacDonnell's absence. Harry King, an ex-policeman prior to joining the RAF and an experienced navigator willingly agreed. The remaining members of the crew of KG374 were "Dickie" Medhurst, Alec Ballantyne and four Army despatchers from No 223 Company RASC – Corporal Nixon and Privates Harder, Ricketts and Rowbotham. By midday, weather prospects seemed to have improved and a little after 1 pm seventeen Dakotas of No 271 Squadron took off. Each was loaded with ammunition panniers destined to be dropped on

DZ – Dropping Zone – "V" on the north-west outskirts of Arnhem, but unknown to the Dakota crews DZ "V" was in German hands. The outward trip was plagued by thick cloud conditions initially although as the aircraft neared Holland this cloud gave way to irregular patches of dense haze. Due to an error in timing the scheduled fighter escort units had already exhausted their fuel and were returning to base but the transport train received no interference from the Luftwaffe en route.

Navigating by DR – dead reckoning – with the help of "GEE" – medium-range radar aid employing ground transmitters and airborne receiver – King gave Lord an estimated time of arrival of 3 pm and minutes before that hour, Lord began to let down through swirling haze. At 1,500 feet he broke into clear sky and saw the Lower Rhine ahead by some four miles. The Dakota was immediately engaged by flak and hit in its starboard engine; a slender streak of eddying smoke bursting into flames. Medhurst punched the fire extinguishing system button while Lord asked King how far to the DZ. "Four minutes, Skipper," replied the navigator. "We're going in," said Lord. As the dropping zone came into view, King went back to help the despatchers and seconds later the aircraft was again hit by flak. The fire in the starboard engine had spread to the wing and it would only be a matter of time before the starboard wing tanks caught alight. In the rear fuselage a green light flicked on and King and the four despatchers started kicking the panniers of ammunition down their roller track. The track jammed, its rollers partly crippled by stray shrapnel. The five men manhandled the cargo out of the open side-hatch. At a mere 900 feet, the bulk of the panniers dropped away smoothly as Lord held the blazing Dakota rock-steady over the DZ. Reaching the end of his run, Lord was then told that two panniers still remained to be dropped. With his starboard wing a roaring furnace, Lord edged the crippled Dakota round for a second run, dropping to some 600 feet and plunging again into the murderous flak.

By then the spectacle of his blazing aircraft struggling to complete its appointed task had gripped the attention of both British and German ground troops and there was an eerie lull in the bitter fighting as all watched the air drama. Flattening out over the DZ, Lord signalled to release the last two containers and then gave the order to bale out, although he made no move to prepare himself. King and Ballantyne started helping the despatchers to don their parachutes and then, as King turned towards the open hatch, he noticed Medhurst coming from the cockpit. The next few seconds were a blur. With a tearing blast of tortured metal, the starboard wing fell away from the doomed Dakota. King was shot into space by the sudden whip of the fuselage and was watched breathlessly by men of the 10th and 156th Battalions of the Paratroop Brigade as he fell to earth. Almost miraculously King's parachute deployed sufficiently to brake his fall and he hit the earth hard, but alive. The time was 3.16 pm. Behind him the Dakota plunged into oblivion, carrying David Lord, Ballantyne, Medhurst and the four despatchers to their deaths.

Joining forces with the complement of a glider which landed near by, Harry King eventually spent that night fighting alongside paratroops of the 10th Battalion Parachute Regiment holding Wolfheze railway station but at 9 am the next morning he and sixty-one others became prisoners. He finally returned to England on May 13, 1945, and when the full story of David Lord's last flight was told, a recommendation was forwarded for the award of the Victoria Cross. This was approved and officially gazetted on November 13, 1945.

In the post-war RAF, Lord's name became perpetuated when his parents presented the Lord Trophy to RAF Transport Command for annual award to the transport squadron considered most proficient in the Support role. On November 11, 1968, David's brother, Wing Commander FE Lord AFC with Flight Lieutenant Harry King in attendance, performed a ceremony of naming a VC 10 – XR810 – of No 10 Squadron RAF at Brize Norton, "DAVID LORD VC".

CHAPTER FOUR

Air Command South-East Asia

ORDE WINGATE AND THE CHINDITS

Major-General Orde Charles Wingate DSO under Wavell's direction, had set out from Imphal plain with seven separate columns during early 1943. His purpose was to filter through the jungle and, after piercing the Japanese cordons, to harry the enemy's rear. Others before Wingate had planned disciplined warfare inside enemy territory; Wingate's special brilliance, in addition to his qualities of leadership, lay in his implicit confidence in air power to keep him supplied. He believed that the answer to the problem of supply, in the absence of bases and roads in North Burma, was to eliminate the risk of ground lines of communications and to bring equipment to the troops from the sky as required.

Wingate went forward from Imphal in February, seemingly in the antique way with pack-mules, bullocks and even elephants. But he took with him RAF liaison officers and radio equipment, so that each column could ask for air aid and supplies when it needed them. A total of 177 supply sorties were flown by night and day for this operation without casualty to aircrews. General Wingate wrote in his report that "supply dropping was a complete success".

The first Chindit operation had little strategic purpose other than the planting of trouble in the enemy's rear. Originally it had been intended to synchronise with a Chinese advance, but when this failed to materialise Wavell decided nevertheless to launch the columns, partly for the sake of experience. From that viewpoint it was successful, and even before Wingate returned Wavell had issued orders for the formation of another brigade on similar lines.

The hard statistics, four bridges were destroyed by the Chindits, thousands of tons of cliffside at Bonchaung Gorge blasted on to a railway line and the track cut in more than seventy-five places over a length of thirty miles.

More men and machines came to India, and the Army trained for new offensives. Additional squadrons arrived in the theatre and the building of airfields and roads went forward. The monsoon of 1943 imposed an interval on the ground, but in the air it was an interval with its own programme.

Supply by air had to continue. The Dakotas of No 31 Squadron followed this outstanding work in feeding the Long Range Penetration Group under Wingate by consistent supply-dropping in jungle country where, without this aid, military operations would have been impossible. The squadron carried out 1,000 sorties during the monsoon, using "parajutes", an Indian jute substitute employed during the world parachute shortage.

Never was a mail service cancelled because of weather, although sometimes it was postponed or diverted because of the flooding of the railways along which mail should have been brought to the air base. In the Chin Hills and in the Fort Hertz area troops were sustained, and at Coppi Bazaar, east of Maungdan in Arakan, where the pass had been washed away and not even mules could climb, the Dakotas delivered the goods. Here they were escorted over Japanese territory by Hawker Hurricanes stepped up high above the storms, with only the lower escorts providing a visual link with the transport aircraft.

At the Quebec Conference held during August 1943, Major-General Wingate, who secretly attended at Mr Churchill's invitation, had been commissioned to lead another Chindit operation into the heart of the Japanese armies.

The Wingate air invasion, which was planned under the code name of *Operation Thursday*, had an interesting origin. In the 1943 operation Chindits who were seriously wounded or ill had little chance of life. Except on the rarest occasion there was no means of bringing them out by air, and often it was impossible to carry them along the ground. When South East Asia Command (SEAC) was created at the Quebec Conference, Admiral Mountbatten, GCVO KCB DSO ADC, formerly Chief of Combined Operations, had been selected as Supreme Commander. Mountbatten discussed the 1944 Chindit operation with Wingate and agreed that a light air-ambulance service should be provided. The Air Commando Group, which eventually carried in the Wingate spearhead and brought out many of the casualties, was Mountbatten's own idea. The force was provided by General HH Arnold, Commanding General of the US Army Air Force, who named them in compliment to Mountbatten for his Commando work from the United Kingdom.

Arnold selected Colonel Philip Cochran to lead the Air Commandos. He arrived on the scene in SEAC with as heterogeneous an array of flying machines and equipment as anyone had previously seen in the theatre. It consisted of North American B-25 Mitchell bombers, North American P-51 Mustang fighter-bombers, the ubiquitous C-47 Skytrain or Dakota, unarmed Stinson L-1 Vigilants and L-5 Sentinel light aircraft, Waco CG-4A Hadrian gliders and Sikorsky R-4 helicopters. Each proved invaluable.

Cochran worked operationally under Air Marshal Baldwin, commanding

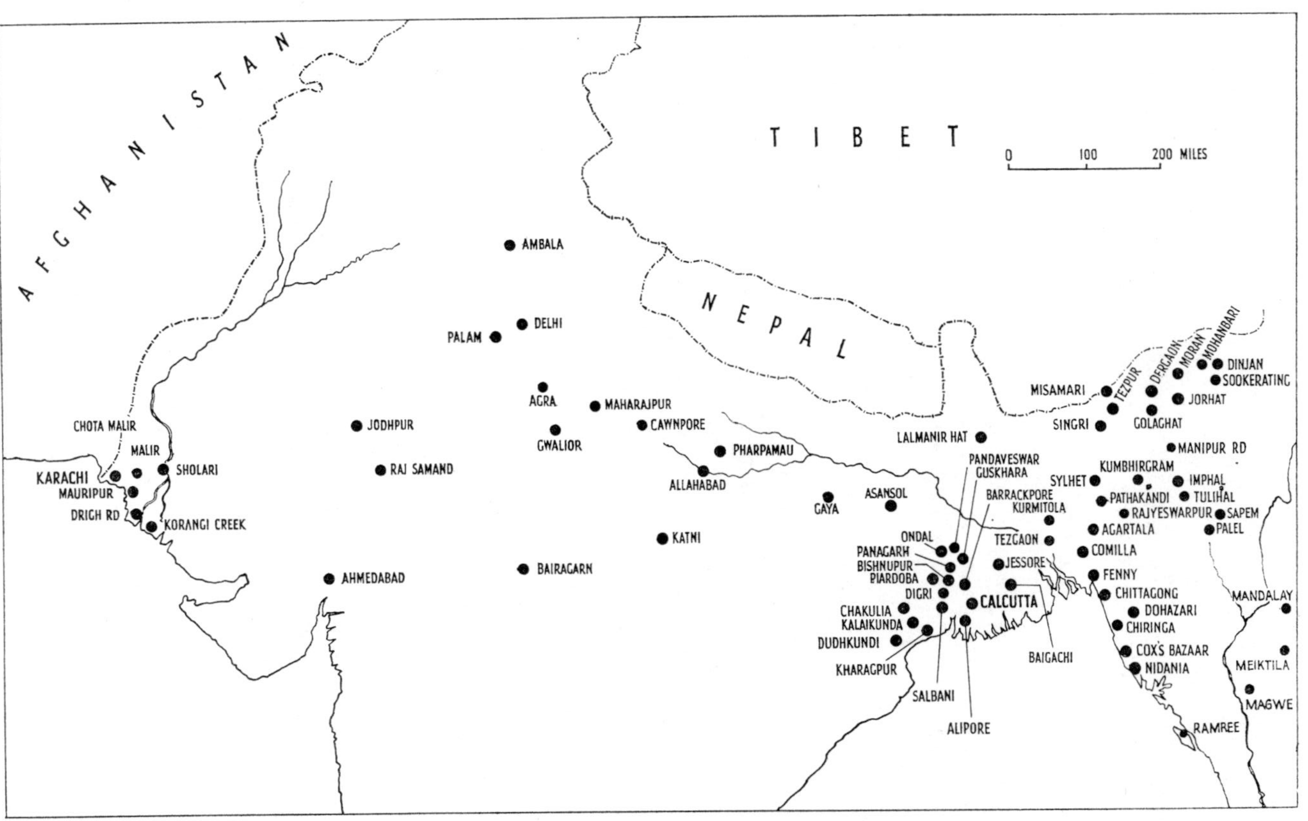

Some of the principal airfields in ACSEA

T.D.—8

Third Tactical Air Force, but he planned direct with Wingate, who became to the Americans as *The Man* or, less reverently, *The Beard*. Although the Air Commandos were scheduled to carry the spearhead, far greater body of troops was to be delivered by both RAF and USAAF squadrons of Troop Carrier Command. Cochran helped to effect the complete liaison with the British forces that was essential for the operation.

The purpose of *Operation Thursday* was to insert about 12,000 men, or the approximate bayonet strength of two divisions, far behind the Japanese armies in north-east Burma. About 10,000 of these men were to be carried by air, the rest to cut their way through the jungle. The intention was to sever the main arteries of supply of the Japanese forces who were opposing General Stilwell's march to Myitkyina. D-Day was March 5, 1944.

It was imperative that any enemy reconnaissance aircraft was prevented from discovering what was afoot, as large forces were now at stake. Near the Chindwin a glider landed a patrol which diverted Japanese attention. Allied heavy bombers dropped such concentrated loads on the Irrawaddy ports that the Japanese feared an invasion from the south. Air Marshal Baldwin kept fifty fighters in hand in case of need.

The airstrip at Lalaghat in Assam, was an impressive sight on that critical Sunday afternoon in March 1944. The Dakota tugs were lined up at one end of the runway, to the right, with the long, nylon ropes lying near by rigged for double-tow since each tug was to haul two gliders. The gliders, eighty Waco CG-4A Hadrians, were massed in a double row on the other side of the runway. General Wingate was directing loading operations from a small tent, whilst most of the other high-ranking officers were talking together – Air Marshal Baldwin, General Sir William Slim, KCB CBE DSO MC, who commanded the 14th Army and was Wingate's Commanding Officer, General Stratemeyer, Air Vice-Marshal Williams, General Old and Colonel Cochran. The soldiers and the aircrews stood about, waiting, many of them silent while the minutes went by to the take-off.

At five oclock an officer ran onto the airfield, holding a still wet photograph – the news he carried imperilled the whole operation. The print showed that *Piccadilly*, code name for the chief strip on which the gliders were to land, had recently been obstructed by the enemy with teak logs laid in rows and hidden by buffalo grass so that the logs could not be seen by high-flying aircraft. The photograph had been taken early that afternoon by Lt Russhon, operating a hand camera from a low-flying North American B-25 Mitchell of the Combat Camera Unit. This aircraft was attached to the Air Commandos to obtain films and news pictures, and it had made the survey at Cochran's request; but the results it brought back now became history as well as news, for the significance of the picture went deeper than the crust of teak logs. As the generals and air officers pored over the print, it appeared to them that here was evidence that the design of *Operation Thursday* was known to the enemy.

The possibility of a breach of security in a plan which had been developed over several months, involving four countries and great numbers of men, was strong, and the discovery was now ominous. The same aircraft had also photographed the proposed landing field at *Broadway* and showed that that was clear of obstruction, with the possible implication that the enemy, having made *Piccadilly* a death-trap for gliders, was massing an ambush at *Broadway*. Take-off was immediately postponed.

Loading, however, continued while the group around the commanders considered the problem, and the grim news was kept from the men. There was a chance that the Japanese action was no more than routine precaution. *Piccadilly* had been used for one solitary landing and evacuation of wounded during the 1943 Chindit action, and a photograph of it had appeared in an American magazine. Through neutral countries, if not from the local Nagas themselves, the news of *Piccadilly* would be known to the enemy. On that reasoning Slim, Wingate and Cochran were ready to take the risk, deleting *Piccadilly* from the plan and concentrating all their gliders for that night on *Broadway*.

When the senior Air Officer, who had the right to the last word in launching the air operation, agreed to this, Cochran went off to tell his aircrews of the perilous change of plan. At eight minutes past six the first gliders shuddered as the Dakota tug aircraft took up the slack of the ropes, then fought for speed through the yellow dust from the runway. They were hardly airborne, struggling to gain altitude with their heavy loads of bulldozers, Chindits and weapons, when things began to go wrong. Gliders bucketed in the evening turbulence and in the slipstream, and some of the nylon rope shredded and broke.

The airstrip at Lalaghat was so dusty that for three or four minutes after a Dakota tug and its pair of gliders got airborne it was impossible to see. The strip was fairly long and there was not much wind so the problem was solved by positioning Dakotas in the middle with take-off in opposite directions. Some Dakotas were equipped to carry five mules in bamboo stalls, and it was often a most difficult task persuading these animals to walk up the ramp into the aircraft. One stubborn mule which refused to go on board the waiting transport was taken for a walk around the Dakota by General Orde Wingate himself, but this tactic by the master was to no avail. Several mules had to be shot as they ran amok.

Four of the powerless gliders came down and were wrecked in the jungle near their point of take-off, three more broke loose east of the Chindwin, two east of the upper Irrawaddy. Co-pilots of the Dakotas, finding that the telephones to their gliders had suddenly gone dead, looked back for reassurance and then to their horror saw they were alone. Glider men watched the blue blobs of the Dakota exhausts ahead of them swaying more and more hectically across their line of vision as the air over the mountains and the slipstream wrenched the aircraft, and then they were left with nothing more than the surge of the wind, and little enough time to choose their landing point in the bamboo or teak.

But for all the misery and death that resulted from the parting of tow ropes, the remarkable truth is that these accidents considerably helped the whole project of *Operation Thursday*. Certain manoeuvres had been planned to deceive the enemy as to Wingate's real intentions, but nothing on the scale that in fact occurred. Five of the severed glider loads by chance put down near Japanese headquarters, and the infantry who escaped injury immediately constituted themselves into minor commando forces, acting as independent scorpions on the enemy's neck. Possibly it was in view of Mountbatten's fame in planning this type of attack when he was Chief of Combined Operations that the enemy wrongly assessed the raid, thinking it was intended to disrupt his own offensive, due in a few days, against the British in Manipur. So the Japanese reaction to the real purpose of *Operation Thursday* was delayed, and when it came it was too late.

The majority of the aircraft continued on their way east until the glinting of the Assam sun on the rifle-barrels and knife-hilts of the infantry died away in the fuselages. The gliders flew for a while in darkness over the Japanese armies and, when the three-quarters moon lit the land, smoke forest fires and ground haze hid the airborne armada from view; so the defenceless aircraft arrived without interference from fighters over the jungle clearing.

These airborne soldiers who wore green battledress, many with beards were men of the Special Force, otherwise known as the 3rd Indian Division, Long Range Penetration Groups, and still better known as Wingate's Chindits. They were so named by him after the Chinthay, mythical griffin, half-lion, half-eagle guardian of the Burmese temples. The title 3rd Indian Division was, in fact, a deception intended for the enemy. Most of its troops were British, drawn from the former 70th Division; the remainder were Ghurkas and West Africans. There were also some American engineer units.

For his 1944 campaign, Wingate proposed to erect strongholds deep in the enemy zone, and, once established, to launch large-scale operations around these fortified bases. It involved flying in not only mobile columns and garrison troops, signal installations, ack-ack and 25-pounder batteries for jungle fortress defence, but also engineer units equipped with bulldozers and mechanical graders to construct airfields capable of handling a regular air supply service. However remote the selected sites might be, the enemy were sure to discover and attack them within a few days. So the sappers had to work fast.

In his own phrase, Wingate aimed "to insert himself in the guts of the enemy". Initially this was to be accomplished by going not where the enemy was, but where he was not. To neutralise the Japanese airfields in North Burma, for example, it would have been necessary to seize them by airborne landings, and this would certainly be stoutly resisted. Far better to pierce the vulnerable arteries which sustained four enemy divisions in the field and a still respectable air force.

The plans had been carefully discussed at the Quebec Conference. Gen Arnold had inquired how he might aid the new South East Asia Command, and Mountbatten put forward his suggestion for a special air unit. No 1 Air Commando was born with Col Philip Cochran and Col Robert Alison at its head. Wingate later recorded that "had this unique force not been provided the operation could never have been carried out". Cochran proved to be a loyal and imaginative comrade of Wingate.

In Cochran's Circus, SEAC found men who had mastered both the art of lifting and towing gliders and the more intricate practice of "snatching" gliders off the ground by Dakota tugs already in the air. The value of this technique in evacuating wounded from inacessible glades and paddy-fields would be demonstrated hundreds of times in the coming campaign.

The co-ordinating air control of *Operation Thursday* had been placed in the hands of Air Marshal Sir John Baldwin, Commander of 3rd Tactical Air Force. The three landing grounds, *Piccadilly*, *Broadway* and *Chowringhee* – the latter named after Calcutta's main street, were situated in the triangle Mogaing –Indaw–Bhamo,and had been earmarked by Wingate from the ground-floor during 1943.

The plan was that the first wave of troop-carrying Hadrian gliders should land, signalling to those following if the enemy was found to be in possession. Once the gliders had cast off their tow-ropes of course, they had to go in, and, once in, they had to stay in. The Dakota tow-ships, stripped bare to haul the heavy loads, had only sufficient fuel after release to return to base over the hostile jungle. The first wave of Chindits would occupy the clearing, fan out, and screen it while the second wave arrived. This would contain more Chindits, bulldozers and graders, and also combat engineers to build an air-strip between dawn and dusk, so that next night the Dakota transports could bring in an army, with its guns, wagons, jeeps, mules and heavy wireless sets.

Once established in this region, the Chindit columns would strike against the railway, road and river systems which served the Japanese army operating against Stilwell's Chinese-American forces. These were approaching from the north through the Hakwang Valley, building the Ledo Road as they went along. To guard Stilwell's right flank, one of Wingate's Brigades, the 16th commanded by Brigadier Bernard Ferguson, DSO, had been marching for a month through the Naga

Hills on the west, parallel with his line of advance. They were nearing the invasion area.

Operation Thursday was until the invasion of Fortress Europe a few months later, the greatest airborne adventure of the war. Long after darkness had fallen the Dakota tugs continued taking off from Lalaghat at five-minute intervals. They were within radio call of base, and linked by telephone with their gliders. Not one in twenty of the airborne troops had ever flown before. No fighters escorted the air armada which travelled without lights and had been ordered to land by no other illumination than that of the moon. All depended on surprise – and no man knew what lay at the end of his journey.

Of the 67 gliders that flew, 32 landed on *Broadway*. None was hit by ack-ack fire, though several were fired on; 9 had come down in the enemy lines and 11 on friendly soil. The remaining 15 were turned back by signal because of the congestion on *Broadway*, and returned safely to their base.

Meanwhile all had not gone according to plan at *Broadway*. The advance party gliders had landed, but the Control Glider had been forced down on the banks of the Chindwin River. No guiding brain, therefore, directed the procession of arrival on the strip. Lacking a ground control, gliders overshot the mark and ploughed through the deceptive ground beyond, which was cut up by timber-hauling ruts and buffalo-holes overgrown with grass. Other Hadrian gliders came to grief on the strip itself, and, as they piled up, the next arrivals crashed into them. On the crowded runway, men heaved frantically and tore their muscles dragging the wrecks clear.

The casualties were lighter than anyone dared expect. Twenty-three men were dead, and as many more injured. Four hundred troops and stores had been delivered. But almost all the mechanical equipment, so necessary for clearing away the debris quickly, had been lost. Brig Calvert, whose 77th Brigade was the spearhead of the air invasion, decided to halt all further traffic towards him.

The code-word tapped out to signify that *Broadway* was closed to further gliders was *Soyalink*. This message was received and acted on and all airborne gliders with their Dakota tugs comprising the second wave were recalled, and turned back to Assam. At his base Wingate did not know if the strip was closed because of ambush, as had been feared, or for any other reason, and when he tried to find out by radio he had no success. It was probably one of Orde Wingate's worst moments.

At first light the engineers of the US Army 900th Field Unit began to level the surface by hand. Thirteen hours later the first Troop Carrier Command Dakota transport landed safely, bringing reinforcements and evacuating the injured. It was piloted by Gen Old. In the meantime the *Broadway* wireless operator tapped out the code word *Pork-sausage*, signifying that all was well and that the strip was held. That night fifty-five

Dakotas came into *Broadway*. This transportation continued without hitch or interference by the enemy for five more nights.

Meanwhile, on March 6, twelve Waco Hadrian gliders had opened up a second strip at *Chowringhee*, south of the Irrawaddy bend, and with the same speed four columns of the 11th Brigade with its headquarters were flown in. Two days later the Dakotas from No 194 Squadron were landing supplies, by day and night, joined by others of Troop Carrier Command.

The operations of Troop Carrier Command were supervised, and its hazardous first flights led, by General Old, who long ago had made himself familiar with these landing grounds by flying low over them in moonlight. The Dakotas made 660 sorties and the gliders 78; they transported 9,052 troops, 1,360 pack-animals and 250 tons of equipment, at a casualty cost of 121 men. Initially not a single Dakota was lost. Four days after they had landed the columns were marching off along the jungle paths to start business on the Japanese communications.

Wingate was determined not to sit upon the doorstep of his achievement. The approach of Fergusson's marching Brigade had raised his strength to 12,000 combat troops. They were planted, in truth, "in the guts of the enemy", and not even yet located by him. But this period of immunity was rapidly running out. Wingate gave the order to abandon *Chowringhee* and move across the Irrawaddy towards a new stronghold which he had planned about forty miles west of the railway. It was named *Aberdeen* after his wife's home.

It was not too soon. The Japanese at last reacted. Two hours after the rearguard had withdrawn from *Chowringhee*, the enemy bombed and strafed the burnt out gliders on that abandoned strip. Within a few days Fergusson had hacked a clearing at *Aberdeen*, and on March 23 a fourth Chindit Brigade – the 14th, commanded by Brig Tom Brodie, was flying in. The initial part of the operation was over.

And then the following day, March 24, when it remained only to reap the harvest that had been sown, Orde Wingate himself was killed while flying towards India in a North American B-25 Mitchell aircraft which encountered a storm. They eventually found the wreckage and thirty yards away lay Wingate's battered "coal-scuttle" topee, which had been a landmark to every man in his command. With this singular soldier perished the American crew and two British war correspondents, Stuart Enemy of the *News Chronicle* and Stanley Wills of the *Daily Herald*.

What Wingate might ultimately have accomplished will never be known. Mystery, and mysticism, too, threaded the man's life. You could never quite distinguish where the real and the romantic merged in him. He survived his adventures long enough to impose much of his pattern on the jungle war. Some critics complained that his Special Force or "Private Army" was an extravagant venture; there is no doubt he demanded – and obtained – for it unusually generous supply. Others considered that there should be no "specialising" anyway, but that all troops in the Burma theatre should be equally well trained and equipped. This was a sincere if unintended tribute to "*the Man*" as Cochran called him.

THE HUMP AND ACSEA

In the period following the launching of the Japanese offensive in December 1941, China's position was early recognised as vital. It was clear that China must be given enough aid to keep her in the war, if not for China's sake, then certainly that her soil might serve later as the base for a counterattack against Japan. The outlook was very gloomy. Japanese air and naval action in the China Sea left seaborne reinforcements out of the question. The fall of Rangoon in March 1942 cut off the flow of supplies by land over the Burma Road. There remained only the air route.

The possibility of establishing a useful air route into China was under serious discussion as early as January 1942. The United States contemplated building up the China National Aviation Corporations fleet of Douglas DC-3 transports to the point where twenty or twenty-five of the aircraft should maintain communications between Calcutta and Chungking. At this time the US Army Air Force was planning to inaugurate a service from Sadiya, a railhead at the eastern extremity of the Brahmaputra River Valley in Assam, 200 miles over the rugged mountains of North Burma to Myitkyina in the upper reaches of the Irrawaddy River. At Myitkyina cargoes were to be loaded on barges, floated 100 miles down the Irrawaddy to Bhamo, there to be transloaded once more for truck shipment over the Burma Road to Kunming and Chunking.

A total of seventy-five aircraft of the US Army Air Force, Douglas C-47 and C-53 transports, allocated to this service were to arrive at Calcutta by June 15, 1942, while work was rushed on the construction of a suitable hard-surfaced airfield at Myitkyina. It was hoped this fleet would be able to deliver 7,500 tons of cargo a month. When the middle of June came, ten C-53s had been delivered to Karachi for the use of either CNAC or the Chinese Government. In addition, a total of thirty-nine aircraft for use by the Army Air Force had been flown out. On May 8 the Japanese took the airfield at Myitkyina, the base that was to have played a key part in the air supply of China.

That disaster left only one means of keeping an airway to China – the grim prospect of direct flight from airfields in eastern Assam across the high Himalayas to Yunnanyi, Kunming, or other points in the Yunnan Province of China. The route from Dinjan, near Sadiya, in upper Assam to Myitkyina had been forbidding enough, but not so difficult as the more northerly route to which Royal Air Force and US Army Air Force Dakota aircrews would now be restricted.

The distance from Dinjan to Kunming was 500 miles by air. The Brahmaputra valley floor lay 90 feet above sea-level at Chabua, a spot near Dinjan where the principal US Air Force base was constructed. From this level the mountain wall surrounding the valley rose quickly to 10,000 feet and higher. Flying eastward out of the valley aircraft first topped the Patkai Range, before passing over the upper Chindwin River Valley, bounded on the east by a 14,000 feet ridge, the Kumon mountains. Then across a series of 14 to 16,000 foot ridges separated by valleys of the West Irrawaddy, East Irrawaddy, Salween and Mekong rivers. The main "Hump", which gives its name to the whole awesome mountainous mass and to the air route which crossed it was the Santsung Range, often 15,000 feet high, between the Salween and Mekong rivers. East of the Mekong the terrain became decidely less rugged, and the elevations were moderate as one approached Kunming airfield, itself 6,200 feet above sea-level.

At minimum altitude on this route violent turbulence was commonly encountered. To avoid this menace pilots had to climb to levels at which severe icing occurred during several months of the year. During March 1943 one pilot reported the icing level commenced at 12,000 feet. A Consolidated C-87 Liberator transport pilot went to 29,500 feet on instruments and was unable to climb any higher, and couldn't get on top of the overcast. It had rained about seven and a half inches in five days. All aircraft were grounded.

The stifling hot ground weather of mid-May ushered in the true monsoon, in which during five and a half months a rainfall of 200 inches is common. To the stark natural hazards of the route were added those of the attacks of the enemy, who was particularly active in the winter months of 1942/43 and 1943/44. The Hump was short in comparison with the long over-water flights of the North Atlantic. Few, nevertheless, will challenge the claim of the men who flew the Hump that theirs was an air transport route of surpassing danger and difficulty.

Its hazards apart, the India–China route had a unique character. The other routes operated by the Royal Air Force and US Army Air Force were extremely important for the strategic supplies, key personnel, and priority mail delivered to combat zones, but not one of them was the sole means by which a theatre of operations was nourished. In contrast, every vehicle, every gallon of fuel, every weapon, every round of ammunition, every typewriter, and every ream of paper which found its way to Free China for either Chinese or US forces during nearly three years of war was flown in by air from India.

India itself was not the source of the military supplies required in China. Most of the goods had to be brought to India by sea or air. Whichever of the major ports – Karachi, Calcutta or Bombay – was the point of debarkation the sea route was long and painfully slow. Once ashore the cargo was still 1,500 miles by a string of primitive railroads of varying gauges and limited capacity from the jumping-off point in Assam. Slow, ancient barges on the Brahmaputra River carried much of the fuel used by aircraft. The Assam and Bengal railroad, built primarily to market the tea crop, had to carry a large part of the load. Between Calcutta and Assam all Hump-bound freight had to be transferred to cars used on the narrow-gauge track up the valley.

In spite of these handicaps, the airlift to China was initiated in 1942 and came eventually to flourish. In July 1942 a handful of US Army Air Force Douglas C-47s delivered a meagre 85 tons of army supplies and passengers to China. In July 1945 the peak was reached with 71,042 net tons from bases in India to China.

During May 1943 the first Royal Air Force pilots were seconded to the China National Aviation Corporation from No 31 Squadron for training on the route to Kunming. The CNAC pilots were very experienced and included several of General Chenaults Flying Tigers. Initial US Army Air Force losses on the "Hump" route were heavy. Regular flights to Kunming by Royal Air Force Dakotas were started in August and increased in frequency as more pilots were checked out on the route.

On November 30, 1943, Dakota Mk I FD820 from No 31 Squadron based at Kharagpur made a typical Hump sortie with Flg Off "Leo" Williams as pilot, Flg Off Jack Morris as observer, Warrant Officer Tom Wright as wireless operator, plus a member of the ground crew. The Dakota flew to Dum Dum, Calcutta, where the aircraft was loaded with supplies for China. It was three and a half hours flying time to Dinjan to refuel. This was an RAF controlled airfield used by the US Army Air Force whose main base in Northeast Assam was at Chabua only a couple of miles from Dinjan. Flying time from Dinjan to Kunming was between three and four hours depending on the winds aloft. Aircraft were required to have sufficient fuel for the return flight over the Hump. The crew stayed overnight in the British Military Mission in Kunming, returning to base the following day after a round trip of about fifteen hours flying. The odd passenger was carried on the return flight to India, but oxygen was available only for the crew and flying at 20,000 feet over the Hump without could be most uncomfortable.

One Royal Air Force Dakota from No 31 Squadron was flying west from Kunming on February 7, 1944, and encountered a headwind which reduced the ground speed to 82 mph and forced the transport to land at Yunnanyi for more fuel after only two and a quarter hours in the air; the rest of the flight to Dinjan taking another three hours and twenty minutes.

It is true that the Hump route tested aircraft and crews, but provided everything worked, there was no special difficulty. In fair weather one could cross safely by way of passes without going higher than 10,000 ft – it is true one of the passes was decorated with a CNAC DC-3, who presumably caught a down-current when cutting it too fine. During the monsoon season it was possible to go onto instruments shortly after take-off from Dinjan and see nothing of the ground until arrival at Kunming. As one veteran Hump pilot of the Royal Air Force disclosed – no memory exceeds the splendour of a clear moonlit night over the Hump with the steady drone of twenty-eight Pratt & Whitney pots and a good programme of classical music from the BBC.

The Air Command, South East Asia, was formed on November 16, 1943, and embraced the whole of the Royal Air Force in South East Asia Command – SEAC – including India, except for a small force for the protection of the North West Frontier which remained under Gen Auchinleck's command.

As the fighter effort gathered strength, with the arrival of the first Supermarine Spitfire squadrons, the scale of operations by the Allied Troop Carrier Command was also increasing. On January 2, 1944, Troop Carrier Command moved its headquarters to Comilla, in order to be near those of the 3rd Tactical Air Force and 14th Army. This led to closer integration, not only in tactical matters but in the complex details of all administration, such as airfield construction, supply loading, and maintenance, that was being undertaken by the 14th Army on behalf of the Royal Air Force.

After the Cairo Conference held on November 21, 1943, all the Allied forces throughout SEAC were now put under Air Chief Marshal Pierse, who became Allied Air C-in-C with Maj Gen Stratemeyer of the US Army Air Force as his second-in-command, and was given direct command of Eastern Air Command which was formed to control those Allied air forces flighting in the Burma campaign. The new Eastern Air Command headquarters which controlled all the operational air units in Assam and Bengal, consisted basically of the Operations Section of the old 10th US Army Air Force organisation in the India-Burma sector, but now also included a Royal Air Force element. The forces under its command were divided into four main components: the 3rd Tactical Air Force under Air Marshal Sir John Baldwin: a Strategic Air Force under Brig Gen – later Maj Gen – HC Davidson of the US Army Air Force: a Troop Carrier Command under Brig Gen William D Old, also US Army Air Force, and a Photographic Reconnaissance Force, under Grp Capt SJ Wise.

At the start of 1942, the Burma-India theatre, because of the poverty of ground communications, needed transport aircraft like the Douglas Dakota, more perhaps than any other zone. The Dakota was to become the most useful and necessary aircraft of the whole SEAC campaign.

A Douglas C-47A-60-DL Skytrain 43-30643 named *Mercury*, equipped as a mobile wireless and cypher station, accompanied the Supreme Commander, Lord Louis Mountbatten, for two and a half years, flying more than 200,000 miles. Preceding his own personal aircraft, a Dakota Mk III FL510 *Sister Ann*, it enabled him from the moment of arrival to be in direct touch with his headquarters, and through them with London and every part of the theatre. This mobile signal headquarters enabled him to avoid imposing extra strain on the cypher staffs of Army, Corps and Group communications – besides greatly speeding up his own communications. A similar aircraft, a Dakota Mk IV KK205 *Hermes*, was later provided for the C-in-C, Allied Land Forces, South East Asia. The idea of these mobile signal stations was instigated by the Signal Officer-in-Chief, Capt M Hodges, RN, who was on the Supreme Commanders staff.

It was clear that, unless Troop Carrier Command which was already engaged and disposed of only eight squadrons – four Royal Air Force units Nos 31, 62, 117 and 194 Squadrons, and four US Army Air Force C-47 Skytrain and C-46 Commando units – received additional aircraft from some other source, it could not bring up reinforcements in time to influence the course of the battle. Air Marshal Baldwin was instructed to request Maj Gen Stratemeyer to take thirty C-47 transports, or their equivalent, off the Hump route, and to place them at the disposal of Troop Carrier Command for transporting the 5th Indian Division to the Central front.

The air-supply situation had been a recurring source of worry, and a request had been made to the US Joint Chiefs of Staff for reinforcements. On March 25, 1944, Gen Arnold offered to set up four Special Combat Cargo Groups for SEAC, each containing 100 C-47 Skytrain transports. and also to build up more Air Commandos. The first of these was to reach SEAC in July, and the remainder at regular intervals during the year.

In the third week of March it was clear that Troop Carrier Command could not undertake to supply garrisons at Imphal and Kohima, in addition to supplying the Special Force, Lt Gen Stilwell's forces, and the 81st West African Division. On March 25 Lord Louis Mountbatten made a request to retain, for longer than the one month for which their loan had been authorised, the twenty Curtiss C-46 Commando transports which had been diverted from the Hump route, for the airlift of the 5th Indian Division. In addition the Supreme Commander asked the Combined Chiefs of Staff to provide a further seventy Douglas C-47 aircraft, or their equivalent, as reinforcements.

The result of this latter request, was the diversion from the Mediterranean theatre of one US Troop Carrier Group of sixty-four C-47 Skytrains for one month, plus a detachment of fifteen Dakota aircraft from No 216 Squadron which would have to return in May. These seventy-nine transports arrived in April, and began to operate immediately. Ten of the C-46 Commando aircraft were returned to the Hump route, the remainder as soon as essential engine repairs had been made. As replacement aircraft arrived in the theatre the seventy-nine transports borrowed from the Middle East were returned in small batches.

During April, transport squadrons, practically unmolested by enemy aircraft, provided continuous air-supply to the 4th Corps. By the middle of the month, however, the garrison required nearly 500 tons a day, and owing to various difficulties, shortage of all-weather airfields, etc, this tonnage could not be met, and 4th Corps had to be reduced to half rations.

On May 17, columns of Galahad force and Chinese infantry who, after an exhausting advance over the Kumon range, had been carrying out an outflanking attack against Myitkyina itself, caught the enemy unawares and captured the airfield just as the monsoon was starting. Troop Carrier Command immediately flew in Waco CG-4A Hadrian gliders and Dakotas, carrying one US airborne aviation engineer company, two batteries of US anti-aircraft artillery, and two troops of light anti-aircraft gunners from the 14th Army. In this airborne operation, which was carried out by day and night under enemy ground fire and air attacks, only one Dakota was shot down and a few destroyed on the ground. Two days after its capture the airfield was in operation, but despite reconstruction and expansion, was overworked. Three more US aviation engineer battalions were flown in, fully equipped, and five more all-weather airfields were built in the area. During this construction work the battalions were supplied entirely by air throughout the monsoon.

No 1 Air Commando, under Col Philip Cochrane, US Army Air Force, which had flown for longer than it had been organised to fly for, ceased to operate in mid-May and was disbanded on May 21. Orders were issued on May 17 for a US squadron of thirteen C-47 Skytrains to be diverted from Troop Carrier Command to the 14th US Army Air Force for the supply of the Yunnan Force. This decision was taken at a moment when the resources of Troop Carrier Command were strained to the utmost.

The air-supply system, which had given recurrent cause for anxiety, had been reorganised both on the ground and in the air. On May 1 the activities of Troop Carrier Command had been co-ordinated with those of the 3rd Air Force under the overall command of Air Marshal Baldwin. As a result of this reorganisation, supplies had been increased; but it had proved impossible to make up arrears, and the troops in the Imphal area remained on a reduced scale of rations. Flying was now restricted by the south-west monsoon to an extent which Air Command had rather under-estimated in the original programme. Moreover the inadequacy of the landing facilities in the Imphal area prevented the Allies from making the best use of the aircraft available.

In the monsoon, only all-weather airstrips could be used; and it was becoming difficult to maintain the only two which came in this category – Palel and Imphal itself – in view of the wear and tear that constant landings and take-offs were inflicting on the surface originally intended for handling fighters. Both airfields were under intermittent shellfire; and Palel was occasionally raided by parties of Japanese infantry, who destroyed a number of aircraft and compelled for a time the airfield to be abandoned. Unloading was handicapped by the lack of sufficient hard-standings; and the congestion on both airfields was such that Dakotas often had to circle for as long as one hour before being able to land, and sometimes had to return to base still loaded. Sometimes supplies were not available at the operating base; and sometimes the loading parties on the despatching airfields were unable to keep pace with the number of transports which needed loading. Bomber aircraft of the Strategic Air Force had already been diverted to transport work, but the position was still deteriorating; the troops were beginning to use their reserves, and these were not being replaced. Fortunately, by the middle of June the lift of supplies by air had steadily improved.

It is difficult to realise that in August 1942 there was only one transport unit in existence in the theatre – No 31 Squadron – equipped with Douglas DC-2K and DC-3 aircraft originally designed for carrying airline passengers, and now impressed as cargo transports. Even with these grossly inadequate means, many isolated parties in difficult hill country were kept supplied, sporadically, it is true, but they were not left to rot unsuccoured. In those early days such problems as the types of stores which could be dropped without a parachute or the type which could not, what ground signals could be sent and what could not, and many other problems were discovered and solved.

By December 1942, internal air services were being maintained by No 194 Squadron flying Hudsons – later Dakotas – and they continued this important work for nine months until replaced by No 353 Squadron, which later was also to re-equip with Dakotas.

Before the end of 1943 the weekly mileage of one transport squadron had risen from 5,000 in December 1942 to 37,000 in November 1943, a seven-fold increase in less than a year. By the beginning of January 1944 it was possible to carry, not battalions or brigades only, but whole divisions by air, and to keep them fully supplied once they reached the battle area. Gen Sir George Giffard, General Officer Commanding, Eastern Army, in October 1943 wrote – "It is not untrue to say that without the assistance of airborne supply to outlying garrisons, we could not have held, during the monsoon, positions we held in May last."

This expansion in all branches of the Royal Air Force – fighters, bombers and transports – was accomplished only by the construction of a large number of airfields. Not until 1943 was it fully realised that the malarial map was as important as the geographic; one airfield, excellent from every other aspect, had been constructed in an area of the Lushai hills where the incidence of malaria was 100 per cent. Here a malignant form of the disease obtained which resulted in streams of small parasites in the blood vessels, sometimes entering the brain. In the new building plan malaria was a chief consideration.

The US field engineering units with their massive and ingenious equipment, were outstanding in the construction of the new airfields, but both Allies learned from each other new ways of getting the job done more solidly and more swiftly. Floodlands were drained and jungle cleared for the long runways, taxi-tracks and hard standings. When the logistics were known the programme rolled forward, giving to each new airfield either 300,000 tons of concrete, or 600 Dakota loads of steel planking, or 200 tons of bitumenised hessian.

In March 1942, precisely four airfields with all-weather runways had been serviceable in the theatre. By the end of the monsoon of 1943 there were 285 airfields completed and more under construction. Some 45 were handed over to the US Army Air Force and facilities given them on Royal Air Force airfields.

Behind the build-up of the transport units of the Allies, had been built an organisation without which the Dakota squadrons and their accompanying Waco CG-4A Hadrian gliders, could not have flown. These were the repair and maintenance units, the ferry units, plus the staging posts, all necessary to keep the transports supplied to the units. The maintenance personnel on the squadrons did a fine job. Always working in the open, in extreme conditions of heat and rain, they kept the serviceability of operational aircraft at a high standard.

With the formation of SEAC on November 16, 1943, this huge support organisation was rapidly built up in readiness to support future requirements. No 322 Maintenance Unit at Chakeri, near Cawnpore, constituted the largest service base repair unit in India. It was the main SEAC servicing base for the Dakota. The Pratt & Whitney Twin Wasp engines were removed and overhauled, tested and modified at Technical Plant No 1 located at the other side of Cawnpore, a non flying unit. Other maintenance units were located at Karachi, Ambala, and Lahore in addition to Cawnpore, with civilian maintenance units at Kanchrapara, Trichinopoly, Cawnpore, Barrackpore, Dum Dum, Calcutta and Poona. The civilian units were organised under the Aeronautical Division of the Department of Supply, which came under being early in 1943, and developed in October into the Directorate General of Aircraft. Hindustan Aircraft Company at Bangalore did sub-contracting. The Royal Air Force maintenance unit at Drigh Road, had serviced the earlier DC-2K and DC-3 aircraft from No 31 Squadron and was now ready to handle the Dakota.

The maintenance organisation in the forward areas consisted of the Repair and Salvage Units – R & SU – supporting squadrons at their airfields and taking on all the work which the flying units could not complete within forty-eight hours. No 2 R & SU was based at Agartala. One remedy for the recovery of crashed or force-landed aircraft away from an airfield was the formation in November 1943 of an Airborne Salvage Section, which could fly to the scene of the crash in a specially fitted transport aircraft which carried spares, tools and engines. On reaching the site, patch repairs were effected and the damaged aircraft nursed to the nearest depot. The Airborne Salvage Unit was given one of the first Dakota transports to be salvaged, and in that aircraft mainplanes of large aircraft and complete fighters like Spitfires were carried. The output of Dakotas from repair rose from two in December 1943 to ten in April and eleven in May. The figures could have been higher still but for the complete lack of certain spares in the Command which had to be demanded from the United States.

No 361 Maintenance Unit was formed at Bihta, near Patra, and was the erection unit for the large number of Waco CG-4A Hadrian gliders arriving from the United States. Dakotas were used as tugs to deliver and test the gliders, and from No 361 MU servicing echelons were formed and went all over the command. No 1 Glider Servicing Flight was formed in June 1944 at Chaklala, later moving to the airfield at Whamial.

No 21 Ferry Control was at Jodhpur in 1943, later at Karachi, and similar units were set up throughout India along with Transport Command staging posts such as those at Mauripur, Allahabad and Alipore, the latter being No 67. Lahore was a huge base, housing a ferry flight, No 47 Staging Post, and was visited by No 1331 Conversion Unit, which moved around the theatre as training requirements demanded.

Recognised as one of the most impressive feats of air organisation in the world was that by which Royal Air Force Transport Command met its heavy and varied commitments in South East Asia, filling its role of handmaiden to the fighting forces with remarkable efficiency.

There are many reasons, but one is outstanding: the "operational" zest of the men and women concerned. Many of these personnel left bomber, fighter or coastal duties in Europe, feeling that a comparatively dull future awaited them in transport, only to discover that the new job could be fascinating, because it was so vitally important to the progress of operations. The five main activities of the Command in India and Burma have been: delivery of supplies to the armies in Burma; evacuation of casualties from forward areas; ferrying all new aircraft to squadrons; control of air trooping into India; and operation of air lines in India and Burma, extending to China and Australia.

In four of these activities magnificent work was done. It is acknowledged, for example, that without the support given by Royal Air Force and US Army Air Force Dakotas of Combat Cargo Task Force, the advance in Burma through some of the most difficult campaigning country in the world would have been impossible. Of all units, those in Transport Command were least affected by a rise or fall in the scale of fighting: the air supply lines, radiating from great bases like Karachi and Calcutta, formed an immense and intricate network on which traffic flowed in an ever-growing volume. The capture of Rangoon certainly ended the most spectacular phase of support from the air for the armies in Burma. The Combat Cargo Task Force lift of more than 330,000 tons of material and men in six months was a joint achievement. After the task force was disbanded in June 1945 the support squadrons of the Royal Air Force fulfilled the obligation alone, and did it in the teeth of appalling weather conditions. There was little relaxation from the strain of the battle while the monsoon was on, and in delivering 9,575 tons in the last weeks of July 1945, the squadrons put up a performance that can only be rightly assessed when one knows from experience the hazards of monsoon flying. Here is an instance of the determination to get the supplies through. On the way to Toungoo a Dakota met a severe storm in the face of which the crew would have been justified in turning back. Wide detours were made and the mission completed, but only after seven hours and a quarter on a trip which would normally have taken one hour and three-quarters. Another example was that of the Dakota which reached its base seven hours after leaving Myingyan with only sixty gallons of petrol in the tanks, the trip being scheduled for an hour and a half. Such risks were not always taken successfully, and the squadrons paid with lives and aircraft, but splendid airmanship kept the cost lower than may be expected.

Civilians also received airborne supplies, dropped in north and north-east Burma in the mountainous regions. An intelligence officer who visited the area between Anisakan and Haipaw, who met the Civil Affairs officer, was asked to assure his Dakota crews of the high degree of accuracy in their supply drops, and to express the gratitude of the civilian population for the prompt and welcome deliveries of food.

When their supply mission was completed, the Dakotas that landed on the forward airfields had an equally urgent job on the return journey, the movement of wounded and sick men back to hospital areas. Many casualties were flown to the airfields in Stinson L-5 light aircraft which picked them up from beaches, roads and small clearings where only these light Sentinel aircraft could land. In the first six months of 1945, 50,000 men were carried back by the Dakota support squadrons to base airfields for eventual transfer to hospital.

Ferrying was the third commitment of Transport Command. From the moment an aircraft arrived in India, either at an airfield or in a packing case on a ship, its swift safe despatch to a squadron was the immediate concern of many people. Pilots, navigators and wireless operators, trained and tested so that their reliability could not be questioned, took the new aircraft in relays over some of the longest air routes in the world, to the places where they were put into service. These ferry pilots duty was an onerous one. They had to see that the squadrons operational strength was maintained and, though the weather may often be atrocious, must deliver their costly article in first-class condition. From the four-engined heavies to the smallest trainer or communications type, the stream from west to east flowed daily.

Air trooping was a feature introduced towards the end of World War 2. A quota of troops were drafted from the United Kingdom in Dakotas, making the flight to Karachi in five days which included a 48-hour halt at Lydda in Palestine. Transit camps were organised and long-distance air travel was warmly approved by the troops.

Finally, there was the air lines which weaved a communication pattern over India and Burma linking up all the main cities, so that they were only a matter of hours apart instead of days or weeks. The service embraced a ground organisation which included the staging posts, radio and meteorological installations and maintenance units which ran with the efficiency of a well-conducted railway system. Astronomical mileage and flying time totals were built up by the air line squadrons, whose aircraft ranged from Rawalpindi in the north-west, Karachi in the west, to Kunming in China over the Hump, to Calcutta, Rangoon, Colombo and most distant of all, Australia. A Liberator express service operated over the Delhi-Colombo-Perth-Sydney route, among its major task being the delivery of mail to the British Pacific Fleet. The mail was carried to the fleet at Leyte by the Dakotas of No 300 Wing. Four and a half million miles were flown by the air lines of Transport Command during the first six months of 1945, when 80,000 passengers, 2,208 tons of mail and 4,548 tons of freight were transported. In 32,000 hours flying during the same period, not one passenger met with injury, and it has been deduced that a person averaging 200 hours annually on Transport Command air lines in South East Asia would have risked a minor accident once in 160 years.

About the time of the fall of Rangoon, the Japanese marched numerous British and Indian POWs northwards until they met advance scouts of the 14th Army; Dakotas from No 238 Squadron along with transports from other units, flew to Payagi near Pegu, taking reinforcement troops and returning with our ex-prisoners. The Dak crews had set out with as many cigarettes as they could muster, and on the return flight it was impossible to see in the cabin for smoke as the passengers chain smoked the first cigarette they'd had for years.

In January 1944 Lt Col Frank Owen started the publication of the daily newspaper "SEAC", the first completely inter-service newspaper to be published in any Command. The original editorial staff comprised an Army and a Royal Marine subaltern and a few other ranks and ratings, drawn from the three services. The paper was printed in Calcutta by courtesy of *The Statesman* newspaper. It immediately became very popular with the services, and was unquestionably a great morale-builder throughout the SEAC campaign. In a very short time its circulation rose from 10,000 to 100,000 copies per day. Throughout the campaign certain formations and units were supplied with "SEAC" by air-drop from Dakotas and in most cases it arrived regularly – daily.

For the device of the command in South East Asia the Supreme Commander obtained the King's consent to use the symbol of the phoenix, a fabulous and fierce bird which arose from the ashes of the fire which could have destroyed anything less adamantine. The choice of emblem appeared not only to have been touched with a sense of poetry but soon was shown also to have been inspired with the gift of prophecy.

The American Stratemeyer, had the qualities necessary for his task, including deep belief in the Allied ideal, and a leaning towards attack. In a General Order he declared "We must merge into one unified force, in thought and in deed neither English nor America, with the faults of neither and the virtues of both. We must establish in Asia a record of Allied air victory of which we can all be proud in the years to come. Let us write it now in the skies of Burma."

Air Marshal Baldwin, who came to ACSEA from Bomber Command in the United Kingdom, in a report concerning *Operation Thursday* said: "Nobody has seen a transport operation until he has stood at *Broadway* under the light of a Burma moon and watched Dakotas coming in and taking off in opposite directions on a single strip, at the rate of one take-off or one landing every three minutes."

On August 6, 1945, an atomic bomb was dropped on Hiroshima followed three days later by a similar bomb on Nagasaki. News was brought to the Supreme Commander on August 10 that the Japanese Government were prepared to discuss terms for the surrender of the Japanese Empire. On August 14, 1945, Japan accepted unconditional surrender. Orders were issued for the suspension of all land, air and sea operations in South East Asia – so far as was consistant with the safety of Allied forces.

Admiral (Hon Lt Gen and Hon Air Marshal) the Lord Louis Mountbatten, GCVO KCB DSO ADC, relinquished his appointment as Supreme Allied Commander South East Asia Command on May 31, 1946. He was created Viscount Mountbatten of Burma the following month, and Earl Mountbatten of Burma a year later.

The atom bomb was the last, as it was the most terrible, of all the levers of war that toppled conquerers of the East to destruction within four years of their greatest triumph.

BRITISH PACIFIC FLEET AND THE DAKOTA

Although it was only operating for fourteen months, No 300 Group of Royal Air Force Transport Command based in Australia, provided one of the most efficient air transport services to serve that country. During that time, seven million miles were flown in 38,681 hours, 72,290 passengers were carried and a total weight of 12,000 tons transported. In 61¼ million passenger miles flown there were only four fatal accidents.

Originally operating as a Wing, No 300 Group was established to provide air transport support for the operations of the British Pacific Fleet. Although the Commander-in-Chief of the Fleet was based on Sydney, Melbourne was chosen as the air headquarters in order to maintain close contact with the Royal Australian Air Force headquarters.

The Wing expanded rapidly after its establishment late in 1944. During November the build-up had commenced in the United Kingdom and it started operations with its Douglas Dakotas with Camden in New South Wales as the nucleus of the units operational activity. Here thousands of tons of equipment required to service the squadrons and to provide maintenance facilities at the many staging posts was based. In the ensuing months many outposts sprang up through the South-West Pacific Area.

Mascot, a civil airport near Camden in New South Wales, became the terminus for the thrice-weekly Royal Air Force trans-Pacific service from San Diego in California, which routed via New Zealand, and which was operated with Consolidated Liberator transports by No 45 Group with its headquarters at Dorval in Canada. The trans-Indian service from Colombo also terminated at Mascot, using Douglas C-54 Skymaster four-engined transports of No 229 Group of SEAC. Staging posts were set up at Guildford and Learmouth in Western Australia, and at Gawler in South Australia, to cater for passengers and aircraft servicing on these two long-distance routes.

The Wing rapidly expanded outside the mainland. Ground personnel arrived by sea from the United Kingdom, and staging posts were established at Townsville, Port Moresby, Manus, Biak, Pelau and at Leyte in the Philippines. When the Japanese at Hong Kong surrendered, an aircraft of 300 Wing was one of the first to land there, and, within a week, the scheduled service from Sydney to the Philippines was extended to Hong Kong. Further services were called for, and in June 1945 a further Dakota squadron – No 238 – was brought from Air Command South East Asia, where it had operated throughout the retreat and subsequent conquest of Burma. This enabled further routes to be opened through

Clonourry, Darwin, and Morotai to Leyte; from Darwin to Balikpapan, Labnan, Saigon and Hong Kong: also from Darwin through Borneo to Singapore, thus linking up with the services provided from Europe, India and Ceylon to Malaya.

In May 1945 No 300 Wing was still in the process of being built up as an air transport organisation to be devoted exclusively to serving the British Pacific Fleet based at Leyte. In addition to No 243 Squadron and No 1315 Flight, each with their thirty Dakotas and forty-eight aircrews, a communication flight was formed consisting of two VIP Liberators, two normal passenger Liberators, two VIP Dakotas, four passenger Dakotas and three Beech C-45 Expeditors.

Great difficulty was experienced in obtaining adequate housing facilities for No 300 Wing in Australia, but after the first six Dakotas had arrived in February 1945, accommodation was found at Camden, near Sydney, in spite of the hangers there being too small to take the aircraft. By February 26 a regular service had commenced between Sydney and Manus, the forward fleet base in the Admiralty Islands, just to the north of the Equator and eastern New Guinea. Subsequently this service was a daily one, and in addition a thrice-weekly service between Sydney and Perth, Western Australia, had been started, in addition to many other special *ad hoc* services for the Royal Navy.

Between February 26 and May 28 a total of 1,251 passengers, 117,650 lb of freight, and 383,200 lb of mail were carried between Sydney, Manus and Leyte, the total mileage flown being 90,662 miles. By this service mail could be delivered to the Fleet at Leyte in an average time of three weeks from posting in London, a very important factor in maintaining morale in the combat area. Many tons of urgent operational stores were also delivered to the Fleet without which it might have been impossible to maintain the offensive.

As demands on this air service increased, more aircraft, up to a minimum of ninety Dakotas, were asked for and also more four-engined transports in order to increase the range between refuelling points. The VIP Liberators at the disposal of the C-in-C British Pacific Fleet, Admiral Sir Bruce Fraser, were in constant use. In spite of operating with inadequate ground staffs and facilities, and while suffering from a shortage of aircrews, a splendid record was being established. The Admiralty emphasised the need to build up further this Transport Command organisation as a matter of great importance to the operation of the British Pacific Fleet.

No 300 Group headquarters were established in a requisitioned old house in Tivoli Place, South Yarra, Melbourne, while base installations were at Parafield near Adelaide; Camden in New South Wales, and Archerfield, near Brisbane. Royal Australian Air Force personnel were loaned to the organisation including the Group's Chief of Staff, Grp Capt

GT Gilbert, Wg Cdr Jack McLean, DSO DFC AFC, an old hand among Burma transport pilots, who was in command of No 243 Squadron at Camden, and Sq Ldr Mervyn Baker, personal Liberator pilot to the C-in-C British Pacific Fleet. Royal Air Force personnel in command included Wg Cdr Reg Bailey who commanded No 1315 Flight at Archerfield, Wg Cdr RS Searle, Admin Officer at HQ No 300 Group, and Flt Lt L Lawler, assistant intelligence officer.

Royal Air Force Transport Command had an even higher safety record in Australia than in the rest of the world. In the early days Transport Command passengers were regarded pretty much as passengers who hitch-hiked on an army truck. By 1945 there was an almost civil airline mentality in the command. Pilots handed out information chits to passengers who were reminded very pleasantly by telephone where to be and when. There was plenty of effort to ensure passengers were comfortable. Ordinary 300 Group briefing for captains by Grp Capt Gilbert were along bedside manner lines.

> "Captains should take the opportunity of introducing themselves to their passengers before taking off; not only will it give them an opportunity to see who is to fly with them, but also the captain can learn a little about the attitude of his passengers to their trip . . . A brief survey of the route when the captain briefs his passengers just before take-off will be of interest to them . . . Throughout the whole trip the captain should keep in touch with his passengers . . . In bad weather a visit from a member of the crew helps a lot to cheer a nervous passenger."

During World War 2 it was Royal Air Force Transport Command, along with the US Army Air Force Transport Command, who introduced thousands of servicemen, more particularly staff officers, to flying in Dakotas as a normal means of fast transport. Such travel was compulsory, free, usually uncomfortable, but incomparably faster than train or troopship.

Today, mention of Transport Command reminds ex-servicemen of scattered staging posts throughout the world, but in the main through the many theatres of war. Their names are imprinted in their memory like hotel labels on a grip.

No 243 Squadron, commanded by Wg Cdr TW Gillen, was formed at Morecambe, Lancashire, on December 15, 1944, and its personnel were fully kitted out there for overseas service. The personnel were members of sixteen aircrews who were to form the advanced echelon of the Squadron, the rear echelon of which was to follow about three months later. They were posted to HQ Transport Command from the following squadrons: Nos 24, 48, 147, 167, 233, 271, 512 and 575. All units which operated the Dakota transport.

After three days at Morecambe the squadron embarked on the *New*

Amsterdam at Greenock, Scotland, and disembarked at Halifax, Nova Scotia, Christmas Day. From Halifax the unit travelled by train to Montreal and thence by bus to the Royal Air Force station at Dorval, the HQs of No 45 Group. Here they underwent a period of training which included both technical lectures and flying on the Dakota Mk IV aircraft for pilots and co-pilots with special emphasis on radio range "Airways" flying as used in the United States. Navigators concentrated on Astro and Wireless-operators on American R/T and W/T procedures. No 45 Group were responsible for the training and for the routing of the aircraft from Dorval to Sacremento in California, on the first stage of the long trans-Pacific flight to Australia.

On completion of the training the squadron took over fifteen Dakota Mk IV aircraft, specially fitted with eight 100-gallon overload fuel tanks rigged in the fuselage. Two flights were formed, "A" Flight with Sq Ldr Coupland in command, and "B" Flight with Sq Ldr Glen, AFC. Flying independantly the Dakotas flew to Nashville, Tennessee. The next stop was Dallas, Texas, where it stayed overnight, proceeding to Tucson, Arizona, the following day. Here the US Army Air Force acted as host.

On January 16, 1945, No 243 Squadron reached Mather Field, Sacramento, where the aircraft were overhauled and the aircrews were processed by the Medical, Intelligence and Security Officer and also the Specialist Briefing Officers. This briefing consisted of a general outline of the long route to Sydney, Australia, and a detailed survey of the first lap of the route, from Sacramento to John Rodgers Field, Honolulu. A feature of the briefing was the showing of films of interesting points which would assist the aircrews in identifying their destinations, showing navigational aids and warnings, views of airfields, and the correct approach and let-down procedures.

Flying individually the Dakotas took off from Mather Field on January 24 and set course for Honolulu, arriving there the following day after a flight of seventeen hours. Leaving Honolulu on January 28 and flying via Christmas Island, Canton Island, Fiji, Auckland in New Zealand, the squadron arrived at Mascot Airport, Sydney, on February 4 where they were accommodated by the Royal Australian Air Force at Bradfield Park for the night.

No 243 left Mascot the following day and flew to Amberley airfield, near Brisbane in Queensland, where it became a lodger unit pending the allocation of a permanent base. Since leaving Montreal the ferry delivery flight had taken eighty flying hours. During its stay at Amberley the Dakotas were serviced and the overload fuel tanks removed.

On February 9 the unit moved to its final destination, the Royal Australian Air Force station at Camden in New South Wales. The station commander was Wg Cdr Newstead, RAAF. Here it was joined by the rest of the unit who had travelled by sea, which included seven aircrews as well as other personnel, making the total strength up to twenty-three aircrews including the squadron commander.

Having settled in, three Dakotas were despatched on February 12 captained by the squadron and two Flight commanders respectively, on a survey flight covering the areas in which it was to operate in the future. These included Queensland, the New Guinea area, and Leyte in the Philippines. The longest of these routes took some thirty hours flying. Regular flights started, consisting mainly of interstate work, with occasional flights to the Pacific Islands and Leyte. Two Dakotas were despatched to Madang, New Guinea, on February 19 with important equipment for No 15 Squadron RAAF which had been posted from Camden, and on February 25 two aircraft were despatched to Auckland, New Zealand, to transport forty Royal New Zealand Navy personnel from there to Sydney.

Since the squadron had become established at Camden on February 9, 1945, it had done a considerable amount of transport work, during which time the crews had become familiar with the peculiar conditions existing in the South-West Pacific Area – the difficult landing strips in New Guinea and other islands, the characteristic weather over New Guinea and the Coral Sea, and the lack of many of the facilities which in Europe ensured safety in navigation and in flight. By this time two services had been inaugurated and the squadron strength was increased by one more Dakota, making sixteen in all.

Back in the United Kingdom, preparations were being made for the organisation and training of the rear echelon of No 243 Squadron. On November 25, 1944, ex-Bomber and Training Command aircrews reported to the newly opened Transport Command airfield at Stoney Cross in Hampshire. Personnel awaited allocation to complete crews, for, unlike the original echelon of No 243 Squadron, the personnel were mainly Australians from many varied squadrons and units. Under the direction of the Transport Command Mobile Training Unit personnel commenced training for transport duties on Dakota aircraft.

No 232 Squadron was formed on January 3, 1945, with the intention of operating to and from India, but was divided the following day into No 1315 Flight and the rear echelon of No 243 Squadron, the latter being commanded by Sq Ldr Warren, DFC. This rear echelon would ultimately join the original echelon of No 243 which by this time was already on its way to Australia. The rear echelon comprised twenty-two complete aircrews, but no co-pilots.

Training was completed by January 6 and the squadron moved to the airfield at Merryfield in Somerset to carry out flying conversion on the Dakota transport. Flying exercises were completed eleven days later, and included both day and night flying, plus further lectures on American equipment, etc from the Mobile Training Unit. On January 25 the inoculation and kitting-out parades commenced.

Leave of absence was granted until February 3 when all personnel were to report to Morecambe, Lancashire, however instructions were received to the effect that the rear echelon aircrews were to be all Australians if it could be arranged, this meant that a reallocation of crews took place and some were transferred to the newly formed No 238 Squadron, also equipping with Dakotas, and who was to join No 300 Group at a later date in Australia. The strength of No 243 Squadron rear echelon was now twenty-four crews.

The aircrews on leave were recalled to Merryfield on January 28 for re-allocation of crews, and the date of the movement to Morecambe was indefinite, as priority of movement was given to No 238 Squadron and this unit was given full use of the Dakota aircraft for training until February 15.

An extra seven days leave was granted to all aircrews who returned on February 13 to be given a new departure date from the United Kingdom of March 7. This enabled intensive flying training to take place which consisted of four or five cross-country flights, with Beam and Radio Range flying, also practice in Astro navigation whilst Link Trainer practice was included on the ground.

After a further amendment the rear echelon of No 243 reported to Morecambe on March 9 from where it left by train for Greenock and embarked on the *Queen Elizabeth* on March 13 which was bound for New York. After berthing at New York six days later, the personnel proceeded by train to Montreal, Canada, finally arriving at the reception depot on March 20.

Flying and technical training was carried out at Dorval, similar to that which the original part of the squadron had experienced about three months earlier, and this was divided into two sections – (a) Crews who were to ferry the Dakotas to Australia, and (b) Crews who were to be flown out as passengers with the former crews.

Leaving Dorval on April 4, 1945, the squadron flew to Sacramento, California, stopping overnight at Elizabeth City in North Carolina and Dallas, Texas, arriving at Mather Field, Sacramento, two days later. After a rest of four days which included the usual briefings, etc by the US Army Air Force, they flew via Honolulu, Canton Island, Nandi in Fiji, Whenupai at Auckland, New Zealand, and finally arrived at the Royal Australian Air Force station at Camden on April 15 after an excellent flight across the Pacific Ocean, with neither casualties or accidents, and the average time taken for the Pacific crossing was seventy-six hours.

On March 5 nine aircraft of the advanced echelon now settled in at Camden, were temporarily based on Menangle landing strip, some ten miles away, whilst the Camden runway was being resurfaced, and the approaches to the runway cleared of prominent trees. This airfield construction work was completed by March 9. It was decided on March 14 to send Liaison Officers to Garbutt airfield, Townsville, and to Momote airfield on Manus Island, in the hope that the inefficiency and confusion which was so apparent at these bases could be reduced. These Liaison Officers were to co-ordinate the demands of the Royal Navy and the various Australian forces with the Officer Commanding Flying at Camden, and with Operations No 300 Wing. This arrangement was quickly appreciated by visiting aircrews, particularly in so far as overnight accommodation was concerned.

A regular scheduled service to Guildford airfield, Perth, was inaugurated on March 16. Stops were made at Essendon Airport, Melbourne, and at Parafield airfield, Adelaide, where the aircraft made a night stop, and at Forrest. During March there was an increase in the weekly number of schedules to Melbourne and Manus Island, together with additional services to Perth and Leyte. Many of the difficulties encountered on these services, particularly the northern one, were surmounted after the arrival of the Liaison Officers who were to stay for an indefinite period of time. Further efficiency was gained when the Royal Navy set up an office and a Movement Officer at Mascot Airport, thus facilitating the loading and despatch of aircraft.

Also during March, seventeen new Dakota aircraft arrived from No 45 Group in Canada, making the squadron strength up to thirty-three aircraft, with twenty-four aircrew units. On March 20, during the ferrying process of these new aircraft, it was reported that Dakota Mk IV KN343, piloted by Plt Off F Carnell, had ditched in the Coral Sea between Port Moresby and Townsville. It was later revealed that the aircraft had been experiencing engine trouble due to lack of oil pressure when flying to Townsville at 9,000 feet. The engine had to be stopped and the propeller feathered. The Dakota was turned around and headed back to Port Moresby, slowly losing height. At 8,000 feet the pilot decided to ditch the aircraft, believing he could not reach land, the nearest being 150 miles distant. All kit was jettisoned and the twenty-four passengers were instructed on the procedure to be adopted, but while the aircraft was losing height, the other engine developed the same trouble and was eventually stopped also, and the aircraft was brought down on the sea, about 120 miles south of Port Moresby. The passengers and crew embarked on the three dinghies, however, twenty-eight persons proved too much for these and some of the passengers had to remain in the sea until relief arrived.

After they had been drifting for just over one and a half hours, a Royal Australian Air Force Short Sunderland flying-boat appeared overhead, but was unable to land because of a heavy swell. Shortly afterwards one of the squadron Dakotas – KN240 – also arrived. These two aircraft dropped seven inflatable dinghies, four of which were secured by the mariners. During the afternoon another of the units Dakotas arrived on the scene and stood watch until a US Army Air Force Liberator showed up during the early evening. The Liberator, after dropping two dinghies, which were not secured, continued on its flight. By nightfall all aircraft lost contact with the dinghies and the watch was abandoned.

Early next day, March 21, a RAAF Sunderland appeared and directed a rescue launch to the scene and all passengers and crew were taken aboard, after having endured life afloat in overcrowded rubber dinghies for over twenty hours. This, however, was not the last of their ordeal, because it was found that the small rescue launch, which was a seaplane tender, could not safely carry its new load. It leaked badly and shipped water over the gunwales, so arrangements were made to transfer most of the passengers and crew to another vessel out of Port Moresby. The transfer was satisfactorily completed and Port Moresby was finally reached before noon, some twenty-three hours after ditching. The crew and passengers were accommodated by the Royal Australian Navy, whose guests they remained for several days. Plt Off F Carnell was later awarded the Air Force Cross, in recognition of his handling of the situation.

Regular scheduled air transport services were inaugurated from Mascot Airport, Sydney, to Tacloban airstrip at Leyte on March 20. Intermediate stops for loading and refuelling were made at Archerfield, Brisbane; Garbutt airfield, Townsville, which was a night stop; Milne Bay in New Guinea; Momote airstrip on Manus Island also a night stop; Sorido airfield on Biak Island; this being later abandoned in favour of Mokmar; Pelelieu Island in the Palan Group for a further night stop. On reaching Tacloban the Dakotas were immediately turned around and despatched as soon as possible so as to avoid congestion on this very busy airstrip. The round flight took seven days, and involved sixty hours of flying.

A special flight was despatched to Perth on April 7 for the purpose of carrying a spare engine for the Governor General's Avro York MW140 "*Endeavour*" which was unserviceable.

With the arrival of the rear echelon in April with its thirteen Dakota Mk IV aircraft and twenty-four aircrews, the squadron strength amounted to a total of forty-seven aircrews.

On April 16 two special VIP Dakota Mk IV aircraft were delivered to the squadron by No 1315 Flight crews. This was followed on April 21 by two more VIP Dakotas. Two of the aircraft were flown to the condemned Narranderra air station in New South Wales, to be used as pantechnicons for transporting any useful furniture that willing hands could secure. In all several trips were made by these two aircraft before the "sack" of Narranderra was completed to the vast improvement of accommodation at Camden.

Special flights for VIPs included one on April 25 for Lt Gen CH Gairdner, CB CBE,* British Army, so that he could visit Melbourne, Canberra and Sydney. After his tour the General and his staff were flown to Manila. Three days later Gp Capt Anderson, DFC AFC, who was going to inspect the staging posts on the route of the normal scheduled service to Leyte, possibly with a view to extending the service, was despatched by VIP Dakota to Manila. One of the VIP Dakotas was put at the disposal of Rear-Admiral Fisher, CB CBE, Rear-Admiral Training, Fleet Air Arm, for an indefinite period commencing on the first day of June. This was for the purpose of visiting the various training centres at Brisbane, Sydney and Melbourne. On the same day eleven aircraft were sent to the Fleet Air Arm station at Schofields to airlift personnel and equipment to Maryborough airfield. Two lifts of 5,000 lb were required of each aircraft.

The month of June proved to be particularly wet and, as a result of widespread flooding, the airfield at Camden was closed to air traffic for three days. All aircraft which were away when the airfield was closed were diverted to Mascot Airport, where they based pending the reopening of Camden.

Wg Cdr WJ McLean, DFC AFC, arrived from Burma on July 1 to take over command of No 243 Squadron from Wg Cdr TW Gillen. Wg Cdr McLean came from No 117 Squadron which was engaged in close support work in Burma with its Dakota transports. Wg Cdr Gillen was to take up duties in India.

Nine Dakotas were detailed to carry out a special flight for the Royal Navy – five aircraft were employed from No 238 Squadron and four from No 1315 Flight. No 243 Squadron were responsible for the briefing. Bad news was received on July 25, when it learned by signal, that Dakota Mk IV KN530 had crashed into the sea, south of Tachloban. The aircraft had exploded on impact and there were no survivors.

The following day the C-in-C British Pacific Fleet, Admiral Sir Bruce Fraser, accompanied by Grp Cpt Gaskell, Liaison Officer with the Fleet, was conducted on a tour of the station by Grp Cpt Anderson and Wg Cdr McLean.

Throughout August 1945, the work of the squadron was still primarily in the transport role, carrying mail, freight and passengers in support of the British Pacific Fleet, which was operating in the Pacific theatre. During the month sixty-two training flights were carried out, including fifty-one

* Prime Minister's and Supreme Allied Commander's representative with Generalissimo Chiang Kai-Shek.

by day and eleven by night. One crew was attached to No. 7 Operational Training Unit at Tocumwal for a Liberator conversion course. On August 22 the Air Officer Commanding No 300 Group at Melbourne, Air Cdre A Earle, visited the squadron on inspection.

The highlight of the month was the visit of the Air Officer Commanding-in-Chief of Transport Command, Air Marshal Sir Ralph Cochrane, KBE CB AFC. He showed considerable interest in the Flights and was particularly interested in the aircrew detail boards.

Hours flown during August were 3,690, the distance flown was 453,856 miles, passengers carried 6,333, mail carried 856,512 lb and freight carried 840,233 lb. By the first day of September, the scheduled flights had been reduced to one per day, carrying through to Hong Kong, however, there was an increase in the number of special flights, and these kept the squadron fully occupied. Special flights were organised to carry Red Cross supplies for ex-prisoners of war, and on one occasion the unit carried ex-prisoners, now released.

On September 14 news was received that Dakota Mk IV KN348 carrying the radio call-sign VM-YAU, pilot Flt Lt Shanley, DFC, had made a successful ditching in the sea at position 19′ 47″ N 118° E. The survivors spent twenty-four hours in their dinghies before being rescued by a Royal Navy destroyer. During their immersion they were sighted by a squadron Dakota – KN350 VM-YBD – which dropped a dinghy and circled the survivors until it was relieved by a Consolidated Catalina flying boat. All mail and freight was lost, but the crew of four and two passengers were uninjured.

The squadron's work estimate for September included the following: 1,904 hours flown, 268,158 nautical miles flown, 4,259 passengers carried, 434,581 lb of mail carried and 347,145 lb of freight.

Pending the move of No 300 Group, plus possibly some of the Camden aircraft and personnel, to Hong Kong, Sq Ldr C. Warren, DFC, carried out a survey of the airfield facilities in that area. Numerous special flights were performed during October, including the carriage of medical supplies, conveyance of urgently required jeeps and the uplifting of ex-POWs at Parafield. With World War 2 over personnel were being prepared for demobilisation, and up to the end of December 1945 over 200 airmen left the station. New scheduled flights for No 243 Squadron were introduced during January 1946. The daily Hong Kong schedule was reduced to three a week, on Mondays, Wednesdays and Fridays. In addition No 243 took over the Singapore schedule flights on Tuesdays and Saturdays, also the Manus run every Wednesday and the Melbourne run on Mondays, Wednesdays and Fridays.

No 1315 Flight seemed to be doing most of the special flights, and No 238 Squadron was virtually broken up, the majority of the crews and some of the aircraft were transferred to No 243 Squadron. No 238 was disbanded on February 8, 1946. The popular supposition that No 243 Squadron would ultimately be posted to Tokio was exploded by information that the schedule flights would terminate about the end of March, and the squadron would disband. The personnel would either go to Air Command South East Asia or return home. When instructions were received for disbanding the squadron, five Dakotas with spares and ground equipment for three months, were flown to Hong Kong to be stationed with No 300 Wing headquarters. These were processed during February. By the end of the month personnel were preparing to clear the station at Camden, and a total of fourteen Dakota Mk IV aircraft were flown to No 389 Maintenance Unit at Singapore for storage and subsequent disposal. Other Dakota transports were flown back to the United Kingdom, an example being Dakota Mk IV KN364 which departed Camden on March 23, 1946, and arriving at St Mawgan in Cornwall eight days later with total ferry flight time of 77 hrs 45 mins. The aircraft was later flown to Blakehill Farm near Cirencester in Gloucestershire.

No 238 Squadron had moved from Comilla, Bengal, with its Dakotas during June 1945, routeing via Ratmalana, Ceylon; Cocos Island in the Indian Ocean; Learmouth, West Australia; Guildford, near Perth, and finally to its new base at Parafield, near Adelaide, in South Australia. A total of thirty Dakotas were involved, three per day being ferried until the move was complete. The Commanding Officer of No 238 Squadron was Wg Cdr H Burton, DSO MBE, who today is Air Officer, Commanding-in-Chief of Royal Air Force Air Support Command.

The Transport Command bases in use with No 300 Group were given staging post numbers. No 189 Guilford, near Perth; No 190 Learmouth, West Australia; No 191 Parafield, Adelaide; No 192 Essendon Airport, Melbourne; No 193 Townsville (Garbutt airfield); No 194 Archerfield, Brisbane; No 195 Tacloban, Leyte in the Philippines; No 196 Palam; No 197 Sorido; No 198 Mamote, Los Negros Island in the Admiralty group; and No 199 Gurney.

No 300 Wing was originally formed at Camden on December 17, 1944, and became No 300 Group on April 24, 1945. It reverted back to Wing status on March 1, 1946, and was finally disbanded at Kowloon, Hong Kong, on April 30, 1946. In the House of Commons during March 1946 the Under Secretary for Air, John Strachey, made a statement to the effect that 40 per cent of the entire manpower of the Royal Air Force was engaged in long distance carriage of men and freight. During World War 2 Royal Air Force Transport Command, although tardy in admitting it, was the flag carrier for British civil aviation.

CHAPTER FIVE

Maple Leaf and Speedbird

ROYAL CANADIAN AIR FORCE DAKOTAS

The Douglas Dakota first went into regular service with the Royal Canadian Air Force on March, 29, 1943, when aircraft No 650 was delivered to No 12 Communications Squadron at Rockcliffe. This aircraft had the Douglas constructors number 9015 and the US Army Air Force serial 42-32789. In April this aircraft went to No 164 Squadron at Moncton, New Brunswick. Dakotas were flown by that unit alongside Lockheed Lodestars until October 1945 when the latter type was retired. On the first day of August 1946 No 164 was renumbered No 435 Squadron, a unit which had flown Dakotas during World War 2 in Air Command South East Asia.

Other RCAF units using the Dakota were No 12 Squadron, which was redesignated No 412 Squadron on April 1, 1947. No 165 Squadron at Sea Island, near Vancouver, which was formed in June 1943 with the Dakota and flew them alongside Lodestars until disbanded on October 31, 1945. No 168 Squadron was based at Rockcliffe for the purpose of flying mail overseas in Boeing Flying Fortress and Consolidated Liberator aircraft with Dakota detachments in England, France and North Africa for onward transport of the vital mail.

As the war progressed, an ever increasing number was taken on strength and units were formed which flew them exclusively. No fewer than 131 of the 200-odd Dakotas used by the Royal Canadian Air Force were ex-RAF, retaining their original serials in most cases. For eight months during World War 2 RCAF Dakotas flew over the Burma "Hump" with Nos 435 "Chinthe" and 436 "The Flying Elephants" Squadrons, while No 437 Squadron was formed on September 14, 1944, at Blakehill Farm near Cirencester in Gloucestershire. It took part in the Arnhem operation towing gliders and dropping supplies.

In the post-war era, Dakotas have carried paratroops, towed troop-laden gliders for the airborne forces school in Rivers, Manitoba, air-lifted passengers and freight, served as air ambulances, navigation trainers and undertaken SAR (Search and Rescue) duties. They have also made good platforms for photo surveys. Equipped with ski-wheel landing gear Dakotas of the RCAF Air Transport Command have been employed as cargo carriers into snow and ice-covered areas along the Mid-Canada Line, the early warning network which roughly follows the fifty-fifth parallel.

Dakotas of Nos 413 and 414 Squadrons assisted in supporting aerial mapping detachments between 1947 and 1950, with the aircraft of No 414 Squadron involved in vertical photography. No 408 "Goose" Squadron was reformed at Rockcliffe with Dakotas in January 1946 and along with Avro Lancaster MR Mk X aircraft was involved in a huge photographic survey.

Riding the flood of World War 2 with its technological spring thaw, the Cabinet Defence Committee in 1947 abandoned the disjointed forays of pre-war mapping for an ambitious long-range programme: map of all Canada at 1: 250,000 scale (about four miles to the inch) in twenty years.

The programme entailed a complete photo survey of Canada, a Shoran-fixed net of control points in the inaccessible north, a denser polkadot of control points fixed by survey parties, and a finished product of 925 gaily coloured maps depicting at a reasonable scale for the first time the uncharted country of Canada – almost 4 million square miles. In 1947, a map of 425 square miles required just under 200,000 man hours of flying, surveying, plotting and drafting. The same map requires about 100,000 man hours today.

This mammoth programme was assigned to the Canadian Armed Forces and the – then – Department of Mines and Resources. It was to be one of the armed forces' major peacetime projects. Over the twenty-year programme, the Royal Canadian Air Force, mainly No 408 Squadron with its Dakotas, flew about 75 per cent of the aerial photography, stretched a Shoran net across the entire country in nine years, and supported the Army Survey Establishment which did about one-third of the total map-making, including a survey of the entire Western Arctic.

Shoran is simply a way to measure distance between widely spaced points using aircraft and electronic pulses. Knowing the position of two points, the ground and air crews can establish the position of a third; then using the last established point, establish a fourth, and so on, slowly extending the net of datum points.

The catch is that each point is a Shoran station, with 13–18 men needing supplies for at least a month plus mail and ration runs every week, and each line between two points has to be flown sixteen times for the ideal accuracy.

Aircraft used in the programme used and operated out of such "glamorous" bases as Frobisher Bay, Yellowknife, Whitehorse, Goose Bay, Churchill and Thule. About 230 air force technicians and ground crew, were lifted as close as possible to their hilltop Shoran sites by Consolidated Cansos and other amphibious types. Then from the nearest point on the lakeshore, the techs, cook, and statisticians, bolstered by the Cansos aircrew, lugged the Shoran components on their back to the summit, and there they remained like bearded eagles for the summer.

While the RCAF staked out northern Canada in broad patterns, army ground parties inched their way around unmapped areas, establishing accurate perimeters, which were filled in by aerial photography. Over the entire programme, No 408 Squadron photographed three and a half million square miles of Canadian territory in 31,000 hours flying time. By the end of 1967 the mapping of Canada, to the NATO standard scale 1: 250,000 was complete. About one-third of Canada has now been mapped at the most useful military scale of 1: 50,000. The rest will take many years.

Until supplemented by the Douglas C-54M North Star four-engined transport, Fairchild C-119 Boxcars, and later Lockheed C-130 Hercules, Dakotas were responsible for carrying supplies, mail, and personnel to northern sites. The principal operators of this veteran transport were Nos 426, 435 and 436 Squadrons. Wing Commander JG Roberts, DFC DFM, went to Canada at the end of 1946 on an exchange posting to the RCAF and spent 1947 with No 435 Squadron based at Edmonton, Alberta. Duties included a daily scheduled flight up the North West highway with stops at Grand Prairie, Fort St John, Fort Nelson, Watson Lake and Whitehorse in the Yukon which was a night stop. Twice a week a scheduled service went the other way to Winnipeg, stopping at Calgary and Regina. Various special flights were flown all over the North West territories to places like Fort Norman, Norman Wells, Yellowknife, Port Radium on Great Bear Lake, Churchill, Coral Harbour, Southampton Island and to Cambridge Bay on Victoria Island where a landing was made with a Dakota on sea ice. Two other places visited were Snag and Aishihik between Whitehorse and the Alaskan border. The winter of 1946–47 was a very cold one and 82 degrees below zero Fahrenheit was recorded at Snag. A Dakota was flown into Watson Lake airstrip at 50 degrees below zero. Aircraft used were Dakota Mk IIIs 960, 964, 963, 968, 974, 655 and 659. Dakota Mk IVs 976, 990.

Dakota Mk III 964, which landed on the sea ice at Cambridge Bay, took off from Churchill in blowing snow when the pilot discovered the undercarriage pins were still in; he could not land again due to visibility being nil, so continued to Edmonton, lost an engine on the way, made a "Mayday" distress call and was guided to Le Pas which was reached after dark. The transport overshot the runway on attempting to land, tipped on its nose, resulting in one of the engine mountings breaking.

The following year, 1948, was spent with No 146 Squadron based at Montreal whose Dakotas were responsible for the other section of the trans-Canada scheduled runs. Stops were made at Ottawa, Winnipeg,

Monkton, Halifax and Goose Bay, with special flights to places like Frobisher – Baffin Island. At this time the unit was re-equipping with the North Star aircraft. Dakota Mk IIIs used included 658, 664 and 965.

Some of the operations in which the Dakota was involved include *Operation Beetle* – this was to provide a supply of base equipment for a weather station at Cambridge Bay, Victoria Island, which was located at 69° N 105° W. Three Dakotas and a Noorduyn Norseman on skis took part. The first stop was Yellowknife on the Great Slave Lake were it was usual in winter to maintain a strip of rolled snow on the lakes ice which was estimated to be seven or eight feet thick. This was a refuelling stop and the next landing was made on an *ad hoc* strip of rolled snow alongside the uranium mine at Port Radium on the Great Bear Lake. The temperature in the morning was 20 degrees below zero F and it took an hour to get the Twin Wasp engines up to starting temperature using ground heaters. The leg to Cambridge Bay had to be flown using gyro and astro compass because of the weak magnetic field in these parts. A strip had been laid out on the sea ice in Cambridge Bay, but the runway turned out to be bare ice with snow drifts across it, this giving the undercarriage a pummeling on landing. This operation took part on April 5, 6, 7, 1947, and one of the three Dakotas which took part was 964. *Operation Sandbag* involved flying men and materials to areas of British Columbia threatened by floods in June 1948. *Exercise Flyrite* was a paratroop dropping exercise held in 1950, whilst *Exercise Sweetbriar* was a similar joint air and ground defence operation.

From 1946 to 1966 RCAF Dakotas amassed a total of close to one million miles in the air, and the aircraft still on inventory, estimated at some seventy-five, are adding a respectable 62,000 flying hours annually. As a tribute to the type, a Mk IV Dakota – KN451 – was retired and placed in the RCAF Museum. On November 1, 1945, No 437 Squadron arrived at Odiham in Hampshire, being joined on April 4, 1946, by No 436 Squadron. No 437 Squadron was disbanded on the station on June 15, 1946, and No 436 had in the meantime flown out to Down Ampney in Gloucestershire, also to be disbanded. Both units later reformed in Canada.

The Dakota has been a workhorse for the United Nations, and has been in service with UN missions in Indonesia, Greece, Palestine, India, Pakistan, in the Gaza Strip and Sinai Desert and in the Congo, not to mention the Lebanon. All these missions have used at least one aircraft – the Congo mission had ten in service at one time. In all cases the aircraft has carried passengers and freight and has also done duties as an ambulance and observation aircraft. The Royal Canadian Air Force, United States Air Force and Italian Air Force and other countries provided the aircraft and crews to the United Nations, but the majority of the Dakotas came from the RCAF.

No 115 Air Transport Unit – UN – is based at El Arish, Egypt, and on June 17, 1958, a Dakota Mk IV – KN666 – was forced by United Arab Republic MiG-15 jets to land at Abu Suer, allegedly for not flying the established air corridor. Other Dakotas used by No 115 ATU were Mk IVs 656, 989, 563 and 511. In July 1964, the Dakotas were replaced by the RCAF de Havilland (Canada) Caribou with several of the UN Missions.

Up to 1958 the Royal Air Force were training navigators with the RCAF at No 2 Air Observer School equipped with Dakotas. Today the Canadian Armed Forces – all aircraft were consolidated in a single inventory under the Canadian Armed Forces on February 1, 1968 – Air Navigation School based at Winnipeg still has twenty-two of these Douglas transports on strength. This unit received national recognition during 1969 for its superb flight safety record covering five years of accident-free flying, involving over 85,000 hours in the air.

The school headed by Lt Col HL Broughton, has the task of training all navigators and observers for the service. Flying the fleet of Dakotas, known more familiarly as Gooney Birds, are some sixty odd pilots headed by Maj TE Scanlon, whose log-book records 8,300 accident free hours. Two veteran transports are based at the school, including the oldest Dakota in service with the CAF No 651 which came into service in April 1943, and, with more than 16,500 hours in its log up to May 1966, is still working hard. The other veteran is a Mk IV KN201, which was one of the first RCAF Dakotas to fly over the Burma Hump during World War 2. Both these aircraft are employed in the schools flying programme which involves flying in excess of 1,200 hours per month.

But flying student navigators on exercises doesn't take up all the unit's time. The Red Cross may need an airlift to set up a blood donor clinic in a northern community; the Lieutenant-Governor of Manitoba or the Commander of Training Command may want to go up to Forth Churchill; or the Rescue Co-ordination Centre may request an aircraft to assist on a search. There may even be a request to airlift canoes or other equipment for use in an exercise.

In 1969 the Air Navigation School Dakotas ranged from Hall Beach on the DEW Line to Texas, and to innumerable Canadian communities. And each year the ANS Flying Squadron contributes aircraft to give air cadets familiarisation flights at points from Lakehead to Vancouver.

The young pilots arrive after taking eighty hours of instruction at the Operational Training Unit at Trenton. As a first officer the young pilots then fly navigation details and long-range trips for experience. Then, after amassing 1,000 flying hours, 500 of them on Dakotas, the young pilots get an opportunity to become aircraft captains. After more experience they become eligible for a long-range captaincy and, after four such trips, and a flawless test ride, they are checked again and qualified to fly over the Rockies. During 1969 the Royal Air Force was represented at the Canadian Armed Forces Air Navigation School by Flt Lt RE Williams, on an exchange agreement.

The major airlines in Canada have replaced their DC-3s with more modern aircraft, and although the Dakota is still rendering yeoman service with the CAF, their demise is only a matter of time.

BRITISH OVERSEAS AIRWAYS CORPORATION

Early in 1941 the Government's attention was drawn to the sad state of the British Overseas Airways Corporation aircraft fleet. This consisted of a motley collection of pre-war British and American aircraft that were inherited from British and Imperial Airways, plus five Douglas DC-3-G102s of KLM which escaped when Holland was overrun during May 1940, along with their crews.

At this time everything was being concentrated on the war effort, so, except for three Boeing 314 flying boats, acquired from Pan American Airways, BOAC soldiered on for another year. On December 17, 1942, a British Member of Parliament, Mr WD Perkins, again drew the House of Commons attention to the plight of BOAC and the inability of its fleet to keep up the demands made of it. This time the Government acted and, through the Lend-Lease scheme, BOAC acquired, together with other aircraft, a number of Douglas Long Beach built C-47-DL Dakota Mk Is which were delivered between February and April 1943. Fitted with strengthened floors, large double freight doors, and bench seats for twenty-seven passengers along the cabin sides, the first six aircraft, which were powered by two 1,200 hp Pratt & Whitney GR-1830-S1C3-G engines, were delivered with military serials, acquiring civil markings on registration.

Although these were the first Dakotas delivered to BOAC, way back in July 1942 a certain Douglas C-49H-DO was briefly registered to BOAC as G-AGEN. This aircraft had started life as a Douglas DC-3-G102A-277D, with constructors number 4118 and built at Santa Monica during 1941. It was delivered to American Airlines as NC33655 on May 5, 1941, thence to Pan American Airways in Africa on July 9, 1941, finally becoming a C-49H serial 42-38251 with the United States Air Transport Command on March 14, 1942. During July 1942 the British Purchasing Commission acquired it for the RAF but on arrival at the Air Reinforcement Centre at Karachi the application for the transport to go to BOAC had been cancelled so it never became G-AGEN, but became MA943 on August 1, 1942, and was delivered to No 31 Squadron eight days later.

Later in 1943 the C-47 Dakota Mk Is were subject to a compulsory modification that changed their 12-volt electrical system to 24-volt, thus bringing them up to C-47A Dakota Mk III standard. A total of thirty

Dakota Mk IIIs were supplied to BOAC between April 1943 and July 1944.

Three Dakota Mk IIIs were diverted to expatriate KLM to replace three DC-3s that had been lost. G-AGBB was shot down over the Bay of Biscay on June 1, 1943; G-AGBC crash-landed in bad visibility at Heston aerodrome on September 21, 1940, and G-AGBI was destroyed by enemy bombing at Whitchurch aerodrome on November 24, 1940. The replacements were C-47A-1-DKs FL589 (G-AGJR), FZ618 (G-AGJS) and FZ617 (G-AGJT) delivered between January and May 1944, and named respectively "Roodborstje", "Spreeun" and "Turelzuur". During January 1946 they were reregistered in Holland as PH-TAY, PH-TAZ and PH-TBA.

Following the C-47A Dakota Mk III came the C-47B Dakota Mk IV powered by Pratt & Whitney GR-1830-S3C4-G engines, twenty-three being supplied between August 1944 and January 1945. These had lengthened carburettor air intakes containing tropical filters, thermostatically operated oil cooler shutters, and a modified hydraulic system whereby a small jack replaced the bunjee cord assistor on the undercarriage lock-up gear. By the end of hostilities BOAC had accepted fifty-nine Dakotas, delivery of the majority being by way of the North Atlantic ferry route under No 45 Group. Most went direct to BOAC but others spent short periods with RAF units beforehand.

BOACs main United Kingdom wartime base was at Whitchurch near Bristol, but from November 1, 1944, operations moved to Hurn, retaining Whitchurch as the maintenance base. Subsidiary bases were at Croydon, Lyneham, Leuchars and, as the war progressed in the Allies favour, Cairo. All aircraft were delivered in a dark green and earth camouflage on all upper surfaces. Some were black underneath and others natural metal. Following the total loss by enemy interception of KLM DC-3 G-AGBB "*Ibis*" on June 1, 1943 – the famous actor Leslie Howard was a passenger – all aircraft were painted black underneath, as crossing of the Bay of Biscay was only permitted during the hours of darkness. Civil registrations were black outlined in silver on the upper wing surface and fuselage side, but either white or black under the wings depending on the finish. Red, white and blue stripes appeared beneath the letters on the fuselage and under the wings, with red and blue stripes under the upper wing registration. Initially a large Union Jack appeared on the nose, but this was later replaced by a large BOAC "*Speedbird*" device, outlined in silver. When flights were made on behalf of RAF Transport Command, aircraft carried military serials instead of civil registrations. Most of the fleet changed guise many times, and even the crews had two sets of uniform. At the end of 1944, additional markings appeared alongside the RAF serial numbers. These were Transport Command four or five letter wireless telegraphy (W/T) call-sign codes in white on the fuselage side, an example being

C-47A-25-DL Dakota Mk III G-AGHK FD860 "ODZHK". The changing of military and civil markings continued until March 1946.

Initial and all subsequent Certificate of Airworthiness (C of A) overhauls were carried out by the BOAC Inspection Unit at Croydon, other maintenance being carried out at Whitchurch, which continued to be used when the British European Airways Division began services from Northolt after the end of World War 2, and during the initial use of Heathrow.

BOAC Dakotas were first introduced in service on the Whitchurch to Lisbon route on May 11, 1943. This replaced the KLM DC-3 service and operated four times a week. During 1943, Dakotas appeared on services to Gibraltar, Madrid, Takoradi and Cairo. On November 20 a Whitchurch to Algiers service was begun, routing via St Mawgan and Gibraltar outbound, and Rabat and Gibraltar on return. Aircraft had RAF markings and crews wore RAF Reserve uniforms. Also during 1943 Leuchars-based Dakotas operated the Stockholm ball-bearing runs, but were replaced by de Havilland Mosquito aircraft as the Dakotas posed a dangerously slow moving target for night-fighters and flak. A longer but safer route via the Norwegian-Swedish border was abandoned as it proved too much a strain on both aircraft and crews. Dakotas were reintroduced on September 1, 1944, when the route once more proved safer for the slow-flying transports. On April 16, 1944, BOAC took over the responsibility from RAF Transport Command of the Whitchurch to Lagos service, routing via St Mawgan, Lisbon, Rabat, Fort Etienne or Dakar, Bathurst, Freetown – occasionally Abidjan – Takoradi and Accra. This was known as Route 23W/24W. The Whitchurch to Algiers service was extended to Cairo via Tripoli on June 27, 1944. Algiers was omitted from October and St Mawgan when the operations transferred to Hurn during November. Also during 1944 BOAC was operating a service from Cairo across Africa to Accra via Wadi Halfa, Khartoum, El Fasher, El Geneina, Maiduguri, Kano and Lagos. This was known as Route 25T/26T, and connected with the Whitchurch, later Hurn, to Accra service. The flight from the United Kingdom to Egypt taking normally five to six days.

As a basis for future postwar airline operations, No 110 Wing and No 46 Group RAF Transport Command, commenced daily Croydon to Paris, Brussels and Lyons services on September 21, 1944. The aircraft used were Dakotas from No 147 Squadron. Subsequently the Lyons service was extended to Marseilles and Naples, and new services commenced to Athens, Prague, Warsaw, Copenhagen and Oslo.

The first Cairo, Lydda, Damascus, Baghdad, Basra service was operated by Dakota G-AGHK on February 18, 1945, Dakotas being used until the end of April. On the Leuchars to Stockholm service, due to the short period of darkness in the summer at Northern latitudes, Dakotas were again withdrawn from regular operations on April 11, 1945.

By the end of hostilities in Europe, on May 8, 1945, of the fifty-nine Dakotas BOAC had acquired, no fewer than fifty-five survived the war – an excellent record gained under arduous conditions. The unlucky four were – G-AGFZ which overshot the runway at Bromma Airport, Stockholm, on April 21, 1944; G-AGIR which crashed into the base of the Atlas mountains, SSW of Casablanca at Telmest on August 28, 1944. Captain LJ White, three passengers and three crew members were killed; G-AGKM had its undercarriage collapse during take-off from El Adam on April 8, 1945. It was operating as KJ992 "OFZM". G-AGNA crashed at Basra on May 1, 1945.

During the first few months of peace the BOAC services continued to expand. The United Kingdom to West Africa and the West Africa to Cairo services were combined. During May daylight flights from Leuchars to Stockholm commenced. On June 3, 1945, Dakota G-AGMZ operated the first twice-weekly Hurn to Karachi service via Istres, Malta, El Adam, Cairo, Baghdad and Sharjah. Lydda and Basra were added on eastbound flights as from early July. Operations located at Leuchars, moved to Croydon on June 5. BOAC lost their first Dakota in peacetime when G-AGHR, operating as FL514 "ODZS", crashed while taking-off from Luqa, Malta, on October 24. KLM operated the Hurn to Gibraltar service under charter, and as from December 5 this was operated by Dakotas of BOAC.

Wartime restrictions on civil flying were revoked on January 1, 1946, and on that day the British European Airways Division of BOAC was formed to take over the services operated by No 110 Wing of RAF Transport Command. Also on that day, the Croydon to Stockholm service was increased from four to six flights per week. On January 2 BOAC took over the United Kingdom to Lisbon service from KLM which operated five times each week. The United Kingdom to Karachi service was withdrawn on January 24, and on February 4 the newly formed BEA Division took over the Continental services operated by No 110 Wing, moving from Croydon to Northolt in the process. These included flights to Amsterdam, Brussels, Helsinki, Lisbon, Paris and Stockholm. Dakotas carried military markings and the crews wore RAF Reserve uniforms.

It was not until March 4, 1946, that the BEA Division began operating under civil markings, the crews wearing BOAC uniform. On March 11 the BEA Division began a thrice-weekly Northolt to Oslo service, followed by a four-times weekly service to Copenhagen the following day. A weekly Northolt to Marseilles, Rome and Athens service was initiated on March 14.

During 1946 BOAC received a further twenty Dakotas from the RAF to augment the BEA Division at Northolt, before it became the British European Airways Corporation on August 1, 1946. Of these, three went direct to Railway Air Services, three were cannabalised at Speke, Liverpool

– BEACs Maintenance base – and two were returned to the RAF.

As 1946 progressed the civil airlines continued to expand at a rapid rate, not the least of them BOAC. Their Dakota services were continually being developed. A weekly Hurn to Lydda service commenced on April 8, and the following month Channel Island Airways operated BOAC Dakotas under charter. The Rome to Athens run was extended to Nicosia, Beirut, Lydda, Baghdad and Tehran on May 9, Dakotas operating the Athens leg only, night stopping at Rome. During June the United Kingdom to West Africa and Cairo service was terminated due to the withdrawal of meteorological services. However the United Kingdom to Kano sector, via Lisbon, Casablanca, Bathurst and Lagos was resumed at the beginning of July. BOAC commenced operations from Heathrow on May 28, their last service out of Hurn being on June 14. A Heathrow to Beirut Dakota service commenced on July 15.

BOAC Dakota casualties during 1946 included G-AHIY whose undercarriage collapsed on January 23 while landing at El Adam. G-AGHK force-landed at Oviedo, Spain, on April 17 with Captain Price-Stephens plus four crew and nine passengers. One passenger was injured. G-AGKD was wrecked in a gale at Luqa, Malta, on December 23.

Training of aircrew in the early postwar period was carried out at the BOAC Training Headquarters at Aldermaston. This was opened on May 9, 1946, and combined the RAF and BOAC school for four-engine training at Ossington and the twin-engine training unit from Whitchurch. White Waltham was used as the engineering base.

The Dakotas of BOAC were now operating on a civil basis, but mention must be made of two further operations with military significance, in which BOAC with Dakotas took part. In 1947 during *Operation Pakistan*, BOAC and three British independent companies carried 7,000 people from Delhi to Karachi, and about 1,500 in the reverse direction. Food, medicine and vaccine were flown to Delhi and Lahore, BOAC operating twelve Dakotas including G-AGFY, G-AGGB and G-AGHE, alongside their two Avro Yorks and one Avro Lancastrian. The operation commenced on the first day of September and ceased fourteen days later and was under the direction of Air Cdre HG Brackley. During the Berlin Airlift in 1948 BOAC operated three Dakotas – G-AGIZ, G-AGNG and G-AGNK – alongside other civil and military operators from October 20 to November 25. The aircraft, based at Hamburg, carried out eighty-one sorties, flew 224 hours and airlifted 294 tons.

The ubiquitous Dakota was just one of the many aircraft types operated by BOAC during World War 2 and the years that followed. The crews came from far and wide, merchant airmen who did their task without fuss or publicity. It is impossible to be pessimistic of a merchant service which is manned by such as these. They served us well.

CHAPTER SIX

Postwar Operations

VIP DAKOTAS

The US Army Air Corps were naturally interested in the commercial Douglas DC-3 that was being produced for the airlines at Santa Monica in the pre-war years. Government defence expenditure was centred on bombers, fighters and training types, leaving very little for transport aircraft. It is believed that one or two of the civil airline DC-3s were purchased from a special fund for General's aircraft, a possible example being the ex-Eastern Airlines C-49B used by Lt Gen Kruger for travelling between San Antonio, Texas and Lake Charles, Lousiana.

In the Middle East during 1941 the Douglas DC-2Ks in use with Nos 31, 117 and 267 Squadrons often operated as VIP aircraft according to demand and serviceability. On September 12, 1941, DC-2K AX755 of No 267 Squadron was flown from Lydda to Heliopolis by Wg Cdr Lord Forbes with Princess Aly Khan and her party on board. As recorded elsewhere the same aircraft flew the Polish Premier to the USSR with the same pilot, who was by then with No 31 Squadron.

Many long distance flights were recorded with VIPs, amongst them flying General Auchinleck from Delhi to Cairo to take over as Commander in Chief Middle East, with Wg Cdr SB Ubee, Commanding Officer of No 31 Squadron as pilot of the DC-2K aircraft. General Wavell was flown from Cairo to Ambala in a DC-2K to take over as Commander in Chief India with Sq Ldr WH Burbury as pilot. Later "Bill" Burbury was to fly General Wavell and his staff to such places as Tehran, Baghdad and Tiflis, just to name a few.

A Dakota Mk I – HK983 – was built up from spare parts at a Middle East Maintenance unit, and Sir Keith Park used this aircraft on his appointment as Air C-in-C South East Asia Command on February 20, 1945. The aircraft remained in the Far East theatre until April 24, 1947, when it was handed over to an Army salvage unit.

A selection of Dakotas of all Mks were converted for VIP use, and No 24 Squadron throughout its long career with Daks flew a selection of personalities which would put any United Nations organisation to shame. The squadron records show that during World War 2 every day brought at least one important flight, and the names of famous War Ministers, Service chiefs and foreign diplomats follow each other in unending procession as the pages of the operational sheets are turned. This carriage of "Very Important Persons" continued well into the post-war years.

During July 1944 HM King George VI visited the Allied forces in Italy, flying out from Northolt in an Avro York aircraft. Whilst visiting troops near the front he used the personal Dakota Mk III – FZ631 – named *Freedom* belonging to Gen Maitland Wilson.

On June 7, 1945, a Dakota Mk IV – KN386 – piloted by Sq Ldr Hinks from No 24 Squadron, flew from Northolt to the Channel Islands with HM King George VI and Queen Elizabeth. Another Dakota, a Mk III – KG770 – accompanied the party.

When Lord Tedder was Chief of the Air Staff, his personal aircraft was a Dakota Mk IV KJ994 *Dulcie* the pride of "B" Flight No 24 Squadron. Personal Pilot was Sq Ldr JA Gibson, DSO DFC, a New Zealander. It was said to be one of the world's most luxurious aircraft. Its floors were carpeted, its fuselage interior panelled in walnut and lined overhead with cream pigskin. Its soft amber interior lights were built in and had push-button switches for each. Five swivelling armchairs, upholstered in brown leather, two settees which could be converted into bunks for flying at night, and two small cream leather covered stools completed the seating accommodation. A concealed radio set provided soft music – the engines were barely audible in the main cabin – and an altimeter, airspeed indicator and clock over the flight door enabled Lord Tedder to keep a personal check on his movements. A folding table was carried which enabled Sgt Dick Graves, airframe fitter in the crew, who also acted as Air Quartermaster, to serve the meals he cooked in the galley aft. The galley had an electric stove on which Sgt Graves cooked many a meal during the world-wide travels with the Chief of Staff.

Field Marshal Montgomery, during his career used a number of Douglas Dakotas for personal use, the first being exchanged in North Africa for his Boeing B-17E Flying Fortress – 41-9082 – in August 1943 because the airstrips in the Allied advance into Sicily were often unsuitable for the larger aircraft. This Dakota followed the advance into Europe but was destroyed by enemy action when the Field Marshal was on a visit to troops in January 1945. General Eisenhower, who had supplied both the Dakota and the Flying Fortress, immediately replaced the loss with a Douglas C-47B-15-DK 43-48804 – which he had originally intended for himself.

Dakota Mk IV KN628 arrived in the United Kingdom from the USA in July 1945, and was flown to an RAF Maintenance Unit at Courtrai in Belgium to be converted to suit Field Marshal Montgomery's personal requirements. This unit had previously converted Dakotas for Air Chief Marshal Sir Sholto Douglas and Air Marshal Sir Arthur Coningham. In August 1945, KN628 was test flown by Sq Ldr Duncan, personal pilot to the Field Marshal. Its weight – 21,846 lb – was heavier than that of the average Dakota but performance did not suffer as a result. From then on until May 1946 "628" took the Field Marshal and many other notables on numerous historic flights.

The aircraft was one of the showpieces of No 24 Squadron. The Field Marshal designed the interior himself, and in workmanship and finish its cabin was not unlike that of Lord Tedder's aircraft. But it had neither bunks or galley, as Monty rarely slept or took meals in the air, but spent most of the time reading and writing. When he flew over his old battlegrounds his main pleasure was to study the terrain from the aircraft. He would follow his course on a series of maps which he always carried with him, and before take-off the navigator always marked the route on the glass-fronted map case which the Field Marshal kept in front of him. Points of interest and landmarks were indicated by numbers, and when the Dakota passed each one the navigator flashed a numbered green light near the VIP seat. These lights were another of Monty's ideas.

Scottish Aviation at Prestwick Airport was one of the many contractors working on Dakota overhaul and conversion programmes, and they converted many Dakotas to VIP standard. These included two for the Royal Hellenic Air Force – KN542 for HM The King of Greece, and KN575 for General Margartin, the Chief of Staff.

Most theatre commanders had their own Dakotas. Air Marshal Sir Arthur Coningham had a Dakota Mk IV KK209 which had a blue overall finish produced by Cellon the aircraft dope specialists. Air Marshal Sir Charles Medhurst used KN377 in the Middle East which was piloted for most of its long career by Flt Lt Neil McGilvray a South African. This aircraft was furnished in pale blue brocade; it had been specially fitted out for Sir Charles and contained two divan beds and four reclining armchairs. There was also a galley and a cocktail cabinet at the rear end. It was very luxurious. Lady Medhurst very often travelled with the aircraft. Lord Tedder took on charge his first Dakota – a Mk II TJ170 – on May 27, 1944, and the following year this aircraft was transferred to No 24 Squadron for use in the VIP role. General Gairdner used a Dakota Mk IV KP230 in the Far East. Most of these aircraft were modified to the specification of the user.

Depending on the situation or the rank of the VIP, crews were either seconded on request from Dakota squadrons operating in the same theatre, or personal crews were selected for the task.

Early in 1961, two Dakotas were chosen and operated by the Queen's Flight in the Nepalese sector of the Asian tour undertaken by HM Queen Elizabeth and the Duke of Edinburgh. They were considered to be the most suitable and proven type for the conditions involved. Katmandu, which was on the Royal route, was the only airfield in the country with an all-weather runway, 800 yds long, and about 4,000 feet above sea-level.

The two Dakotas employed were KN452 which had been used by the Air Officer Commanding Malta, and KN645 which was used by Viscount Montgomery after the war and which was to be the aircraft selected to be placed in the Royal Air Force Museum at Hendon, to take its pride alongside other veterans. Its last assignment was as a VIP aircraft with the Commander in Chief Allied Forces Northern Europe – AFNE – and based at Fornebu near Oslo.

ALL-WEATHER SERVICE, FIREDOG AND GRAPPLE

The problems of all-weather flying is fundamental to air transport, whether military or civil. Transport Command decided, therefore, in August 1945 to set up an experimental all-weather route between two terminals. Prestwick, Scotland, and Blackbushe in Hampshire were selected. The route of some 400 miles was chosen because it passed through areas notorious for bad weather and poor visibility. The original intention was to study as many as possible of the aids then available for airfield and runway approach. These included Very High Frequency – VHF – and High Frequency – HF – Direction Finding, low power Medium Frequency beacons, Eureka beacons, Blind Approach Beam System – BABS Mk II – and SCS 51 and Ground Control Approach – GCA – radars. In addition to examining radio problems, there were many allied matters to be examined, such as the use of fog dispersal apparatus – FIDO – the effect of severe turbulence, and aircraft icing difficulties.

The service was operated by Dakota aircraft from No 24 Squadron which was then based at Hendon just north of London. Passengers were not carried when the forecast weather conditions for landing were below those normal for passenger operations, and the scheduled traffic was one flight in each direction every day.

On September 16, 1945, the service was initiated by No 24 Squadron and terminated on August 31, 1946. Of the 728 flights planned, 726 were carried out, and this high performance resulted in an operational efficiency of 99·73 per cent. Of the two flights cancelled, the first was the return northbound flight on October 26, 1945, owing to cumulus-nimbus cloud and excessive turbulence associated with a cold front of exceptional violence. The other occurred on January 11, 1946, when the northbound service could not take-off owing to cross winds. On this occasion a gusty 40-knot wind, blowing across both runways at Blackbushe, had made landing at the end of the southbound flight extremely difficult, and as conditions did not improve, it was decided to cancel the return flight.

In no case was it necessary to land at an airfield other than the scheduled destination. The schedules were never delayed on account of weather, although occasional technical snags, plus delays on the incoming transatlantic service at Prestwick caused the inevitable delay. FIDO was used as a landing aid at Blackbushe on five occasions, but it was not available at Prestwick. Passengers were carried on 660 of the flights planned.

An analysis of the weather experienced by the crews on the all-weather service revealed that poor visibility of less than 1,000 yards was experienced eleven times at Blackbushe, and only three times at Prestwick. Turbulence or severe wind conditions occurred six times at Blackbushe, and five times at Prestwick. Icing was not found to cause serious difficulties in handling the Dakotas. There were numerous reports of ice causing whip aerials to break off, but this caused no embarrassement. The Meteorological Office reported that gales that winter were perhaps rather more frequent, and of greater severity than usual.

Commanding Officer of No 24 Squadron at this time was Wg Cdr ELA Walter, DFC AFC, and on February 25, 1946, the squadrons base moved from Hendon to Bassingbourne in Hertfordshire. Six of the units Dakotas were already at Bassingbourne on a demonstration of airfield aids as used on the All-Weather Air Service, which was given to a delegation from the Provisional International Civil Aviation Organisation – PICAO – consisting of civilian and military representatives of the international aviation world. This was held from February 16 to February 26 when the six Dakotas flew nearly sixty-five hours on demonstration sorties.

A further demonstration was being organised by Transport Command for September 1946, and during June four Dakotas and crews were detached to Brize Norton in Oxfordshire for training on various navigation aids. Initially two aircraft and three crews had commenced the all-weather service from Blackbushe and records reveal that Dakota Mk IV KN433 operated the schedule on September 27, 1945. This was timed to fit in with the North Atlantic arrivals at Prestwick.

There is no doubt at all that the All-Weather Service, operated by the Dakotas of No 24 Squadron, was a success. The regular operation of the service afforded the aircrews involved – the crews were changed frequently – useful experience on the various approach systems available. This experience enabled Royal Air Force Transport Command to demonstrate let-down aids, including GEE, BABS, SCS 51, the Orbit Meter and all methods of blind flying aids, as support to the scheme for standardising the procedure throughout the world and placing English blind-flying procedure in the front line. PICAO – from late 1946 it became ICAO – is today the world organisation responsible for the strict regulation of safety standards, airworthiness, requirements, airfield standards, navigational control, meteorological services, international air maps and charts, and a host of other essential adjuncts to a smooth-working international transport system for civil airlines and operators.

The winter of 1946/47 was a particularly severe one, when huge snowdrifts enveloped parts of the country for many weeks. During early February Royal Air Force Transport Command Dakotas were called to drop rations to 1,200 Royal Air Force personnel including some WAAFs, who had for days been snowbound and isolated at the airfield at Binbrook in Lincolnshire.

On March 7 a report was received from Mr Edwards at Gaginwell Farm, Enstone, near Woodstock in Oxfordshire, stating that he was completely cut off by deep drifts of snow and required fodder urgently for over 350 pedigree pigs, who would otherwise starve.

As a result of an urgent telephone call from the RSPCA, RAF Abingdon, which was one of the few airfields open for traffic in the area, thanks to an excellent snow clearance plan, fodder was loaded into a Dakota Mk IV KN424 from No 238 Squadron, which was flown by the Commanding Officer, Wg Cdr DE Bennett, with Fg Off Rice as co-pilot.

In spite of severe snowstorms and low cloud, the Dakota succeeded in free dropping all the fodder close to the oil-fire marker, and thereby saved the farmer from ruin. This humane effort was entirely due to the skill of the crew of the Dakota from No 238 Squadron. The operation received a worthy mention in the RSPCA Annual Report for 1947.

At this time No 238 Squadron was operating a regular service to Europe with freight, passengers, diplomatic mail, etc. A typical flight involving Dakota Mk IV KN493 took place on June 10, 1947, to Vienna, the flight continuing to Budapest, Bucharest, and Sofia with Dakota Mk IV KN382, returning to base on June 20.

Training with the airborne forces was continued by Dakota units in the United Kingdom, and on July 7 *Operation Blithe Spirit* was held involving fifty Dakotas towing Airspeed Horsa gliders. A Dakota Mk IV KN402 from No 238 Squadron piloted by Wg Cdr DE Bennett led this mass glider lift.

During the summer of 1948 Royal Air Force Dakotas were involved in a mercy mission in India when food supplies of grain and rice were dropped to the civil population over large areas stricken by disastrous floods.

June 1948 saw the beginning of operations in support of security forces against terrorists in Malaya – *Operation Firedog* – in which Dakotas were used for supply dropping, Air Sea Rescue, marker dropping for the Avro Lincoln bombers of the Royal Australian Air Force, while one RAF unit – No 52 Squadron – fought a psychological warfare campaign with its "Voice" Dakotas broadcasting to the communist terrorists.

The first Voice aircraft was operated by the RAF in Malaya in March 1953. Original trials in broadcasting messages to the communists over the jungle were made by a Douglas C–47 Skytrain loaned by the US Air Force. The trials proved satisfactory and two Vickers Valetta aircraft were equipped with broadcasting facilities, and operated by the Far East Transport Wing detachment, based at Kuala Lumpur.

The Valetta did not prove a satisfactory aircraft for voice hailing due to the high engine noise, its comparatively high hailing speed of 90 to 100 knots, and the orbiting technique required to give adequate coverage.

An urgent request by Gen Templer, High Commissioner and Director of Operations, Federation of Malaya, resulted in the loan of a Dakota from the Royal Australian Air Force. This aircraft was fitted with the broadcasting equipment from one of the Valettas, then comparative trials were held in January 1954, in which the Dakota gave superior audibility, greater clarity and an audible signal for two or three minutes when flown in a straight line.

It was therefore recommended that two Dakota aircraft which were available in the United Kingdom, should replace the two Valettas. One of the latter types was withdrawn, and the other along with the Dakota continued to operate until February 23, 1954, when the Valetta crashed on Mount Ophir, 4,187 feet high, in Jahore, with the total loss of the aircraft, crew and equipment.

Demands for Voice aircraft were on the increase and it was decided to form a Voice Aircraft Flight. This became "C" Flight of No 267 Squadron based at Kuala Lumpur. The Flight was established with three Dakotas and two Taylorcraft Auster aircraft. Broadcast trials from an Auster had been made in January 1954 and proved very satisfactory.

The first RAF Dakota arrived on June 12, 1954, and by June 23 was ready for operation, when the RAAF Dakota was returned to Australia. A second RAF Dakota arrived on July 13 and the strength of aircraft was up to establishment by October 1, 1954.

No 267 Squadron changed to No 209 in November 1958, and Voice aircraft continued to operate from Kuala Lumpur until January 1959, when due to the elimination of the communist terrorists White Areas were declared in the southern part of Malaya. The Voice Flight was moved to Penang to be nearer the remaining Black Areas in North Malaya. Due to the more dense jungle, and more mountainous terrain in North Malaya, the two Auster aircraft were disposed of at the same time. On January 26, 1959, one Voice Dakota crashed on take-off from Kuala Lumpur and was destroyed.

In November 1959 No 209 Squadron moved from Kuala Lumpur to an airfield on Singapore Island, and consequently the Voice Flight was transferred yet again to another unit; this time to No 52 Squadron with its base at Kuala Lumpur, the flight remaining as a detachment at Penang.

To achieve the maximum psychological effect upon the communist terrorists, following an encounter by the ground security forces, Voice aircraft were used with the minimum amount of delay while morale was low. The message was broadcast from four speakers mounted on a jettisonable boom slung under the Dakota at an angle of 45 degrees to the vertical, and directed to the port side. Tape recorded messages were used against the terrorists, but live broadcasting was possible, and had proved useful during Search and Rescue operations. Broadcasting in or above cloud, or in rain, gave unsatisfactory ground reception.

Successful ground reception was achieved by flying the Dakota at a speed of 70 knots, at 1,750 rpm, with sufficient boost to maintain 70 knots, which was about 24/25 inches. The wings had to be kept level, or the message, which was beamed by the set angle of the speakers, would be thrown off the target. Flying under these conditions with turbulence in the Malayan mountains, and with the Dakota flying near stalling speed, made these operations dangerous.

Until the emergency campaign ended in 1960 the Voice Flight remained at the civil airport of Bayan Lepas on the beautiful island of Penang. Civil Dakotas of Malayan Airways and Thai Airways used the airport, and the Royal Air Force Dakotas were distinguished by the four large yellow speakers slung under the fuselage. The Flight used three Dakota Mk IV transport aircraft converted for the unique psychological task – KP277 "Faith", KJ955 "Hope", and KJ810 "Charity". In order to keep trained pilots available for the No 52 Squadron Voice Flight detachment, No 240 Operational Conversion Unit, here in the United Kingdom, retained a flight of Dakotas for this purpose, as it had converted to the Valetta like all other Transport Command units which had been equipped with the ubiquitous Dakota.

For the long twelve years of *Operation Firedog* the Dakota played its part in Malaya, over jungle so thick that light had difficulty in penetrating, over trackless evergreen forest, which assisted in the deadly game of hide and seek with the communist terrorists.

The three Dakotas from the Voice Flight were flown to No 390 Maintenance Unit at Singapore, and the last test flight of a Royal Air Force Dakota in the Far East took place on September 5, 1962, when Flt Lt FC Heavery, AFC DFM, the units test pilot, accompanied by Flt Lt SA Lynch, flew KP277 "Faith". The aircraft was later sold to the Philippine Air Lines.

During the second half of 1951 a variety of aircraft from the British independant airlines were hurriedly put to use on a large-scale airlift of troops to the Canal Zone of Egypt. Under the terms of the Anglo-Egyptian Treaty of 1936, the aircraft, which included Douglas Dakotas, Avro Yorks and Handley-Page Hermes, could not be operated in their civil registration and markings, so they were allocated Royal Air Force serials which they used only on flights to and from the Canal Zone. Crews were issued with Royal Air Force uniforms. Once more the Dakota had a very brief opportunity to be put to military use on behalf of Royal Air Force Transport Command.

"Christmas Island Airways" was formed with three Transport Command Dakotas at Dishforth in 1956 and allotted to *Operation Grapple* for the series of nuclear weapon tests in the Pacific. These Dakotas were ferried out to Christmas Island via the United States, and became No 1325 Flight under the operational care of No 160 Wing. They were used for communications between Christmas Island and the target island at Malden some 400 miles south. They also provided excellent grandstands for viewing the nuclear tests.

Initially the aircraft were restricted to supporting *Operation Grapple*, but after completion of the first series of tests, they were flown to Australia to work with the Royal Australian Air Force, flying supplies from Edinburgh Field near Adelaide, to the Weapons Research Establishment – WRE – at Woomera. They were recalled to Christmas Island for a follow-up of nuclear tests in the *Grapple* series.

On completion of their task the aircraft were ferried to No 389 Maintenance Unit at Seletar, Singapore, on May 23, 1960. The aircraft carried full Royal Air Force Transport Command livery and all three were Dakota Mk IV aircraft. KN434 "A" *Polynesian Princess*; KN598 "B" *Coral Queen*; KJ945 "C" *Island Romance*. For a short time No 1325 Flight had the loan of Dakota Mk IV KP277 from the Voice Flight of No 52 Squadron which was based at Penang.

THE BERLIN AIRLIFT

Six Douglas Dakotas airborne under an Operational Order known as *Knicker*, provided the pattern upon which the most colossal air operation in history was built.

The Berlin Airlift began in June 1948. It was initiated to defeat the blockade which had been gradually imposed by the USSR upon the three Western sectors of the city. For political purposes, the Russians had suspended all traffic by road, rail and inland waterway between Berlin and the Western Zone of Germany, which was controlled by France, the United Kingdom and the USA.

First signs that the Western Sector of Berlin might have to rely entirely upon an air freight service for its existence were noticed in the spring of 1948, and it was in April of that year that plans were made for meeting such a contingency. Contrary to popular belief at the time, therefore, the RAF was fully prepared to meet the emergency when the sealing up of surface communications between Berlin and the Western Zones became a reality.

Knicker was put into operation on the morning of June 24, 1948. The six Dakotas plied between Wunstorf in Hanover and Gatow in the British sector of Berlin. They carried between them a daily load of 60 tons of food and other essential supplies, and most people accepted the service as a supplementary one to the normal road, rail and canal supply routes, which would last perhaps a few days – until repairs, which the Russians said they were carrying out to the railway line, were completed.

But hardly had *Knicker* begun when the situation worsened, and a more elaborate air freight service took its place, and four days later *Knicker* became *Carter Paterson*, and three weeks later *Plainfare*.

When the Soviet blockade became complete, the US Air Force in Germany, with its Headquarters at Wiesbaden, conceived the idea of trying to feed the entire population of the western half of the city of Berlin. Under the operational code name *Vittles*, it assembled a fleet of twin-engined Douglas C-47 Skytrain transports at their Wiesbaden Air Force base and began despatching them up the southern corridor to Templehof, each laden with three short tons of supplies. A short ton equals 2,000 lb.

A telephone call from the Air Ministry to Transport Command Headquarters at Bushey Park, near Teddington, Middlesex, made in the early morning of Saturday, June 26, set into motion the biggest and most important peacetime air operation ever undertaken by a single Command of the RAF, and one equal to many of the most hazardous undertaken in war.

From Transport Command Headquarters Operation Order No 9 was issued on June 30, 1948, to reflect a Cabinet decision. It stated, uncompromisingly:

"1. Following the breakdown of the surface communications between the British Zone of Germany and the British Sector in Berlin, the latter will be supplied completely by air.

2. The airlift into Berlin is to be built up as rapidly as possible to 400 tons per day and maintained at that level until July 3, 1948. Therefrom it is to be increased to 750 tons per day by July 7, 1948.

3. In Phase I up to July 3 inclusive, Dakotas of Nos 46 and 38 Group operating under the control and direction of Air Headquarters, British Air Forces of Occupation (Germany), will provide the 400 tons per day lift."

They were intended to be supplemented by the four-engined Avro Yorks from No 47 Group for Phase II.

The airlift was given over-riding priority over all other Transport Operations. It involved the cessation of all Transport Command training, and the cancellation of most of the scheduled services. It was planned to start with an initial lift of 400 tons daily, increasing to 750 tons when the permanent runway at Gatow was completed. Experience soon showed, however, that this 750 tons added to the US Air Force lift from Frankfurt to Templehof of some 1,500 tons daily, was still insufficient to meet the needs of the Western Sectors of the City, and the target was increased almost every week the blockade continued.

The Douglas Dakota was available in large numbers, however, not in squadron service, but in storage at the Maintenance Units located at Silloth and Kirkbride in Cumberland, and at Little Rissington, Gloucestershire. Stored in the open the aircraft were subject to the unpredictable weather experienced in the United Kingdom. The largest unit operating the Dakota in the RAF at this time was No 240 Operational Conversion Unit at Dishforth in Yorkshire, and it was soon supplying both crews and aircraft to *Plainfare*.

Of the squadrons involved in the Berlin Airlift, some had operated the Dakota transport for no more than a few months, others were remnants of disbanded wartime units.

No 10 *Squadron* was disbanded in the Far East on December 20, 1947, after operating Dakotas since it left the United Kingdom after the end of hostilities in Europe. On November 5, 1948, No 238 Squadron at Oakington, equipped with Dakotas, was renumbered No 10. Final disbandment with Daks took place on February 20, 1950.

No 18 *Squadron* had been equipped with de Havilland Mosquito aircraft at Kabrit until it disbanded on November 15, 1947. On December 8, 1947, it was reformed at Netheravon with Dakotas and was disbanded again on February 20, 1950.

No 24 *Squadron* had operated the Dakota since April 1943, and crews from the Commonwealth air forces of South Africa, Australia and New Zealand, came over to assist and fly the Dakotas on the airlift, flying VIPs from Northolt and maintaining a detachment in Germany at Buckeburg. On November 15, 1950, No 24 Squadron disposed of its Dakotas to No 30 Squadron.

No 27 *Squadron* was based in the Far East on Air Search Jungle Rescue until February 1, 1946. On November 24, 1947, the aircrews of No 46 Squadron at Abingdon were retitled No 27 and moved to Oakington to fly Dakotas as a unit of Transport Command. The squadron returned from the airlift in September 1948 to resume its normal role. It was finally disbanded at Netheravon on October 28, 1950, after operating its Dakotas in the role of airborne support.

No 30 *Squadron* was flying Hawker Tempests in the Far East until disbanded on December 1, 1946. Reformed at Oakington with Dakotas on November 24, 1947, it flew the type until fully re-equipping with the Vickers Valetta in December 1950.

No 46 *Squadron* had joined Transport Command on January 9, 1945, with Short Stirling transports, its task being that of trooping to India. It was based at Stoney Cross and re-equipped with the Dakota in 1946, took part in the airlift and disbanded on February 20, 1950.

No 53 Squadron like No 46, had been flying the routes to India and the Far East since June 1945, but with the Consolidated Liberator transport. It was disbanded on June 15, 1946. On November 1, 1946, the unit was reformed at Netheravon with Dakotas, moving to Waterbeach just a year later, losing its identity as a separate unit as did all the Dakota squadrons during the airlift, and was disbanded in July 1949.

No 62 Squadron received its first Dakotas during July 1943 whilst in India and remained in the Far East until disbanded on March 15, 1946. Most of its Dakotas were deposited and stored with No 107 Maintenance Unit at Kasfareet in the Canal Zone of Egypt. On September 1, 1946, No 62 reformed at Mingaladon from No 76 Squadron as a general transport unit with Dakotas, being disbanded in India on August 10, 1947. Reformed once more with Dakotas at Manston in December 1947 No 62 took part in the airlift before its final disbandment on June 1, 1949.

No 77 Squadron along with No 10, was a wartime Handley-Page Halifax unit, re-equipping with Dakotas after VE-Day and moving to the Far East with Transport Command. Whilst in SEAC it was renumbered No 31 Squadron on November 1, 1946. However, one month later No 271 Squadron at Broadwell, a veteran Dakota unit, was retitled No 77 and after operating on the airlift was disbanded on June 1, 1949.

For *Operation Plainfare*, these Dakota units were reinforced with retired aircraft from the Maintenance Units. Operations began with the first of six Dakotas which took off from Wunstorf at 0645 hours on June 28, 1948, with a load of supplies for Berlin. Almost every serviceable transport aircraft was sent to Germany, when the emergency first arose, but it was found that the loading aerodrome at Wunstorf became too congested, and that the most practical force which could be efficiently operated from there was 43 Avro Yorks with 60 crews, and 50 Dakotas with 63 crews. The surplus aircraft were returned to the United Kingdom to act as a reserve backing.

During December 1947 No 30 Squadron, under Sq Ldr AM Johnstone, was based at Waterbeach, and operating alongside Nos 10, 27 and 46 Squadrons with a total of thirty-two Dakotas. Training under peace-time conditions were being carried out, and included a week at the Transport Command Support Practice Camp at Netheravon when they practised container, package and paratroop dropping plus glider towing with Airspeed Horsas.

In April 1948 No 30, along with No 27 Squadron, sent a detachment of Dakotas including Mk IVs KN238, KN410, KN442, KN498, KN507, KN512 and KN518, to another Transport Support Practice Camp at Schleswingland, Germany, where the two Dakotas and one Handley-Page

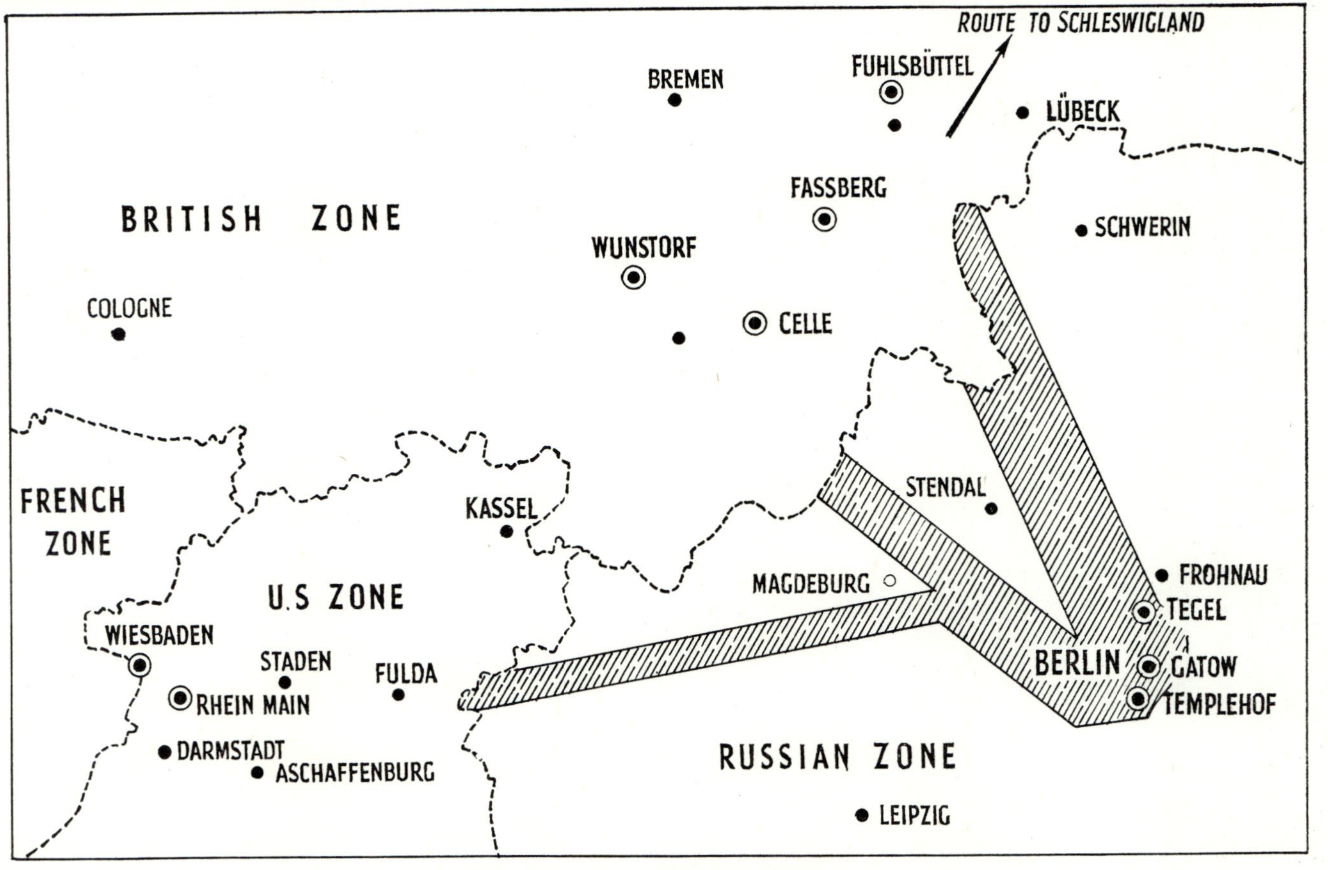

The Berlin Airlift "Operation Plainfair"

Halifax A IX Squadron co-operated with the airborne troops and the Glider Pilot Regiment. However, after completing only fifty hours for each pilot, which included formation flying, various forms of paradrops, plus glider towing, the Berlin Airlift emergency intervened.

With the arrival at Wunstorf of the Avro Yorks it was evident the aerodrome was overcrowded so the Dakotas were moved to Fassberg and sorties continued on July 19 when Dakotas from Nos 18, 53, 62 and 77 Squadrons which had been based at Waterbeach, and Nos 10, 27, 30 and 46 Squadrons, ex-Oakington, flew eighty sorties to Berlin carrying over 250 tons of supplies. In the first few weeks of the airlift the Dakotas, which operated in a common pool, had mainly carried food, flour and hay, but from Fassberg the cargo carried was nearly always coal from the Ruhr into Berlin, returning with freight or passengers.

During September 1948, the US Air Force, with Douglas C-54 four-engined Skymaster transports, were moved into Fassberg, so once more the Dakotas were on the move due to overcrowding, this time to Lubeck and the crews were pleased to return to flying foodstuffs into Berlin. No 30 Squadron with its detachment of Dakotas remained at Lubeck for just two weeks before moving to Buckeburg, to assist in the scheduled passenger service operated by No 24 Squadron between Buckeburg and Gatow, which was increased in frequency. After two weeks the aircraft and crews returned to Lubeck and carried just about everything into the beleagured city of Berlin – boots, baby food, newsprint, fish, just to name some of the commodities.

On the night of November 17, 1948, Dakota Mk IV KP223 was returning to Lubeck in bad weather and crashed in the Soviet Zone whilst doing a Blind Approach Beam System – BABS – approach. The pilot Master Pilot Trezona, and crew were killed.

The airfield at Tegel in the French Zone of Berlin, which had been completed in three months, was brought into service on November 18, 1948, and was used by Dakotas of No 30 Squadron until mid December, when they reverted to Gatow. The building of Tegel was probably the most remarkable of achievements in an operation in which remarkable achievements became commonplace. Sq Ldr Johnstone, CO of No 30 Squadron piloted the first aircraft to land at Tegel, a Dakota Mk IV KN446 loaded with tyres for tractors, drums of cooking oil and crates of condensed milk.

It was fortunate that Transport Command had taken the precaution of ordering all squadrons to attain maximum serviceability; ground crews were working non-stop and aircrews were standing by – even No 240 OCU at Dishforth with its Dakotas, was on a wartime footing for the early days of the airlift. By the end of August 1948 it had become apparent that a settlement on the Berlin dispute was not going to be found without prolonged negotiation, and the daily requirement was raised to 4,300 tons to cover any anticipated rise in coal and food consumption, and to "stock pile" for the winter months.

The RAF Dakotas were assisted in *Plainfare* by Avro Yorks and later Handley-Page Hastings, plus many civilian operated aircraft. A total of seventy-two Dakotas were able to fly to Germany when the initial call came from Transport Command, but it was certain that these were not sufficient for the need.

Transport Command had its Major Servicing Unit based at Honington which was responsible for seeing that aircraft supplying the marooned city of Berlin with the necessities of life were never kept on the ground for lack of vital spares. The unit had six Dakotas which it operated as a *Plumber Flight*, which each month flew 60,000 miles and carried between 400 and 500 tons of spares, not only to airlift bases in Germany, but to Transport Command bases in the United Kingdom. Dakota aircraft employed on the Berlin Airlift had a much higher landing rate so the strain on tyres, brakes and undercarriages increased generally. The US Air Force often helped out from their store at Burtonwood in Lancashire.

Civil contractors were called in to assist with the refurbishing of stored Dakotas. Scottish Aviation Limited at Prestwick overhauled a total of seventy-one Dakotas between August 17, 1948, and May 25, 1949, all for use on the airlift. Airwork Limited at Eastleigh, Southampton, did major servicing on Oakington-based aircraft. During February 1949 Dakotas Mk IV KN397 and KN657 from No 30 Squadron were ferried in for overhaul and Mk IVs KJ977 and KN379 collected, Sywell was also a Dakota overhaul base. During this period KK121 was ferried in and KJ997 collected. Every civilian aircraft contractor with knowledge of the Douglas Dakota was called in to assist. Field Aircraft Services at their Tollerton base was handling major overhauls, whilst their engine division overhauled the Pratt & Whitney engines at Croydon, Surrey. Marshalls of Cambridge had previously overhauled Dakotas under contract to BOAC so they were naturally included.

Operation Plainfare was the greatest air transport operation of all time, and keeping it going was an extremely complicated business. So many aircraft were flying along the narrow corridors that special flight rules had to be devised to prevent collisions. The utmost aircrew accuracy was needed to keep the aircraft in their correct positions in the streams that flowed day and night into Berlin. Pilots were required to exercise greater skill than ever before, particularly when making their approaches to the three Berlin airfields – Gatow, Templehof and Tegel. For, if they could not land at the first attempt, they could seldom land at all, but had to return to their parent bases, for there was seldom any question of keeping aircraft orbiting in circuits which had become the busiest in the world. At times the weather was below the pilots minimum. On the night of July 2, 1948, it rained so hard at Wunstorf that twenty-six Dakotas were put out of service by electrical faults.

There were many incidents both on the ground and in the air involving the Dakota. During the first full month of the Berlin Airlift, there were twenty-seven assorted incidents involving Transport Command aircraft. At Wunstorf a German driver of an RAF vehicle hit a Dakota and damaged the pitot head. An Army driver backing up to another Dakota misjudged the distance and hit the fuselage. At Fassberg, a Dakota being parked after unolading was found to have a damaged aileron. An unauthorised airman driving a petrol bowser hit a parked Dakota and damaged the leading edge of the starboard wing. An airlift Dakota landing at Buckeburg swung off the runway and was damaged.

Flt Lt HCM Holmes was flying a Dakota from Wunstorf to Gatow when a piston in the port engine failed. He jettisoned half his load of hay, and managed to return to Wunstorf on one engine. Another aircraft bound for Gatow had a fuel leak and returned on one engine. Carburettor trouble caused another Dakota to land at Wunstorf shortly after take-off. Dakota Mk IV KN641 had to make a forced landing at Schiphol, Amsterdam, with engine failure, and another Mk IV KN252 crashed after a fire in the air.

The Dakota squadrons from No 46 Group Transport Command had started the airlift from Wunstorf. They had been expelled from there to make way for the Avro Yorks. Then they were evicted from Fassberg so that the Douglas C-54 Skymasters could come in. The first sortie from Wunstorf was on June 30: the first from Fassberg was July 19: the first, by a service aircraft, from Lubeck on September 6, all done by the ubiquitous Douglas Dakota. Initially they had flown into Gatow. On November 12 they had been switched across the city to Templehof, only to be diverted back to Gatow four days later. After the visit by Sq Ldr Johnstone in KN446, the Dakotas started to use Tegel – which was without Ground Control Approach – GCA – and Blind Approach Beam System – BABS.

On December 11, 1948, a normal flow of Dakotas arriving at Gatow were joined by a number of Douglas C-54 Skymasters diverted from Templehof resulting in a total of 112 runway movements in two hours, or nearly one a minute. This total included arrival and departures. An Avro York MW232 carried the 100,000th ton of freight into Gatow on December 17, and six days later the 50,000th *Plainfare* landing was made at Gatow. Before the end of the month, another 2,031 landings were made, bringing the December total to 6,737.

The overall statistics were encouraging and by the end of December, the airlift had been operating into Gatow for 187 days, and an average of 278 landings had been made every 24 hours. Gatow, the busiest airfield in the world, had handled 321,620 metric tons of freight. The Ground Controlled Approach radar had assisted 3,654 aircraft, and only a small percentage had been forced to overshoot. Due to fog, landings at Gatow on December 22, 23 and 24 were curtailed.

During January 1949, it was decided that *Operation Plainfare* would be regarded as a long-term commitment covering a period of at least two years. Headquarters No 46 Group, which dealt with the general operational control of the British effort, was transferred to Luneburg. New flight rules were drawn up. From 1100 hours on January 15, 1949, all aircraft from Celle, Lubeck and Wunstorf were to fly to Gatow. From Fassberg, Fuhlsbuttel and Scheswigland, they would go to Tegel.

On January 24, Dakota Mk IV KN491 arrived at Gatow with a load of Ruhr coal from Lubeck. It was required to return with twenty-three passengers so the transport was swept out and seats fitted. On making an approach to land at Lubeck the aircraft crashed near the Anglo-Russian border near Schonberg. The wireless operator and five passengers were killed.

By March 9, the 50,000th passenger was back-loaded from Gatow to Lubeck in a Dakota. It was a girl, and she was seen off by the Station Commander, Grp Capt Yarde, and welcomed on arrival at Lubeck by the Station Commander, Grp Capt Biggar.

An Avro York, with Sq Ldr Best and crew, plus the AOC-in-C, Air Marshal T Williams, as second pilot, flew the millionth airlift ton into Gatow on February 18, 1949. The last RAF York sortie was flown into Gatow on August 26, and the civil aircraft had completed their sorties by August 15. The US Air Force and US Navy Skymasters ended their effort on the last day of September, whilst the Handley-Page Hastings had delivered the last load of coal on September 6, 1949.

On September 23, 1949, the last Dakota – a Mk IV KN652 – piloted by Master Pilot Brown and with Grp Capt Biggar on board, took off from Lubeck at 1830 hours arriving at Gatow 52 minutes later. It bore the insciption – Positively the last load from Lubeck – 73,705 tons – Psalm 21, Verse 11. "For they intended evil against thee: they imagined a mischievous device, which they are not able to perform."

By the end, the RAF had flown in a total of 394,509 short tons of cargo in 65,857 sorties. At the peak of the operation, in May 1949, it had about forty Avro Yorks, forty Dakotas and fourteen Hastings engaged on the operation.

A great victory had been won by Maj Gen William H. Tunner, USAF, Commander of the Combined Air Lift Force, and former Officer Commanding of the wartime India-China operation over the Himalayan Hump route, and his second-in-command, Air Cdre JWF Merer, AOC No 46 Group RAF. Higher Command over the Task Force was shared by Air

Marshal Sir Arthur Saunders, succeeded in November 1948 by Air Marshal TM Williams, and their American opposite number, Lt Gen John K. Cannon.

It was May 1949 before the Russians eventually reopened the surface routes into Berlin. So ended the greatest humanitarian supply operation in the history of aviation.

RESEARCH AND DEVELOPMENT, FOREIGN SALES

Despite the introduction of new transport aircraft into Royal Air Force Transport Command after World War 2, the Dakota remained in use in large numbers with various units and establishments both at home and overseas. The Airborne Forces Experimental Establishment – AFEE – had moved from Sherburn-in-Elmet, Yorkshire, to Beaulieu in Hampshire and used the Dakota until its closure in the 1950s when all airborne supply research was incorporated with the Air and Armament Experiment Establishment – A&AEE – at Boscombe Down in Wiltshire. During 1946 AFEE at Beaulieu had used Dakota Mk III FD943, whilst Boscombe Down had done smoke trials with another Mk III KG402 as early as 1944. Asymetric flight trials were carried out with FZ563 during 1945, whilst a Certificate of Airworthiness – C of A – for maximum safe operational weight was carried out with KN407 a Mk IV during 1947. Trials involving paradrops and radio altimeter tests were carried out with equipment fitted in the versatile Dakota.

A Dakota Mk IV – KJ839 – ex-Royal Air Force Transport Command, with low airframe hours and unfurnished, was selected by Armstrong Siddeley to have its Pratt & Whitney Twin Wasps replaced by the company's Mamba turboprops. Scottish Aviation at Prestwick were largely concerned with the modification work and the first flight was at Bitteswell near Rugby on August 27, 1949. The aircraft was later re-engined with the Mamba 3s and flew many hours as a flying test-bed for engine research before the Twin Wasps were reinstalled and the aircraft sold in 1958.

On the first day of June, 1949, a Dakota Mk IV – KJ829 – arrived at Hucknall near Nottingham for Rolls-Royce to replace the Twin Wasps with the Dart turbo-props. On March 15, 1950, KJ829 made its first flight and became a flying test-bed for future models of the successful Dart, and Rolls-Royce eventually purchased the aircraft on August 22, 1956. The Dakota continued to fly with Darts installed until November 1961, by which time Rolls-Royce had purchased two civil Dakotas for conversion. During April 1950 KJ829 was flown to Boscombe Down for take-off tests with its Dart engines. The Dart Dakota was well proven when British European Airways operated the type on a freight schedule. Rolls-Royce officials enjoy telling the story of a surprised Boeing B-29

Superfortress crew who had a strange looking DC-3 formate with them over East Anglia at 30,000 feet. The DC-3 airliner, the model T of the air had suddenly joined the jet age.

A Dakota Mk III – TS423 – was acquired by the Ferranti Flying Unit based at Turnhouse Airport, Edinburgh, on August 15, 1949, with only 766 hours on the airframe. Under a Ministry of Aviation contract TS423 was heavily modified. The fuselage furnishings were stripped and a work bench installed along the starboard side with four observer seat positions. Various experimental units were installed on the bench and throughout the aircraft. A special petrol-driven auxiliary power unit – APU – to generate AC power supply, was installed and the aircraft used on distance measuring trials.

In 1951 the existing nose was extensively modified and extended to accept a gimbal supported and hydraulically controlled gun turret. The turret was manually operated by an observer and access was gained from the co-pilot's position which was radically changed in appearance. The nose profile was slightly unorthodox compared to the standard Dakota.

The nose profile was again altered in 1952, this time to accept a bullet shaped structure to carry an Airpass Radar. A periscope structure was installed in the cabin, extending about two feet through the upper fuselage for forward viewing by the observers.

Subsequent modifications were incorporated and various installations carried out throughout the years, but the basic Airpass shape was retained for the 1,300 hours flown in these roles. The addition of a temporary structure on the upper fuselage and christened the "hen-coop" was designed to carry a sight and a forward looking camera, and was also accessible for visual observations by the test observers.

Short Brothers & Harland Limited at West Malling near Maidstone, Kent, took over TS423 during 1967. In November 1968 it was overhauled by Scottish Aviation at Prestwick before being acquired by Marshalls of Cambridge Limited on May 14, 1969, for use on a Ministry of Technology contract with the Royal Aircraft Establishment, West Freugh, near Stranraer, Scotland. This is one of the last Dakota aircraft to operate in the military markings of the Royal Air Force. During May 1971 a surplus C-47A-60-DL 42-24338 of the Canadian Armed Forces – 661 a Dakota Mk III – was refurbished by Scottish Aviation and delivered to RAE West Freugh to work alongside TS423.

When Air Vice-Marshal "Batchy" Atcherley was Air Officer Commanding No 12 Fighter Group with its headquarters at Newton in Nottinghamshire, he acquired a Dakota Mk IV KN 369 which was intended for transporting staff officers en masse to take part in the very individual brand of AOCs inspections which Batchy inflicted on his stations. The aircraft was used for giving air experience to the Air Training Corps cadets and personnel of the Royal Observer Corps. It was loaned to neighbouring stations from time to time in order to transport sports teams to away fixtures.

Field Aircraft Services at Tollerton, Nottingham, had for some years after World War 2 held overhaul contracts with both the Air Ministry and the United States Air Force for Dakota and C-47 Skytrain aircraft. The British Government decided to return fifty surplus Royal Air Force Dakotas to the United States as a gift, and in 1954 a contract was given to Fields to refurbish, test fly and deliver these aircraft. The surplus transports were located at No 8 Maintenance Unit at Little Rissington in Gloucestershire, and at No 12 MU at Kirkbride and No 22 MU at Silloth, both located in Cumberland. These fifty aircraft were delivered in United States Air Force markings, and for the first time carried the serial number allocated to them on the production line at the Douglas factory, but replaced by the Royal Air Force serial. The United States reallocated the refurbished C-47 transports within the network of the North Atlantic Treaty Organisation – NATO – air forces. It was a kind of reverse Lend-Lease. At least ten of the aircraft were handed over to the German Air Force who for many years used the Dakota as one of its support transport for tactical units. The US Air Force retained quite a few aircraft for use on its bases throughout Europe, and at one time every Air Attache had the use of at least one C-47.

After World War 2 thousands of war-weary Dakotas were in storage in the Maintenance Units strung across the globe. It was natural that with the build-up of postwar civil aviation the Dakota had a potential use, and was on the market in large numbers. The result was that nearly 300 Dakotas appeared on the British Civil Register, most of them ex-Royal Air Force, and in many cases flown by crews who had flown the type in the service.

When Dakota C4 – KN645 – landed at RAF Kemble in Gloucestershire on April 4, 1970, with Sq Ldr Neil Franks at the controls, there ended a phase in the career of a unique transport aircraft which had faithfully served in the Royal Air Force for more than a quarter of a century. Placed in temporary storage with No 5 MU KN645 will eventually be placed in the RAF Museum – at London's historic Hendon aerodrome – alongside other veterans, few of which can claim such a varied career as that of the "Dak".

On the morning of May 18, 1970, Dakota Mk IV KP208 was flown from No 5 MU at Kemble to Odiham in Hampshire with Wg Cdr EL Connor as pilot, Sq Ldr AC Edmunds as co-pilot, and Flt Lt C Stephen as navigator. The flight took one hour making the total flying time 4,164 hours. On June 27, 1970, KP208 was formally handed over to the Colonel Commandant of the Parachute Regiment as part of the Airborne Forces

Day ceremonies. The aircraft now stands outside the Airborne Forces Museum at Aldershot so that ex-parachutists can confer their ultimate accolade on the charlady of wartime aircraft – the Douglas Dakota.

It is felt that the final tribute to the Royal Air Force Dakota in this volume should come from the aircrew themselves who flew in the transport during World War 2. Here are a few extracts from the hundreds of letters received.

"Having notched up over 8,000 hours on the Dak I have nothing but affection and admiration for the old dear, and I can think of no other aircraft that could have taken the punishment that Daks received weather-wise in SEAC for instance. I have had landing lamp glasses smashed by hail stones, wing rivets pulled, and the webbing straps that held the stretchers in position broken in turbulence, and still the old lady flew on. I remained on Daks by choice, until almost the end of their service in BEA."

"I am afraid that my history of the 'ole lady is restricted to only No 24 Squadron. Mark you that covered five years and includes trips pretty well world-wide on VIP duties, including Royalty, Prime Ministers, etc – Yalta and Potsdam Conferences. Still there is nothing terribly interesting about that as many chaps did exactly the same. However it certainly provided me with an everlasting affection for the Dakota."

"I was a member of the flight which ran the All-Weather Air Service between Prestwick and Blackbushe. This was the first All-Weather flight and service set up, and it ran for a year with practically 100 per cent regularity. It is quite a story in its own right. After this I left and flew as a civil pilot with various airlines flying for some years on DC-3 and their converted C-47 equivalent aircraft. I also flew the type in West Africa during the war as well as an impressed US civil DC-3 which was used as a hack transport and regular service aircraft by West Africa Command in 1942–44 supplying and providing passenger services for this far flung command."

"I was a pilot in No 238 Squadron in 1945. I believe we had 30 Dakotas, which we flew from Merryfield, near Ilminster, Somerset, to Comilla, Bengal. They were part of what was called Combat Cargo Task Force. US Army Air Force C-47s and C-46s outnumbered us. We plied between Comilla and Burma like a bus service. From Comilla with overload tanks fitted, we flew to Adelaide, South Australia, and ferried naval personnel and supplies around Australia and way up beyond New Guinea."

"I don't know whether 'Lummy' Lord did much flying between returning to the United Kingdom and Arnhem. He had quite a stack of hours before leaving No 31 Squadron – well over 2,000. He thought a lot of FD787 – he used to call her 'D' for Dover – maybe we all used to dream of the white cliffs at times when sweating it out there. My favourite kite was FD811 followed by FL555. I think the latter aircraft was the first one I flew in fitted with two-speed blowers – it enabled you to get that little extra height when flying over the Hump."

"Checked through my old log books the other day and found I completed 374 parachute descents from the Dakota over the years. As you can imagine a good few old memories come to mind."

"I remember the flight very well; it lasted for one hour which was terminated by a perfect three-point landing following a rather undignified bounce."

"We also had a meat, vegetable, poultry and egg run. The smell in the aircraft was atrocious, and we would remove the aircraft rear door, in order to drag out the smell when airborne – never broke one egg, but lost countless Indian chickens who forced their way out of the bamboo cages, and disappeared through the rear doorway over the Chin hills."

"I remember the long one month's wait at Mather Field, California, until at last we received a forecast of favourable winds so that we could make the trip direct to Honolulu. This we did in the good time of 15 hours, and KK155 was definitely not my favourite Dakota as regards airspeed and fuel consumption."

"From 1956 to 1959 I flew the C-47 on Combat Readiness Training, when I was on an exchange with the United States Air Force, it was much more convenient to fly than the T-33 Shooting Star jet, as I could take my gold clubs in the Dak."

"I thought the 14th Army were the tops, they did a marvellous job in vile conditions. I never knew them capture or build a strip without their next task being the erection of a tea tent for the aircrews. We had little to offer in return except to write out the latest war news that we'd picked up on the aircraft radio, and pin the digest to the tent pole."

"I was in command of FZ582 when we burnt out on landing at 'Clydeside' on May 12, 1944. I still have the headset I was wearing and did not take off as we went through the escape hatch – I think I went in a straight leap. This was my second write-off in a week as on May 7 I had gone off the runway at Jorhat and wrote off the undercarriage of FL506. This was due to what we now know as aquaplaning in strong cross wind and sliding off the runway when one wheel bogged and that was that. On June 26, 1944, in FD878 we were doing a supply drop on Fort Keary when the hydraulic system exploded. We got down at base, Agartala, and trundled slowly off the end of the runway and no more damage. I still have great nostalgia for those Dakotas in the Royal Air Force."

"The Navigation School uses the Dakota aircraft as its basic trainer, currently operates some 18 aircraft and there is no doubt that the Dak is still a very fine machine. In addition Canadian Search and Rescue squadrons still operate a number of this type. It is highly probable, I suspect, that the morning line-up at Winnipeg is one of the largest Dakota formations left in the world."

"I was posted from a fighter Blenheim unit to No 24 Squadron in December 1941 and was on the Long Range flights with them on Hudson aircraft and we just converted on the squadron to Dakotas in 1944/45. I left No 24 in September 1946 and then went to Japan – Iwakuni – again on Dakota aircraft on No 1315 Flight, and flew routes to Australia, Hong Kong, etc, but mostly to Tokyo. The Commanding Officer of No 24 Squadron during my period with them were Wg Cdr Collins, DFC, Wg Cdr Archbell, DFC, and the Flight Commander of No 1315 Flight – Sq Ldr Murphy, OBE. I remained with No 1315 in Japan until the British element of the occupation forces withdrew and we flew the aircraft to the MU at Seletar, Singapore."

"One day we were doing a very intensive shuttle with supplies between Kumbirgram and Imphal. I had seen a particular Dak taxi out and take off quite normally, and was surprised to see it back in about 20 minutes. I jeeped over to its dispersal to find the pilot complaining that the 'bloody aeroplane wouldn't climb – couldn't get her above 4,000 feet'. A knowledgeable Flight Sergeant then looked inside and found that it had been loaded twice – with bags of grain. The normal load – 6,000 lb – was two layers deep. This time it was four. The max all up weight of the Dak was 31,000 lb. We estimated this one had taken off at 37,000 lb and landed at not much less."

A recent report by the Institute of Strategic Studies revealed that out of ninety-four countries included in their annual survey, at least sixty-six are still using variants of the Douglas C-47 as a military transport. According to the records the following air forces purchased surplus Royal Air Force Dakotas during or after World War 2 – Australia, Belgium, Brazil, Burma, France, Germany, Greece, Ethiopia, India, the Netherlands, Pakistan, Rhodesia, South Africa, Spain, Sudan, Thailand, South Vietnam, Norway, the United States, plus Royal Kymer Aviation, the Cuban Army, the French Aeronavale and Jugoslav air force.

It was General Dwight D Eisenhower who once said that the Dakota belonged alongside the jeep, bulldozer, amphibious duck and two and a half ton truck as the "equipment most responsible for Allied victory in World War 2". Thousands of veterans would agree.

On November 26, 1965, the United States announced the arrival of the 4th Air Commando Squadron (Fire Support) in the Republic of Viet-Nam. The squadron was equipped with the Douglas AC-47 aircraft fitted with three side firing 7·62 millimeter miniguns each capable of firing 6,000 rounds per minute. The organisation was commanded by Lt Col Max T Barker and was initially formed in the summer at Forbes Air Force Base in Kansas. A prototype aircraft had undergone a test programme in the Republic of Viet-Nam for the past year where it had become known to the ground forces as "Puff, the Magic Dragon". The nickname is derived from the roar of the guns which have a combined fire power of 18,000 rounds per minute and the flame from the tracer bullets which often forms a solid stream of fire from the aircraft to the ground.

The reputation of the Douglas DC-3 and her elder sisters has not diminished since wartime days. It has done its job safely and well for more than a quarter of a century. Aeronautical experts believe that in another quarter of a century there will still be DC-3s bringing air services to small airfields of the world. Records will probably show that some of these DC-3s served in the Royal Air Force as Dakotas.

CHAPTER SEVEN

Dakota Squadrons of the Royal Air Force

NO. 24 SQUADRON

In omnia parati – Ready for all things

In April 1942 No 24 Squadron was transferred to Ferry Command, the predecessor of Transport Command and in the same month began flights to Malta with passengers and mail using unarmed Lockheed Hudson aircraft. Its base was Hendon and during 1943 it had a wide variety of aircraft types on its inventory, these included de Havilland Dominie and Flamingo transports, Vickers-Armstrong Wellingtons converted as transports, the Lockheed 12A and Hudson, Airspeed Oxfords which were used as ambulance aircraft, a Stinson Reliant light aircraft plus a Grumman Goose amphibian.

March 1943 saw the introduction to the squadron of the Douglas Dakota transport, which, from that date, began to play an increasingly large part in the squadron duties. The operational records reveal that on March 4, 1943, Flt Lt EG Fraser flew Dakota Mk I FD772 from Hendon to Portreath in Cornwall with two passengers and 3,047 lb of freight. The following day the passengers and freight were flown to Gibraltar returning three days later with two additional passengers and 2,029 lb of mail.

On March 7 the establishment for No 24 Squadron was ammended with the addition of a fourth flight of twelve Dakota aircraft – Mk I and Mk III models. By the middle of April Dakotas were flying regular trips to Gibraltar, returning with German and Italian prisoners of war for internment. On May 4, Dakota Mk I FD826, brought Field Marshal Messe, General Beradi, General Orlando and Lt Calacchi to Hendon, whilst Generals Von Arnim and Kramer arrived in FD879 on May 16. The Commanding Officer of the squadron at this time was Wg Cdre HB Collins, DFC.

More and more Dakotas for the Royal Air Force were being ferried across the Atlantic to Prestwick, and as the new transport became available they were collected by ferry crews. A Lockheed Hudson usually flew the ferry crew to Prestwick, but on occasions the crew went by rail. During the first few months of 1944 the squadron was still adding Dakotas to its strength, some aircraft being collected from Doncaster which was a holding and modification unit for the type.

On D-Day the squadron was actively engaged in the carrying of supplies to our attacking forces. These were all special outbound flights, but on the return journeys the crews used their own initiative and evacuated casualties, prisoners of war, etc according to the demands of the moment.

In the last phase of World War 2, in both the European and Far East theatres, No 24 Squadron followed up the fighting forces, carrying VIPs to vital points as the battle progressed. Among other duties carried out at this time was the movement of doctors and Commissions to the notorious German concentration camps. Flights were also carried out to the United States and Canada, an example being the flight by Dakota Mk I FD797, captained by Sq Ldr EDM Higham, AFC, which departed Hendon on August 3, 1944, landing at Northolt, Iceland, Bluei West I, Goose Bay, Hamilton Falls, Dorval, La Guardia, Mingam and Rockcliffe. The aircraft and crew arrived back at base on August 26.

On September 1, the same aircraft and crew flew Air Chief Marshal Sir Frederick Bowhill and Air Cdr Brackley to Paris.

As the Allied armies liberated more of Europe, the extent of overseas flights increased and in October 1944 the squadron was reorganised. In place of the collection of antique types, the Dakota became the standard equipment of the unit, with a flight of Avro Ansons for short-range work. Wg Cdr TH Archbell had taken over command during September, whilst a casualty was a Dakota Mk III FL559 with Fg Off GW Rowe on October 2.

The RAF Form 540 shows that during October 1944 the Squadron flew a total of 1,188 hours, carried 236,290 lb of freight and carried 1,556 passengers. The unit consisted of 107 officers, 48 other ranks and 6 WAAFs. A total of 19 Dakotas and 8 Ansons were on charge.

The same document for May 1945 shows 1,434 hours flown, 183,920 lb of freight carried and 3,425 passengers carried making a total of 198,388 track miles flown. Aircraft strength was 30 Dakotas but only 3 Ansons. An Airspeed Oxford MP350 was used for training purposes. The older Dakota Mk III aircraft were allocated out including FL518, FL584, FL634 and FZ629, to be replaced by the Mk IV transport, including KN386, KN433, KN488, KN489, KN495, KN508, KN512, KN515, KN522, KN574.

Many of the passengers carried by the squadron were VIPs. On November 9, 1944, Sq Ldr CH Willis, AFC, in Dakota Mk III flew the Prime Minister and Mrs Churchill and the Rt Hon Anthony Eden and staff from Northolt to Orly. The following day Sq Ldr ED Higham, AFC, in Dakota Mk I FD795 flew General Sir Alan Brooke, General Ismay, Sir Alec Cadogen, Cdre Hardy and four other passengers from Northolt to Orly. Dakota Mk IV KJ979 with Sq Ldr SR Hinks, AFC, flew Winston Churchill, Field Marshal Sir Alan Brooke plus staff from Northolt to Y55 an American landing strip somewhere on the Continent. These VIP flights resulted in many complimentary letters being received by the squadron.

The all-weather service from Blackbushe to Prestwick, commenced on September 16, 1945, and operated for a period of twelve months, and was a noteworthy achievement carried out by the squadron. Two Dakota aircraft and three experienced crews of the squadron commenced a service designed to fit in with the North Atlantic arrivals at Prestwick. Flights departed the Scottish airport at 1030, arriving at Blackbushe two hours later and departing again for Prestwick at 1430.

After a period of over thirteen years, most of them eventful, based at Hendon, the squadron moved to Bassingbourne in Hertfordshire on February 14, 1946, and settled down to continue the heavy flying duties involved by the peace, which necessitated flying to all parts of the world including the United States, Canada, Russia, India, Italy, Poland, Ceylon, Burma, South Africa, the Middle East, Iceland and almost all parts of Europe. In order to fulfil a programme of this nature aircraft and crews were at constant standby, ready to fly to the furthest parts of the earth at a few hours notice. On July 1, 1946, No 24 Squadron absorbed No 1359 VIP Flight with its five Avro Lancastrians, five Avro Yorks plus twelve Dakotas Mk III and Mk IV aircraft.

Two PICAO demonstations took place at Bassingbourne during February and September 1946, when six specially modified Dakotas and six crews supplied by the squadron took part in the demonstration of letdown aids and all methods of blind flying aids, as a support to the scheme for standardising the procedure throughout the world and placing English blind flying procedures in the front line. These demonstrations were attended by almost all the civilian and military representatives of the international aviation world.

During April 1947, authority was given by the Air Ministry for No 24 Squadron to be reorganised to include Dominion representation, and to be renamed "No 24 Commonwealth Squadron". The reorganisation allowed for the establishment of twenty-eight crews of which five were Royal Australian Air Force, three South African Air Force, and two Royal New Zealand Air Force. These ten crews being provided on an exchange basis for a tour between one and a half and two and a half years duration. The post of Squadron Commander being filled by each of the Dominions and the Royal Air Force in turn.

The task of the squadron at this time was to carry out special flights, the carriage of service VIPs and when necessary civilian VIPs, using Dakota, York and Lancastrian aircraft. Because of these VIP flights a number of well-known political and military figures passed through Bassingbourne, although for the most part VIPs were carried to and from Northolt, the aircraft using Bassingbourne for base facilities. During March and April 1947 there were frequent movements between Bassingbourne and Moscow: this was for the important Moscow Conference of Foreign Ministers, attended by George Marshall of the United States, Mr Vishnisky and Mr Molotov from the USSR, Mr Bidault of France and Ernest Bevin from the United Kingdom. For this, twenty Russian aircrew were attached to Bassingbourne having the task of flying the Berlin to Moscow leg of the journey. The erection of the Western Alliance, conferences in Europe, the Independence of India, etc all meant work for the squadron.

Field Marshal Viscount Montgomery and Marshal of the Royal Air Force Lord Tedder, flew most months with the squadron to various parts of Europe. The Secretary of State for Air used squadron aircraft at a rate averaging one flight per week, and as a result was presented with a log-book commemorating his flights.

Wg Cdr ELA Walter had taken over command of the squadron during October 1945, to be relieved by Wg Cdr CWA Nicholls, DSO OBE, in September 1946. Wg Cdr PH Lombard, DFC, took over command during March 1948.

If, however, the ferrying of VIPs appeared to be a glamorous activity, there was less spectacular though important work to be done. Despite, or because of, the Moscow Conference, relations between the USSR and the Western Allies deteriorated until in June 1948 the Russians cut the land communications between the Western Zone of Berlin and Western Germany. For almost a year, until May 1949, all commodities consumed in West Berlin were flown in; British aircraft flew up to 75,000 tons in the peak month. The Dakota aircraft of No 24 Squadron played a prominent part in the Berlin Airlift flying from Northolt and Bassingbourne, plus maintaining a detachment at Buckeburg in West Germany.

After a period of routine work No 24 Squadron moved to Waterbeach on June 8, 1949, but on February 20, 1950, moved to Oakington where it received its first two Vickers Valetta aircraft. Wg Cdr Lombard was posted overseas and replaced by Wg Cdr CF Read, DFC, of the Royal Australian Air Force. On April 27, 1950, the AOC-in-C Transport Command, Air Marshal Sir Aubrey Ellwood, KCB DSC, visited the station and inspected York and Dakota aircraft of the squadron.

The following flights were carried out by "B" Flight between November 1 and November 15, 1950, after which date the Dakota and Valetta aircraft were transferred to No 30 Squadron.

Two VIP UK internal flights with
Air Marshal Sir William Dickson
Air Marshal Sir Victor Goddard

One tour of the Middle East with up to eleven passengers on Dakota Mk IV KP220

One passenger UK internal flight carrying twenty members of No 607 Squadron

One VIP tour of Germany with Field Marshal Viscount Montgomery

No 24 Commonwealth Squadron moved from Oakington to Lyneham between November 24 and 29, and on arrival at Lyneham "B" Flight was re-equipped with Handley-Page Hasting transports. The remaining two Avro York aircraft – MW199 and MW319 – were flown to the maintenance unit at Silloth in Cumberland.

No 31 SQUADRON

In caelum indicum primus

One of the transport units during World War 2 was No 31 Squadron. A true description of one of its claims to fame is to be found in its motto – "In caelum indicum primus – First into Indian skies", but naturally it cannot add that it has flown the longest in India skies, or that it has a record second to none for continuous service overseas. That it was the pioneer squadron for supply dropping in the Far East, and for a long time the only RAF unit capable of carrying out this task, is a fact little publicised.

The origin of the squadron dates back to the autumn of 1915 when A Flight was formed with five BE2c aircraft, four officers and forty-four other ranks, early in October from No 1 Reserve Squadron, Farnborough, and, under the command of Capt CR McDonald, was earmarked for duty in India where it remained until the end of World War 2.

As the last years of peace before World War 2 were enjoyed by the world in general, No 31 Squadron from Fort Sandeman, participated in the Waziristan revolts against the administration, then had a spell at Lahore and its old station at Peshawar and, under the command of Wg Cdr Reid, watched and waited.

Vickers Valentias, ex No 216 Squadron, had arrived in August 1939, and the squadron was redesignated Bomber Transport and moved to Lahore, but the Faqir of Ipi could not endure a settled routine, and in 1940 they were back in the continuing task of keeping law and order. Towards the end of October 1940, Wg Cdr Nicholls took over from Wg Cdr Reid, and in February 1941 the squadron helped in the movement of No 27 Squadron to Singapore and No 60 Squadron to Rangoon. A return to Lahore was recorded in March, but only for a short time, because with Allied forces in the Middle East being fully committed in the Mediterranean area, the military control of Iraq had been passed to India Command, and trouble was brewing.

On April 3, 1941, an Iraqi politician, Rashid Ali, backed by four generals, seized power in Baghdad. Scenting danger, the Regent Abulla Illah had fled the previous day to the protection of the RAF at Habbaniya from where he was flown first to Basra where he took refuge in a British warship, and subsequently to Transjordon. Rashid Ali and his generals were known to be employed by the Germans and on April 16 were informed of the British intention to use the treaty right to pass military forces along the Iraqi lines of communication.

Even before Rashid Ali was ready, troops from India Command left for Iraq by sea, and seven Vickers Valentias of A Flight plus four Douglas DC-2Ks from B Flight, began to transport an additional forty men of the 1st Battalion KORR from Karachi to Shaibah. In this task they were assisted by four Armstrong Whitworth Atlantas. The period commencing April 12, 1941, was spent by No31 Squadron converting B Flight crews to the first six DC-2Ks, as the new transports were known in the RAF inventory. Sq Ldr WH Burbury was the flight commander and they became operational on April 16. The following day four of the DC-2Ks (DG468, 469, 470 and 471) under Sq Ldr Burbury, flew to Shaibah where they remained as a detachment. During the next three days four more American civil registered DC-2s were taken over at Shaibah from their American crews. One Valentia was lost at LG/K4, and on April 19 the detachment moved to Basra and continued flying men, stores and equipment to Habbaniya daily. When Rashid Ali began his attacks on May 2, 1941, the transports flew into Habbaniya to evacuate the women and children. Even during the siege of this British base, occupied in 1937 and designated the permanent HQ of the RAF in Iraq, the DC-2Ks and Valentias of No 31 Squadron arrived from Shaibah with more men of the KORR and returned with more evacuees.

B Flight had the misfortune to lose one DC-2K (NC14290) and two Valentias during a low-flying attack made by six Luftwaffe Messerschmitt Bf 110s from Mosul. The Allies were unaware of the presence of German aircraft in Iraq, and at the time of the attack the No 31 Squadron detachment had six of its transports lined up on the aerodrome at Habbaniya.

By the end of May the Iraqi forces had been defeated and Rashid Ali had fled. Operating from Habbaniya the squadron detachment continued to transport troops as far as Mosul, then took part in the operations in Syria and Iran. It was during the latter operations, when six Valentias flew a company of infantry up to Haft Kel to protect the oilfields on August 25; that the unit had to write-off two Valentias which crashed on landing. There were no casualties.

Wg Cdr SB Ubee had taken over command of the squadron in April and B Flight with its DC-2Ks had moved back to Karachi at the end of August. Many long-distance flights were recorded with VIPs as passengers including the transportation of General Auchinlech from Delhi to Cairo to take over as C-in-C Middle East with Wg Cdr Ubee as pilot. Sq Ldr Burbury flew General Wavell from Cairo to Ambala to take over as C-in-C India. There were many more such flights.

In October 1941 command of the squadron passed to Wg Cdr HP Jenkins who took another detachment of DC-2Ks (DG468, 469, 471, 473, 476, 477 and 478) to the Egyptian Canal Zone and based at Bilbeis they joined a detachment of DC-2Ks from No 117 Squadron. Here they were used for supply carrying to forward areas in the Western Desert and evacuating casualties. Throughout its four months at Bilbeis the detachment carried out many flights to Cyprus, and one to Stalingrad.

The squadron recorded the arrival of the first Douglas DC-3 (LR230) on April 19, and the following day received LR232 and 16094 (which became LR231) delivered by Flt Lt Howell on his return to the unit after sick leave. These three plus AX769 (a DC-2K) formed a detachment that moved to Dinjan on April 22 and immediately joined in the operations and dropped food and medical supplies on the three routes along which the evacuation of civilians from Burma was taking place, and also flew out wounded and civilians, from Myitkyina to Dinjan. The remainder of the squadron aircraft retired to Lahore where they underwent a much needed overhaul.

The work carried out by the detachment was continually hampered by heavy rain over the northern Assam Valley and the hills, which were 8,000 feet high in places, on the route from Dinjan to Myitkyina, plus the complete lack of any navigational aids. It was an extremely dangerous business and was carried out entirely by the three DC-3s, as by this time the weary DC-2Ks, owing to lack of spares, were too unreliable. It must be remembered that these DC-2Ks and DC-3 transports used by the RAF were already veterans. Some of the engines, a mixture of Wright Cyclones and Pratt & Whitney Twin Wasps, already had a history of 10,000 hours when the RAF took them over from the United States.

By May 7 the squadron had a total of six DC-3s on strength, and in addition to the Japanese the weather had moved in. Bombardments of the airfield at Myitkyina increased in intensity, but the rescue work continued through the gathering storms until May 6, when the first two RAF DC-3s to land were attacked by Japanese dive-bombers. In one aircraft two women passengers and a child were killed. As the remainder of the refugee passengers tumbled out of this aircraft the Japanese returned and machine-gunned them.

From all Burma during the retreat, but mostly from Myitkyina, 8,616 men, women and children were brought out by air, over 4,000 of these being airlifted by the Douglas transports of No 31 Squadron. After the fall of Myitkyina the squadron did supply drops at Fort Hertz, and on two occasions – May 31 and June 13 – DC-3 LR234, piloted by Sq Ldr KF Mackie landed on a paddy field strip at Fort Hertz to evacuate twenty-three Army and civilian personnel each time before the Japanese surrounded the area. On these missions aircrews were flying as many as five sorties a day over the mountains in an effort to compensate in exertion for the lack of aircraft. Curtiss Mohawks from No 5 Squadron based at Imphal provided fighter escort when the DC-3s were supply dropping in the forward areas of Burma, but quite often the fighters had to return to base before a mission was completed due to fuel shortage. No supply parachutes were then available and so all drops were of the free variety. The DC-3s had been stripped of all their airline furnishings and the doors removed. At the beginning of June Wg Cdr WH Burbury took over command and was given a great welcome.

Mention should be made of the DC-3 (MA925) which was detached to Delhi with Sq Ldr DWT Withers for just over a month during June 1942 on the occasion of the visit by HRH the Duke of Gloucester.

A detachment was posted out to Tezpur, and reconnaissance flights were recorded as well as trooping duties and the transportation of supplies to the forward areas. The detachment at Tezpur was commanded by Sq Ldr EB Fielden, and consisted of three DC-3s and three Lockheed Hudsons. Two of the latter were lost in the region of Sumprabum when on a supply drop. It was never known whether they were shot down or crashed when dropping supplies from a low altitude. The award of DFCs to Wg Cdr Jenkins Burbury and Sq Ldr Mackie, for their work in Burma and Assam, made the squadron realise that the good work they had carried out had not been overlooked.

The supply dropping for the first Wingate expedition was carried out by a detachment from No 31 Squadron operating from Agartala. It consisted of five DC-3s and five Hudsons loaned with crews from No 194 Squadron. General Wingate will long be remembered by No 31 Squadron crews who had many headaches trying to locate the elusive columns in the massive jungles of Burma. However the transports were able to make use of the Chindwin and Irrawaddy rivers as navigation aids which proved of immense value to the crews winging their way to the dropping zones set up by the Chindits. The feats of operations carried out by the Chindits against all odds including malaria and the dreaded monsoon will live forever in the memory of squadron members of that period, and the Chindits forever held in high esteem. This was during March 1943 and except for a few isolated supply drops, all were carried out at night.

From its base at Agatarla the squadron was kept busy supplying the Chindits. On April 25, 1943, Dakota Mk I (FD787 "D-Dover" and the favourite transport of Fg Off DSA Lord), crewed by Lord, Fg Off Barry, a New Zealander, and WO T Wright, took off with 6,000 lb of supplies. One passenger was William Vandevert, a US war correspondent representing *Life* Magazine. After locating the DZ it was noticed that the troops were making words with the parachutes from the supply packs. After completion the message read "PLANE LAND HERE NOW". David Lord briefed the crew in preparation for an attempt to land on the 800-yard strip, but after three approaches in vain the transport had to return to base. A few days later a Dakota from the squadron, piloted by Fg Off Mike Vlasto managed to land on the strip and fly out seventeen sick and wounded Chindits who would not otherwise have survived. Fg Off Vlasto was later awarded the DFC for this heroic deed. He had earlier helped to pioneer the Hump route for the RAF, and later as Sq Ldr was transferred to No 52 Squadron at Dum Dum.

In June 1943 command of No 31 passed to Wg Cdr HA Olivier, and amongst the duties carried out by the squadron was the dropping of supplies at Fort Hertz, where the Kachin levies were trained, and at Goppi Bazaar in the Arakan, as well as flights over the Hump to Kunming. Even in the monsoon season the unit recorded over 1,000 sorties.

Amongst the decorations awarded to members of the squadron in 1943 was the DFC to Fg Off RE Dyson and Fg Off DSA Lord. "Lumme" Lord had joined the squadron in India on October 7, 1939, and had served in Iraq and Egypt with the detachments. Returning to Burma he continued to fly many hours on Douglas DC-2Ks, DC-3s and Dakotas, until his total hours stood at around 2,500. He was transferred to the United Kingdom in January 1944 and joined No. 271 Squadron at Down Ampney. He was promoted to Flt Lt and received the Victoria Cross for an act of gallantry at Arnhem in September 1944, an act which cost him his life.

By May 1, 1943, the squadron had eleven Dakota Mk Is on strength these being increased to twenty by the end of the month. During May a move was made from Dhubalia to Khargpur. Dakota Mk I FD820 was grounded for spares and robbery was suspected. Another Dakota (FD801) swung off the runway at Khargpur, was extensively damaged and repaired on site by No 2 Repair and Salvage Unit based at Agatarla. The squadron Engineering Officer was complaining of tool kits missing from new aircraft delivered, and the situation became so serious that the Douglas representative, Mr Achelle, was called in to investigate. As a result of missing American tool kits two Dakotas were cannibalised (FD811 and FD844).

On January 1, 1944, Wg Cdr Burbury returned from Air HQ India to take command once more, and February saw the introduction of a hard six months flying during which the squadron recorded a total of 13,200 operational hours flown for a loss of six aircraft.

The battle of Kohima, the most hard fought and critical action of the whole Japanese campaign to take the Imphal and breach the Assam Valley and the strategic railway, must be mentioned. On the first day of the Kohima siege a supply drop was desperately needed for the British garrison which consisted of an understrength battalion and some detachments. The DZ was a very small area of ground, approximately 200 yards by 60 yards and surrounded on all sides by the Japanese. Despite intense enemy ground fire No 31 Squadron managed a successful supply drop. For the next fourteen days the Dakotas continued to supply the Kohima garrison.

The siege at Imphal was no light task, and in July the squadron was moved out of Agatarla and sent to Basal for a rest which was spent carrying out a heavy training programme, including paratroop dropping by day and night, and in formation with other Dakotas. The training culminated with a large-scale exercise in which four squadrons of Dakotas (Nos 31, 62, 435 and 436), the latter two, RCAF units, carried out a combined paratroop drop with a Brigade of Ghurkas.

The award of a DFC to Fg Off WA Russell and a DFM to F Sgt WH Perry, was added to the squadron's list of honours and awards before they moved back to Agatarla from where they carried out routine supply drops over the Chin Hills and the Arakan, and helped to build up supplies in Tiddim.

Offensives were based on the possibility of transport aircraft bringing in the supplies and meant hard work for the Dakotas of No 31 Squadron; but there were no failures on the part of the men. By the end of 1944 awards of DFCs to Sq Ldr P. Bray, Sq Ldr RG Honeyman and WO OF Horry, had been announced.

A move to Hathazari took place early in 1945, and Wg Cdr RO Altman took over command from Wg Cdr Burbury in February as the squadron continued to work in support of the 14th Army during the advance on Rangoon, during which, in April alone it logged close on 4,000 operational flying hours. Soon after the occupation of Rangoon in May 1945 the squadron moved to Ramree Island, and a detachment was based at Toungoo to supply Force 136 in the Shaw Hills, but as the war moved to a close orders became a little difficult to follow as HQ tried to keep pace with movements.

With the end of the war in the Far East the squadron flew into Singapore and from here took part in *Operation Mastiff*, carrying out ninety sorties in three weeks to bring aid to, and airlift out, Allied prisoners of war. One Dakota was lost. In this month Flt Lt N Currell made the first RAF flight to Kuching, Sarawak, when he flew Wg Cdr Reynolds in to take over from the Japanese. A detachment was also sent to Batavia, and in November 1945 they suffered the loss of two Dakota aircraft in unfortunate circumstances. One Dakota being shot down when in the circuit at Soerabaya by the Indonesians, and another which crashed in Batavia was found later with the crew and passengers butchered.

For its last few months of service Sq Ldr DW Evans took over command of No 31 Squadron which at the end of September 1946 was disbanded at Komanjoran after completing close on thirty-one years service. However it was only a break for one month for No 31 Squadron came back on the active list under the command of Wg Cdr JM Cooke, DSO, DFC when No 77 Squadron was renumbered No 31 at Karachi in November 1946. For just over a year it continued to operate over its old hunting grounds and then, once again, it was disbanded at Mauripur on the last day of 1947. This time it was the end of its service in India.

The conquest of Burma from the mountains in the north had proved a doctrine new in warfare – that air power can carry, supply and support an army independently of ground channels. This was Air Command South-East Asia's contribution to the art of war, a war in which No 31 Squadron operated with considerable distinction as a transport unit, taking part in every major operation of the Burma Campaign.

No 48 SQUADRON

Forte et fidele – Strong and faithful

It was on February 16, 1944, that No 48 Squadron, based at Gibraltar with Lockheed Hudson aircraft, received instructions from the Air Ministry to move to the United Kingdom with the utmost despatch. The squadron had arrived in Gibraltar during December 1942 from Gosport, when the North African operation was at its height, whilst heavy attacks by U-boats in the local areas to the east and west of the Rock were increasing.

Whilst the squadron prepared for the move, the Hudson aircraft kept up their patrols for the enemy, and on February 21, after some of the unit had left by air for the UK, two Hudson aircraft crashed – EW906 "Q" Queenie at Monte Majialegre in North Portugal, and "H"-How at Sierra de Estrella, also in Portugal.

The unit history records that the squadron move was probably unique in the history of Coastal Command and possibly the RAF, both for its size, its method of transportation, which was by air in Dakotas, and its speed of execution.

On February 23 the nucleus of the new squadron was formed after flying all personnel from Gibraltar to Hendon in Dakotas. It was not until arrival of the squadron in the United Kingdom that it transpired that the unit was to be transferred from Coastal Command for operational work with Transport Command at Down Ampney. Three days later the first Dakota arrived to initiate cockpit drills.

For the first two weeks of March the squadron was busy converting its crews to Dakotas, and on March 19 airborne forces training commenced at Netheravon with paratroop drops followed by supply dropping four days later. The new role of the squadron had commenced. Of the forty crews posted in only six had previously flown the Dakota, and in ten days all Captains had converted to the type. Several days were spent at Hampstead Norris on glider towing with Airspeed Horsas, whilst detachments to Netheravon enabled twenty complete crews to have roller-conveyer supply dropping experience.

Night flying commenced on March 25 and by the end of the month twenty-nine crews had been checked out. The squadron strength was 66 officers, 161 senior NCOs and 325 airmen. The Commanding Officer was Wg Cdr TFU Lang, AFC, who recorded that their new home at Down Ampney was in an unfinished state.

Exercises were commenced with its neighbouring units, Nos 271 and 233 Squadrons, also with Dakotas, and these exercises included code names such as *Otis*, *Dreme*, *Mush*, *Tour* and *Roger*. On April 23, 1944, the first operational flights since its inception into Transport Command took place when five Dakotas – KG439 "YI", KG317 "D", KG428 "XI", KG337 "DI" and KG364 "F" – were employed in leaflet dropping raids over occupied France, the targets being Laval and Argantan.

The AOC Transport Command, ACM Sir Frederick Bowhill, CBE KCB CMG DSO, visited the station on April 28 from his headquarters at Harrow, Middlesex, accompanied by the AOC No 46 Group, Air Commodore AL Fiddament, DFC. In honour of the VIPs 40 Dakotas – 20 from No 48 Squadron and 20 from No 271 Squadron – took off with Horsa gliders in 26 minutes for release over Down Ampney.

Visitors during early May included ACM Sir Trafford Leigh-Mallory, KCB DSO, C-in-C Allied Expeditionary Air Force, and Lt Gen Browning, CB DSO, Commander of the Airborne Forces. These visits by VIPs provided an opportunity for a demonstration of Dakota tugs and Horsa gliders.

As the great day drew nearer exercises were held more frequent and on a larger scale. Paratroops of the 1st Polish Battalion and the 22nd Independent Paratroop Battalion, were dropped by night at a dropping zone near Langford in Exercise *Nark*, while Exercise *Consternation* involved landing seventy-five gliders on Netheravon aerodrome. It took just ten minutes for them to land after being cast off. Nursing orderlies were carried on navigation exercises for air experience as they were to play a vital part in the evacuation of the wounded later on. Sq Ldr Daniell took four crews and a Dakota to Doncaster to take part in a Transport Command exercise of moving a complete squadron.

On June 2 the Station Commander of Down Ampney, Grp Capt Bradbury, DFC, announced that the camp was sealed forthwith, and the briefing for D-Day was held the following day.

A total of thirty Dakotas from No 48 Squadron, accompanied by Horsa gliders were involved in a formation of seventy-two aircraft during the night of June 5–6, 1944. *Operation Overlord* had commenced. A Dakota Mk III KG439 "UY" was hit by enemy gunfire, and another Mk III KG426 "UV" was shot down. Flg Off J Le Huray was airborne at 1850 hours and released his Horsa glider at 2107 hours. Two minutes later his Dakota was hit in the starboard engine and began to loose height. The pilot ordered Flg Off Woodcock and Sgt Carr to bale out and successfully crash-landed the transport, enabling the pilot and Flg Off Furrell to get out safely. Woodcock and Carr had parachuted into a canal where Sgt Carr drowned before assistance could be rendered. The survivors arrived back in the United Kingdom on June 7.

Marshal of the Royal Air Force, Lord Trenchard, visited the squadron on June 12. Wg Cdr Lang was promoted to Grp Capt and posted to India during early July. Wg Cdr JA Sproule took over command on July 16. A highlight of the month was a visit by HM Queen Mary also on July 16, who was shown over Dakota Mk III KG419 "AV". Six aircraft and crews were detached to Northolt for VIP duties between the United Kingdom and the Continent. Among the many passengers carried were ACM Bowhill and Lt Gn Browning.

The briefing for *Operation Comet* was held on September 7, this being designed to land airborne troops and gliders in the Nijmegan, Grave and Arnhem areas and so hold the Rhine bridges intact. This operation was delayed and it was September 16 before the Dakotas and Horsas were marshalled in readiness for *Operation Market Garden.* The following day No 48 Squadron despatched twenty-three of the forty-nine crews detailed for the first part of the huge air armada. The first aircraft was airborne at a few minutes before ten o'clock, and the last one eighteen minutes later on that fateful morning. Throughout the Arnhem operation the squadron flew in supplies, troops and gliders, despite heavy enemy opposition. However the unit was not without its losses and on September 19 lost two Dakotas – KG401 and KG428 – over the battle area, whilst six – FZ620, KG346, KG350, KG404, KG417 and KG579 – were lost two days later.

The crossing of the Rhine followed in March 1945, and No 48 was once more engaged in towing gliders from its base in the UK. It continued the task of lifting freight and passengers to the continent, returning with casualties. As the Allied Forces advanced the Dakotas followed close behind and were often the first aircraft to land on the improvised landing strips constructed of pierced steel planking or PSP as it was known to many who used it.

It flew its Dakotas into many of these improvised airfields. It flew No 91 FSB into B2 Bazenville-Crepon, with seven aircraft, flying out fifty-five casualties; No 126 Wing into B4 Beny-ser-Mer-Douvres, with five Dakotas airlifting 95 wounded out; No 247 Wing into B6 Coulombs with seven aircraft bringing out 115 casualties. One aircraft took part of No 143 Wing into B8 Sommervieu lifting 23 wounded back home, and five Dakotas took No 125 Wing into B11 Longues, airlifting 63 casualties on the return flight. There were many such flights as the battle pierced deep into enemy occupied territory.

Even these supply flights were not without incidents. On January 9, 1945, Dakota Mk IV KN270 "UY" was destroyed at B56 Evere due to an explosion caused by a Boeing B-17 Flying Fortress of the US Air Force landing with a full bomb load on board. The Dakota crew escaped unhurt. On April 27 Dakota Mk III KG411 "UH" crashed into Lake Drummer while making an approach to B114 Diepholz with a load of petrol from Blakehill Farm. The pilot, Flg Off LA Abbey and crew escaped. Weather conditions at the time were atrocious with cloud on the surface.

The work continued even after VE-Day. On July 12, 1945, the squadron ran a special schedule service to Berlin with food and champagne for the *Big Three* conference. Two days later the unit commenced a fourteen-day training programme prior to its move to SEAC. Its scheduled duty with No 46 Group ceased.

With the end of the war in Europe, No 48 left the United Kingdom during August for service in the Far East, flying their Dakotas 7,000 miles to Patenga near Chittagong in Bengal. It arrived just in time to hear the news of the Japanese surrender on August 14. There was, however, plenty of work to be done, flying food and other essentials to garrisons in remote locations.

Wg Cdr M Hallam, DFC, had taken over command on September 11, 1944, and was succeeded by Wg Cdr PD Squires, DFC, on February 15, 1945.

September 1945 was the first full month of operational flying by the squadron in SEAC. During this month the unit transported large quantities of freight including mail, fresh victuals to locations in Burma and Eastern Bengal, returning with casualities and passengers. Supply drops of mail and essential freight were made to isolated units.

On September 5 the squadron was extremely unfortunate in loosing Flg Off Jones and crew in Dakota Mk IV KN532 which crashed in the Irrawaddy Valley with a full complement of passengers. Sq Ldr Wheatley-Smith carried out an investigation at the scene of the crash and reported that the aircraft broke up in severe weather conditions. The Dakota had taken off from Meiktila.

The weather was generally bad at the beginning of September, with towering cumulus nimbus cloud up to 40,000 feet. Towards the end of the month the weather began to show an improvement. Total flying hours for September were 1,736. Casualties carried were 160 stretcher cases, and 1,212 sitting wounded.

Whilst at Pantenga No 48 Squadron was visited on December 7 by AVM JDI Hardman, AOC No 232 Group.

During the last month of 1945 the squadron had been particularly active with numerous sorties flown to Singapore, Batavia, Penang and Bangkok. Crews were flying in some cases over nine hours at a time. Reinforcement troops to the 12th Army at Rangoon, food to No 505 District plus mixed freight and personnel. Supply drops with food and mail to the 32nd Division at Taungup and Sandaray. The December total included 238 sorties, 1,472 flying hours, 3,320 passengers, 232 casualties, 591 tons of freight landed and 27 tons dropped.

The squadron records indicate that hopes were raised that the squadron would not be disbanded after a visit by the AOC No 232 Group. However, on December 28, 1945, news was received that the squadron with effect from January 16, 1945, would disband, so ending, for the time being, a magnificent record of achievements in Coastal and Transport Commands during World War 2.

On February 15, 1945, just one month after being disbanded, the nameplate of No 48 Squadron was transferred to No 215 Squadron at Kallang in Singapore. Thus No 48 continued to operate in the transport role, flying Dakotas. One detachment was maintained at Hong Kong, whilst later in 1946, the squadron moved to Changi, Singapore, operating services to Rangoon via Butterworth, and Hong Kong via Saigon.

Wg Cdr JR Gordon-Finlayson, DSO DFC, took over command on October 31, 1946, followed by Sq Ldr RN Wheatley Smith on September 15, 1947.

In October 1947 the squadron gave birth to a notable baby. In that month the VIP and Special Duties Flight became a separate unit under the designation, Far East Communication Squadron.

With the outbreak of hostilities in June 1948, against communists in Malaya, No 48 Squadron, along with Nos 52 and 110 Squadrons, evolved a technique of supply dropping in the mountainous jungle which enabled them to drop supplies to troops and police all the year round. Numerous bases and forts deep in the mountains came to depend entirely on air supply for their existence.

This demanding flying over difficult terrain in swiftly changing monsoon weather took its toll, and up to 1957 the squadron lost four Dakotas with their crews in operations over Malaya.

In 1951, after a short spell at Kuala Lumpur, the squadron returned to

Changi to convert to Vickers-Armstrong Valetta transports, and routes were flown to Hong Kong, Iwakuni, Butterworth, Negombo and Kuala Lumpur, in addition to supply dropping duties.

No 48 continued its transport role in the Far East, and during October 1957, whilst commanded by Sq Ldr L Hague, the award of a Standard was approved, the unit having completed twenty-five years faithful service.

No. 52 SQUADRON

Sudore quam sanguine – By sweat rather than by blood

On the first day of July 1944 No 52 Squadron was reformed at Dum Dum, Calcutta, from "C" and "D" Flights of No 353 Squadron with Dakotas. It carried on the work of flying the Hump route to China as well as providing air transport schedules to forward airfields in Burma. Among many special flights was the evacuation of British personnel from Kweilin in China which was threatened by a Japanese advance, as well as evacuation from the battle area, VIP flights, etc. All of which was carried out without serious delay or accident over some of the most difficult air routes in the world. These flights set the standard of the squadron for post-war operations. In May 1945 the squadron received the No 229 Group Airmanship Cup. Since it had reformed it had flown 19,000 hours without accident and its navigational record was first in No 229 Group and third in Royal Air Force Transport Command.

After the war the squadron continued flying transport schedules moving to Mingaladon in October 1946 and to Changi in 1947. Its strength was then reduced from twenty to eight Dakotas, and while it still carried out many special route flights, some as far afield as Australia, Hong Kong, Japan, Burma, Siam and Indo-China, its major role became transport support to the Army.

In June 1948 the crews and aircraft were detached to Butterworth, and during that month flew the first sortie in support of the security forces engaged in anti-communist terrorist activities. The squadron was engaged in non-stop air supply operations in the Federation of Malaya. It moved its bases to Changi, Kuala Lumpur and Seletar as necessary, but always maintained detachments wherever needed to supply the ground forces. In 1951 the old faithful Dakota was replaced by the Vickers Valetta transport.

The Air Supply Force Malaya was formed at Kuala Lumpur in January 1957 from the elements of Nos 48, 110 and 52 Squadrons, plus No 41 Squadron of the Royal New Zealand Air Force. The force was always commanded by an officer from No 52 Squadron.

In July 1959 it became the specialist squadron for air supply, and was again posted to Kuala Lumpur. In November it took over the Dakota Voice Flight detachment from No 209 Squadron which was operating from Penang with loud hailing equipment on psychological operations against the communist terrorists. This detachment operated until the official end of the emergency in July 1960.

No 52 Squadron was unique in that it was the only unit in the Royal Air Force that operated continuously in air supply operations in Malaya since the beginning of the emergency. In its work it had been ably supported by No 55 Company Royal Army Service Corps, some of whom, together with aircrew of the squadron, lost their lives in supply operations in the early days.

Dakotas of No 52 Squadron were detached to Colombo on Air Sea Rescue duties; they also did marker dropping for the Avro Lincoln bombers of the Royal Australian Air Force, in addition to the psychological warfare work mentioned earlier. Their Dakotas also dropped leaflets over the thick jungle. For many years it was a Dakota aircraft from No 52 Squadron which calibrated all the numerous navigation aids in the Far East Air Force theatre.

The squadron was lucky in that, even in peacetime, its task was productive and demonstrably played a vital part in the success of the ground forces in maintaining law and order. Tangible proof that in postwar years the squadron had maintained the high standard set by the original members, can be seen from the high number of awards received by both air and groundcrews; more indeed than were won by the squadron in World War 2. The Malayan Government recognised the squadron services by the presentation of a ceremonial kris in 1960, and by the award of an Ahli Manjku Negara in 1964. The members of the squadron who coined the squadron motto in 1939, when it was a training unit, could not know how appropriate it had been to members as they flew over the tropical jungles of the Far East.

No 117 SQUADRON

It shall be done

No 117 Squadron was formed at Khartoum on April 30, 1941, under the command of Wg Cdr WE Rankin, from a detachment of another famous transport squadron, No 216, and became as famed as its worthy forbear. It began its life quietly with a mixture of aircraft, including Bristol Bombays, Italian Savoia-Marchetti SM 79s, Vickers Wellesleys, Lockheed 12As, etc and was employed on the Takoradi to Cairo route ferrying supplies and spares for the army in the Western Desert. This was known to many as the "*Bush Bus*" route. In October 1941, it began to convert to the Douglas DC-2K and the following month moved to Bilbeis, between Cairo and Alexandria, leaving its other types behind. It was engaged in training for its future role of transport support, meanwhile continuing the constant build-up of vital supplies for the army. At this time, civilians were evacuated from the hard-pressed fortress of Malta, and General Alexander was flown by Wg Cdr Rankin to India to take over command in Burma.

Lockheed Lodestars and Hudsons were added to the unit strength after May 1942 while the DC-2Ks were handed over to No 31 Squadron, although occasional use was made of the DC-2K and DC-3 until August. Wg Cdr RG Yaxley, DSO MC DFC, had taken over the squadron on July 8, 1942, and under his leadership No 117 began to play a large part in the advance from El Alamein. A detachment moved up the desert on the heels of the 8th Army, supporting the forward fighter squadrons with personnel, bombs, ammunition and stores to forward airstrips.

The Hudson aircraft carried casualties back to Egypt on the return flight. During the advance Wg Cdr Yaxley was promoted to Group Captain to take over No 249 (Transport) Wing, and was relieved by Wg Cdr J Goodhead. The final defeat of the Afrika Corps found No 117 at Castel Benito near Tripoli preparing for the invasion of Sicily. Unfortunately both Group Captain Yaxley and Wg Cdr Goodhead were shot down over the Bay of Biscay when returning from a visit to the United Kingdom in a Hudson. Wg Cdr WE Coles, DFC, assumed command of the squadron on June 30, 1943.

In June Dakotas began to replace the Hudsons, but the latter remained in service with the unit until late August. Preparations were begun for the first attack on the Fortress Europa, via Sicily. The now familiar Dakotas were there, ferrying – often under fire – stores, food, ammunition, etc to the troops on the island, and evacuating casualties back to North Africa. Even before Sicily fell, a forward detachment from No 117 Squadron was based at Catania.

September 3, 1943, found the unit at Catania in Sicily carrying on with its all important task into Southern Italy. By a month later the unit was based at Bari and fulfilling its transport supply role. However this was short-lived, for on October 25 orders were received for No 117 to leave the Middle East and move to India to help in the Burma campaign. Seven days later the bulk of the unit was at Rawalpindi.

Then followed a period of intensive training for a new type of transport support, namely training paratroops of the 50th Indian Para-Brigade and supply dropping with Wingate's columns training for the second penetration of Northern Burma. Hitherto, supplies had been ferried from rear to forward airstrips but in Burma there were no airstrips and little suitable terrain for landing near to the front line troops. Supplies had, therefore, to use an expression of General Wingate's "to come down the chimney", and it was for this type of work that the squadron was now preparing. The stay at Rawalpindi, far removed from the heat and dust of the desert, was very welcome and the amenities of the town more than compensated for the drop in temperature over the winter. No 117 Squadron now at Dhamial formed part of No 177 Wing based at Rawalpindi with No 62 Squadron at Chaklala and No 194 Squadron at Basal.

By February 1944, training was complete and the squadron moved to Lalmai in Eastern Bengal to begin its new task initially dropping supplies to surrounded troops in the Arakan. At this time preparations for the battle of Imphal, which was to become only the beginning of the long trek to Rangoon and beyond, was soon to be in full swing when day after day, night after night, men, guns, food and ammunition were flown into Imphal and non-combatants were evacuated, leaving the town garrison with more than a sting in it. However, early in March came Orde Wingate's second expedition into Northern Burma, but this time the Chindits, with all the paraphernalia to equip them for months in the jungle deep behind the enemy lines, were flown to hurriedly made strips carved out of the jungle.

No 117 Squadron carried a variety of loads including 221 mules and 47 ponies into the strips at *Broadway*, *White City*, *Chowringhee*, *Aberdeen* and *Clydeside*. When their task was completed, the Dakotas evacuated many of the Chindits back into Assam just before the Japanese captured the strips. The squadrons part in *Operation Thursday*, as the initial fly-in was called, was acknowledged by the award of the American Distinguished Flying Cross to the Commanding Officer, Wg Cdr WE Coles, DFC AFC, who himself had flown into all the strips in use in Dakota Mk IIIs FD834 "E-Easy", FD967 "L-Love", FD937 "H-How" and FL512 "D-Dog". The squadron was given unofficial permission to wear the coveted Chindit badge, which was, however never worn.

On June 6, 1944, Wg Cdr Coles returned to the United Kingdom to take over command of No 233 Squadron at Blakehill Farm also equipped with Dakotas. It was learned later that he was awarded a bar to the DFC for operations south of Lake Indanaugi in May. He was succeeded by Sq Ldr WJ McLean, AFC, later to be awarded the DSO and DFC, who had joined the squadron as a Plt Off in the autumn of 1941 – he made his first sortie with the unit on October 25 of that year – and a more popular choice could never have been made. Under his leadership new records were made and broken.

The battle of Imphal was won and the advance to the south began over terrain where few vehicles could operate so that supply had perforce to be by air. Everything the army needed, from darning needles to guns, was dropped to them by parachute or free drop and on at least one occasion sacks of flour and rice were dropped clean through the Quartermasters stores. One could ask for no better service than that. The advance proceeded and the squadron kept pace by moving southwards too, but kept to the west side of the hills, to Sylhet, and later Agartala.

At the end of October 1944, after enduring its first monsoon, a spell of it at a spot only forty miles from the world's wettest place, although some believed that Sylhet was even wetter, the squadron was withdrawn for a well-earned rest. This proved to be a misnomer, but the change of climate and environment at Risalpur was both beneficial and welcome. But after only three weeks No 117 was moved to Bikram where intensive glider towing was carried out for a fortnight, after which on December 10, 1944, the squadron moved back into the operational area at Hatazari near Chittagong.

At Hatazari the unit heard of the fall of Mandalay, and from there all previous records of hours flown and loads carried per month were broken. New names came into the picture, Meiktila, Toungoo, and numerous dropping zones tucked away by the road to Rangoon. At Meiktila many crews came under fire from the Japanese who surrounded the strip and who came out at night to recapture it, only to be driven off next morning. During May 1945 the astonishing figures of 4,396 hours flown and over 9,230,000 lb of freight carried were achieved and it is believed that this is a record for any transport squadron in any theatre of war.

The long haul to Rangoon was considerably shortened by the move, in May, to Ramree Island which was a veritable paradise in comparison with previous locations. Here on the very doorstep was a beach with excellent bathing facilities, and everyone benefited alike from the sea air. Whilst the squadron was at Ramree, Wg Cdre McLean was repatriated to Australia and Wg Cdre AJ Samson, DFC, succeeded him. The squadron gave Wg Cdre McLean a rousing send off at a birthday party, and gave the new Commanding Officer an equally warm welcome.

But the stay at Ramree, like many other good things, did not last long and a month later the squadron was back at Chittagong, this time at Patenga strip. The reason for the move was so that No 117 could cover the Central Burma supply route, while other squadrons based on Rangoon dealt with the Southern area. In some ways, the move was a good thing, for the monsoon was just beginning at Ramree and the accommodation there left a good deal to be desired, but Patenga was not too pleasant with its leaky bashas and permanently water-logged ground. Here the weather was the worst enemy, particularly in the Akyab area, and whilst the squadron was operating in the area a total of five Dakotas were lost, with only two crews saved.

By this time the war with Japan was nearing its end, and VJ-Day found No 117 standing by for a new and more pleasant task, that of evacuating our prisoners of war from French Indo China and Siam. For this purpose, an operational detachment flew to Hmawbi, near Rangoon, on August 19, 1945, and after a fortnight of waiting and filling in time by transporting loads of medical and other supplies from Akyab to Mingaladon in preparation for the reception of the ex-prisoners, the first shuttles to Bangkok and Saigon began on September 3, 1945. Then followed weeks of flying in weather which was very variable, but on a task into which everyone threw his heart and soul. Unfortunately two Dakotas were lost, one of them, flown by the Commanding Officer, Wg Cdre Samson, whilst carrying thirty-one ex-prisoners and other passengers from Saigon to base. The other aircraft crashed between base and Bangkok whilst carrying twenty-one occupation troops. Both crashes were presumed to be due to bad weather.

One of the Dakotas, piloted by Warrant Officer MH Wilby, had the honour of being the first allied aircraft to land at Moulmein since before the Japanese invasion in 1942. He was forced to land there owing to bad weather whilst returning to base from Bangkok. There was a number of Japanese on the strip, and while Warrant Officer Wilby was uncertain of their intentions or of the accuracy of their intelligence, he declined to stay and take the surrender of the garrison.

During the last few months of the squadron's life, under a command of Wg Cdr LT Bryant-Fenn, DFC, new fields were visited, the shuttles being transferred to airfields in Malaya and Singapore, the task being to ferry supplies and men required for the occupation forces. These shuttles continued up to, and after, the date of disbandment on December 17, 1945.

The figures for the total war effort of the squadron are indeed impressive. They are as near accurate as possible, some of the Middle East records do not include, in one or two cases, the total passengers or freight carried.

The list of awards which the squadron gained is not so impressive as that of its achievements, but it includes two DSOs, at least twelve DFCs, four AFCs, one American DFC, and eleven mention in despatches. The squadron can be proud of the recipients.

Thus ended the career of No 117 Squadron, which, considering that its life was only a little more than four and a half years, is a shining example of what can be done by perseverance and the indefinable something which can only be called *esprit de corps*. One can take hope for the future when one realises that these results were brought about, not by a body of supermen, but by ordinary mortals, but with the difference that they were working hand in hand with one single purpose in mind. If this spirit could be extended to public life there would be no need to fear for the future.

No 117 Squadron flew 17,972 sorties in South East Asia. During the period from May 1, 1941, to December 17, 1945, it flew a total of 87,595 hours of which 81,677 were on operations. During that period it carried 44,639 short tons of freight – a short ton equals 2,000 lb – carried a grand total of 102,223 passengers which included 3,014 prisoners of war evacuated and 18,972 casualties. The experts with their slide rule calculated that for over four and a half years, No 117 Squadron had continuously, every hour of every day, approximately two and a half aircraft airborne, each carrying approximately two and a half passengers and 2,250 lb of freight – or a total load of 2,750 lb.

Author's note: This history was compiled by the unit Orderly Room staff whilst No 117 Squadron was based at Hmawbi, and except for the odd correction or addition is reproduced in its entirety.

No 194 SQUADRON
The Friendly Firm

No 194 Squadron was formed on October 13, 1942, at Lahore, Punjab, in North India – not far from the notorious North West Frontier – under the command of Wg Cdr AC Pearson who had been a Flight Commander with No 31 Squadron. Sq Ldr Thirlwell and Sq Ldr Frankie Bell were appointed Flight Commander of "A" and "B" Flights respectively. The squadron badge depicted a flying elephant and the squadron adopted the motto – *The Friendly Firm* – but, although the entire fleet of Lockheed Hudson and Douglas Dakota aircraft carried the crest throughout the Burma campaign, it was never officially recognised by Royal Charter.

The day following formation it was announced that the squadron strength would be sixteen Lockheed Hudson aircraft controlled by Air HQ India through No 226 Group. The unit history records that No 82 Squadron personnel were posted in from Karachi making a total unit complement of 312 personnel.

Local flying commenced on October 15 and nine days later Wg Cdr Pearson with crew of three took a Hudson Mk VI to Dum Dum, Calcutta, for stores. More aircraft arrived for the squadron, until by the end of the month the strength was thirteen transport Hudsons. Total flying for the first month was seventy hours plus forty-four hours link trainer time.

On November 5 Wg Cdr Pearson flew a survey flight to Delhi with the object of putting into operation a transport service with squadron aircraft. The proposed schedule was to depart Lahore every Saturday en route for Delhi, Bhopal, Bangalore, Trichinopoly, Colombo and return. The survey flight was satisfactory and so No 194 Squadron commenced air communication work within India and Ceylon on November 21, so preserving the vital links in the Far East chain of command essential to the war effort.

Ports of call soon included such famous places as Bombay, Madras, Calcutta, Allahabab, Cochin, Chittagong, Feni, Armada Road, Cultack, Magpur and Vizaga Patam. Initially the Calcutta to Bombay leg was not flown until completion of the airfield at Nagpur.

Meanwhile more Hudson aircraft were being ferried to the squadron – FK586 arrived on November 20 via Waterloo, West Africa. The unit strength was then 17 aircraft, 11 officers and 96 airmen. Earlier in the month two aircraft took part in an ARP demonstration, over Lahore in company with six Hawker Hurricanes during which 50,000 leaflets were dropped. Sq Ldr Thirlwell and Plt Off Barrier in Hudson FK411 had commenced an India to Ceylon flight, taking 10,000 lb spares southbound, and ferry pilots on return. This first schedule took five days to complete.

On November 23, Maj Gen HTD Hickman, CB OBE MC, and Lt Col CM Hutchings, OBE, were flown to Agra and became the first of many VIPs to be carried by No 194 Squadron. The following day a detachment was flown to Dum Dum with six Hudsons including FK474, FK485, FK493. During the next few days Army co-operation and the first paratroop trips were flown. The Hudson FK411 had returned after completing the first schedule, and prisoner-of-war mail for Tokyo was carried to Delhi. Hudson FK584 arrived from Takoradi via the Air Reinforcement Centre at Karachi bringing the unit strength to twenty aircraft. On the last day of the month records show that fourteen Hudsons were serviceable, others being modified by having the gun turret removed. It must be remembered that the Lockheed Hudson was originally a maritime reconnaissance aircraft used by Coastal Command. The unit had fifty-three airmen maintaining the aircraft. There was complete harmony and co-operation throughout the squadron.

The Colombo mail service was commenced on December 5 with Hudson FK488 piloted by Plt Off Mellsop with ten passengers. The same day Hudson Mk VI EW946 with Sgt Curtis and crew departed for the Middle East – Cairo and return – with 830 lb freight and ten passengers. This was followed on December 6 by FK469 with Sq Ldr Thirlwell returning ferry pilots to the Middle East. FK504 was handed over to the AOC in Delhi and FK488 crashed on take-off at Bangalore when it hit a Consolidated Catalina aircraft. This aircraft was Cat B and handed over to the Hindustan Aircraft Company.

On December 9 the AHQ Bengal Command requested a daily service by the Dum Dum detachment for mail, AOG parts, medical stores, etc. The route was Fenney via Chittagong calling at Agartala on alternate days.

Hudson Mk VI FK474, piloted by Flg Off Salveson, flying from Dum Dum to Chittagong on December 16 was over Sitakund on their third trip of the day when attacked by two Japanese Zero fighters. The unarmed transport was badly hit and with the undercarriage unserviceable crash-landed on the muddy beach, it being low tide. With only minor injuries the crew walked seven miles to the nearest Police Station at Sitakund and received attention. They were later flown back to base from Chittagong. The following day FK431 belonging to No 353 Squadron, attached to No 31 Squadron, but with a No 194 Squadron crew was reported missing.

On December 25, 1942, the Squadron Commander and his officers visited the airmen's mess in the customary tradition. Supply dropping to the 77th Army Brigade was carried out two days later. A detachment to Tezpur was effected on December 30, whilst on New Year's Day Wg Cdr Pearson flew FK481 to Jodhpur with ferry crews to pick up FK596 and FK607. Four days later Wg Cdr WH Burbury from No 31 Squadron arrived in Douglas DC-2 HK821 "M" with the kit of the deceased crew of FK431. Lt JH Van Rooyan of the South African Air Force was posted in from the PRU at Dum Dum on January 15. By the end of the month No 194 Squadron had twelve aircraft at Lahore, five at Dum Dum and three at Tezpur.

The body of the late HH Maharajah of Bikaner was flown from Bombay to Bikaner, its last resting place, by Hudson FK481 on February 3, 1943. Pilot was Sgt Patin accompanied by crew plus eight passengers. Three days later Hudson FK411 was attached to Indian National Airways with Sgt Gambas for use on mail runs.

The squadron moved to Palam by rail, road and air on February 18. Hudson FK485 crash-landed at Bangalore and collided with two parked aircraft causing considerable damage two days later. The new Calcutta to Bangalore mail service was inaugurated on February 27. The squadron transported a film unit from Amala to Peshawar on March 10 in FK411. They were engaged in making the film *Behind the Wings*. Whilst at Nagpur three days later, Sq Ldr Bell took His Excellency the Governor of the Central Provinces, Sir Henry Twynham, for a twenty-minute flight in Hudson FK493. The Indian National Airways mail run was continued at the end of the month using EW972 piloted by Plt Off Clark.

In May 1943, in accordance with the policy laid down by AHQ India the squadron converted from the Hudson to the Douglas Dakota. It took on loan two Douglas DC-3 transports from No 31 Squadron – MA943 and LR235 – for two months. LR235 crashed at Tezpur and MA943 was sold to Indian National Airways. On May 29, Dakota Mk I FD812 "K" was allocated to No 194 Squadron, this being the first of many Dakotas it was to operate in the months to come. As the new Douglas transports were ferried in, the Lockheed Hudsons were flown out.

The July 1943 statistics totalled 637 flying hours, 715 passengers and 115,891 lb of freight carried. This was the highest figure for any one month and mostly due to the Indian National Airways mail service which the squadron had taken over. During August there were two accidents with Hudson aircraft – FK966 crash-landed on August 4 at Dum Dum during a heavy rain storm and was severely damaged. The pilot was Plt Off Moreland. On August 27 FK584 crashed one mile from Allahabad piloted by Plt Off Brookman. Passengers on this aircraft included Maj Gen TGG Heywood, Brig Gen HP Radley and Mr Rand of the US Lend-Lease mission.

No 353 Squadron took over the Indian National Airways mail commitment on September 16 and No 194 Squadron was moved to their new home at Basal for training with their ten Dakota and two Hudson aircraft. It was during August that Grp Capt George Donaldson arrived at Rawalpindi, Punjab, to form No 177 Wing – its role was to be the development of the use of airborne forces with paratroops and gliders for use on the Burma front. The Wing had initially three units – Nos 62, 194 and 267 Squadrons. On September 20, 1943, *The Friendly Firm* became No 194 Airborne Forces Squadron.

Visitors to the squadron on October 2 included ACM Sir REC Pierse and Air Commodore HJF Hunter. On October 11 the first anniversary of the squadron was recorded in the Operational Record Book (ORB).

No mention of No 194 Squadron is complete without including Orde Wingate and his Chindits. During the first legendary Wingate expedition into Burma during 1943 the units Dakotas had assisted No 31 Squadron on special supply dropping missions in support of the Chindits from a base at Tezpur in Assam. The Hudsons had also played a large part in this operation.

General Wingate and his men will long be remembered by No 194 Dakota crews who had many headaches trying to locate the elusive columns in the massive jungles of Burma. However, the squadron was able to make use of the great Chindwin and Irrawaddy rivers in Burma as navigation aids which proved of immense navigational value to the crews winging their way to the jungle dropping zones set up by the Chindits. The small wireless pack sets carried by the columns also proved to be invaluable on many a dicy occasion. The feats of operations carried out by the Chindits against all odds including malaria and the dreadful monsoon will live forever in the memory of squadron members of that period, and the Chindits forever held in high esteem.

Towards the end of 1943 the units comprising No 177 Wing, including No 194 Squadron had completed airborne forces training at the Air Landing School located at Chaklala. All the Wireless Operators went along for training as jumpmasters and forty-seven out of fifty volunteered and completed the necessary training. "A" Flight with Sq Ldr Thirlwell in command, moved in as "A" Flight from No 62 Squadron moved out and back to Basal. "B" Flight did cross-country flights from Peshawar before a training detachment at Chaklala. AVM Baker, No 223 Group, SEAC and Grp Capt Donaldson visited the squadron during this intensive training period. This was followed by exercises involving an average of fifteen Dakotas – *Tiger*, *Dove*, *Pigeon*, *Jupiter*, *Snipe*, *Grouse* were some of the code names used.

A sad blow to the squadron was the sudden death of Flg Off JS King who was buried in Rawalpindi cemetary with full military honours on December 23, 1943. Over one hundred personnel from the squadron attended.

No 194 became operational with Allied Troop Carrier Command under Brig Gen William D Old, US Army Air Force, on January 1, 1944. Throughout the next two months the airborne forces exercises continued and included *Goldcrest* and *Pheasant*. On February 4 the squadron was instructed to move to Comilla and five days later this was complete. Supply drops were carried out in the Arakan area at night with ten Dakotas. On February 14, Dakota Mk I FD911 "C" piloted by Flg Off Carter and with DO Williams as crew member, encountered light enemy ground fire whilst operating over the dropping zone. A bullet pierced the propeller dome of the port engine allowing egress of oil making it necessary to cut the engine. The crew despatched the load of vital supplies into the jungle approximately ten miles from the dropping zone. The Dakota pilot managed to maintain height and even increased it sufficiently to cross the Chin Hills and back to the Assam base at Agartala. FD911 had been flying on one engine for nearly two hours. Unfortunately FD911 crashed in a very severe gusty cross wind taking-off from Palel airfield on April 9, 1944, whilst evacuating personnel of a Hawker Hurricane squadron from the front line.

To the Eastern Air Command, The Arakan Naval Coastal Forces and the 14th Army.

"Since the formation of the Eastern Air Command and the 14th Army you have given the Japanese a crack they will remember. You have come victoriously through your first battle.

The Japanese are learning that battles are not won by surprise attack, just as they have learned that wars cannot be won by treacherous assaults. A large and formidable force was sent through the jungle three weeks ago by the enemy to cut your lines of communications and attack you in the rear, with the hope of defeating you and sweeping into India they launched a major offensive in the Arakan. Although many of you were cut off and encircled, dependant on supplies dropped from aeroplanes, everyone stood firm, inspired and strengthened by the knowledge that powerful support was at hand from land, sea and air. You met the onslaught with courage, confidence and resolution. The Japanese attack has now been smashed, after bitter fighting in the jungles and in the skies. The threatened passes are clear; the roads open; the enemy forces which infiltrated to your rear have been scattered. A complete victory is yours. When I visited you recently your splendid spirit was clear to me. That spirit, that tenacity, that courage, has now been demonstrated to the enemy and to the world. I salute you." Signed: *Louis Mountbatten.*

The above was endorsed with similar messages from Troop Carrier Command, No 114 Brigade, Air Commander Eastern Air Command and 15th Indian Corps.

Supply dropping operations began in earnest on the first day of March 1944. The following day Operations Order No 13 was issued despatching 13 Dakotas and 70 personnel to Tulihal, near Imphal, for the purpose of landing two Brigades 200 miles behind the Japanese lines. This was a strenuous month for No 194. They flew day and night with troops, equipment, mules, ammunition and food behind the enemy lines. Supply dropping in the Arakan and evacuating the sick and wounded from the forward areas. On March 18 came the order to airlift 123rd Brigade from Dohazari to Imphal, this involving 15 Dakotas.

Operation Thursday was launched from Lalaghat on March 5 and No 194 Squadron, along with No 1 Air Commando and other transport units, were involved. Two aircraft flew to Lalaghat to load supplies to be dropped on *Broadway*, these being the first two British aircraft to fly over the strip – Wg Cdr AC Pearson piloted Dakota "F" and Sq Ldr JFM Bell piloted "K". Grp Capt George Donaldson flew Air Marshal Sir John Baldwin into both *Piccadilly* and *Broadway* in a Dakota Mk III FL513 from No 194 Squadron. The rest of the crew were Flt Lt Mayer and Flg Off Shepherd. The first aircraft to land at *Broadway* was a Douglas C-47 Skytrain piloted by Brig Gen William D Old of the US Army Air Force.

The following day the squadron contributed twelve Dakotas to the airlift into *Broadway* with jeeps, mules and equipment. Two aircraft were damaged on landing, but were repaired and flown out three days later. From then on No 194 gave full support to the campaign, alongside its fellow Dakota units.

As the occasion arose, five more air strips for the landing of Dakotas behind the enemy were built by Cochran's engineers, and about one hundred small strips for the landing of the Stinson L-5 Sentinel aircraft which were later to be added to the strength of No 194. *White City*, *Blackpool* and *Clydeside* were the familiar names given to three of the rough strips cut through paddy fields and thick jungle growth. *Chowringhee* was another strip, named after Calcutta's main street, and *Aberdeen* was a strip named after Orde Wingate's wife's home.

On April 7, Sq Ldr JFM Bell, Commanding Officer of "B" Flight, was shot down over *Aberdeen* by a Japanese night-fighter. The pilot, with both engines out manged to crash-land on the strip without serious injury to the occupants. Four days later Flg Off Mellsop, a member of the Royal New Zealand Air Force, serving with No 194 Squadron, crashed into a hillside whilst going in to land at *Aberdeen* – of the twenty-eight passengers, only twelve survived.

The strips opened earlier were still very active and the resupply Dakotas provided a round the clock service in all weathers. During the night of May 5–6 Dakota Mk III FZ599 piloted by Flt Lt PWHF Wood, crashed on take-off from *Broadway* fully loaded with troops and four mules. Six days later Dakota Mk III – FZ582 – with Flg Off JG Simpson at the controls, broke its starboard undercarriage leg on landing at *Clydeside*. The cargo consisted of 6,000 lb of petrol and two bags of mail. Fortunately the crew had time to escape through the cockpit escape hatch unhurt. However, Flg Off Simpson remembered the mail bags and with utter disregard for his own personal safety he dashed back and entered the blazing wreckage and retrieved them.

By May 12, 1944, Troop Carrier Command had completed 69,000 sorties, carried 18,371 tons of freight, airlifted 32,312 men and carried 8,580 casualties. The Friendly Firm can claim their share of these figures.

On May 17 the Commanding Officer of No 194, Wg Cdr "Fatty" Pearson, was awarded the American Distinguished Flying Cross, in recognition of the squadron's part in landing the 2nd Wingate expedition deep in Burma, 200 miles behind the Japanese lines. The strain of flying long hours over most difficult terrain, made ten times worse by appalling weather conditions had tested the health and nerves of the unit's aircrew to the limit. Nine crews from No 99 Squadron and three crews from No 215 Squadron were moved in to enable No 194 to have a well earned rest.

The flying hours for May were 2,040. On May 10 alone Troop Carrier Command completed 6,000 sorties and Eastern Air Command exceeded 1,000. Two days earlier Dakota "A" had crash-landed at Jorhat, and four days later "C" crashed and caught fire. Two aircraft, "H" and "V", had flown supplies to *Blackpool*, only to find the enemy in possession of the strip, so the supply drop was abortive.

On June 4 Wg Cdr AC Pearson and Sq Ldr JFM Bell were awarded the Distinguished Flying Cross, and on June 6 Wg Cdr RT Chisholm from No 117 Squadron was nominated to assume command. The posting of Wg Cdr "Fatty" Pearson from the squadron was a blow felt by many, and in recognition of his popularity he was presented with a silver plate which was engraved with the signature of every officer on the squadron. Later in the month the Distinguished Flying Cross was awarded to Sq Ldr JD Thirlwell, "A" Flight Commander.

Troop Carrier Command had been inactivated on June 4 so No 194

Squadron came under Headquarters 3rd Air Force. The unit figured prominently in activities in the relief of Kohima and the Imphal siege. Some familiar places to No 194 during the Kohima battle and the Imphal siege were Dimapur, Manipur Road, Palel Kangla, Jorhat, Silchar. Sylhet and Dozazari. However there were incidents. Warrant Officer BR Christie in Dakota Mk III FZ600 took off from Agartala with 6,000 lb of supplies to drop at Kohima, but during bad weather struck a hill and crashed. The date was June 19. Three days later four Dakotas with air and ground crews were detached to Dergaon for *Operation Bustle* which was to keep the 23rd Brigade in Burma supplied from the air. Flg Off Brown was in charge, so naturally the detachment was nicknamed the *Brownbirds*. On June 26 the detachment was increased to twelve transports and Flt Lt Davidson was put in charge.

June 6 was one memorable day with the squadron. Seven Dakotas carried out 15 sorties. They all carried out a Basal, Kangla, Jorhat, Imphal, Box shuttle, carrying a total of 71,500 lb of supplies and 225 men. Places like Namun, Thetsemi, Somra, Chosumi, Jessami, Mokochung and Fort Khary were becoming familiar to the pilots and crews.

Dakota Mk III FZ504 "D" with Sgt OE Sheppard as pilot took off with a load of barbed wire and just over an hour later crashed at Imphal. The crew were slightly injured. Date was June 23. The same day Sgt SH Carr in Dakota Mk III KG493 "C" crash-landed at Imphal in adverse weather conditions.

The Operational Record Book for No 194 contains the following dated July 1, 1944. "It has taken on occasion six to seven days of battling through torrential rain, strong winds, and 10/10 cloud down to 200 feet to fulfil one mission, but it has been done and the squadron is very proud of its record of no failures to date."

July records six crews detached to Imphal. Six crews arrived from the squadron training unit at the Air Landing School at Chaklala making forty-one complete crews. The Dergaon detachment was moved to Imphal. It was reported that some jute chutes failed to open. Two Dakotas were slightly damaged by enemy ground fire whilst supply dropping on July 26.

Major Rigby of No 5 ASD was instructed to congratulate Plt Off S Hart on accurate drop carried out in bad weather condition over DZ RK 724888. Load included gelignite, anti-tank mines and weapons and was delivered within five hours of demand made by Brigade. As a result of this flight a pocket of Japanese resistance and four tanks were wiped out. Message came direct from General Messervy who was commanding the 33rd and 39th Brigade who were directly involved. Lt Gen CEN Stopford, CB DSO MC, was Commander of the 33rd Indian Corps. By August 1 the squadron was airlifting the casualties from Imphal.

Air Commodore CEN Guest, Air Officer Commanding No 229

Transport Group, visited the squadron on August 12. Flg Offs Brown, Kaitty and English were repatriated home to Canada and records show that Flt Lt AW Chalmers was the unit Adjutant. A Dakota Mk III FZ550 failed to take-off on August 24 and the pilot, Plt Off Howie, received slight injuries. An order for the squadron to move to Kangla on August 27 was cancelled and changed to Imphal. The total supplies dropped for the month of August was 2,099,873 lb.

The squadron had assisted to transport the 5th Indian Division, lock, stock and barrel from the Arakan to reinforce beseiged Imphal, evacuated their casualties and continued to fly in the supplies, so vital to the advancing army. After the Imphal siege and following a brief well earned rest period at Basal in the Punjab, No 194 Squadron moved back into the Imphal Valley airstrip and carried out intensive supply drops in the Meiktila area, the scene of many heavy battles during the final push against the Japanese in Burma.

On the first day of December 1944 twelve Dakotas were engaged in a local exercise dropping paratroops in the nearby Kutcha Strip. No 53 Glider Course was held at Fatehjang and there was a briefing for *Exercise Pongo* 1, scheduled for December 3 at Chaklala. The squadron establishment was increased to 81 pilots, 41 navigators and 41 Wireless Ops. A further move to Agatarla and Imphal was implemented on December 9 to relieve two US Army Air Force Combat Cargo Squadrons. No 436 RCAF Squadron assisted and the move was completed by December 13.

Eight Dakotas flew 12 sorties on December 11, dropping 81,500 lb of supplies to 33rd Corps with an escort of 6 Republic P-47 Thunderbolt fighters. A total of 52,627 lb of freight was delivered to Taukkyan by 8 aircraft, each making one sortie and returning with 23 casualties. Due to the large number of passengers at Indianggale awaiting transport to base, and the amount of freight to be delivered, 27 sorties were made to clear this backlog. The total freight flown to Indianggale was 163,291 lb and 64 casualties on stretchers, plus 438 passengers flown out. Yazagyo received a visit from the shuttle aircraft with 4,000 lb flying thence to Tamu with 1,860 lb and return to Yazagyo with 2,000 lb making a total of 228,818 lb airlifted.

A number of squadron pilots were posted out to No 9 Ferry Unit and the Transport Support Training Unit based at Chaklala. Wg Cdre RC Crawford was mentioned in the ORB as the new Commanding Officer. A number of aircrew reported various occurrences on December 24 which had an important bearing on supply dropping. Warrant Officer EJ Woodwiss, pilot of Dakota Mk III KG520 reported that 75 per cent of the sacks containing grain were rotten and allowed it to trail on the floor during despatching and consequently making it a most dangerous occupation for aircrews standing and working near the open cargo doors. Flg

Off Murray, pilot of Dakota Mk III FZ839, reported difficulty in identifying the recognition word on DZ SQ381654. Ground troops in this area used white strips against an almost white base. Flg Off B Shelly in Dakota Mk III KG520, reported hearing a report resembling flak in the vicinity of Kalela, although no smoke puffs were visible. Records show that a further 301,935 lb of supplies were dropped.

Wg Cdre RC Crawford made a COs report at the end of 1944. At the beginning of December, the squadron was just getting into its stride on training and had reached the stage of live paratroop dropping and glider towing in formation. Due to outside committments it was suddenly ordered to move to Agatarla and Imphal on December 9, 1944, and it had moved and was operating from both aerodromes by December 13. Since then the unit has been flying at a rate of well over 3,000 hours per month in spite of the lack of essential aircraft spares. The main item in short supply during December was main wheel tyres which were responsible at one period for holding five Dakotas on the ground.

The moral of both aircrew and groundcrew was exceedingly good, and it appeared as if they preferred to be at Imphal doing operational work than training at Basal.

Christmas went off well, although the amenities were not as they were to have been at Basal. A very good show was put on, and I can say without the slightest doubt that all members of the squadron had an enjoyable time.

By the beginning of January 1945 No 194 Squadron was flying well over forty sorties per day, the only factor causing hindrance being the frequency of bad weather which occurred during the first week of the year.

The squadron establishment was again considerably increased on January 27 with receipt of signal LWE/SEA/TC/1218, which catered for a substantial increase in both aircraft and personnel. The new order allowed for eight Stinson L-5 Sentinel light aircraft together with five pilots, five Beechcraft C-45 Expeditor transports, plus three Avro Anson aircraft.

Grp Capt PWM Wright from HQs No 229 Transport Group visited on January 2, and the first Sentinel pilots arrived – Flt Sgt Western and Flt Sgt Brodie. These light aircraft would be used for Jungle Rescue. On the lighter side mention must be made of the classical records supplied by No 221 Group for use on the squadrons own broadcasting system "NBG" with its motto "We aim to entertain you, but the best policy is to entertain yourself, if you won't, we can't". Sgt Fletcher was NCO in-charge.

Engine blowers in new Dakota aircraft were giving trouble, aircraft tyres were in bad condition, but replacements including engine spares were received regularly, plus new Dakota Mk IV aircraft.

Aircraft incidents during January 1945 included a forced landing at night by Dakota Mk IV KJ894 "L" piloted by Flt Lt DS Forster, on the YE-U strip on January 19. Just nine days later Flt Sgt CA Walton in

Dakota Mk IV KJ944 "Y" blew a tyre on take-off at Imphal causing the starboard undercarriage to collapse.

On January 31, 1945, the elephant badge unofficially adopted by No 194 Squadron since its inception and used throughout its service in India and Burma, was submitted to Chester Herald for official approval, but unfortunately the design of the flying elephant was described as unsuitable.

Dakota Mk III FL644 piloted by Flg Off F. Gillan Bremner, suffered a blown tyre at Imphal on February 12. Four days later Warrant Officer Haywood, flying Dakota Mk IV KJ898 "P", reported seeing a crashed Dakota at SR 2910. It had yellow "S" ident letter and the airframe serial number was K867. The unit checked with No 435 RCAF Squadron but their ident letter colour was red. This same Dakota – KJ898 – but flown by Warrant Officer Strongman hit some telegraph wires over the Chindwin River after take-off from Monywa and had to make a forced-landing. A further case of overloading a Dakota was reported during February with Mk III KG762 and Flt Lt GM Metcalf at Monywa.

The squadron moved from Imphal to Akyab on March 19 and operated alongside No 436 RCAF Squadron who also operated Dakotas. The gallant 14th Army under General Sir Bill Slim, was pushing forward towards Rangoon, but not before being involved in further heavy fighting on the Arakan front around Buthidaung and Maungdaw. The Dakotas followed and supplied the troops all the way. On March 20 Dakota Mk IV KK175 "D" was shot up near Meiktila and the pilot, Warrant Officer Smith, was wounded. Another Dakota Mk IV KK170 groundlooped five days later piloted by Warrant Officer J McGoff, and KK121 another Mk IV landed in a paddy field on March 29 and overturned. The pilot was Flg Off JH Murray. The five Sentinel aircraft were kept busy and on March 21, Warrant Officer Brodie took the 14th Army Commander, General Slim, from base to Monywa, Mandalay, Tardu and back to base on a visit to troops in the field.

Awards to No 194 Squadron personnel during April 1945 included the DFC to Flt Lt J Davidson, Flg Off DR Dossetor, Flg Off NC Brown, Warrant Officer EJ Woodwiss, and the AFM to Flt Sgt C Bruce. Air Marshal Sir Keith Park, KCB KBE MC DFC, visited the unit, and the Commanding Officer of No 194 was still Wg Cdre Robert C Crawford.

Airstrips used by the squadron included Magwe, Myingyan, Ywataung, Mingaladon – after the fall of Rangoon – and Tayatkwa. On April 7 Dakota Mk III KG762 "V" requested an emergency landing at Myitche after the pilot discovered the transport was grossly overloaded. The aircraft was wrecked on landing.

During *Operation Dracula* on May 1, 1945, No 194 Squadron completed twenty-two supply dropping sorties to Elephant Point, Syrtan and Government House. A detachment to Meiktila was effected during May, and Dakota Mk IV KN202 "Y", piloted by Flt Sgt Walton, was reported missing after take-off at 0455 hours with supplies for Payagyi – reference QF 9820.

From the period January 1 to April 8, 1945, the following tonnages were dropped to the 14th Army and 15 Corps. Supply dropped 20,202, landed 109,535, free dropped 7,767, making a total of 137,504. No 194 Squadron was now under No 341 Wing in the newly formed No 232 Group.

On April 11, 1945, the following message was received from the Commander-in-Chief Transport Command – Air Marshal Sir Ralph A Cochrane, KBE CB AFC, "Recent figures showing results achieved by squadrons of the newly formed No 232 Group make impressive reading and reflect high credit on all concerned. Well done."

Fall of Rangoon messages included one from the Supreme Commander, Lord Louis Mountbatten to Air Marshal Sir Keith Park. "Please convey my warmest congratulations to Stratemeyer, Coryton, Vincent, Evans and all concerned for their share in the extremely valuable capture of Toungoo airfields; only the closest co-operation between the Army and the Allied Air Forces could have made this possible."

With the end of World War 2 on August 14, 1945, No 194 Squadron moved from Akyab to Mingaladon, Rangoon, on about August 22, and it is believed the unit had a temporary Commanding Officer – Sq Ldr Bristow. Dakota Mk III FZ673 ran off the runway at Akyab whilst taking-off on August 24. The squadron operated a shuttle service to Don Muang, Bangkok in Siam, evacuating prisoners of war including British personnel who had been forced to work on the fateful and tragic Burma railway. This was perhaps the happiest, yet the saddest period for the squadron. The unit was again associated with its old friend, Grp Capt GFK Donaldson, DFC AFC, with the formation of No 118 Wing to which No 194 belonged. One of the first Dakotas to land at Bangkok was piloted by Flt Lt Arnold Boakes, later Sq Ldr and OC "B" Flight, accompanied by NS Greene as Navigator.

The unit was not without its personalities. The OC "A" Flight about this time was Flt Lt, later Sq Ldr, Joe Rank, nephew of Lord Rank. Flg Off Freddie Cox, later to be very involved in the FA Cup plus manager of Portsmouth and Bournemouth, had many hours to his credit in the Dakota. During early 1946 the Commanding Officer was Wg Cdr Penman, DSO DFC, and ex-No 617 Dambuster Squadron pilot.

After a few months of general transport duties No 194 Squadron was disbanded on February 15, 1946, having every good reason to be proud of its record. It took part in the Wingate Expedition of 1943, the Arakan campaign, and the Second Wingate airborne armada in 1944, the siege of Imphal and the Battle of Burma 1944–45, all campaigns in which air supply, with its Dakotas, was a deciding factor.

Credit and indeed praise must surely go to all personnel. Ground staff and aircrews alike who served with the squadron, whose wonderful team work and team spirit under good leadership throughout contributed everything to the efficiency of No 194 Squadron – The Friendly Firm – and its truly fine and successful achievements of which all No 194 personnel can feel justly proud.

On February 1, 1953, No 194 Squadron reformed at Sembawang, Singapore, with Westland Dragonfly helicopters for co-operation with the security forces fighting the Communist guerillas in the Malayan jungle. In 1954, the Dragonflies were supplemented by Sycamores and in June 1959, the squadron merged with No 155 to form No 110 Squadron.

No 271 SQUADRON

Death and Life

No 271 Squadron was reformed from No 1680 Flight on March 28, 1940, as a transport squadron under the control of Fighter Command. It was equipped mainly with Bristol Bombay and Handley-Page Harrow transport aircraft, but, in addition, it took over some of the aircraft belonging to civil air lines which had been impressed into military service. These included Ford and Savoia Marchetti tri-motor types. In April 1940 No 271 Squadron was transferred to the control of Bomber Command, and subsequently to Ferry Command, with which it remained until the formation of Royal Air Force Transport Command in 1943.

During the withdrawal from France in 1940 it was called upon to provide many services between the United Kingdom and the Continent, and for the next three years it provided internal transport services in the United Kingdom between RAF stations, transporting kit and personnel as well as urgent freight. It also provided the first transport service to our forces in Iceland. Throughout this period the squadron was based at Doncaster in Yorkshire.

Towards the end of 1943 it began re-equipping with Dakota transports, these being ferried from Prestwick after delivery from the United States. Early Dakota Mk III transports collected by squadron crews included FZ615, FZ633, FZ649 and FZ667. At Doncaster the aircraft were given a final check and brought up to date with modifications, plus new equipment. When re-equipping was complete No 271 Squadron had thirty new Dakota aircraft and on February 29, 1944, it moved to Down Ampney near Cirencester in Gloucestershire, where it was to be based with Nos 48 and 233 Squadrons also equipped with the Dakota.

An intensive training period followed during which numerous exercises were held with the airborne forces in parachute dropping at Netheravon in Wiltshire, and glider towing at Brize Norton in Oxfordshire and Hampstead Norris near Newbury in Berkshire. In addition it retained five Handley-Page Harrow aircraft which were operated as the *Sparrow* Ambulance Flight until November 1944.

In April 1944 the squadron, by then part of the newly formed No 46 Group of Transport Command, made its first sorties into occupied Europe. A member of "C" Flight was Flt Lt Jimmy Edwards, who was allocated a Dakota Mk III KG444 which he named "*The Pie Eyed Piper of Barnes*" after his birthplace. His first Nickel raid, as the leaflet operations were called, was on April 25. One of the units most important tasks came on the night of June 5–6, 1944, when it was among the first to drop paratroops on French soil. Dakota KG444 towed a heavily laden Airspeed Horsa glider and was damaged by enemy anti-aircraft fire over the French coast. The aircraft landed back at base safely, with no hydraulics, brakes or flaps. Supplies were dropped to the invasion troops near Caen the following day and Dakota Mk III FZ615 was used by Flt Lt Edwards while KG444 was repaired. This was a daylight sortie and involved towing a Horsa glider. The squadron flew many resupply missions to the airborne troops in France.

Along with other transport units, No 271 Squadron began a regular shuttle service between the United Kingdom and France, returning home with casualties and transporting supplies on the outward flight. Dakota KG444 and its pilot made their first landing in France on July 2 at strip B8 located at Sommervieu with equipment for No 39 Wing. Sixteen casualties were brought back by KG444 on the following day. Blood plasma was flown into B14 Amblie and twenty-four casualties flown out on July 10. The first aircraft to land at B17 Caen/Carpiquet was a Dakota Mk III KG500 from No 271 Squadron flown by Jimmy Edwards on August 22. The rest of August was spent flying into A50 Bricy with food for the citizens of Paris.

The second great event in the units history was *Operation Market Garden*, the airborne assault at Arnhem. On September 17, 1944, No 271 provided twenty-four Dakota aircraft, including KG444, and crews for the glider-borne force. A similar number was provided on the second day, and on the third, when the situation was becoming critical, seventeen Dakotas dropped supplies to the encircled troops. It was on this third day, September 19, 1944, that Flt Lt DSA Lord, DFC, gave his life in Dakota Mk III KG374 whilst on a resupply mission.

On September 21, Dakota KG444, piloted by Jimmy Edwards, was shot down by a Focke Wulf Fw 190 fighter south-east of Nijmegan whilst on a resupply mission. Three of the crew baled out safely of which two were taken prisoner, and three Royal Army Service Corps despatchers were killed. The pilot was wounded but landed safely in friendly territory.

After the Arnhem operation the squadron resumed its supply and casualty evacuation services until called upon to take part in the final great airborne operation of World War 2, the Rhine crossing in March 1945. A total of twelve Dakotas from No 271 Squadron towed Horsa gliders from the United Kingdom to a point just north of Wesel on the east bank of the river. The following month the unit joined in the agreeable task of flying home liberated Allied prisoners of war from Germany, a task which continued until after VE-Day. By May Flt Lt Jimmy Edwards was back on flying status, and flew Dakota Mk IIIs KG621, KG668 and KG564 to Europe with supplies, returning with casualties.

In the months following the war, transport services had to be maintained undiminished. On August 9, 1945, Flt Lt Jimmy Edwards DFC was posted to No 24 Squadron based at Hendon near London, having flown approximately 450 hours on the Dakota, all with No 271 Squadron. At the end of August No 271 was moved to Odiham from where it continued to operate passenger and freight services between the United Kingdom and the Continent. A further move was made in October, this time to Broadwell in Gloucestershire, and on the first day of November 1945 the squadron began the important task of operating a trooping service to India, which lasted several months. When this was completed a passenger and freight service to Naples was begun, later extended to Malta and Gibraltar, as well as frequent flights to the Control Commission headquarters in Germany. These services were still in operation when No 271 Squadron was renumbered No 77 on December 1, 1946.

His Majesty King George VI approved a badge for the squadron in November 1944. The design was indicative of the unit's aircraft carrying paratroops, bombs, etc, on their outward journeys and casualties on their homeward one.

No 435 SQUADRON

Determined on Delivery

When Wingate's raiders set off on their epic expedition into Burma, they chose as their emblem the Chinthe, a mythical monster, half-dog, half-lion, ferocious and externally watchful, images of which stand guard over the Burmese pagodas.

When No 435 Squadron began operations with its Dakotas, in support of the 14th Army it, too, adopted the Chinthe as the squadron badge, combining it with the motto – *Certi Provehendi.*

The Chinthe squadron more than lived up to its motto. After commencing operations in December 1944, it chalked up a record unsurpassed by any other unit in the Combat Cargo Task Force in South East Asia Command. The Chinthes followed the 14th Army all the way from Kawlin to Meiktila and Thazi. They flew the first Dakota transport to cross the Irrawaddy in support of the 14th Army bridgehead. Their jump-masters played a prominent role in the airborne operation against Rangoon. They flew by day and they flew by night. They flew with and without fighter escort. They landed at airfields which were under enemy fire and at airfields whose ownership at any future moment could not be vouched for by briefing officers. They dropped on dropping zones no bigger than geranium pots. They braved Japanese fighters and ground fire to deliver their loads. But the Chinthes always delivered the goods, and they brought back their cargoes of army casualties without suffering a single loss.

No 435 Squadron was one of two Royal Canadian Air Force transport units which went out to India in September 1944. Its first Commanding Officer was Wg Cdr TP Harnett. Before commencing operations, the Chinthes embarked on a programme of intensive training at Gujrat in the north of India. Particular attention was paid to paratroop exercises.

In November the Chinese armies began to retreat before the hard-pressing Japanese. In order to meet this situation, several of the US Army Air Force transport squadrons supplying the 14th Army were hurriedly moved to the Chinese front. The Chinthe squadron was ordered to move up to fill the breach immediately. By flying twenty-eight out of thirty-six hours, the squadron flew to its new base at Tulihal in Assam in little more than a day. On December 19, 1944, the squadron was operational.

There was no surplus of air transport, and in order to keep the army supplied, it was necessary to eke the last ounce of air tonnage out of every available aircraft. On its record day the squadron flew in 199 tons of supplies, its aircraft flying as much as 13 and 14 hours per day. Turn around was cut down to an almost unbelievable fine limit. Frequently the Dakotas unloaded their 7,000-odd lb of supplies and were airborne again within ten minutes of touching down. One enthusiastic crew established an all-time record of eight minutes for this task – that is, from touch-down to take-off.

The squadron flew Christmas puddings, rum, turkeys and mail to the 14th Army on Christmas Day, which was then in the Kawlin and Yazagio area. On New Year's Day the squadron was airborne on normal supply dropping operations.

On January 9, 1945, the 14th Army had fought its way into the town of Shwebo, an important road junction about sixteen miles west of the Irrawaddy. A dropping zone – DZ – was marked out some four miles east of the town, almost within range of the Japanese guns. On January 12 the squadron went out in force to carry out a drop on this DZ near Shwebo.

As the Dakotas came in, they joined the dropping-circuit, until there were six or seven of them over the DZ unloading a portion of their cargo on each circuit. Sq Ldr HL Coons, DFC, was in charge of this flight his Wireless Operator Warrant Officer RO Buckmaster, was in the astro-dome, keeping a look-out for enemy aircraft.

It was not long before Buckmaster warned the pilot of a Japanese Zero fighter making an attack on the Dakota. Coons cut his throttle and hit for the deck – then he opened up and headed north. The Zero made four passes at the Dakota, its guns blazing each time. Cpl AM White, one of the groundcrew who came along as cargo "kicker" was hit in the chest with a bullet. After the fifth attack Coons managed to break free and head for home. He arrived with the transport full of holes and minus four feet of wing tip. For his coolness and courage under fire, Sq Ldr Coons was awarded a Bar to his DFC.

Meanwhile the other Dakotas were hard pressed. According to reports by ground observers, there was a dozen Zeros in the circuit diving on the defenceless transports. Flg Off JK Ramsay in his Dakota didn't have a chance, the Zero got him first time, and his aircraft plunged to earth, enveloped in flames. Only the co-pilot, Flg Off AL Thomson, survived. The third aircraft to be attacked was piloted by Flt Lt RF Simpson, the units only English skipper. Flg Off T Jordan-Knox was co-pilot. The bulk of their load was ammunition. One Japanese shell properly placed and they were goners. They received a blast, LAC RG Evans, a groundcrew kicker, was hit in the arm. Warrant Officer DG Cotter received a cannon shell in his abdomen and fell to the floor, groaning. Flg Off AE Foster, who had come along for the ride, had two bullets rip his shirt, cutting deep grooves in the flesh of his back. The ammunition caught fire, the tail caught fire, and the port engine caught fire. Foster started to get rid of the blazing ammunition, and the navigator, Flg Off LB Dumont, beat out the tail fire with his bare hands. Simpson picked out a jungle clearing and brought the blazing Dakota in for a perfect crash landing. They evacuated the blazing aircraft as fast as their legs could carry them, made Dave Cotter comfortable, while the ammunition went off in all directions. Cotter died in hospital a few days later. For his skill and courage in crash-landing under extraordinary difficult conditions, Flt Lt Simpson was awarded the DFC. The hard-pressed British troops had watched the battle above them, unable to assist their Canadian friends.

In view of the increased Japanese fighter activity, it was decided to start making deliveries at night. After dark the Chinthe flare-path became a scene of bustling activity. The Dakotas took off at intervals of three minutes, turning off their navigation lights as soon as they left the circuit. At that time the squadron shared its airfield with a US Army Air Force troop carrier squadron equipped with C-47 Skytrains. The two units together put up thirty aircraft per night, each of which flew two sorties. The landing strip was no more than six to eight miles from the nearest Japanese troops.

On January 14, the 14th Army established a bridgehead across the Irrawaddy, near Singu, forty miles from Mandalay. During the next few days it was touch and go. The Chinthe squadron had the distinction of flying the first transport Dakota to cross the Irrawaddy in support of the bridgehead. The pilot of this aircraft was Warrant Officer FM Smith. No sooner had the transport entered the dropping circuit at 500 feet, when they saw tracers coming up at them. Smith made three circuits, and on his third his groundcrew kicker, Sgt Nick Jarjour, was wounded an the foot and arm. While first-aid was applied, Smith made two more iruns. By this time Jarjour was in a bad way, but there was still one-quarter of the load left – priceless cargo for the men at the bridgehead. Smith solved the problem by flying Jarjour back to the field hospital at Shwebo. Then he took off again and returned to the bridgehead, but the DZ was too hot for safety. Smith dropped a note informing the troops he intended dropping his cargo on a nearby strip of sandy beach. He arrived home safely, with nine bullet holes and minus one crew member.

The day after Smith's adventure, another of No 435 Squadron's Dakotas picked up a bellyfull of bullets over the DZ. The pilot was Fg Off WJ Bill Rogers, with co-pilot Flt Sgt WB Bill Rogers. They made four circuits over the DZ dropping each time. On the fourth trip they ran into trouble. One bullet cut the electric control cable. Another pierced the hydraulic fluid tank. Knowing that the aircraft was seriously damaged, Rogers set out for base. He landed, and switched the remainder of his cargo to another Dakota, took off and returned to the bridgehead only to find the DZ markings had disappeared. They dropped the remainder of their load on the beach without mishap.

The month of February provided a particularly hectic period for the Chinthe squadron. After some fierce fighting the army broke through towards Meiktila, south of Mandalay on the Rangoon railway, and perhaps the second most important communications centre in Burma. They raced on to occupy the vital airfields. Thabukton was occupied on February 27. On the following day transport aircraft came in with supplies and reinforcements. By day the British Army made strenuous efforts to keep the airfields clear for their transport squadrons. By night the Japanese attacked.

The units fighting for Meiktila had no solid rear, so all their supplies, from food to ammunition, had to be flown in. Despite enemy ground fire the Dakotas kept the troops supplied.

In the battle for Mandalay during March, the Chinthe squadron again figured prominently. The first Dakota to arrive dropped on a hurriedly improvised DZ at the foot of Sacred Hill. The DZ itself was approximately

50 yards wide by 100 yards long – tiny enough when you consider that at a dropping speed of 120 mph an aircraft traverses 100 yards in little better than one-and-a-half-seconds. The wonders of modern bomb-sight coupled with an electro-magnetic release had no application here. The drops were made visually, and the cargo was unloaded by hand, the trick being to drop as many parcels as possible per circuit, and to drop them all accurately. The situation did not improve until the 14th Army captured the airfield at North Mandalay and transport aircraft were able to land supplies.

After Mandalay had been taken, the Chinthe squadron was assigned to fly out the heroic 36th Division, which had fought almost 400 miles from Myitkyina to Mandalay. At the height of the battle, the Chinthe squadron had dropped the Division 50,000 cigarettes out of their own issue. They fully realised that battle is precisely the time when a man needs a cigarette most. When they flew the 36th out, the Chinthes were thanked profusely for their generosity.

Allied plans called for the continued advance of the 14th Army down the Mandalay-Rangoon railway, coupled with an air and sea operation against Rangoon itself. The airborne operation took place on May Day, and again the Chinthe squadron figured in the news.

Both Nos 435 and 436 Squadrons had concentrated on paratroop exercises during their training in North India. The troops who took part in the final assault on Rangoon where the same troops with whom the Canadian squadrons had trained. However, the aircraft provided in the operation were provided by the US Army Air Force squadrons of the Combat Cargo Task Force, but the paratroops, not unnaturally, asked that their original jumpmasters be allowed to travel with them. This request was granted and the Chinthes provided twenty jumpmasters and twenty by their sister squadron.

In Transport Command the wireless operator is trained as jump-master, and he is rarely mentioned in accounts of airborne operations, and still more rarely given credit for the importance of the work. A skilled jump-master, commanding the confidence of the paratroops under him, can make all the difference in the world to the success of a drop. It is the task of the jump-master, working on signals from the pilot, to see that the troops are dropped accurately and as rapidly as possible. A good jump-master working with experienced troops can get a "stick" of twenty men away in 16 to 18 seconds, and a "stick" of ten in half that time.

Before embarking on the final operation, the USAAF C-47 Skytrains, the Canadian jump-masters, and the British and Indian troops went through a final rehearsal. The drop was 100 per cent successful. Then on May 1, 1945, they took off for Rangoon, their target. Again the drop was 100 per cent successful. Not one man missed the dropping zone; not a single casualty was suffered. This was something completely unheard of.

The men of the Combat Cargo Task Force had to cope with other enemies than the Japanese. For a time in February vast forest fires swept through the jungles of Burma, and the Chinthes flew through the dense smoke which billowed up to 15,000 feet and more, with horizontal visibility virtually nil.

They had to fly over some of the worst jungle in the world and through what is unquestionably the worst weather in the world. In Burma the monsoons break near the end of May, and continue with fluctuating intensity until September. They are characterised by swiftly changing weather, much rainfall, and frequent and violent thunderstorms. Over the Chin Hills the storms are especially widespread and violent. Several of the Chinthe squadron Dakota pilots had unnerving experiences whilst flying during the monsoon season.

With the Japanese driven out of Burma, things were rather quiet for the squadron. For some weeks in June and July, most of their work consisted of freighting rice for the communities of North Burma, where the food situation was acute as a result of the ravages of war. Some of the rice was landed at airfields, much of it was dropped on the little villages on DZs set up by the Army Civil Affairs Officer in charge of the local food distribution.

On the eve of their departure for the United Kingdom, the Chinthes were called upon to carry out one of their most trying assignments. Southeast of Toungoo, several groups of British guerillas were fighting desperately against surrounding Japanese forces. When the transport squadrons supplying the guerillas were called away on other duties, No 435 Squadron were asked to fill the breach. A total of three detachments of Dakotas were sent to Toungoo, operating for four or five days before returning to base.

When operations ceased at Tulihal in the last days of August 1945, the Chinthes had completed just over eight months with the Combat Cargo Task Force. During those eight months the squadron had flown 29,873 hours on 16,592 sorties, averaging almost 120 hours per day throughout the whole period. Its Dakotas consumed over 1,760,000 gallons of gasolene and covered more than 4 million miles. The average Dakota flew seven hours per day. The cargo delivered totalled 27,460 tons, in addition to which 14,440 passengers and 851 casualties were carried.

With meagre equipment the groundcrew worked wonders. Engine changes, normally a job for repair depots were carried out in half a day and less. Serviceability during the crucial months was kept up around the 90 per cent mark. A truly amazing figure for a tropical station. When they travelled as kickers, as they often did, they shared the dangers of flying. Their work on the ground was routine, tedious, exacting. But without their efforts the fine showing of the squadron would have been unattainable.

After VJ-Day, which the Chinthes celebrated at the estate of the Maharajah of Manipur, the squadron prepared to fly back from Burma to the United Kingdom. Late in August the first wave of Dakotas left Tulihal, followed at intervals by other groups, until the last departed on September 11. Their homeward course took them via Alipore, Maharajpore, Karachi, Masirah, Aden, Wadi Halfa, Lydda, El Adam, El Aouina and Istres, to Down Ampney in Gloucestershire.

When No 435 Squadron arrived at Down Ampney, Wg Cdr CCN McVeigh, AFC, the commander of the training unit, succeeded Wg Cdr Harnett as Commanding Officer of the squadron.

Teamed in a Wing with two other Royal Canadian Air Force Dakota squadrons – Nos 436 and 437 – the Chinthe unit embarked on a new phase of transport work, carrying supplies and personnel to and from many places on the continent. Istres, Ghent, Brussels, Naples, Hamburg, Copenhagen, Oslo and Buckeburg were the principal ports of call. These operations continued for several months. Then on March 31, 1946, No 435 Squadron was officially disbanded overseas, and the twenty-five Dakota transports flown home to Canada.

Within a few months, the squadron number was revived by the re-designation of No 164 Squadron as No 435 on August 1, 1946. From their new base at Edmonton, the Chinthes embarked upon another tour of transport operations, adding fresh laurels to those won in two overseas theatres.

Canada may well be proud of its Chinthe Squadron and cherish the memory of those Chinthemen who gave their lives while carrying the means of battle to the Army in Burma.

Author's note:—

Space has prevented more than eight of the 50–odd Dakota squadrons in the RAF/RCAF being represented.

COMMAND BADGES

SQUADRON BADGES

DAKOTAS

"Oh, where are you going to all you Dakotas,
With Lord Louis airlifts, above the green trees?"
"We are going to fetch you your biscuits and bully,
Your sardines and curry, rice, atta and cheese."

*

"And where will you fetch it from, all you Dakotas,
I'll 'likh' you a 'chitti' while you are away"
"We fetch it from Chitters, Comilla and Dum Dum –
Address us at Akyab, Rangoon or Magwe."

*

"But if anything happened to all you Dakotas,
And suppose you were 'pranged' in the jungle afar?"
"Then you'd have no siyas or slingers for khana,
And you'd have no wads to eat with your 'char'."

*

"Then I'll pray for the fine weather for all you Dakotas,
For no monsoon rain, and headwinds so high."
"Oh, monsoon and winds don't bother Dakotas,
We've less hours on the ground than we have in the sky."

*

"Then I'll build a new airstrip for all you Dakotas,
With plenty of 'homers' to bring in your crew."
"Oh, the air and the ground's full of R/T already,
With Air from Sigs types bawling:
'Speak up – you're through'."

*

"For the 'roti' you eat, and the hard tack you nibble,
The fags that you puff, and replacements of men,
They are brought to you hourly by all us Dakotas
And if anyone hinders our coming – Amen."

E. C. DANIELS.

THE DC-3

1. In fifty one they tried to ground the noble DC-3
And so some lawyers brought the case before the C.A.B.*
So the board examined all the facts behind their great oak portal
And then pronounced these simple words, "The Gooney Bird's Immortal"
Chorus
They patched her up with masking tape, with paper clips and strings
And still she flies, she never dies, Methuselah with wings.

2. The Army toast their Skytrain in lousy scotch and soda
The Tommies raise their glasses high to cheer their old Dakota
Some claim the C-47's best, or the gallant R4D.,
Forget that claim, they're all the same, they're the noble DC-3

3. Douglas built this ship to last, but nobody expected
This crazy heap would fly and fly, no matter how they wrecked it
While nations fall and men retire, and jets go obsolete
The Gooney Bird flies on and on at eleven thousand feet

4. No matter what they do to her the Gooney Bird still flies
One crippled plane was fitted out with one wing half the size
She hunched her shoulders then took off (I know this makes you laugh)
One wing askew, and yet she flew, the DC two and a half

5. She had her faults, but after all, who's perfect in this sphere?
Her heating system was a gem and we loved her for her gear.
Of course the windows leaked a bit when the rain came pouring down
Sh'ld keep you warm, but in a storm, its possible you'ld drown.

6. Well now she flies the feeder routes and carries all the freight
She's just an airborne office, a flying twelve ton crate
They patched her up with masking tape with paper clips and strings
And still she flies, she never dies, Methuselah with wings.

(Writer unknown.)

*Civil Aereonautics Board.

DOUGLAS DAKOTA SPECIFICATION

Powered by: Two Pratt & Whitney Twin-Wasp R.1830-90C nine-cylinder engines, each driving a 12 ft 0 in diameter three-blade propeller.

Wing span: 95 ft 0 in. Length: 64 ft 6 in

Wing area: 987 sq ft. Gross weight: 31,000 lb

Max cruising speed: 192 mph at 10,000 ft

Max range: 2,125 nautical miles

Passenger/troops: 28

Crown Copyright

Appendix

Royal Air Force
Douglas DC-2K, DC-3 and Dakota
Serials

Douglas DC-2K	AX755	1
	AX767 to AX769	3
	DG468 to DG479	11
	HK820 and HK821	2
	HK837, HK847, HK867, NC14279	4
Douglas DC-3	LR230 to LR235	6
	MA925 and MA943	2
Dakota Mk I	FD768 to FD818	51
	HK983 built up from spares	1
	HK993	1
Dakota Mk II	FJ709 to FJ712	4
	HK867	1
	MA928 and MA929	2
	TJ167 and TJ170	2
Dakota Mk III	FD819 to FD967	149
	FL503 to FL652	150
	FZ548 to FZ698	151
	KG310 to KG809	500
	TS422 to TS427	6
	TS431 to TS436	6
Dakota Mk IV	KJ801 to KJ999	199
	KK100 to KK220	121
	KN200 to KN701	502
	KP208 to KP279	72
	TP181 to TP187	2
		Total: 1,951

NOTES:

FG857 listed as Dakota Mk I: but no records.

TJ168 and TJ169 allocated but not delivered.

Ground Instructional Dakota Aircraft

3493M		US 8th Air Force – No 1 Parachute Training School (PTS) Ringway 1943
3494M		US 8th Air Force – No 1 Parachute Training School (PTS) Ringway 1943.
4838M	42-22422	Mk III allocated from Prestwick 1944.
4844M	42-24068	Mk III No 107 Operational Training Unit, Leicester East. Direct from USA.
4957M	KG593	Mk III.
4981M	KG639	Mk III.
4989M	KG527	Mk III.
5254M	KG796	Mk III No 105 Operational Training Unit, Edzell.
5351M	FD826	Mk III No 512 Squadron, later No 1 Parachute Training School, Brize Norton.
5566M	KG590	Mk III.
5567M	KG418	Mk III cancelled.
5742M	KG214	Mk III No 1336 Heavy Conversion Unit (HCU), Welford, Warwickshire.
5749M	FL546	Mk III No 1381 Transport Conversion Unit (TCU), Bramcote, Warwickshire.
5949M	FD772	Mk I School of Air Support, Old Sarum, Wiltshire.
6252M	TJ167	Mk II (C-53) converted February 3, 1947, for No 5 Maintenance Unit.
6253M	FL561	Mk III School of Air Support, Old Sarum, Wiltshire.
6410M	FL584	Mk III Converted to instructional aircraft August 15, 1947.
6731M	KP231	Mk IV School of Technical Training, St Athan, Glamorgan.

The Douglas DC-3: Family Tree

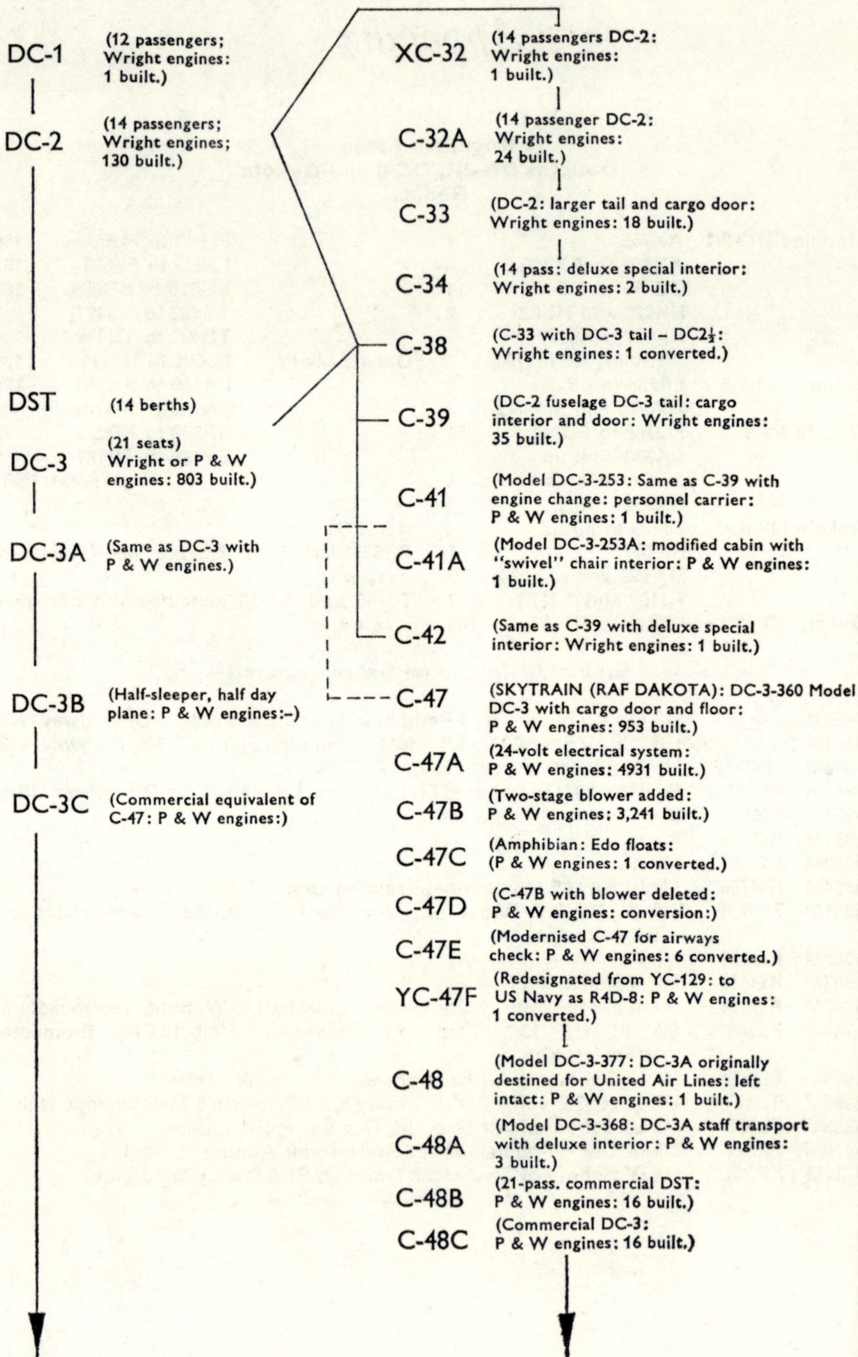

C-49 (Model DC-3-384: 24-pass. DC-3 built for TWA: Wright engines: 6 built.)

C-49A (Model DC-3-385: 21-pass. DC-3 built for Delta: pass door on left-hand side: Wright engines: 1 built.)

C-49B (Model DC-3-387: As Navy R4D-2: door on right-hand side: built for Eastern: Wright engines: 3 built.)

C-49C (Model DC-3-386: Troop-cargo heavy deck: small pass. door: side seats: built for Delta: Wright engines: 2 built.)

C-49D (Model DC-3-389: Same as C-49C. Built for Eastern: Wright engines: 11 built.)

C-49E through H (DC-3 taken from airlines and converted to troop carriers. Wright engines: 58 built.)

C-49J and K (DC-3: Trooper interior: Wright engines: 57 built.)

C-50 (Model DC-3-396: 21-pass.: door on left: built for American Airlines: Wright engines: 4 built.)

C-50A (Model DC-3-401: Trooper interior: built for American Airlines: passenger door: Wright engines: 2 built.)

C-50B (Model DC-3-397: C-50A with minor interior changes: Built for Braniff: Wright engines: 3 built.)

C-50C (Model DC-3-391: 21-pass. transport, built for Penn-Central Air Lines: Wright engines: 1 built.)

C-50D (Model DC-3-392: Trooper interior: built for Penn-Central Air Lines: Wright engines: 4 built.)

C-51 (Model DC-3-390: Trooper interior, right-hand door: built for Canadian-Colonial Air Lines: Wright engines: 1 built.)

C-52 (Model DC-3-398: Trooper interior: right hand door: built for United Air Lines: P & W engines: 1 built.)

C-52A (Model DC-3-394: Trooper interior: built for Western Air Lines: P & W engines: 1 built.)

C-52B (Model DC-3-395: Trooper interior: built for United Air Lines: P & W engines: 2 built.)

C-52C (Model DC-3-402: Trooper interior: built for Eastern Air Lines: P & W engines: 1 built.)

C-53 SKYTROOPER: Model DC-3-405: Troop transport: left-hand door: P & W engines: 193 built.)

XC-53A (Full-span flaps: hot air wing and tail interior de-icing: P & W engines: 1 converted.)

C-53B (First "winterised" C-53: P & W engines: 8 built.)

C-53C (Minor interior changes: P & W engines: 17 built.)

C-53D (First C-53 with 24-volt electrical system: P & W engines: 159 built.)

C-68 (DC-3A with 21- passenger interior: Wright engines: 2 built.)

C-117A and B (Army version of DC-3A: reconverted from C-47B: P & W engines: 17 built.)

C-117C (Revised C-47: P & W engines: 11 converted.)

YC-129 (Re-designated YC-47F: to US Navy as R4D-8: P & W engines: 1 converted.)

DC-3D (Douglas name for re-converted C-117s.)

XCG-17 (C-47 with engines removed and used as glider: 1 converted.)

Civil Douglas DC-2 aircraft impressed into use by the RAF

RAF Serial	Douglas c/n	US Civil Registration	Unit(s) and History
AX755	1301	NC14268	267 Sq: 31 Sq: Delivered to Delta Air Lines. Transferred to No. 31 Sq at Bilbeis in October 1941 and flown to India with squadron in Feb. 1942. Operated from Akyab in Feb. and Dum Dum in March. Written off at Akyab April 13, 1942. Engines salvaged. SOC after total flying hours of 504.45.
AX767	1238	NC13712	117 Sq: 31 Sq: Delivered to Transcontinental & Western Airlines Inc. Sold to US Treasury on July 5, 1941, for the British Purchasing Commission. Flown from Miami in American Airlines livery by a crew from Pan American Airways and arrived at Khartoum on October 14, 1941. After conversion, was allotted to No 117 Sq and used in the Western Desert until April 1942 when it was transferred to No. 31 Sq in India. Due to engine failure on April 25 force-landed 30 miles north east of Khanpour and received Cat.B damage. Removed to Delhi and leased to Indian National Airways on September 25, whilst under repair and became VT-ARA. Flown uncamouflaged as AX767/VT-ARA until its return to the RAF in September 1945.
AX768	1406	NC14966	117 Sq: 31 Sq: Delivered to American Airlines. Sold to US Treasury in March 1941. Flown from Miami by crew of Pan American Airways and arrived at Khartoum on October 14, 1941. After conversion allotted to No. 117 Sq and used in the Western Desert until April 1942, when it was transferred to No. 31 Sq in India. Flew into a hillside while flying in cloud over the Nandi State Forest during a flight to Bangalore on July 24, 1942. Cat. E.
AX769	1310	NC14277	117 Sq: 31 Sq: Delivered to American Airlines Inc. Sold to the US Treasury on July 5, 1941, for the British Purchasing Commission. Flown from Miami by crew of Pan American Airways and arrived at Khartoum on October 14, 1941. After conversion was allotted to No 117 Sq and used in the Western Desert until April 1942, when it was transferred to No. 31 Sq in India. Undershot the runway at Lahore on September 27, 1942, and its undercarriage struck a pile of cement and collapsed. The damaged airframe was dismantled and conveyed to Bangalore, where it was finally SOC on April 1, 1943.
DG468	1314	NC14281	31 Sq "D": Delivered to American Airlines Inc. Sold to the British Purchasing Commission on December 5, 1940. Allotted to Govt. of India as VT-AOU in April 1941, but was delivered to No 31 Sq and saw service in the Iraq rebellion and later in the Western Desert. Returned to India in February 1942 and took part in the Burma campaign. Retired to Lahore in April for overhaul and released to Tata Air Lines Ltd. on July 7 for operation on their Karachi to Ceylon freight service. Last known to have returned to Lahore on August 1, for transfer inspection. Actual fate not known.
DG469	1315	NC14282	31 Sq: Delivered to American Airlines Inc. Sold to the British Purchasing Commission on November 29, 1940. Allocated to Govt. of India in March 1941 as VT-AOQ, but delivered to No. 31 Sq in April and saw service during the Iraq rebellion and later in the Western Desert. Returned to India in February 1942 and took part in the Burma campaign. Retired to Lahore in April for overhaul and from May 23 to July 4 it was loaned to No. 301 Maintenance Unit at Karachi for supplying much needed equipment to RAF units. On August 22, 1942, it was transferred to Tata Air Lines Ltd. at Bombay and flew with them for the remainder of its life. SOC on June 21, 1945.
DG470	1316	NC14283	31 Sq "R": Delivered to American Airlines Inc. Sold to the British Purchasing Commission on November 29, 1940. Allocated to Govt. of India in March 1941 to become VT-AOR, but delivered to No. 31 Sq in April and saw action during the Iraq rebellion. Remained in India whilst rest of unit in the Middle East. After taking part in the Burma campaign, it was

RAF Serial	Douglas c/n	US Civil Registration	Unit(s) and History
			retired to Lahore in April 1942 and remained on squadron charge until it was withdrawn from service and SOC on November 8, 1943.
DG471	1244	NC13718	31 Sq: Delivered to Transcontinental and Western Airlines Inc. Sold to Cox & Stephens Inc. on February 19, 1941, for the British Purchasing Commission. Allocated to Govt. of India in April as VT-AOS, but delivered to No 31 Sq. Detached with three others to Shaibah on April 16 to help quell the Iraq rebellion and returned to India in May only to return to the Middle East in October with seven other unit DC-2Ks to work with No. 117 Sq at Bilbeis. On October 23, 1941, crashed on take-off from Drigh Road, Karachi. Loaded with ammunition for Iraq, the cases being heavy and looked a small load; some loader seeing this, added another load, which no one observed before the intended early morning take-off. Fire broke out on impact and the aircraft was destroyed. Crew included pilot Flg Off Mehar Singh and Mike Vlasto as co-pilot who escaped unhurt.
DG473	1308	NC14275	31 Sq: Delivered to Delta Air Lines. Bought by the British Purchasing Commission in February 1941 and allocated to Govt. of India as VT-AOV but was delivered to No. 31 Sq. Detached to the Middle East with seven others in October, returning to India in February 1942. On June 14 force-landed 60 miles east of Bangalore, in the Kolar Goldfields, during monsoon weather and its undercarriage collapsed on hitting a small bank. Fire broke out and the aircraft damaged beyond repair. SOC on October 20, 1942, as Cat. E.
DG474	1407	NC14921	31 Sq: Delivered to Delta Air Lines. Sold to British Purchasing Commission in February 1941. Allocated to Govt. of India as VT-AOW in March, but delivered to No. 31 Sq in April and saw service in India and Burma. Destroyed during a Japanese air raid on Mingaladon airfield in January 1942 and was SOC on February 3 with total hours of 303.15.
DG475	1410	NC14924	31 Sq: Delivered to Delta Air Lines. Sold to the British Purchasing Commission in February 1941. Allocated to the Govt. of India as VT-AOX in March but was delivered to No 31 Sq. Detached with seven others to Middle East in October but was shot down by three Me. 110s on December 25. Aircraft crash landed, pilots Warrant Officer David Lord and Flt Lt Howell safe; one passenger killed. Aircraft Cat. E.
DG476	1251	NC13725	31 Sq "Y": Delivered to Transcontinental & Western Airlines Inc. Sold to Cox and Stephens Inc on February 11, 1941, for the British Purchasing Commission. Allocated to Govt. of India in April as VT-AOY, but delivered to No. 31 Sq via No. 103 MU instead. Detached to the Middle East in October along with seven others, to work with No. 117 Sq at Bilbeis, returning to India in February 1942. Withdrawn at Bangalore while awaiting new engines and SOC on November 8, 1943.
DG477	1237	NC13711	31 Sq "Z": Delivered to Transcontinental & Western Airlines Inc. First production Douglas DC-2. Sold to Cox & Stephens Inc on February 26, 1941, for British Purchasing Commission and allocated to Govt. of India as VT-AOZ in April, but delivered to No. 31 Sq via No. 103 MU. Detached with seven others to the Middle East in October and returned to India the following February. Remained on unit charge at Bangalore after April 1942 and was SOC on November 8, 1943, while awaiting new engines. Believed to be DC-2 named *Ally Sloper* remains of which were seen on an aircraft dump at Juhu, Bombay in 1947.
DG478	1403	NC14923	31 Sq: Delivered to Delta Air Lines. Sold to the British Purchasing Commission in February 1941. Allocated to Govt. of India in April as VT-APA, but delivered to No. 31 Sq. It saw

RAF Serial	Douglas c/n	US Civil Registration	Unit(s) and History
			service in the Middle East and Burma, but was badly damaged at Chittagong in February 1942. Temporarily repaired and flown out only to be grounded at Lahore for extensive airframe repairs. Repairs started but abandoned and the aircraft SOC on June 30, 1944.
DG479	1240	NC13714	31 Sq "B": Delivered to Transcontinental & Western Airlines Inc. Sold to Cox & Stephens Inc. on February 26, 1941, for the British Purchasing Commission. Allocated to Govt. of India in May as VT-APB, but delivered to No. 31 Sq on May 23 Used by the squadron from Akyab and Dum Dum during the Japanese advance in Burma. Made the units last operational sortie on March 19, 1943, when it flew from Tezpur to Agartala. Withdrawn in serviceable condition at Lahore and SOC on November 8, 1943.
HK820	1350	NC14290	31 Sq: 117 Sq: Delivered to Pan American Airways. Taken over by No. 31 Sq at Shaibah and operated during the Iraq rebellion. Badly damaged by Me. 110s during a strafing raid at Habbaniya and left behind when the squadron returned to India. Repaired and joined No. 117 Sq in July 1942 and was last used by them on July 2, 1943. Fate not known.
HK821	1304	NC14271	31 Sq: 117 Sq: 31 Sq "M": Delivered to Pan American Airways. Taken over by No. 31 Sq at Shaibah on April 17, 1941, during the Iraq rebellion. Left behind when the squadron returned to India, May 1941. Transferred to No. 117 Sq in November. Rejoined No. 31 Sq in India during April 1942 and remained with the unit at Lahore until withdrawn in serviceable condition and SOC on November 8, 1943.
HK837	1371	NC14950	31 Sq: 117 Sq: Delivered to Pan American Airways. Taken over by No. 31 Sq at Shaibah and operated during the Iraq rebellion. Left behind when the squadron returned to India in May. Delivered to No. 117 Sq in October and operated by them in the Western Desert. Although transferred to No. 31 Sq in April 1942, was retained by No. 117 Sq until May 1943. Subsequent fate unknown.
HK847	1313	NC14280	31 Sq: 117 Sq: 31 Sq: Delivered to American Airlines Inc. Sold to US Treasury in 1941 for the British Purchasing Commission. Taken over by No. 31 Sq at Shaibah in April 1941 during the Iraq rebellion. Left behind when the squadron returned to India. Transferred to No. 117 Sq in October. Rejoined No. 31 Sq in April 1942 but in July the airframe became unserviceable and whilst under repair at Delhi it was bailed to Indian National Airways on September 25 and became VT-ARB. SOC on June 30, 1944, and dismantled and returned to the RAF in March 1945.
HK867	1311	NC14278	Delivered to American Airlines Inc. Sold to US Treasury in May 1941 for the British Purchasing Commission. Allotted to No. 267 and the RAF serial allocated. Ferried from USA via Brazil, Natal, Freetown, Ascension, reaching Sierra Leone on September 7, 1941. While landing at Hasting's Site, near Freetown, that same day it came into collision with a Hawker Hurricane Z4257 of the Fighter flight from No. 95 Sq. The pilot of the DC-2 lost control and the aircraft dropped heavily causing the undercarriage to collapse. Both aircraft were Cat. E. Note HK867 was re-allotted to a Dakota Mk. II by No. 267 Squadron in 1942.
Nil	1312	NC14279	Delivered to American Airlines Inc. Sold to US Treasury in May 1941 for the British Purchasing Commission but crashed at Bathurst, Gambia, on August 2, 1941, while en-route to the Canal Zone and the RAF.

Note:—SOC – Struck off Charge.

Civil Douglas DC-3 aircraft impressed into use by the RAF

RAF Serial	Douglas c/n	US Civil Registration	USAAF Serial	USAAF Model	Unit(s) and History
LR230	4173	NC300004	42-14297	C-48	31 Sq "D": Delivered to Defence Supply Corporation and then to US Army Air Force. Delivered to No. 31 Sq in April 1942 and immediately detached to Dinjan on April 20 for operations against the Japanese in Burma. While taking off from Myitkyina during a Japanese attack on May 6, 1942, a bomb fell in front of the port wing causing the aircraft to crash. Written-off on June 15, along with LR231 having completed 138.05 hours.
LR231	1915	NC16094	42-38252	C-49G	117 Sq: 31 Sq "E": Delivered to Eastern Airlines Inc. Delivered to No 117 Sq from West Africa on April 15, 1942, and was delivered to No 31 Sq at Delhi as N16094 on April 20 by Sq Ldr Howell. Camouflaged as LR231 was detached to Dinjan for ops against the Japanese in Burma. Set on fire during Japanese air attack at Myitkyina on May 6, 1942. SOC on June 15 along with LR230, having completed 504.15 hours.
LR232	4130	NC33675	42-38253	C-49H	31 Sq "S": Delivered to Capital Airlines, and to No 31 Sq in April 1942. Detached to Dinjan April 20 for operations against the Japanese in Burma. Landed on one engine at Allahabad on November 3 and serviced overnight by No 308 MU. While on air test the following day both engines failed and aircraft crashed with undercarriage retracted one mile east of the aerodrome. Repairs were started but later abandoned and aircraft was SOC on September 4, 1943.
LR233	1923	NC17313	42-38256	C-49H	31 Sq "H": Delivered to Transcontinental & Western Airlines Inc. To No 31 Sq towards the end of April 1942. By September 1 aircraft had been grounded at Dinjan for an engine change. SOC on October 25, 1942, as Cat. E1.
LR234	3276	NC25623	42-38258	C-48C	31 Sq "K": 194 Sq: US civil operator not known. Delivered to No 31 Sq in April 1942. Transferred to No 194 Sq on April 29, 1943, but on June 26 it was offered for sale to Indian National Airways and became VT-ARH on August 31, 1943.
LR235	1949	NC16082	42-38255	C-49G	31 Sq "J": 194 Sq: Delivered to Eastern Airlines Inc. Received by No 31 Sq towards the end of April 1942. Transferred to No 194 Sq on April 29, 1943, but crashed at Tezpur and was SOC on September 4, 1943.
MA925	4116	NC33653	42-38250	C-49H	117 Sq: 31 Sq: Delivered to American Airlines Inc. Sold to US Government on July 9, 1941. Received in the Middle East from USA by No 117 Sq on May 7, 1942, and was ferried to Lahore as N33653 for No 31 Sq. Later became MA925 and transferred to AHQ India Communications Flight, New Delhi, on September 19, 1942. Put up for sale on June 26, 1943, and sold to Indian National Airlines as VT-ATB.
MA943	4118	NC33655	42-38251	C-49H	31 Sq: 194 Sq: Delivered to American Airlines Inc. Sold to US Government July 9, 1941. Received by Air Reinforcement Centre, Karachi, in July 1942 and was temporarily

RAF Serial	Douglas c/n	US Civil Registration	USAAF Serial	USAAF Model	Unit(s) and History
					allocated to BOAC as G-AGEN but registration cancelled and aircraft delivered to No 31 Sq as N33655 on August 9. Converted to MA943 on major inspection at Dum Dum on September 25. Transferred to No 194 Sq on April 29, 1943. On June 26 it was offered to Tata Airlines but operated by Indian National Airways as VT-ARI from August 31, 1943. Registration cancelled in 1954.

Note: The above information was taken from several different sources, including Douglas Aircraft records, US Army Air Force records, Air Historical Branch record cards, squadron histories of the units involved, and there are certain facts which require clarification. However the author feels that the above table is an accurate a record as yet published.

Re-Arming and Location Programme – Home Units – Transport Command – No. 4 Group – Sept 1st, to Dec 1st, 1945

Unit	Present location	Aircraft type and Mk	To re-arm type/Mk	To move or to be formed at	Target date	Date operational
No 10 Squadron	St Mawgan	Dakota Mk IV	Liberator	ACSEA	Sept 1, 1945	In transit to SEAC
No 76 Squadron	Portreath	Dakota Mk IV		ACSEA	Sept 1, 1945	In transit to SEAC
No 77 Squadron	Broadwell	Dakota Mk IV		ACSEA	Sept 25, 1945	
No 78 Squadron	Breighton	Dakota Mk IV		Middle East	Sept 4, 1945	
No 102 Squadron	Pocklington	Halifax Mk VI	Liberator Mk VI	Bassingbourne	Sept 10, 1945	Dec 1, 1945
No 346 Squadron	Elvington	Halifax Mk VI				
No 347 Squadron	Elvington	Halifax Mk VI				
No 426 Squadron	Tempsford	Liberator Mk VI				Oct 1, 1945
No 466 Squadron	Driffield	Halifax Mk VI	Liberator Mk VI	Bassingbourne	Sept 10, 1945	Dec 1, 1945
No 512 Squadron	Holme	Dakota Mk III/IV		Down Ampney		Mid-Nov, 1945
No 6 LFS	Oakington	Oxford Mk I Lancaster Mk I/III Dakota Mk III				
No 1332 HCU	Riccall	Oxford Mk I Liberator Mk III York Mk I		New station		
No 1333 TSCU GPU Flight	Leicester East.	Oxford Mk II Dakota Mk III/IV Horsa Mk II Oxford Mk II Auster Mk III		New station		

Notes: ACSEA – Air Command South-East Asia

No 346 and 347 Squadron were Free French and eventually took their Halifax aircraft back to France

Driffield was to become a Transport Command station

Holme-on-Spalding Moor and Melbourne were placed under Care and Maintenance (C & M)

New locations to be agreed on for Nos 1332 and 1333 HCU and TSCU

No 10 Squadron never did receive Liberators as indicated but took its Dakotas to SEAC

No 426 Squadron was Royal Canadian Air Force

No 466 Squadron was Royal Australian Air Force

Major operations in which the Dakota was used in the paratrooping and glider-tug role

North Africa	November 1942	1st Parachute Brigade dropped from C-47 Skytrains from No 60 Group US Army Air Force
Sicily	July 9–10, 1943	*Operation Ladbrooke* – gliders
	July 13–14, 1943	*Operation Fustian* – paratroops and gliders
Greece	August 15, 1943	Cos: 11th Parachute Battalion – paratroops
	November 1–2, 1943	Samos: Greek Sacred Squadron – paratroops
Italy	June 1, 1944	*Operation Hasty* – paratroops
Normandy	June 5–6, 1944	*Operation Overlord* – paratroops and gliders
S. France	August 10, 1944	*Operation Bigot Dragoon* – paratroops
	August 15, 1944	*Operation Anvil Dragoon* – paratroops
Greece	September 14, 1944	*Operation Manna* – paratroops
Arnhem	September 17, 1944	*Operation Market Garden* – paratroops and gliders
Rhine	March 24, 1945	*Operation Varsity* – paratroops and gliders
Burma	March 5, 1944	*Operation Thursday* – paratroops and gliders
Rangoon	May 1, 1945	*Operation Dracula* – paratroops

Dakotas of the RCAF

RCAF Serial	RAF Serial	Douglas c/n	USAAF Serial	Taken on Strength	Struck off Strength	Unit(s)	Fate and Remark
650		9015	42-32789	31.3.43	2.2.53	Eastern Air Command 1943	Instr. A 508 12.7.4
651		9290	42-23438	20.4.43			Active 1.2.68
652		9108	42-32882	27.4.43	14.11.55	No. 164 Sq 1943	Instr. A 509 12.7.46
653		9415	42-23553	3.5.43	15.8.52		
654		9595	42-23733	17.6.43	15.8.52	No 165 Sq 1943	
655		9831	42-23969	14.7.43			Active 1.2.68
656		9832	42-23970	14.7.43			Active 1.2.68
657		9834	42-23972	14.7.43			Active 1.2.68
658		9830	42-23968	14.7.43			Active 1.2.68
659		9833	42-23971	19.7.43			Active 1.2.68
660		10199	42-24337	16.9.43			Active 1.2.68
661		10200	42-24338	16.9.43			Active 1.2.68
662		10201	42-24339	16.9.43			Active 1.2.68
663		10202	42-24340	16.9.43			Active 1.2.68
664		10203	42-24341	16.9.43	28.2.50		W/O Ski-wheel u/
960		12267	42-92464	18.2.44	1.11.51		Instr. A 628 14.2.59
961		12289	42-92483	18.2.44	17.8.64	No 9 (T) Group 1946	Sold
962		12544	42-92713	24.2.44	25.10.46		Crashed Esteven Sask. 16.9.46
963		12543	42-92712	3.3.44		No 435 Sq 1947	Active 1.2.68
964	KG381	12411	42-92593	9.3.44			Active 1.2.68
965		12876	42-93012	13.4.44		Radio trainer	Active 1.2.68
966		12877	42-93013	13.4.44	11.8.44	No 165 Sq	Crashed 18.7.44
967		13086	42-93201	23.4.44	14.2.47		Crashed Gandar Nfld. 27.9.46
968		13087	42-93202	29.4.44		No 165 Sq 1945	Active 1.2.68
969		13343	42-93432	23.5.44		AFHQ 1944	Active 1.2.68
970		13342	42-93431	1.6.44			Active 1.2.68
971		13925/25370	43-48109	27.7.44		No 105 CR Flight 1956	Active 1.2.68
972		13926/25371	43-48110	28.7.44		Photomod.8.2.47	Active 1.2.68
973		13923/25368	43-48107	31.7.44		No 14 Photo Sq	Active 1.2.68
974		13924/25369	43-48108	3.8.44	17.8.64	No 165 Sq 1944	Sold
975		14558/26003	43-48742	18.9.44	29.7.59	No 168 Sq 1944	W/O

RCAF Serial	RAF Serial	Douglas c/n	USAAF Serial	Taken on Strength	Struck off Strength	Unit(s)	Fate and Remarks
976		14557/26002	43-48741	19.9.44		No 435 Sq 1947	Active 1.2.68
977		14560/26005	43-48744	21.9.44		No 412 Sq 1956	Active 1.2.68
978		14559/26004	43-48743	25.9.44	4.7.45		Crashed RAF Biggin Hill 25.1.45
979		15196/26641	43-49380	21.11.44		No 414 Sq 1949	Active 1.2.68
980		15199/26644	43-49383	21.11.44	20.5.52		Crashed Frobisher 6.5.52
981		15198/26643	43-49382	25.11.44		No 168 Sq 1945	Active 1.2.68
982		15197/26642	43-49381	28.11.44	5.5.49	No 168 Sq 1945	W/O
983		15688/27133	43-49872	17.1.45	12.3.63	c/s VC-BNA	Indian Air Force
984		15690/27135	43-49874	20.1.45	10.7.58		Crashed St Hubert 28.7.52 Instr. A 597 26.8.52
985		15935/32683	44-76351	16.2.45	19.2.53	Target tow 23.5.51	Lost
986		15933/32681	44-76349	16.2.45	12.11.46		Crashed Goose Bay 29.3.46
987		16367/33115	44-76783	1.5.45	27.1.49	No 9 (T) Group 1945	W/O
988		16368/33116	44-76784	1.5.45		No 9 (T) Group 1945	Active 1.2.68
989		16718/33466	44-77134	19.6.45	12.3.63		Indian Air Force
990		16719/33467	44-77135	19.6.45		No 9 (T) Group 1946	Active 1.2.68
991		16959/34218	45-956	28.9.45	27.12.54	No 414 Photo Sq 1949	W/O
992	FZ658	12217	42-92419	26.8.46			Active 1.2.68
993	KG448	12483	42-92658	20.7.46			Active 1.2.68
994	KG659	13476	42-93552	20.7.46	30.10.62		Indian Air Force
1000	KN665	16620/33368	44-77036	1.8.46		VIP aircraft	Active 1.2.68
10910	FD941	9862	42-24000	30.5.51			Active 1.2.68
10911	FD824	9186	42-23324	30.5.51			Active 1.2.68
10912		4441	USN01985	11.6.51			Active 1.2.68
10913		18986	42-100523	20.6.51			Active 1.2.68
10914		16123/32871	44-76539	15.1.52			Active 1.2.68
10915	KP229	16702/33450	44-77118	12.4.52			Active 1.2.68
10916		16095/32843	44-76511	5.6.52			Active 1.2.68
10917		15629	43-49809	14.6.52			Active 1.2.68
10918	FZ665	12238	42-108839	20.7.46			Active 1.2.68
	FD824		See RCAF "10911"				
	FD941		See RCAF "10910"				
	FL595	12004	42-92227	22.12.43	5.12.45	No 32 OTU	Sold
	FL598	12007	42-92230	5.1.44	19.2.46	No 32 OTU	Sold
	FL615	12026	42-92247	5.1.44	19.2.46	No 32 OTU	Sold
	FL616	12027	42-92248	4.1.44	5.12.45	Converted Syn. Trainer 1.3.44	Sold
	FL618	12039	42-92258	11.1.44	5.12.45	No 32 OTU	Sold
	FL621	12042	42-92261	11.1.44	5.12.45	No 32 OTU	Sold
	FL636	12063	42-92280	15.1.44	19.6.46	Eastern Air Command	
	FL650	12079	42-92294	31.1.44	12.6.45	No 32 OTU	Crashed 6.11.44
	FZ557	12092	42-92306	5.1.44	19.2.46	Eastern Air Command	Sold
	FZ558	12093	42-92307	5.1.44	2.3.46	No 22 (SR) Unit Seal Island	Sold
	FZ571	12106	42-92319	7.1.44	21.12.45	No 6 OTU Comox	Sold
	FZ575	12110	42-92322	5.1.44	5.12.45	No 32 OTU	Sold
	FZ576	12111	42-92323	5.1.44	14.8.44	No 32 OTU	Crashed 23.5.44
	FZ581	12116	42-92328	11.1.44	17.4.44	No 32 OTU Pat Bay	Crashed 26.2.44
	FZ583	12138	42-108829	15.1.44	23.8.45	No 6 OTU	Missing 27.6.45
	FZ584	12139	42-92348	18.2.44	19.2.46	No 32 OTU	Sold

RCAF Serial	RAF Serial	Douglas c/n	USAAF Serial	Taken on Strength	Struck off Strength	Unit(s)	Fate and Remarks
	FZ586	12141	42-92350	18.2.44	5.12.45	No 32 OTU	Sold
	FZ596	12151	42-92359	11.1.44	9.10.44	No 6 OTU	Lost at sea 22.8.44
	FZ634	12191	42-92395	25.5.44	19.2.46	Western Air Command	Sold
	FZ635	12192	42-92396	15.1.44	5.12.45	No 32 OTU	Sold
	FZ658		See RCAF "992"				
	FZ665		See RCAF "10918"				
	FZ669	12254	42-92452	26.8.46			Active 1.2.68
	FZ671	12256	42-92454	26.8.46		No 437 Sq	Active 1.2.68
	FZ678	12273	42-92469	20.7.46	23.6.49		W/O Stn. Fort Nelson
	FZ692	12295	42-92489	26.8.46			Active 1.2.68
	FZ694	12300	42-92493	26.8.46			Active 1.2.68
	FZ695	12301	42-92494	20.7.46		CEPE, Alberta	Active 1.2.68
	KG312	12307	42-92500	26.8.46			Active 1.2.68
	KG317	12314	42-92506	26.8.46	10.5.50		Crashed Summerside PEI 29.4.50
	KG320	12317	42-92509	20.7.46			Active 1.2.68
	KG330	12327	42-92518	20.7.46			Active 1.2.68
	KG337	12344	42-92533	26.8.46			Active 1.2.68
	KG345	12352	42-92540	26.8.46			Active 1.2.68
	KG350	12357	42-92545	26.8.46		No 426 Sq	Active 1.2.68
	KG354	12363	42-92550	26.8.46			Active 1.2.68
	KG368	12377	42-92563	9.9.46	22.9.47	No 9 (T) Group	Sold
	KG381		See RCAF "964"				
	KG382	12412	42-92594	22.2.44	19.2.46	No 32 OTU	Sold
	KG389	12419	42-92600	26.8.46		No 3 OTU, No 408 Sq	Active 1.2.68
	KG394	12424	42-92605	20.7.46			Active 1.2.68
	KG395	12425	42-92606	26.8.46			Active 1.2.68
	KG400	12435	42-92615	20.7.46			Active 1.2.68
	KG403	12438	42-108859	20.7.46			Active 1.2.68
	KG414	12449	42-92627	26.8.46	6.11.62	No 102 KU, Trenton	Indian Air Force
	KG416	12451	42-92629	28.8.46	13.6.52		Crashed Winnipeg Man. 18.4.52
	KG423	12458	42-108861	1.10.46			
	KG430	12465	42-92642	26.8.46	6.7.51		Crashed Summerside PEI 26.6.51
	KG441	12476	42-92652	26.8.46			Equipped with snatch gear Active 1.2.68
	KG455	12490	42-92664	20.7.46			Active 1.2.68
	KG448		See RCAF "993"				
	KG479	12591	42-92755	7.3.44	19.2.46	No 32 OTU	Sold
	KG485	12597	42-92761	10.3.44	5.12.45	No 32 OTU	Sold
	KG486	12598	42-108875	20.7.46			Active 1.2.68
	KG526	12930	42-93060	13.4.44	21.11.45	Western Air Command, Vancouver	Sold
	KG545	13028	42-108918	26.8.46			Active 1.2.68
	KG557	13149	42-93257	20.7.46			Active 1.2.68
	KG559	13151	42-93259	20.7.46	6.11.62	Stn. Whitehorse	Indian Air Force
	KG562	13154	42-93262	1.10.46			Active 1.2.68
	KG563	13155	42-93263	1.10.46			Active 1.2.68
	KG568	13160	42-93267	26.8.46	6.11.62	No 111 Comm Flt. Winnipeg	Indian Air Force
	KG577	13300	42-93393	26.8.46			Active 1.2.68
	KG580	13303	42-93396	20.7.46			Active 1.2.68
	KG587	13310	42-93402	26.8.46			Active 1.2.68
	KG600	13331	42-93421	17.6.46	23.11.60		Instr. A 601 26.8.63
	KG602	13333	42-93423	9.9.46			Active 1.2.68

RCAF Serial	RAF Serial	Douglas c/n	USAAF Serial	Taken on Strength	Struck off Strength	Unit(s)	Fate and Remarks
	KG623	13383	42-93468	9.9.46			Active 1.2.68
	KG632	13392	42-93476	17.6.46			Active 1.2.68
	KG634	13394	42-93478	20.7.46		No 1 Air Division No 435 Sq	Active 1.2.68
	KG635	13395	42-93479	20.7.46	6.7.49	No 9 (T) Group	W/O
	KG641	13453	42-93531	20.7.46			Active 1.2.68
	KG659		See RCAF "994"				
	KG660		See RCAF "10199"				
	KG665	13482	42-93557	17.12.46			Active 1.2.68
	KG668	13485	42-93560	17.6.46			Active 1.2.68
	KG692	13559	42-93626	4.7.44	19.2.46	Western Air Command	Sold
	KG693	13560	42-93627	4.7.44	19.2.46	Western Air Command	Sold
	KG713	13580	42-93645	2.7.46			Active 1.2.68
	KG769	13868/25313	43-48052	25.7.44	21.11.45	Western Air Command	Sold
	KG808	14040/25485	43-48224	20.7.46			Active 1.2.68
	KG827		See "KJ827" as KG827 is a Liberator serial				
	KG828		See "KJ828" as KG828 is a Liberator serial				
	KG936		See "KJ936" as KG936 is a Liberator serial				
	KJ827	14166/25611	43-48350	2.9.44			Active 1.2.68
	KJ828	14167/25612	43-48351	21.8.44			Active 1.2.68
	KJ936	14664/26109	43-48848	3.10.44	2.3.50	No 9 (T) Group No 412 Sq AO-H	W/O
	KJ956	14803/26248	43-48987	7.9.51			Active 1.2.68
	KK101	14995/26440	43-49179	16.11.44	17.10.47	Western Air Command	492.25 hours
	KK102	14996/26441	43-49180	4.11.44			Active 1.2.68
	KK143	15281/26726	43-49465	20.7.46			Active 1.2.68
	KK160	15299/26744	43-49483	14.12.44			Active 1.2.68
	KN200	15456/27004	43-49743	8.1.45			Active 1.2.68
	KN201	15457/27005	43-49744	22.1.45			Active 1.2.68
	KN256	15739/27184	43-49923	20.7.46		No 437 Sq	Active 1.2.68
	KN258	15142/27187	43-49926	20.7.46		No 435 Sq	Active 1.2.68
	KN261	15745/27190	43-49929	17.6.46		No 435 Sq	Active 1.2.68
	KN269	15757/27202	43-49941	20.7.46			Active 1.2.68
	KN270	15758/27203	43-49942	4.6.46		No 435 Sq	Active 1.2.68
	KN277	15767/27212	43-49951	20.7.46		No 437 Sq, No 436 Sq, No 435 Sq	Active 1.2.68
	KN278	15769/27214	43-49953	20.7.46	8.8.63	No 414 Sq, No 418, Sq, No 437 Sq	W/O
	KN281	15773/27218	43-49957	20.7.46		No 437 Sq	Active 1.2.68
	KN291	15792/32540	44-76208	3.7.46		No 437 Sq	Active 1.2.68
	KN392	16065/32813	44-76481	23.11.51			Active 1.2.68
	KN427	16107/32855	44-76523	20.7.46			Active 1.2.68
	KN436	16117/32865	44-76533	20.7.46			Active 1.2.68
	KN443	16125/32873	44-76541	17.6.46			Active 1.2.68
	KN448	16170/32918	44-76586	17.6.46			Active 1.2.68
	KN451	16174/32922	44-76590	5.8.47		Instr. A 655	National Aviation Museum
	KN485	16215/32963	44-76631	6.3.52			Active 1.2.68
	KN511	16298/33046	44-76714	20.7.46			Active 1.2.68
	KN665	16620/33368	44-77036	1.2.46	11.7.47	No 109 (KU) Flight, Marville	Sold
	KN666	16621/33369	44-77037	20.7.46	6.11.62	No 2 (F) Wing No 121 (KU)	Indian AirForce
	KN676	16636/33384	44-77052	17.6.46	6.11.62		Indian Air Force
	KN655		See RCAF "1000"				
	KP221	16689/33437	44-77105	20.7.46		No 437 Sq, No 436 Sq, No 435 Sq	Active 1.2.68

RCAF Serial	RAF Serial	Douglas c/n	USAAF Serial	Taken on Strength	Taken off Strength	Unit(s)	Fate and Remarks
	KP224	16693/33441	44-77109	20.7.46		No 436 Sq, No 435 Sq	Active 1.2.68
	KP227	16697/33445	44-77113	20.7.46		No 435 Sq, No 437 Sq BW-G	Active 1.2.68
	KP229		See RCAF "10915"				
	TS422	19345	42-100882	20.7.46		No 4 OTU Trenton	Active 1.2.68
	TS425	19353	42-100890	20.7.46			Active 1.2.68

Douglas Dakotas operated by BOAC

Douglas Model	Civil Registration	RAF Serial	W/T Call-sign	Remarks
DC-3-G102A	PH-ALI-G-AGBB			Ex KLM "Ibis"
DC-3-G102A	PH-ALR-G-AGBC			Ex KLM "Reiger"
DC-3-G102A	PH-ARB-G-AGBD			Ex KLM "Buizard"
DC-3-G102A	PH-ARZ-G-AGBE			Ex KLM "Zilverreiger"
DC-3-G102A	PH-ARW-G-AGBI			Ex KLM "Wulp"
DC-3-G102A-277D	NC33655-G-AGEN	MA943		Ex C-49H-DO 42-38251 c/n 4118
C-47-DL	G-AGFX	FD769	ODZBK	
C-47-DL	G-AGFY	FD770	ODZCK	
C-47-DL	G-AGFZ	FD771	ODZEK	
C-47-DL	G-AGGA	FD777	ODZDK	
C-47-DL	G-AGGB	FD773	ODZAK	
C-47-DL	G-AGGI	FD796	ODZFK	
C-47A-1-DL	G-AGHE	FD827	ODZGK	
C-47A-1-DL	G-AGHF	FD824	ODZZ	
C-47A-1-DL	G-AGHH	FD825	ODZY	
C-47A-25-DL	G-AGHJ	FD867	ODZX	
C-47A-25-DL	G-AGHK	FD860	ODZHK	
C-47A-25-DL	G-AGHL	FD861	ODZJK	
C-47A-30-DL	G-AGHM	FD901	ODZW	
C-47A-25-DL	G-AGHN	FD868	ODZV	
C-47A-40-DL	G-AGHO	FD941	ODZU	
C-47A-25-DL	G-AHGP	FD862	ODZT	
C-47A-50-DL	G-AGHR	FL514	ODZS	
C-47A-50-DL	G-AGHS	FL516	ODZR	
C-47A-50-DL	G-AGHT	FL520	ODZQ	
C-47A-50-DL	G-AGHU	FD942	ODZP	
C-47A-1-DK	G-AGIO	FL548	ODZLK	
C-47A-1-DK	G-AGIP	FL544	ODZO	
C-47A-1-DK	G-AGIR	FL568		
C-47A-1-DK	G-AGIS	FL607	ODZM	
C-47A-1-DK	G-AGIT	FL560	ODZN	
C-47A-1-DK	G-AGIU	FZ561	ODZK	
C-47A-1-DK	G-AGIW	FZ630	ODZJ	
C-47A-1-DK	G-AGIX	FL628	ODZH	
C-47A-1-DK	G-AGIY	FZ567	ODZL	
C-47A-1-DK	G-AGIZ	FL647	ODZMK	
C-47A-1-DK	G-AGJU	FZ614	ODZG	
C-47A-1-DK	G-AGJV	FZ638	ODZF	
C-47A-1-DK	G-AGJW	FL641	ODZD	
C-47A-1-DK	G-AGJX	FL604	ODZC	
C-47A-1-DK	G-AGJY	FL608	ODZB	
C-47A-1-DK	G-AGJZ	FL629	ODZA	
C-47A-1-DK	G-AGJR-PH-TAY	FL589		PH-AZR never used. "Roodborstje"
C-47A-1-DK	G-AGJS-PH-TAZ	FZ618		PH-AZS never used. "Spreeuw"
C-47A-1-DK	G-AGJT-PH-TBA	FZ617		PH-AZT never used. "Turelzuur"
C-47B-1-DK	G-AGKA	KJ802	OFZY	
C-47B-1-DK	G-AGKB	KJ804	OFZX	
C-47B-1-DK	G-AGKC	KJ807	OFZW	
C-47B-1-DK	G-AGKD	KJ811	OFZV	
C-47B-1-DK	G-AGKE	KJ867	OFZU	
C-47B-1-DK	G-AGKF	KJ868	OFZT	
C-47B-1-DK	G-AGKG	KJ879	OFZS	
C-47B-1-DK	G-AGKH	KG871	OFZR	
C-47B-5-DK	G-AGKI	KJ928	OFZQ	

Douglas Model	Civil Registration	RAF Serial	W/T Call-sign	Remarks
C-47B-5-DK	G-AGKJ	KJ933	OFZP	
C-47B-5-DK	G-AGKK	KJ929	OFZO	
C-47B-5-DK	G-AGKL	KJ935	OFZN	
C-47B-10-DK	G-AGKM	KJ992	OFZM	
C-47B-10-DK	G-AGKN	KJ990	OFZL	
C-47B-10-DK	G-AGMZ	KJ985	OFZK	
C-47B-10-DK	G-AGNA	KJ976	OFZJ	
C-47B-15-DK	G-AGNB	KK137	OFZH	
C-47B-15-DK	G-AGNC	KK145	OFZG	
C-47B-15-DK	G-AGND	KK142	OFZF	
C-47B-15-DK	G-AGNE	KK139	OFZD	
C-47B-20-DK	G-AGNF	KK201	OFZC	
C-47B-20-DK	G-AGNG	KK216	OFZB	
C-47B-20-DK	G-AGNK	KK206	OFZA	
C-47A-10-DK	G-AGYX	KG437		Delivered January 1946
C-47A-5-DK	G-AGYZ	FZ681		Delivered January 1946
C-47A-10-DK	G-AGZA	KG420		Delivered February 1946
C-47A-1-DK	G-AGZB	FZ624		Delivered February 1946
C-47A-5-DK	G-AGZC	FZ622		Delivered February 1946
C-47A-10-DK	G-AGZD	KG415		Delivered Croydon February 22, 1946 as KG415
C-47A-10-DK	G-AGZE	KG386		Delivered March 1946
C-47A-5-DK	G-AHCS	KG341		Delivered Croydon March 11, 1946, as KG341
C-47A-5-DK	G-AHCT	KG313		Delivered Croydon March 11, 1946, as KG313
C-47A-25-DK	G-AHCU	KG621		Delivered March 1946
C-47A-10-DK	G-AHCV	KG408		Delivered April 1946
C-47A-25-DK	G-AHCW	KG585		Delivered Croydon April 8, 1946, as KG585
C-47A-25DK	G-AHCX	KG604		Delivered Croydon April 10, 1946, as KG604
C-47A-5-DK	G-AHCY	KG348		Delivered April 1946
C-47A-1-DK	G-AHCZ	FL563		Delivered April 1946
C-47A-1-DK	G-AHDA	FZ622		Delivered Croydon May 2, 1946, as FZ622
C-47A-1-DK	G-AHDB	FL649		Delivered Croydon May 15, 1946, as FL649
C-47A-25-DK	G-AHDC	KG664		Delivered June 1946
C-47A-25-DK	G-AIAZ	KG647		Delivered June 1946. Returned RAF November 1946
C-47A-40-DL	G-AIBA	FD939		Delivered June 1946. Returned RAF November 1946

Notes: FL544/G-AGIP recorded with No 512 Squadron in Middle East November 26, 1943
FL607/G-AGIS recorded with No 271 Squadron at Doncaster December 20, 1943
FL604/G-AGJX recorded with No 512 Squadron at Melton Mowbray December 30, 1943
recorded with No 107 OTU at Leicester East on May 13, 1944
recorded with No 271 Squadron at Doncaster on January 24, 1944
FL608/G-AGJY recorded with No 512 Squadron at Melton Mowbray January 2, 1944
recorded with No 107 OTU Leicester East May 13, 1944
FL629/G-AGJZ recorded with No 271 Squadron at Down Ampney February 14, 1944
recorded with No 107 OTU at Leicester East May 13, 1944

Douglas Dakota Aircraft of the RAF overhauled by Field Aircraft Services Ltd for the USAF in Europe – USAFE

Contract No 61 (514)-779 Aircraft converted at Tollerton, near Nottingham
No 8 Maintenance Unit – Little Rissington, Gloucestershire

Model	RAF No	USAF Serial	Arrival Date	Departure Date	Remarks
C-47B	KN482	44-76628	July 24, 1954	January 30, 1955	
C-47B	KN521	44-76732	July 28, 1954	December 10, 1954	ex No 240 OCU
C-47B	KN356	44-76388	July 29, 1954	February 14, 1955	ex No 27 Squadron
C-47B	KN506	44-76706	August 7, 1954	March 3, 1955	ex No 27 Squadron
C-47A	KJ887	43-48656	August 5, 1954	February 12, 1955	
C-47B	KN388	44-76431	August 6, 1954	February 19, 1955	ex No 27 Squadron
C-47A	FL542	42-24355	August 16, 1954	February 12, 1955	
C-47B	KN369	44-76407	August 13, 1954	April 14, 1955	ex No 27 Squadron
C-47B	KN361	44-76396	August 14, 1954	March 22, 1955	ex No 240 OCU
C-47B	KN360	44-76393	August 26, 1954	June 21, 1955	ex No 27 Squadron

Model	RAF No	USAF Serial	Arrival Date	Departure Date	Remarks
C-47B	KP251	44-77221	August 25, 1954	June 21, 1955	ex No 24 Squadron
C-47B	KK106	43-49295	August 27, 1954	May 27, 1955	
C-47B	KN354	44-76385	September 1, 1954	June 21, 1955	
C-47B	KJ983	43-49160	September 2, 1954	June 21, 1955	ex No 240 OCU
C-47B	KN561	44-76844	September 7, 1954	June 21, 1955	
C-47B	KP217	44-77099	September 7, 1954	July 15, 1955	ex No 27 Squadron
C-47B	KP215	44-77097	September 11, 1954	July 12, 1955	ex No 82 Squadron
C-47B	KP265	44-77235	September 17, 1954	July 12, 1955	ex No 216 Squadron
C-47B	KN373	44-76412	September 10, 1954	August 31, 1955	
C-47B	KN290	44-76207	September 24, 1954	September 21, 1955	
C-47B	KK209	43-49728	September 21, 1954	September 12, 1955	to West German Air Force
C-47B	KP258	44-77228	November 12, 1954	April 18, 1955	ex No 24 Squadron
C-47B	KP248	44-77218	September 6, 1954	March 24, 1955	ex No 24 Squadron
C-47B	KN285	44-76200	October 6, 1954	September 13, 1955	
C-47B	KJ840	43-48364	October 12, 1954	September 25, 1955	
C-47B	KN547	44-76821	September 9, 1954	February 21, 1955	ex No 52 Squadron
C-47B	KJ981	43-49158	September 21, 1954	February 25, 1955	
No 22 Maintenance Unit – Silloth, Cumberland					
C-47B	KN577	44-76871	October 19, 1954	October 4, 1955	ex No 77 Squadron
C-47B	KN498	44-76689	October 21, 1954	October 14, 1955	ex No 46 Squadron
C-47B	KN656	44-77021	October 27, 1954	December 8, 1955	to West German Air Force
C-47B	KN514	44-76720	November 3, 1954	November 4, 1955	ex No 27 Squadron
C-47B	KN499	44-76692	November 9, 1955	December 7, 1955	to West German Air Force
C-47B	KP250	44-77220	November 24, 1955	December 8, 1955	ex No 77 Squadron
C-47B	KN328	44-76304	March 28, 1955	July 17, 1956	
C-47B	KN393	44-76482	February 11, 1955	February 1, 1956	ex No 53 Squadron
C-47B	KN597	44-76906	March 11, 1955	February 21, 1956	
C-47B	KN622	44-76941	February 23, 1955	February 27, 1956	to West German Air Force
C-47B	KN651	44-77012	May 21, 1955	April 30, 1956	to French Air Force
C-47B	KJ801	43-48324	March 29, 1955	March 19, 1956	ex No 78 Squadron
C-47B	KJ905	43-48675	April 27, 1955	April 6, 1956	
C-47B	KJ939	43-48851	June 13, 1955	May 8, 1956	ex No 620 Squadron
C-47B	KK135	43-49455	June 6, 1955	May 22, 1956	ex No 77 Squadron
C-47B	KK197	43-49713	July 4, 1955	June 25, 1956	ex No 252 Squadron
C-47B	KK200	43-49716	July 4, 1955	July 2, 1956	to West German Air Force
No 12 Maintenance Unit – Kirbride, Cumberland					
C-47B	KN572	44-76862	December 1, 1954	January 10, 1956	to West German Air Force
C-47B	KN541	44-76811	March 16, 1955	February 28, 1956	ex No 27 Squadron
C-47B	KN534	44-76757	June 9, 1955	January 16, 1956	
C-47B	KN467	44-76609	June 17, 1955	January 11, 1956	
C-47B	KN386	44-76428	June 21, 1955	January 16, 1956	to French Air Force
C-47B	KN383	44-76425	June 17, 1955	February 9, 1956	ex No 27 Squadron

Dakota squadrons of the RAF

Sq No	Name	Code	Example	Theatre of Operation
10		ZA	KN555 ZA-V	SEAC – UK – Berlin Airlift
18	"Burma"		KN446	UK – Berlin Airlift
21			KJ955	Middle East
24	"Commonwealth"	NQ	KP251 NQ-K	UK – Berlin Airlift
27			KN410	UK – Berlin Airlift
30		JN	KN360 JN-K	UK – Berlin Airlift
31			FD809 "A"	SEAC
45			KN487	Far East
46	"Uganda"	XK	KN241 XK-K	UK – Berlin Airlift
48		12	KG317 12-AA	UK – Far East
52			KN467 "A"	SEAC – Malaya
53		PU	KN490 PU-B	UK – Berlin Airlift
62	"Northampton"		KK185	SEAC – Berlin Airlift
70			KP263	Middle East
76		MP	KN559 MP-S	SEAC
77	"Lancaster"	DV	KG358 DV-A	SEAC – Berlin Airlift
78	"Preston"	EY	KP274 EY-P	Middle East
82	"United Provinces"		KN650 "L"	Middle East
96			KN467 "X"	Middle East – SEAC
110	"Hyderabad"		KJ989 "N"	Far East
113			KN675	Middle East
114	"Hong Kong"		KP263	Middle East

Sq No	Name	Code	Example	Theatre of Operation
117			KN209 "W"	Middle East – SEAC
138		AC	KN499 AC-AW	UK
147		CMV	KG771 CMV-99	UK
167	"Gold Coast"		FZ696	UK
172				UK
173				Middle East
187			KP215	UK – SEAC
194	"The Friendly Firm"		FD894 "F"	SEAC
204			KJ934	UK – Middle East
206		TJ	KN701 TJ-C	Azores
209			KP277	Malaya
215			KN254 "U"	SEAC
216			KN218	Middle East – SEAC
231			KN673	Canada
232				SEAC
233		5T	KG559 5T-	UK – SEAC
238			KN540 VM-YDP	SEAC – Australia – UK
241				UK
243			KK149 VM-YAL	Australia
267	"Pegasus"		FD863 "A"	Middle East – SEAC
271		YS	KN274 YS-Z	UK – Belin Airlift
353			FZ643	SEAC
357				SEAC
510				UK
511			FL547	UK
512		HC	KN499 HC-AW	UK – Middle East
525		WF	KN497 WF-C	UK
575		19	KG630 19-Q	UK – Palestine
620			KJ939	UK
657		TS	KN840 TS-L	UK
Royal Canadian Air Force				
408	"Goose"			Canada
412	"Falcon"	AO	KN277 AO-V	Canada
414	"Imperial"	AQ	KG423 AQ-K	Canada
422		DG	KG615 DG-615	Canada
426	"Thunderbird"			Canada
435	"Edmonton"	BW	KP227 BW-G	SEAC – UK – Canada
436	"Montreal"	FM	TS423	SEAC – UK – Canada
437	"Husky"	Z2	FZ669 Z2-DQ	UK – Canada

Note: Many squadrons had codes allocated but rarely or never used them. The RCAF squadrons are representative only.

Trooping serials allocated to British civil Dakota aircraft and used between 1951 and 1956

RAF Serial	Civil Reg.	Original RAF Serial	Douglas c/n	USAF Serial	USAF Designation	Airline or Operator
WZ984	G-AGWS		6208	41-38749	C-47A-1-DL	Scottish Airlines
WZ984	G-AGZF	FD812	9174	42-23312	C-47A-1-DL	Scottish Airlines
WZ985	G-AGZG		9803	42-23941	C-47A-35-DL	Scottish Airlines
XE280	G-AMRA	KK151	15290/26735	43-49474	C-47B-15-DK	Airwork
XF619	G-AMYX	KN509	33042/16294	44-76710	C-47D-30-DK	Silver City
XF623	G-AMYV	KN469	16195/32943	44-76611	C-47D-30-DK	Silver City
XF645	G-AMVC	KN681	16642/33390	44-77058	C-47D-30-DK	BKS
XF646	G-AMSF	KJ886	14380/25825	43-48564	C-47B-15-DK	BKS
XF647	G-AMVB	KJ915	14637/26082	43-48821	C-47B-15-DK	Scottish Airlines
XF648	G-AMSH	KN642	16583/33331	44-76999	C-47B-35-DK	BKS
XF649	G-AMSF	KJ886	14380/25825	43-48564	C-47B-15-DK	BKS
XF667	G-AMSH	KN642	16583/33331	44-76999	C-47B-35-DK	BKS
XF746	G-AMVL	KN698	16660/33408	44-77076	C-47B-35-DK	JA Wilson
XF747	G-AMYJ	KN353	15968/32716	44-76384	C-47D-30-DK	BKS
XF748	G-AMZG	KN700	16668/33416	44-77084	C-47D-30-DK	Cambrian
XF749	G-AMVL	KN698	16660/33408	44-77076	C-47D-30-DK	JA Wilson
XF756	G-AMPP	KK135	15272/26717	43-49456	C-47B-15-DK	Scottish Airlines
XF757	G-AMJU	KJ894	14489/25934	43-48573	C-47B-15-DK	Starways

Notes: G-AGWS was the first civilianised DC-3 to be converted in the United Kingdom. Converted by Scottish Aviation at Prestwick. It was operated on the Berlin Airlift during 1948–49.
XF619 used the Transport Command radio call/sign "MODWA"
XF623 used the Transport Command radio call/sign "MODWB"

Photographic Credits

Airborn Forces Museum 311
Air Britain Photo Library 253
American Airlines 268
Armstrong Siddeley 237, 252, 253
Aviation Photo News 291, 307, 314
Wing Commander DE Bennett 269, 270 (2)
Peter Berry, Air Britain 241
BOAC 246
British Army 299
Canadian Armed Forces 256 (2), 257 (2), 258 (2), 259, 260 (2)
Commanding Officer RAF Gatow 226, 242
Daily Sketch 276
Douglas Aircraft 251, 265 (2), 267
John Ellis 316
Ferranti 309, 310
Field Aircraft Services 316, 317, 318
Flight 250, 254, 312, 313 (2), 319, 320
Fox Photos 248, 249, 251 (2)
Wing Commander SJ Hubbard 288
Hunting Percival 317 (2), 318
Imperial War Museum 245, 248, 249, 250, 251, 269, 271, 272, 273 (2), (2) 274 (2), 275, 276, 277, 279 (2), 280 (2), 281 (2), 282 (2), 284 (2), 285 (2), 286 (2), 288, 289 (2), 290 (2), 292, 293, 294 (2), 295 (2), 296 (2), 297 (2), 299, 300, 301, 302, 304 (2), 305 (2), 306 (2), 307, 311
RC Jones 317
WT Larkins 263 (2), 264 (2)
Ministry of Defence 243 (2), 244 (2), 247 (2), 278 (2), 288, 291 (2), 292, 310, 312
James Muncie 293
A Pearcy 314, 315
A Pearcy Photo Library 259, 283, 287, 302, 303 (2), 319, 320
Real Photos 245
Rolls-Royce 254, 255 (2)
Royal Australian Air Force 298 (2), 299
CP Russell-Smith 316
Scottish Aviation Ltd 282, 283
Eric Taylor, Air Britain 315
John WR Taylor 318
Temple Press 286
United Nations 261, 262 (2)
United States Air Force 266 (2), 309
United States Air Force (via John WR Taylor) 277
BC Whittaker 301 (2), 308 (2)

Men and machines were recalled for Operation Plainfare in 1947. Still in drab wartime camouflage Dakotas of No 271 Squadron are seen at Fassberg. "YS-H" is KN696 C-47B-30-DK 44-77074 c/n 16658/33406. Note RAF Transport Command badge on nose.

BERLIN AIRLIFT

As the Dakotas employed on the Berlin Airlift were withdrawn for major overhaul the drab camouflage was removed. Taken at Wunstorf in 1947 with damaged Luftwaffe aircraft and hangars in the background. Photo shows Dakota Mk IV KN518 "XK-Y" of No 46 Squadron.

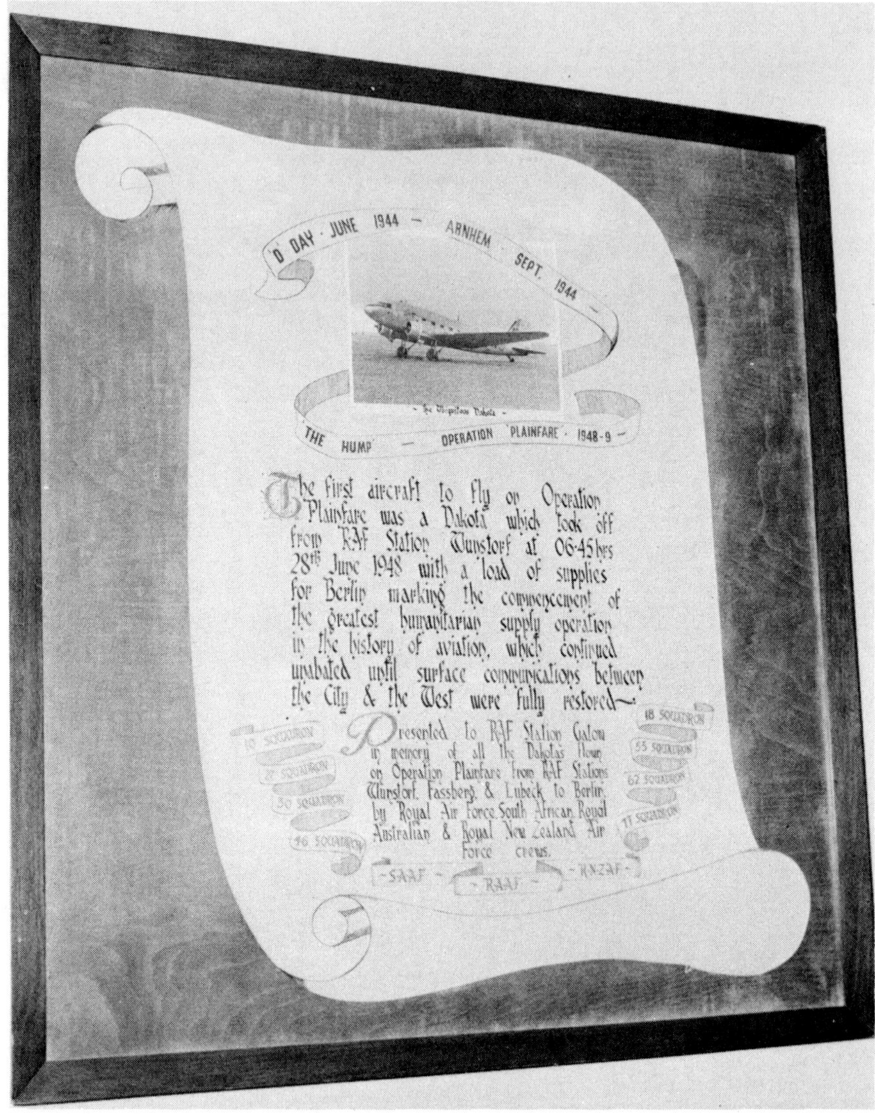

This plaque is a tribute to the ubiquitous Dakotas and was presented to RAF Gatow by the crews from the RAF, SAAF, RAAF and RNZAF who flew on Operation Plainfare with the eight Dakota Squadrons involved. The plaque is still on display in Station Headquarters at RAF Gatow.

A typical scene during Operation Plainfare – the Berlin Airlift. Dakotas being refuelled and loaded with freight before flying to the beleagured city. The airman is giving Aldis lamp signals to the taxying Dakota.

During the Berlin Airlift Dakota aircraft and crews of RAF Transport Command were operated in a pool. Photo shows a typical hangar scene in Germany with servicing crews checking a Pratt & Whitney Twin Wasp engine for a possible oil leak. WAAFs played their part in keeping the aircraft in service.

Bowsers refuel the thirsty Dakotas ready for another mercy flight to Berlin. Crews worked day and night to keep the aircraft in the air in this the greatest humanitarian supply operation in the history of aviation. Dakotas of the RAF, USAAF and the civil airlines played a great part.

Fortunately some of the ex-Luftwaffe hangars at bases such as Wunstorf were still intact. Dakotas were normally parked out in the open, but cover was necessary for aircraft requiring more than the normal daily inspection. Photo shows a typical hangar scene in Germany.

BOAC operated 59 Dakotas of various marks during World War 2 in both civil and military guises on many overseas routes. This landing shot depicts G-AGGB ex FD773 C-47-DL which was delivered to the UK in February 1943, and registered to BOAC the following month. In 1949 it was sold to South Africa and was last registered in Israel.

BRITISH OVERSEAS AIRWAYS CORPORATION

BOAC Dakota G-AGFZ seen taking aboard a spare tyre at BOACs main UK wartime base at Whitchurch near Bristol. Note RAF fin flash. A C-47-DL 42-5637 c/m 6225 FD771 with radio call sign "ODZCK" G-AGFZ overshot the runway at Bromma Stockholm on April 21, 1944, and was sold as spares.

BOAC Dakota G-AGNG C-47B-30-DK 43-49736 c/n 15552/26997 KK216 "OFZB" seen flying over the new site at Heathrow which was still under construction. This aircraft crashed at Quebec on January 16, 1956. It belonged to Quebecair and was registered CF-GVZ.

BOAC Dakota G-AGHE C-47A-1-DL 42-23327 c/n 9189 FD827 "ODZGK" seen flying in postwar markings. The aircraft was sold to Malayan Airways during August 1948 and became VR-SCR and later 9M-ALR.

AIRBORNE FORCES

Rare photograph depicting a Dakota and an Armstrong Whitworth Whitley from No 1 Parachute Training School, Ringway, operating over the dropping zone at Tatton Park near Manchester. As opposed to the Whitley which only carried 10 paratroops in uncomfortable conditions, the Dakota carried 20 in comparative luxury.

Dakota Mk III FZ566 C-47A-1-DK 42-92314 c/n 12101 seen in operation from No 1 PTS Ringway near Manchester. This aircraft survived World War 2, was sold to Air Algerie as F-BCYO only to crash at Lyon-Bron Airport on January 8, 1949.

Royal Air Force Transport Command used the "snatch" method for glider pick-up at the end of World War 2. A Glider Pick-Up Flight was established at Ibsley in Hampshire with Dakotas and Hadrian gliders. Photo shows a Hadrian being snatched by a Dakota.

View of an Airspeed Horsa glider from a Dakota tug. The Horsa was the RAFs first operational troop carrying glider, had a crew of two pilots and could carry 20–25 troops. It was also used by the US Army Air Force in the European theatre.

Flt Lt David Samual Anthony Lord who served with No 31 Squadron in India and the Middle East, and after D-Day with No 271 Squadron here in the United Kingdom. He was awarded the Victoria Cross – posthumously – which was approved and gazetted on November 13, 1945.

Although otherwise in full RAF colours, this Dakota doing a glider "snatch" carries its US Army Air Force serial 315070 on the fin, indicating it is a C-47A-80-DL 43-15070 c/n 19536 which after World War 2 went to Sabena as 00-CBT.

Unique photo taken from the cockpit of a Horsa glider showing the tow-line and Dakota Tug. The circumference of the tow-rope is four inches and is 350 feet long. The glider pilot must watch his position behind the Dakota tug at all times.

Admiral the Lord Louis Mountbatten, GCVO, KCB, DSO, ADC, Supreme Allied Commander in SEAC from November 16, 1943, until May 31, 1946, visited Field Marshal Montgomery in Normandy and are seen here in conference.

Operation Varsity. Dakotas and Horsas seen over the Rhine when 440 gliders carried the British 6th Airborne Division on the last airborne forces operation of World War 2.

Formed at Ibsley after World War 2 the Glider Pick-Up Flight operated with Dakotas modified for glider-tug "snatch" with Waco Hadrian gliders. The system was demonstrated to the public at the RAF Display Farnborough in 1950 as seen by the photo. The Hadrian still retains its US Army Air Force serial 274521.

Dakotas continued to take part in exercises involving airborne forces until well into the 1950s when a replacement aircraft, the Valetta was introduced. This is a typical scene over the Wiltshire Downs with the ground covered in the multi-coloured parachutes which have carried supplies.

Deployed parachutes float gently to the ground during a postwar exercise while the Dakota cargo transports return for more paratroops and supplies. The Douglas Dakota was used by many of our Allies during World War 2 for the carriage of airborne troops and supplies.

Dakota and Waco CG-4A Hadrian Glider enaged in a glider "snatch" exercise. The Dakotas were fitted with a glider pick-up winch installation which in most cases was fitted before the aircraft arrived in the United Kingdom.

TURBO-PROP DAKOTAS

Dakota Mk IV KJ839 C-47B-1-DK 43-48362 c/n 14178/25623 was the first of its type to be fitted with turbo-props. With two Armstrong Siddeley Mambas it made its first flight on August 27, 1949. The aircraft was later re-engined with Pratt & Whitney Twin Wasps and sold in 1958 to Skyways as G-APNK and later to Bahamas Airways as VP-BAB.

Powered by two Armstrong Siddeley Mamba turbo-prop engines developing 1,420 eshp. Dakota KJ839 flew many hours as a flying test-bed for engine research from its Bitteswell base.

Airborne photo depicting Dakota Mk IV KJ839 which had previously served with No 147 Squadron, No 1382 Transport Conversion Unit and No 240 Operational Conversion Unit. It was struck off charge from the RAF in 1958 and sold.

KJ839

Rolls-Royce purchased Dakota Mk IV KJ829 on August 22, 1956, when it was registered in class "B" marks G-37-2 for engine tests with Dart 510/506 engines. It eventually became G-AOXI still fitted with Darts, but after being re-engined with Twin Wasps it was sold to Tyne Tees Airways.

In flight photo of the Mamba powered Dakota flown by the company's two pilots – W. Price-Owen and J. B. Starkey. The small Mamba turbines were fitted in the rather large nacelles to reduce the cost of conversion which was largely done by Scottish Aviation at Prestwick.

Making its first flight with Rolls-Royce Dart turbo-prop engines on March 15, 1950. Dakota Mk IV KJ829 proved so successful that British European Airways operated two on scheduled freight services. Photo shows the clean installation of the Dart.

Along with its two civil counterparts, Dakota Mk IV KJ829 C-47B-1-DK 43-48352 c/n 14168/25613 is reputed to have tested every model of Rolls-Royce Dart engine.

The RCAF used the Dakota extensively during and after World War 2. Depicted is a Mk III FL618 "DM" C-47A-1-DK 42-92258 c/n 12039 flying over the Canadian seaboard. This aircraft went to the RCAF in 1944 and later flew with Trans Canada Airlines as CF-TDQ and was last registered in the USA as N4995E with Frontier Airlines.

ROYAL CANADIAN AIR FORCE

When operating in sub-zero temperatures it takes approximately one hour to generate sufficient heat to start the Pratt & Whitney Twin Wasps of the Dakota. Fitted with ski attachment to the undercarriage the RCAF Dakota operated perfectly from snow and ice covered surfaces as depicted in this photo.

Unusual head-on view of RCAF Dakota Mk III KG423 c-47A-10-DK 42-108861 c/n 12458. Many Dakotas are still flying in Canada both with the Canadian Armed Forces and the civil operators. They are in use as general transports and are forecast to remain in faithful service for some years to come.

Dakota Mk III "964" X-Xray was operated with No 435 Squadron RCAF as KG381 C-47A-10-DK 42-92593 c/n 12411 and was taken on charge March 9, 1944. Still in use with the Canadian Armed Forces in the SEARCH & RESCUE and navigation trainer role.

Depicting an unusual fin flash marking is the RCAF Dakota "652" C-47-DL 42-32882 c/n 9108 which was taken on charge April 27, 1943, and although struck off charge on November 14, 1955, was retained as a ground instructional trainer with serial A509.

Still in use with the Canadian Armed Forces as a navigation trainer is "651" C-47A-20-DL 42-23428 c/n 9290 which was taken on charge on April 20, 1943. Note the radar bulge below the fuselage.

RCAF Dakota Mk III.

A late addition to the RCAF inventory was this Dakota Mk IV KN485 C-47B-30-DK 44-76631 c/n 16215/32963 which served initially with the RAF was sold to the Central Air Transport in China as XT-801 before joining the RCAF on March 6, 1952. It is depicted here in Air Defence Command – 5 Air Division – markings.

Not all RCAF Dakotas retained their RAF serial number. Fine study of Dakota Mk IV RCAF 1000 C-47-B-30-DK 44-77036 c/n 16620/33368 KN655 used extensively by RCAF Air Transport Command on VIP duties. Served as "PU-H" of No 53 Squadron sold to RCAF in 1946, declared surplus in 1967 and sold as CF-WQN.

Taken over by the RCAF in August 1946 from the RAF Dakota Mk III KG568 C-47A-20-DK 42-93267 c/n 13160 was modified for RESCUE operations. One of the eight Dakotas donated to the Indian Air Force in November 1962 by the RCAF.

UNITED NATIONS

Lt Gen ELM Burns (Canada) handed over command of the United Nations Emergency Force to successor Maj Gen PSG Yani of the Indian Army on Dececember 28, 1959. Gen Burns is seen here boarding his personal Dakota, giving a last salute to the men he had commanded since 1956 when the UNEF was set up.

The United Nations Emergency Force in the Middle East consisted of RCAF aircraft including Dakotas, many of which were ex-RAF. Taken in March 1957 at Gaza, a United Nations white Dakota is shown alongside a United Nations Otter, both ex-RCAF.

Dakota "656" ex-RCAF C-47A-40-DL 42-23970 c/n 9832 which was taken on charge July 14, 1943. Supplies are brought by to the UNEF post at the Gulf of Agaba, end of the International Frontier.

Douglas DC-3/DST production line at Santa Monica, California, in September 1936. Deliveries of the new transport averaged six aircraft per month.

The one and only Douglas DC-1 transport X223Y seen in TWA markings and photographed in July 1, 1933. This unique aircraft was later registered in the United Kingdom to Lord Forbes as G-AFIF and ended its days in Spain.

Douglas DC-3-G102-277B c/n 2198 NC21793 of American Airlines in flight. This aircraft was completed at Santa Monica on February 24, 1940, and during the late 1950s was registered in Canada with Pacific Western Airlines as CF-PWH.

Field Marshal Montgomery flew many hours in his personal Dakota Mk IV KN628. Photo shows the arrival of "Monty" during one of his many visits to troops in the field. Wg Cdre – now Air Commodore – Wakeford is to the right of the group. Note tail insignias.

VIPs

Monty and Air Commodore Fielden seen at Blackbushe after the Field Marshal's arrival in his Dakota Mk IV KN628. No 167 Squadron equipped with Dakotas was based at Blackbushe at this time, as will be noted from the steps in the background.

Rare photograph taken at Blackbushe in 1945 showing – left to right – Air Chief Marshal Sir Frederick Bowhill, AOC Ferry and later Transport Command, Air Commodore Fielden of Queen's Flight fame, Wing Commander DE Bennett, OC Flying at Blackbushe and Sq Ldr Nobby Clark.

Dakota Mk IV KN628 was taken over by Field Marshal Montgomery in July 1945 and personal pilot was Sq Ldr GH Duncan. The full crew plus Monty are seen here at Blackbushe 1945. The aircraft was sold to Derby Airways – later British Midland – as G-AOGZ and was resold to the USA during 1969.

Field Marshall Montgomery talks to General Omar Bradley who, unfortunately hides the identity of this RAF Dakota which carries the five-star insignia and Union Jack on the fin. It is reputed that "Monty" used as many as five Dakotas throughout his career during and after World War 2.

Air Chief Marshal Sir Frederick W Bowhill, GBE, KCB, CMG, DSO, took over Royal Air Force Ferry Command on July 18, 1941, and continued with Royal Air Force Transport Command until February 15, 1945.

Air Marshal Sir Charles EH Medhurst, KCB, OBE, MC, took over Middle East Command from Air Marshal Sir Keith R Park on February 8, 1945. Sir Charles and Lady Medhurst flew thousands of miles in their personal Douglas Dakota transport.

VIP Dakota Mk IV KN386 from No 24 Squadron with the Royal Standard Flying. Photo was taken during the Royal visit to the Channel Islands in June 1945. Transport Command Mod. NO66 dated August 9, 1945, was carried out to all VIP Dakotas of No 24 Squadron and was to indicate to ground crews and reception parties when a passenger aircraft has Particularly Important Passengers on board. The quickly erectable flagstaff could carry flags and ensigns up to 36 in in length.

Once the invasion of Europe commenced Dakota squadrons received visits from members of the Royal Family. HRH Princess Mary is seen here visiting a Dakota Squadron "somewhere in the UK" on July 9, 1944, accompanied by Grp Capt Bradbury.

One of the VIPs flown in Dakota of No 24 Squadron was HRH the Duke of Windsor seen here at Hendon talking to the press after arrival in Dakota Mk III KG624 C-47A-25-DK 42-93469 c/n 13384 which was sold to Malayan Airways as VR-SCW, later serving with Malaysia-Singapore Airlines as 9V-BAL.

Prime Minister Winston Churchill is seen here arriving from one of his many overseas visits. The US Army Air Force C-47 Skytrain shown in the background was placed at his disposal. Note the two-star General insignia. Aircraft is a VC-47B-10-DK 43-49208 c/n 15024/26469 which remained in Europe after World War 2 serving as a VC-47D at both Rhein Main and Wiesbaden with different USAF units.

Wing Commander Johnny Johnson greets Monty at Copenhagen. The Dakota in the background was a gift from General Eisenhower after Monty's original aircraft was lost due to enemy action. Aircraft is a C-47B-5-DK 43-48804 c/n 14620/26065. Note the insignia on the fin.

Sir Arthur Tedder steps from his personal Dakota Mk II – a Douglas C-53-DO-TJ170. It was manufactured at the Santa Monica factory. Note single door.

HM King George VI, followed by General Alexander, steps down from General Maitland Wilson's personal Dakota Mk III, FZ631 named Freedom, *a C-47A-1-DK 42-92391 c/n 12187. This was in Italy on July 23, 1944, and one of the few occasions when the King flew in a Dakota. This aircraft was later sold to Australia – Qantas – as VH-EAN in 1949.*

On June 7, 1945, HM King George VI and Queen Elizabeth flew from Northolt to the Channel Islands in a Dakota Mk IV KN386 from No 24 Squadron. This aircraft as C-47B-25-DK 44-76428 c/n 16012/32760 was one of 50 RAF Dakotas returned to the USAF in the 1950s and during 1958 was based at Alconbury in Huntingdonshire. HM King George is seen in this photo stepping from the aircraft on arrival in the Channel Islands.

On December 8, 1944, HRH the Duchess of Kent visited Down Ampney where she witnessed the arrival of wounded soldiers from Belgium. Accompanied by Grp Capt GR Howie, the Station Commander, the visitor watches as stretchers are taken out of a Dakota transport.

The first aircraft to land on a permanent airfield in France after D-Day was this Douglas C-47 Skytrain transport of the US Army Air Force bringing in supplies for the airborne troops. Note PSP runway – pierced steel planking – and oil drum runway markers.

EUROPE

Carrying an RAF fin flash this Long Beach built C-47-DL 41-38592 c/c 4541 is one of the many of its type which served the Allies. Note the supply canisters carried on external racks below the fuselage. After World War 2 this aircraft served in South America before delivery to the French Air Force in 1957.

Reputed to be the most decorated aircraft in the RAF. Dakota Mk IV KN628 C-47B-35-DK 44–76950 c/n 16534/33282 was used extensively by Field Marshal Montgomery from July 1945 to January 1956, when it was purchased by Derby Aviation and registered G-AOGZ, Derby Dale.

Nose decoration on Monty's Dakota Mk IV KN628 included the Eighth Army's Crusader shield, the Control Commission badge, and the crest of the Royal Air Force Transport Command with its motto – "Feri Ferendo".

Hendon was the home base of No 24 Squadron throughout World War 2. Dakota Mk III KG647 C-47A-25-DK 42-93536 c/n 13459 is shown shortly after delivery to the squadron. This transport survived World War 2 and was sold to Australia after a period in the UK as G-AIAZ.

Douglas C-47-DL 41-7817 c/n 4316 an early Long Beach production Skytrain seen at Prestwick, Scotland. The building behind the aircraft is now Redbrae, the Scottish Air Traffic Control Centre. This aircraft was later sold to Italy as I-LEON and was last reported to be with the Italian Air Force.

Douglas C-47A-40-DL 42-24051 c/n 9913 and coded "CN-N" of a 9th Air Force Troop Carrier Squadron, US Army Air Force, seen flying over Bastoigne. Personnel from No 48 Air Despatch, Royal Army Service Corps, were used to drop supplies to the 101st US Airborne Division who were surrounded.

Wartime scene at Whitchurch near Bristol the UK base for BOAC operations. A KLM Douglas DC-3 PH-ARB Buizerd *which escaped the invasion of the Netherlands is seen in the foreground, with a de Havilland Albatross G-AFDM in the background plus other Dakotas.*

Not an unusual sight during World War 2. A total of 36 Douglas Dakotas complete with D-Day invasion stripes set out on a supply dropping mission to "somewhere in Europe".

Douglas Dakotas in a mass fly-past before setting course for the DZ – dropping zone – many rehearsals were necessary before D-Day and involved many men and machines.

"Combined Ops". A US Army Air Force Douglas C-47 Skytrain tows off a British built Airspeed Horsa glider, both complete with the familiar black and white invasion stripes.

Mass fly-past of Douglas C-47 Dakotas at a transport base in the United Kingdom. The black and white invasion stripes were applied to most aircraft of the Allies participating in the invasion of Europe which commenced on D-Day June 6, 1944.

Photographed at Hendon in March 1943, Dakota Mk I FD772 C-47-DL 42-5639 c/n 6227 was coded "ZYOK" of the resident No 24 Squadron, and was named Windsor Castle. *This was the fifth Dakota to be delivered to the RAF.*

Douglas Dakota Mk III FL559 C-47A-1-DK 42-92151 c/n 11920 photographed during overhaul by Scottish Aviation at Prestwick. After World War 2 this aircraft was sold to Argentina as LV-AOP.

Douglas C-47-DL 42-32910 c/n 9136 coded "E5-H" of a 9th Air Force Troop Carrier unit, photographed at Prestwick during overhaul by Scottish Aviation Limited. This aircraft later went to South America, to Aviance as HK-117.

Douglas C-47-DL 41-18608 c/n 4769 "Q-Quebec" manufactured at Long Beach during 1942 and based at the A&AEE Boscombe Down, Wiltshire, during World War 2 for trials.

Led by a Douglas Dakota Mk IV KN427 "AY" C-47B-25-DK 44-76522 c/n 161016/32854 transports of RAF Transport Command are seen flying over the city of Copenhagen at the end of the War in Europe.

Photo of Dakota Mk IV KN512 "AKW" C-47B-30-DK 44-76713 c/n 16297/33045 taken September 25, 1945. Note Transport Command badge on nose. "AKW" is the radio call-sign for this particular aircraft.

Photo of invasion troops with Dakotas on a rough strip on the Continent, taken July 21, 1944. Note the black and white invasion markings on the aircraft.

PSP – pierced steel planking – which was in constant use during and after the war, being unloaded from a Dakota Mk III FZ592 "UZ" from No 48 Squadron. Aircraft is a C-47A-1-DK 42-92356 c/n 12147 manufactured at the Douglas Oklahoma City factory.

Dakota Mk IV KJ994 C-47B-10-DK 43-49174 c/n 26433 was modified as a VIP aircraft for Air Chief Marshal Sir Arthur Tedder and named Dulcie. *Note rank badges above the fin flash, plus extra windows in the roof of the fuselage. KJ994 was also on the strength of No 24 Squadron on VIP duties.*

With the US Army Air Force serial 348266 this C-47B-1-DK 43-48266 c/n 14082/25527 has RAF markings plus invasion stripes and is depicted on its way to France with supplies shortly after D-Day. The port wing shows clearly where the USAF insignia was. The aircraft was later returned to the US forces and was seen by the author at Northolt in September 1949.

Douglas Dakota of RAF Transport Command landing at Croydon Airport, Surrey. Avro Yorks and Dakotas plus a Rapide and an Oxford can be seen parked in the background.

Wounded being loaded on to Douglas Dakota transports for return to base hospitals in the United Kingdom. A total of 24 stretcher cases could be accommodated in each Dakota transport.

The last Douglas Dakota for delivery by No 45 Group in Canada to the United Kingdom is seen with Royal Air Force personnel before final delivery. It arrived from Oklahoma City on June 15, 1946, and was a C-47B-35-DK 44-77119 c/n 16703/33451 and ended its days at RAF St Athan in South Wales as 6731M – a ground instructional trainer.

MIDDLE EAST

Douglas Dakota Mk IV KN377 C-47B-25-DK 44-76417 c/n 16001/32749, the personal aircraft of Air Chief Marshal Sir Charles Medhurst, seen flying over the pyramids in Egypt. This aircraft flew many thousands of miles in the Middle East theatre, and was later returned to the United States Air Force.

Dakota Mk IV KN452 of the Middle East Communications Squadron was based at Khormaksar until the RAF withdrawal from Aden. This was the first RAF Dakota to land on Egyptian soil since Suez when it refuelled at Cairo on its delivery flight back to the UK. Photo shows KN452 flying over typical "crater" terrain in Aden.

Air Vice Marshal W Elliot, CB, CBE, DFC, Air Officer Commanding the Balkan Air Force, had the unique experience of having a varied force of both aircraft and personnel under his command. These included Russian and American units.

A Douglas Dakota from No 267 Pegasus Squadron stands in the mud "somewhere in Italy" during the Allied advance in 1943. The versatile Dakota braved the elements from the equator to the North and South Poles.

Takoradi, the ferry base on the Gold Coast and the delivery point for Lend-Lease aircraft including Dakotas after crossing the South Atlantic. Two Dakotas are seen in this photo plus an Avro Anson and a Vickers Armstrong Wellington or Wimpey as it was known to many.

Two principal air commanders who had their own personal Douglas Dakota VIP transport aircraft – Air Chief Marshal Sir Arthur W Tedder, GCB, with Air Vice Marshal – later Air Marshal – Sir Arthur Coningham, KCB, DSO, MC, DFC, AFC, who commanded the Second Tactical Air Force.

A No 267 Squadron Dakota after taking off from Araxos, Greece, during September 1944. This unit played a large part in the war in the Balkans.

Dakota Mk III KG511 from No 267 Pegasus Squadron lands at an airfield in the Middle East. In the background is parked a Lockheed Hudson transport, a type which did excellent work before and after the arrival of the Douglas Dakota.

Interior view of Dakota Mk IV KJ955 which, until destroyed by a terrorist bomb, was used in Aden with the Middle East Communications Squadron as a freight aircraft.

Interior view of Dakota Mk IV KN452 which was fitted out as a VIP aircraft and used by the British High Commissioner and his staff in Aden before being replaced by a Hawker Siddeley Andover aircraft.

The two Dakotas of the Middle East Communications Squadron in flight over Aden. Both Mk IV transports KN452 was a C-47B-30-DK 44-76591 c/n 16175/32923 and KJ955 was a C-47B-10-DK 43-48986 c/n 14802/26247.

Silhouetted against the Rock of Gibraltar a Douglas Dakota of RAF Transport Command prepares for a flight back to the United Kingdom.

Photographed in rugged surroundings at Habalyn airstrip in Aden during August 1966 is Dakota Mk VI KN452 of the Middle East Air Force. It had previously served with No 10 Squadron, and with the AOC Gibraltar. Many sorties into the Radfan area were flown with this aircraft.

Dakota Mk III KG754 C-47A-30DK 43-48037 c/n 13853/25298 surrounded by peasants at Araxos landing strip in Greece during September 1944. This aircraft was later sold to Air India as VT-CCA and crashed at Bangalore on September 15, 1951.

Photo taken at a landing strip near Taranto on September 7, 1943, showing bombs being unloaded from a Dakota Mk I transport. Aircraft in the background are P-40 Tomahawks of an unidentified unit.

A Middle East Dakota squadron parades its personnel at an investiture held in the desert on November 18, 1943. The transport crews from No.216 Group Middle East Air Force followed the armies in their advance from Africa to Italy.

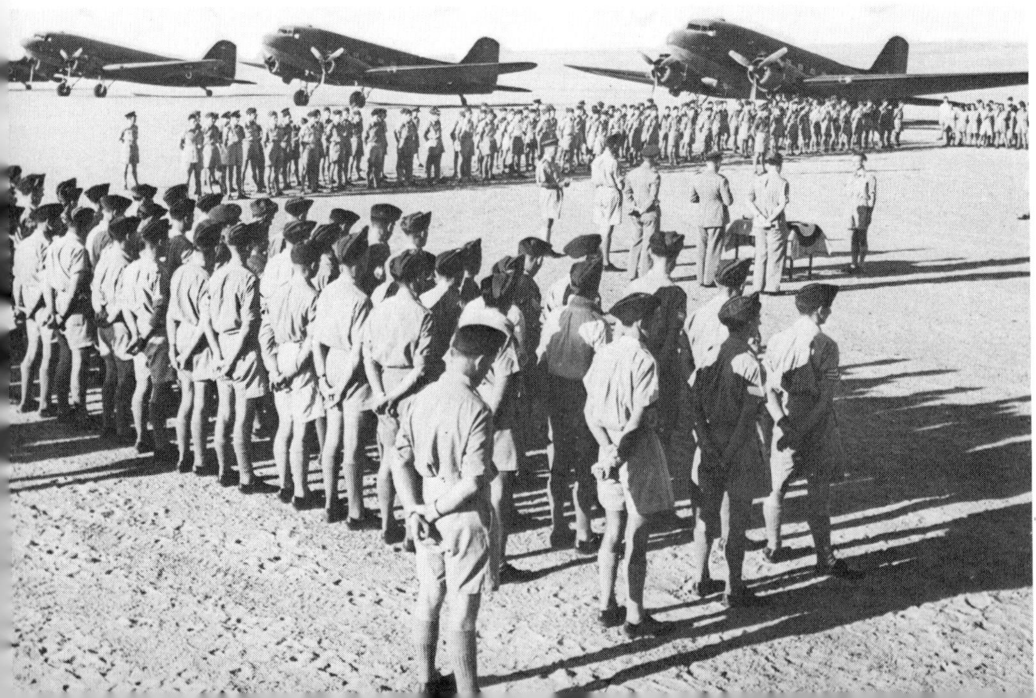

Dakota Mk IV KN482 named Rapier *a C-47B-30-DK 44-76628 c/n 15212/32960 was the personal aircraft of Brigadier General Sir Brian Paget. Photo was taken on July 26, 1945. The aircraft was one of many returned to the United States Air Force during 1954.*

Loading casualties onto a Royal Air Force Dakota with US Army Air Force fin serial. It is a Douglas C-47-dl 41-18529 c/n 4621 which until quite recently was serving with the Brazilian Air Force as FAB-2082. Note that the ambulances are American.

Dakota Mk III KG537 C-47A-20-DK 42-93141 c/n 13020 from No 267 Pegasus Squadron. photographed on January 4, 1945.

A Douglas Dakota from No 267 Pegasus Squadron Royal Air Force Transport Command, stands out in the rain "somewhere in Italy" during the winter of 1943/44.

Camouflaged Dakotas of No 267 Pegasus Squadron parked at Bari, Italy, during 1944. Dakotas Mk III KG496, FL586 and FD857, are in the foreground. Other types identified in the photo include Thunderbolts, Lightnings, Liberators, Fortresses and, of course, many more Dakotas.

Dakota Mk III FD857 "S-Sugar" C-47A-20-DL from No 267 Pegasus Squadron flying over the picturesque Grecian Islands near Missolonghi, on the way back to the Araxos airstrip during October 1944.

FAR EAST

The last Dakota sortie which was flown by the Royal Australian Air Force from Butterworth, Malaya, on December 10, 1968, had British air despatchers on board. Crew commander; Corporal Youngman, Second-in-command; Lance Corporal Brown, Crew: Driver Carr and Driver Jones all from the Royal Corps of Transport – RCT. The drop was to a police field force fort along the border of Thailand and West Malaysia.

The last supply sortie by RAAF Dakota from Butterworth with four British despatchers of the RCT on board. This was the 313th drop by RAAF Dakotas. As of March 1970 the Australians still had six Dakotas based at Butterworth. Photo shows the Dakota on the last sortie getting airborne.

Disbandment parade of No 389 Air Despatch Troop RCT being inspected by Air Commodore Steege, RAAF, during December 1968 at Butterworth.

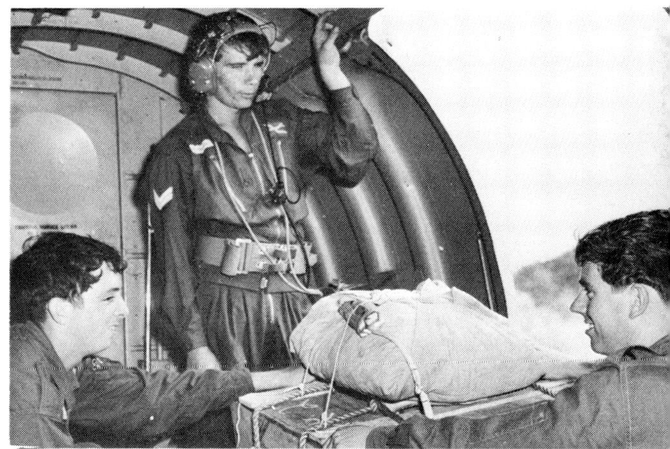

Approaching the DZ – Dropping Zone – on the last Dakota sortie on December 10, 1968, Cpl Brown awaits signals from the pilot before the vital supplies are dropped.

A Dakota transport from No 131 Squadron taking off in monsoon rains from a strip in Burma. In the background is a Vultee Vengeance dive-bomber which was used in large numbers in South-East Asia Command.

Still carrying its US Army Air Force fin number, Dakota "BH" from No 31 Squadron is depicted at an airfield somewhere in South-East Asia with native labour in the foreground.

After VJ-Day the transport squadrons had the task of flying home the thousands of prisoners held by the Japanese in Java, Sumatra, etc. Photo shows a happy crowd of released prisoners alongside the Dakota Mk I FD864 a C-47A-25-DL 42-23548 c/n 9410 which survived service with the RAF and went initially to KLM as PH-TCY.

A Waco CG4A Hadrian glider on the airstrip at Lalaghat, India, from where Operation Thursday was launched with 80 of these US designed and built gliders. It was a combined effort and the US gliders carried both British and Indian troops behind the Japanese lines.

Major-General Orde C. Wingate, DSO, confers with Colonel Philip Cocgrane, US Army Air Force who from January 1, 1944, to May 21, 1944, commanded No 1 Air Commando which was formed to carry Wingate's Chindits during Operation Thursday.

The three Dakotas from No 1315 Flight, No 160 Wing, parked on PSP – pierced steel planking – at one of their many Far East bases. Initially ferried out from the UK via the USA to Christmas Island, these transports visited many countries including Australia and Malaya. Note varied insignia on nose of aircraft.

Air Chief Marshal Sir Keith R Park, KCB, KBE, MC, DFC, took over Air Command South-East Asia on February 25, 1945, and is seen here with Air Vice-Marshal the Earl of Bandon, CB, DSO (with arms folded), who commanded No 224 Group.

"Christmas Island Airways" was formed to support Operation Grapple and its three Dakota Mk IV aircraft are depicted on their last flight as a unit to No 389 MU Singapore for disposal. The aircraft are KN434 "A" Polynesian Princess, *KN598 "B"* Coral Queen *and KJ945 "C"* Island Romance.

Typical scene in the SEAC theatre when everything except the kitchen sink was supplied to General Orde Wingate and his Chindits. Here a mule is carefully persuaded to take a flight in a Dakota of the Third Tactical Air Force. Aircraft were interchangeable as seen by the USAAF fuselage markings.

Dakota Mk IV KP275 "U-Uncle" from No 31 Squadron, a C-47B-40-DK 44-77245 c/n 16829/33577 flying along the route of the Siang River with supplies stacked in the open door ready for dropping. This transport also served with No 77 Squadron and was reduced to spares on June 30, 1950.

The Pratt & Whitney R-1830 Twin Wasp power-plant supported thousands of Dakotas of the Allies during and after World War 2. Taken in the Far East this photo is a typical scene in any theatre showing the "erks" servicing the Twin Wasp of a Royal Air Force Dakota.

Air Marshal Sir Keith Park, KCB, KBE, MC, DFC, Allied Air Commander in Chief during the latter part of the SEAC campaign, talks to Dakota crews. His first personal aircraft was a built-up Dakota HK983 Backsheesh *which was replaced by Dakota Mk IV KN561* Backsheesh II *piloted by Flt Lt Joseph Rank.*

Groundcrew from No 194 Squadron, known throughout SEAC as "The Friendly Firm" look over a Pratt & Whitney Twin Wasp of one of the units Dakotas. Formed with Lockheed Hudson transports at Lahore on October 14, 1942, No 194 served throughout the theatre until disbanded on February 15, 1946.

Dakota Mk IV KJ816 C-47B-1-DK 43-48339 c/n 14155/25600 with jeep and equipment being loaded in SEAC. This transport survived World War 2 and became G-AMWV. It was built at the Oklahoma City factory of the Douglas Aircraft Corporation.

Taken on July 19, 1944, probably at Lalaghat, photo shows mules being loaded onto a Dalota which is an early C-47-DL 41-18420 "M-Mother" c/n 4482 of No 1 Air Commando. Note the Waco CG-4A Hadrian glider in the background.

Dakotas were used by aircraft salvage units to recover crashed aircraft and transport spare fuselages, etc. Taken on September 17, 1944. Photo shows the fuselage of Spitfire Mk VIII JG199 waiting to be loaded into a SEAC Dakota.

Dakota Mk III KG459 C-47A-1-DK 42-92668 c/n 12494 in SEAC markings with a jeep loaded. This aircraft was one of the many Dakotas returned to the United States during and after World War 2.

Dakota Mk III FL-503 C-47A-50-DL which served with both Nos 216 and 353 Squadrons, parked on a strip in India with steel-helmeted Ghurkas ready to board the transport.

Dakota Mk IV KN372 with radio call-sign VM-YCL on the fin named Spirit of Lancashire *from No 243 Squadron No 300 Group based at Camden, Australia, in support of the British Pacific Fleet.*

Dakota Mk III FD-946 "Y-Yoke" from one of the two RCAF transport squadrons which served in SEAC. A C-47A-40-DL 42-24005 c/n 9867. Note the canister racks under the fuselage. Nos 435 and 436 Squadrons were part of the huge Combat Cargo Task Force made up of many Allied transport units.

Dakotas Faith, Hope *and* Charity *from the Voice Flight of No 52 Squadron operated from Bayan Lepas civil airport on the Island of Penang during the Malayan conflict which commenced in 1954. Photo shows Dakota Mk IV KP277* Faith *C-47B-35-DK 44-77247 c/n 16831/33579 at Kuala Lumpur. Note the loudspeaker system below the fuselage.*

This nose photo of Dakota Mk IV KN434 "A-Able" Polynesian Princess *carries the Kiwi symbol of New Zealand and the Kangaroo symbol of Australia, denoting just two of the many countries visited by the three transports from No 1325 Flight.*

The unit noticeboard which was erected outside the Headquarters of No 1325 Flight on Christmas Island. The name "Christmas Airways" was most appropriate as the three Dakotas flew many miles during their short tour on Operation Grapple.

POST WAR

Constructed at Oklahoma City as a TC-47B-30-DK 44-76534 c/n 16118/32866, this photo depicts 0-76534 as an AC-47 "Gunship" aircraft at Tan Son Nhut Air Base in South Vietnam during 1965. This is the latest role for the "Grand Ole' Lady".

Photo showing the installation of the Airpass radar unit into the nose of the Dakota Mk III TS423. This aircraft was a flying test-bench for the radar which is now fitted to the English Electric Lightning supersonic interceptor. TS423 flew many hours with this unique installation.

Dakota Mk III TS423 C-47A-75-DL 42-100884 c/n 19347 was acquired by Ferranti in 1949 with only 766 hours on the airframe. During 1951 the existing standard nose was extensively modified to accept a gimbal supported and hydraulically controlled gun turret as this rare photo shows.

Dakota Mk III TS423 as she is employed at the Royal Aircraft Establishment, West Freugh, near Stranraer, on a Ministry of Defence (Aviation Supply) contract, and operated by Marshalls of Cambridge Ltd. The "dustbin" type nose is the result of the many "transplants" performed whilst the transport was with Ferranti.

Above left: *Airborne Forces Day at Aldershot on May 27, 1970, when Dakota Mk IV KP208 was dedicated to the memory of the thousands of Red Berets who flew in Dakotas during World War 2. Lt-Gen Sir Mervyn Butler, KCB, CBE, DSO, MC, Colonel Commandant The Parachute Regiment, received the aircraft from Air Vice-Marshal AD Frank, CB, CBE, DSO, DFC, BA, Senior Staff Officer at Air Support Command.*

Above right: *Air Marshal The Hon Sir Ralph A Cochrane, KBE, CB, AFC, took over command of Royal Air Force Transport Command on February 15, 1945.*

Last operational flight of Air Support Command Dakota C.4 KN645 was from Fornebu, Norway, to Northolt. Photo shows the crew. Left to right – Pilot Sq Ldr Neil Franks, Radio Operator Ron Radford, Co-pilot Flt Lt John Wells, Chief Tech Les Barnes, Navigator Flt Lt Bill Couper.

On April 4, 1970, Dakota C.4 KN645 C-47-B-35-DK 44-77003 c/n 16587/33335 was flown from Northolt to Kemble, Gloucestershire. Pilot was Sq Ldr Neil Franks. Aircraft was placed in storage with No 5 Maintenance Unit pending display in the Royal Air Force Museum at Hendon.

Cockpit photo of Dakota C.4 KN645 which has changed very little from the Douglas DC-3 which was first flown in 1935 at Santa Monica, California. However, one item of modern equipment installed is the UHF radio equipment. The dialling box is top centre of the photo.

Operated by NATO with the Allied Forces Northern Europe in Oslo, Norway, Dakota C.4 KN645 had a VIP interior as depicted in this photo. This aircraft was also used by Viscount Montgomery of Alamein after World War 2.

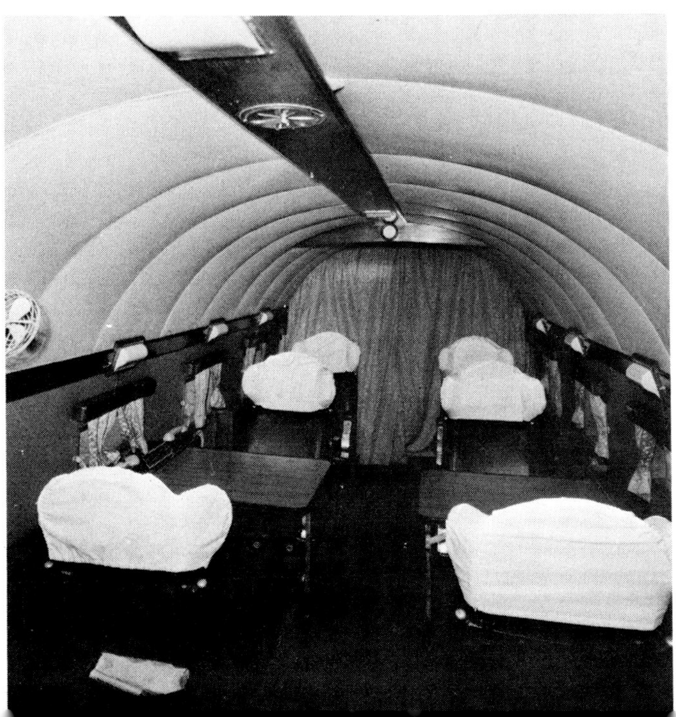

Photographed at Northolt Dakota C.4 KN645 is depicted after its last operational flight from Norway. It was delivered to the RAF from the Douglas factory at Oklahoma City on May 19, 1945, with total of two hours 15 minutes on the airframe. By 1967 it had accumulated nearly 5000 hours.

Dakota Mk IV KP208 C-47B-35-DK c/n 16670/33419 served with HQs RAF Command from February 1953 until replaced by a Varsity, and was based at Bovingdon, Hertfordshire. It later served as a VIP aircraft with the Air Attache in New Delhi.

A lasting tribute to the Red Berets is Dakota Mk IV KP208 which now stands outside the Airborne Forces Museum at Aldershot, Hampshire. It was flown from storage at No 5 MU Kemble to RAF Odiham on May 18, 1970, and then dismantled and taken by road. Total flying time 4,164 hours and 5 minutes.

Typical postwar hangar scene in the United Kingdom after World War 2 when hundreds of surplus RAF Dakotas were converted for civil use. Dakota Mk IV KN509 C-47B-30-DK 44-76710 c/n 16294/33042 is shown being converted to G-AMYX for Silver City.

Several civil Dakotas were impressed into temporary military service during the 1950s. Seen at Blackbushe Airport is XF619 ex G-AMYX of Silver City. During World War 2 this aircraft, as KN509 served with No 46 Squadron as XK-Q for Quebec.

Seen in Nicosia during 1956 with trooping serial WZ985 this C-47A-35-DL 42-23941 c/n 9803 was the first postwar civil Douglas DC-3 to be converted by Scottish Aviation Limited at Prestwick when it was registered G-AGZG. This aircraft was later sold to the French Air Force as 23941.

"Before and after" photo taken at Little Rissington showing dilapitated KP258 C-47B-40-DK 44-77228 c/n 16812/33560 before conversion with a resuscitated C-47 alongside in USAF markings. Ex No 24 Squadron KP258 went to the 7272nd Air Base Group at Wheelus, North Africa, after conversion to 0-477228.

Fuselage of KK135 "M-Mike" on a Queen Mary transporter at Silloth, Cumberland, ready for the journey to Tollerton for rebuild. Ex No 77 Squadron KK135 C-47B-15-DK 44-49456 c/n 15272/26713 was a Dakota Mk IV.

Typical example of a stored Dakota left out in the open to brave the elements. This photo shows clearly the ease with which the Pratt & Whitney Twin Wasp engines could be detached completely with fuel lines, etc.

The 100th aircraft to be overhauled for the United States Air Force (Europe) by Field Aircraft Services Ltd being handed over to the ferry crew at Tollerton by Col Goodrich, USAF acceptance pilot, with Mr Cronk of Fields – test pilot – on right of photo. Ferry crew were from 7531st Air Base Squadron at Bovingdon – right to left – Capt Paul Carr, Lt Williams and S/Sgt Garner. Aircraft was a C-47B-5-DK 43-48675 c/n 14491/25936 ex KJ896 a Dakota Mk IV.

Three rather derelict RAF Dakotas seen at the MU at Silloth, Cumberland. They include KN499 C-47B-30-DK 44-76692 c/n 16272/33024; KN514 C-47B-30-DK 44-76720 c/n 16304/33052; KN656 C47B-30-DK 44-77021 c/n 16605/33353. Two of these transports – KN499 and KN656 – eventually went to the German Air Force.

Dakota Mk IV KP251 NU-G-George C-47B-30-DK 44-77221 c/n 16805/33553 from No 240 Operational Conversion Unit was stored with No 8 MU at Little Rissington in April 1951, and in 1954 was refurbished and handed over to the USAF at Wiesbaden, Germany. Later going to the German Air Force as CA-011.

Many foreign air forces were supplied with surplus Dakotas by the British Government. Photo shows Dakota Mk IV KN527 C-47B-30-DK which was one of a number supplied to the Greek Air Force and seen at Luqa, Malta, on November 22, 1965.

FOREIGN

Polish Li-2 transports seen at Lezno in 1958. The Russian built version of the Douglas DC-3 was allocated the code name "Cab" with the North Atlantic Treaty Organisation. Over 2,000 were produced in the Soviet Union during World War 2 and many are still serving with communist-controlled countries.

Royal Australian Air Force Dakota A65-101 a C-47B-30-DK 44-76780 c/n 16364/33112 which flew alongside Royal Air Force Dakota units during Operation Firedog, the campaign in Malaya. RAAF Dakotas were also involved in the Korean conflict and often carried British medical orderlies during casualty evacuation (CASEVAC) flights. Photo taken in the Middle East during 1953.

Douglas C-53 Skytrooper transports with US Army Air Force markings erased ferry Chinese troops to combat areas. The Douglas DC-3 transport with its many military and civil variants was reputed to have been in use with every country in the world.

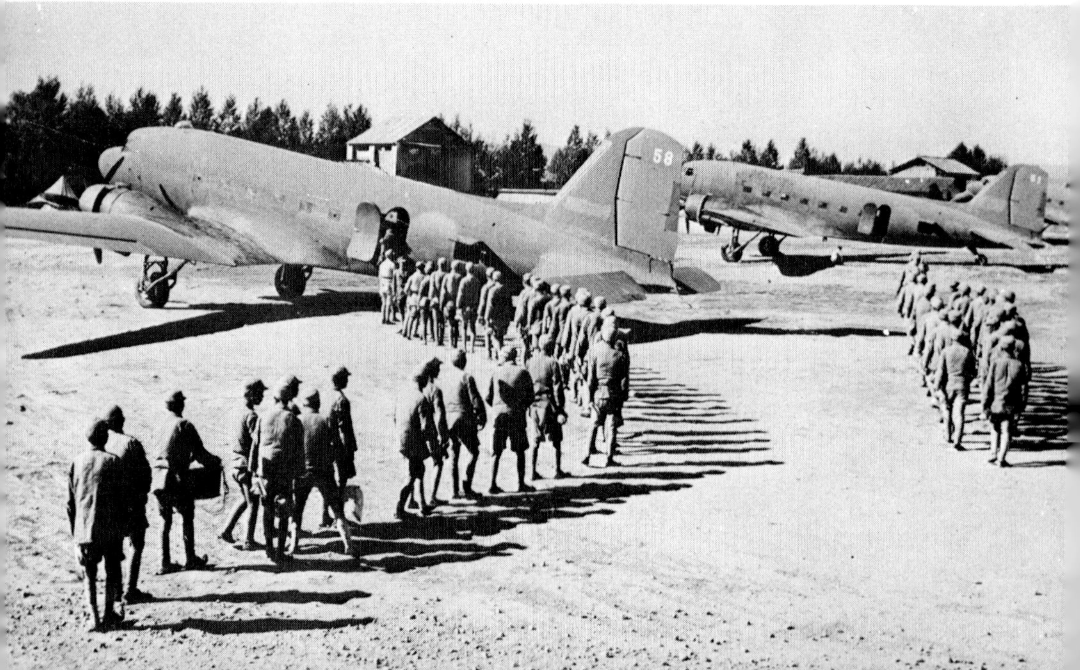